3. Provide lots of reading and thinking practice. Students learn the skills not just by hearing about them but also through hands-on practice. In a fifteen-week course, I spend the first ten weeks covering the ten skills in Part I of the book. I average one skill a week, and I also review each skill with several of the mastery tests in Part II. In the last five weeks, students read two selections a week from Part III. They also do the remaining mastery tests, including the combined skills tests.

4. Use a workshop approach. Here's the nitty-gritty of how I cover a skill in class: I'll work through a chapter page by page, alternating between putting some of the material on the board and explaining or reading some of it aloud. For example, for the second chapter, "Vocabulary in Context," I might write "forbearing" on the board and ask students if they know what it means. Then I'll say, "Look at the sentence in the book that contains the word 'forbearing.' See if there are clues in the sentence that help you figure out what the word means. Which of the three meanings that are shown would you choose?"

When I get to a practice in a chapter, I'll typically say, "Everyone take a couple of minutes to do the practice." Then I'll wait until about half the students in the class have done the practice. (If you wait until every single person finishes, the class momentum can sag.) Next I'll say, "OK, let's go over this practice quickly. Sherrie, why don't you read the first question and answer it?" And if she's right, "Good, Sherrie, that's exactly right. Let's move on now. Carl, do the second one."

My experience is that you can call upon students to read a sentence or so and answer a question without causing them undue nervousness. (I would not, on the other hand, call upon students to read an entire paragraph—here their limited reading skills might be apparent and make them very anxious or embarrassed. Note that almost all the practices in the book require only a one-sentence or shorter answer.) If you ask students to volunteer, it can slow things down. If you "volunteer" them, it keeps them on their toes, and you can proceed more rapidly. And if students see you are going to volunteer them, they will tend to start raising their hands, and so you will have a choice of people to call upon.

5. Use a small group approach at times. Let's say you've covered the chapter on supporting details up to the review tests. At this point, divide the class into groups of four. Then ask each group to work together to do the answers for Review Test 1. Say to them, "When you're done and you all agree on the answers, send a representative to the board to write down the group's answers. Let's see which group gets done first."

Put a grid on the board something like the following:

	Test 1:	1	2	3	4	5
Sherrie's Group						
Robert's Group						
Nelson's Group						
Wanda's Group						

Students enjoy these competitive situations, and peer pressure keeps everyone alert and involved. Also, you can focus discussion afterwards on just those answers on which groups disagree.

6. Use a pairs approach at times. For example, after students read the selection at the end of a chapter, have pairs of students work together on the comprehension questions that follow the selection. Students will be energized by working with another person, just as they are energized by working with a group; in both situations, they will help teach one another. After about half of the student pairs have done the questions, go over the material by having a student in each pair read and answer each question.

7. Use a one-on-one approach at times. If you have fewer than twenty students in a class, you can ask them to work on their own on a given chapter, reading the explanations and doing the activities. Put your desk in a corner, and call students up individually to check their answers and to conference on the skill. The conferences must be short—about five minutes or less for each student—but some students really benefit from the individualized and personal connection.

8. Evaluate frequently. Students have been conditioned by their past schooling to "turn it on" and work hard in test situations. Take advantage of this conditioning by giving lots of tests. The tests give students a chance to see they are learning the material and to confirm they are capable of success. The tests also are loud and clear signals to students who are not learning the materials. Note that there are over sixty tear-out mastery tests in Part II of the book, as well as seventy other tests in the Instructor's Manual ready for duplication.

When you grade a test, by the way, try to include a word or two of praise: "Good job, Carl," or "Promising," or "Well done," or "Excellent." The value of such positive comments can hardly be overstated. Think of the praise as water to what may be a very thirsty plant.

9. For variation, make some tests count and some not. Suppose you are giving students a mastery test. Say, "OK, let's take a test on this skill. Turn to page _____, put your name on top, and then do the test. I may or may not count this test."

Since you might count the test, students will give it their full effort. But at times you can then say, "Instead of collecting these papers for a grade, let's just go over them now in class." Afterwards, you can give another mastery test which will count for a grade.

Note that when you do mastery tests in class, you can provide instant feedback—and save time—by having students grade the papers right away. I often collect test papers as students finish and distribute them to students in other parts of the room. (Some students resist putting X's on a paper that belongs to the person sitting next to them.) Then have class members read and answer each question, with students marking the answers and then writing the number correct at the top.

10. Require some writing at the end of a class. To help students consolidate what they've learned in a given class, wait until the last ten minutes and ask them to write about it. One summarizing assignment that I give is to ask students to write a "Dear _____" letter to a missing classmate. I say, "Explain in a nutshell to _____ what we learned in class today. Pass in your letters as you leave class. I'll read them myself and then send them all to _____."

We wish you luck!

John Langan
Bill Broderick

TEN STEPS TO BUILDING COLLEGE READING SKILLS

SECOND EDITION

JOHN LANGAN
ATLANTIC COMMUNITY COLLEGE

BILL BRODERICK
CERRITOS COLLEGE

TOWNSEND PRESS   Marlton, NJ 08053

The Other Books in the Townsend Press Reading Series:

GROUNDWORK FOR COLLEGE READING
GROUNDWORK FOR COLLEGE READING II
TEN STEPS TO IMPROVING COLLEGE READING SKILLS
TEN STEPS TO ADVANCING COLLEGE READING SKILLS
IMPROVING READING COMPREHENSION SKILLS

Books in the Townsend Press Vocabulary Series:

GROUNDWORK FOR A BETTER VOCABULARY
BUILDING VOCABULARY SKILLS
IMPROVING VOCABULARY SKILLS
ADVANCING VOCABULARY SKILLS
BUILDING VOCABULARY SKILLS, SHORT VERSION
IMPROVING VOCABULARY SKILLS, SHORT VERSION
ADVANCING VOCABULARY SKILLS, SHORT VERSION

Supplements Available for Most Books:

Instructor's Edition
Instructor's Manual, Test Bank and Computer Guide
Set of Computer Disks (Apple, IBM, or Macintosh)

Copyright © 1993 by Townsend Press, Inc.
Printed in the United States of America
ISBN 0-944210-58-9

Send book orders and requests for desk copies or supplements to:
Townsend Press
Pavilions at Greentree—408
Marlton, NJ 08053

For even faster service, call us at our toll-free number:
1-800-772-6410

Or FAX your request to:
1-609-772-9611

ISBN 0-944210-58-9

Contents

Preface to the Instructor   vii

How to Become a Better Reader and Thinker   1

PART I
Ten Steps to Building College Reading Skills   7

 1 Dictionary Use   9
 2 Vocabulary in Context   29
 3 Main Ideas   45
 4 Supporting Details   68
 5 Locations of Main Ideas   85
 6 Implied Main Ideas   103
 7 More About Supporting Details   125
 8 Transitions   147
 9 Patterns of Organization   168
10 Inferences   199

PART II
Mastery Tests (6 tests per skill)   217

Dictionary Use   219
Vocabulary in Context   231
Main Ideas   243
Supporting Details   255
Locations of Main Ideas   267
Implied Main Ideas   279
More About Supporting Details   291
Transitions   303
Patterns of Organization   315
Inferences   327

Combined-Skills Tests   339

PART III
Ten Reading Selections   351

1 Disaster and Friendship *Chuck Wilson*   353
2 Read All About It *Fran DeBlasio*   362
3 Adult Children at Home *Marilyn Mack*   370
4 Winners, Losers, or Just Kids? *Dan Wightman*   379
5 Shyness *Richard Wolkomir*   387
6 False Ideas About Reading *Robert and Pam Winkler*   397
7 Are You a Good Listener? *Robert L. Montgomery*   405
8 Getting Words on Paper: Where to Begin *Richard P. Batteiger*   415
9 Dealing with Feelings *Rudolph F. Verderber*   426
10 Childhood Stress and Resilience *Diane E. Papalia and Sally Wendkos Olds*   436

Limited Answer Key   445

Acknowledgments   449

Index   450

Reading Performance Chart   *Inside back cover*

Note: A reading selection concludes each of the ten chapters in Part I. Here are the titles, authors, and page numbers of these ten selections:

1 The Gentle Giant and the Reluctant Robber *Tom Hinkle*   24
2 Victims Versus Oppressors *Clark DeLeon*   40
3 Group Pressure *Rodney Stark*   63
4 Touch Sparks Love *Phyllis Spangler*   79
5 Body Language *Beth Johnson Ruth*   97
6 Messages from a Welfare Mom *Ramona Parish*   120
7 Behind Closed Doors: Violence in the Family *Michael S. Bassis, Richard J. Gelles, and Ann Levine*   141
8 Responsibility *M. Scott Peck*   163
9 How To Make It in College, Now That You're Here *Brian O'Keeney*   190
10 Exam Anxiety and Grandma's Health *Charles G. Morris and John J. Chiodo*   211

Preface to the Instructor

We all know that many students entering college today do not have the reading skills needed to do effective work in their courses. A related problem, apparent even in class discussions, is that students often lack the skills required to think in a clear and logical way.

The purpose of TEN STEPS TO BUILDING COLLEGE READING SKILLS, Second Edition, is to develop effective reading *and* clear thinking. To do so, the book first presents a sequence of ten word and reading skills that are widely recognized as essential for sound comprehension:

- Using the dictionary
- Recognizing vocabulary in context
- Understanding main ideas
- Understanding supporting details
- Locating main ideas in different parts of paragraphs
- Determining implied main ideas
- Locating major and minor details
- Identifying transitions
- Identifying patterns of organization
- Making inferences.

In every chapter in Part I, the key aspects of a skill are explained and illustrated clearly and simply. Explanations are accompanied by a series of practices, and each chapter ends with three review tests. The last review test includes a reading selection, so that students can apply the skill just learned to real-world reading materials, including newspaper and magazine articles and textbook selections. Together, the ten chapters provide students with the skills needed for a solid understanding of reading materials.

Part II is made up of six mastery tests for each of the ten skills, as well as six combined-skills tests. The tests progress in difficulty, providing students with the additional practice and challenge they may need for the solid learning of each skill. While designed for quick grading, the tests also ensure that students must think carefully before answering each question.

Part III consists of ten additional readings that will help improve both reading and thinking skills. Each reading is followed by a series of *Vocabulary Questions* and *Reading Comprehension Questions* so students can practice the skills presented in Part I and reinforced in Part II. In addition, an *Outlining* or *Summarizing* activity after each reading helps students think carefully about the basic content and organization of a selection. Finally, *Discussion Questions* provide teachers with an opportunity to engage students in a variety of reading and thinking skills and to deepen their understanding of a selection.

Important Features of the Book

• **Focus on the basics.** The book is designed to explain in a very clear, step-by-step way the essential elements of each skill. Many examples are provided to ensure that students understand each point. In general, the focus is on *teaching* the skills—not just on explaining them and not just on testing them.

• **Frequent practice and feedback.** In the belief that it is largely through abundant practice and careful feedback that progress is made, this book includes numerous activities. Students can get immediate feedback on the practice exercises in Part I by turning to the limited answer key at the back. The answers to the review tests in Part I, the mastery tests in Part II, and the readings in Part III are in the *Instructor's Edition* as well as in the *Instructor's Manual*.

The limited answer key increases the active role that students take in their own learning. They are likely to use the answer key in an honest and positive way if they know they may be tested on the many activities and selections for which answers are not provided. (Answers not in the book can be easily copied from the *Instructor's Manual* and passed out at the teacher's discretion.)

• **High interest level.** Dull and unvaried readings and exercises work against learning. Students need to experience genuine interest and enjoyment in what they read. Teachers as well should be able to take pleasure in the selections, for their own good feeling can carry over favorably into class work. The readings in the book, then, have been chosen not only for the appropriateness of their reading level but also for their compelling content. They should engage teachers and students alike.

• **Ease of use.** The straightforward sequence in each chapter—from explanation to example to practice to review test—helps make the skills easy to teach. The book's organization into three distinct parts also makes for ease of use. Within a single class, for instance, teachers can work on a new skill in Part I, review skills with one or more mastery tests in Part II, and provide variety by having students read one of the selections in Part III. The limited answer key at the back of the text also makes for versatility: it means that the teacher can assign some chapters for self-teaching. Finally, the mastery and combined-skills tests—each on its own tear-out page—make it a simple matter for teachers to test and evaluate student progress.

• **Integration of skills.** Students do more than learn the skills individually in Parts I and II. They also learn to apply the skills together through the reading selections that close the chapters in Part I, through the combined-skills tests in Part II, and through the readings in Part III. They become effective readers and thinkers through a good deal of practice in applying a combination of skills.

• **Thinking activities.** Thinking activities in the form of outlining and summarizing are a distinctive feature of the book. While educators agree that such organizational abilities are important, they are all too seldom taught. From a practical standpoint, it is almost impossible for a teacher to respond individually to entire collections of class outlines or summaries. This book is designed, then, to create activities that truly involve students in outlining and summarizing—in other words, that truly make students *think*—and yet that enable a teacher to give feedback. Again, it is through continued practice *and* feedback on challenging material that a student becomes a more effective reader and thinker.

• **Supplementary materials.** The three helpful supplements listed below are available at no charge to instructors using the text. Any or all can be obtained quickly by writing or calling Townsend Press (Pavilions at Greentree—408, Marlton, New Jersey 08053; 1-800-772-6410)

1   An *Instructor's Edition*—chances are you are holding it in your hand—is identical to the student book except that it also provides both of the following: 1) hints for teachers (see the front of the book); and 2) answers to all the practices and tests.

2   A combined *Instructor's Manual, Test Bank, and Computer Guide* consists of the following:

　　a   Suggestions for teaching the course, a model syllabus, readability levels, a complete answer key, and writing activities for each reading selection.

　　b   Four additional mastery tests for each of the ten skills and four additional combined-skills tests—all on letter-sized sheets so they can be copied easily for use with students.

    c A computer guide that reproduces the two additional mastery tests for each skill that are on the computer disks available with the book.

3   A *set of computer disks* (in Apple, IBM, and Macintosh formats) that contain two additional mastery tests for each of the ten skill chapters in the book. The disks are self-booting and contain a number of other user- and instructor-friendly features: brief explanations of answers, a sound option, frequent mention of the user's first name, a running score at the bottom of the screen, and a record-keeping score file.

        Since the disk tests are reproduced in the *Computer Guide*, teachers can readily decide just how to use the materials without having to work through each test on the computer. And teachers without a computer lab can copy these tests for use in class as additional mastery tests.

• **One of a sequence of books.** This is the basic text in a series that includes two other books. TEN STEPS TO IMPROVING COLLEGE READING SKILLS is an intermediate text, and TEN STEPS TO ADVANCING COLLEGE READING SKILLS is an advanced text.

        The BUILDING book is suited for a first college reading course. The IMPROVING book is appropriate for the core developmental reading course offered at most colleges. The ADVANCING book is a slightly higher developmental text than the IMPROVING book. It can be used as the core book for a more advanced class, as a sequel to the intermediate book, or as a second-semester alternative to it.

        A companion set of vocabulary books, listed on page iv, has been designed to go with the TEN STEPS books. Recommended to accompany this book is BUILDING VOCABULARY SKILLS or BUILDING VOCABULARY SKILLS, SHORT VERSION.

        Together, the books and their full range of supplements form a sequence that should be ideal for any college reading program.

        To summarize, then, TEN STEPS TO BUILDING COLLEGE READING SKILLS, Second Edition, provides ten key reading skills to help developmental college students become independent readers and thinkers. Through an appealing collection of readings and a carefully designed series of activities and tests, students receive extensive guided practice in the skills. The result is an integrated approach to learning that will, by the end of a course, produce better readers and stronger thinkers.

Changes in the Second Edition

We are grateful for the helpful comments from the many teachers who have communicated with Townsend Press about the book over the last couple of years. Based on their suggestions and our own classroom use of the text, we have made some major changes:

- *More progression in the mastery tests from easier to more difficult material.* Students are given a greater challenge, especially with the fifth and sixth tests, which usually feature textbook excerpts.

- *Integration of the individual comprehension skills with the reading selections.* A reading selection now follows each chapter in Part I, so students can immediately apply the skill they have learned to an actual reading. As students move from one chapter to the next, they both apply the new skill learned and review the skills covered in earlier chapters.

- *More tests and practice materials.* There are now six mastery tests instead of four, and there are twenty reading selections, compared to fifteen in the first edition. Completely new are brief content tests for each of the ten skills chapters in Part I; these tests begin the final review test in each chapter. Also new are six combined-skills tests—short reading passages followed by questions on a variety of skills. The passages and tests approximate those in typical standardized reading tests. These combination tests will help prepare students for such standardized tests, which are often a requirement at the end of a semester.

- *Many revisions and additions throughout the text.* Adopters of the first edition will note, for example, that a second color is now used to make the content more readable and visually appealing. They will see that seven of the readings are new and that six of these readings have been taken from college textbooks; that the chapters on main ideas and supporting details have been resequenced to better help students' understanding of these closely-related skills; that the chapter on transitions now directly precedes the chapter on patterns of organization; and that there have been changes of some kind on virtually every page of the text.

- *An* Instructor's Edition *of the book.* In this special teacher's version of the book, users now have at their fingertips the answers to all of the tests and practices. And starting on the inside front cover is a series of teaching hints that may be of help—especially for people teaching a reading course or using this book for the first time.

Acknowledgments

We are grateful for reviewer comments, especially from Jane Kennedy of Brevard Community College. Thanks to the exceptional design skills of Janet M. Goldstein, the book enjoys a remarkably clear and "user-friendly" format. We owe appreciation as well to others who have helped along the way: Dot Carroll, Amy Fisher, Elaine J. Lessig, and Beth Johnson Ruth. We value especially the exceptional editorial role played by Carole Mohr, who has worked closely with us for months on every page of the book. Thanks to her insights into the nature of each skill and her sensitivity to the needs of students, the text is significantly better than it would have been otherwise. It has been a special pleasure to work with colleagues who aspire toward excellence. With them, we have been able to create a much better book than we could have managed on our own.

John Langan
Bill Broderick

How to Become a Better Reader and Thinker

The chances are that you are not as good a reader as you should be to do well in college. If so, it's not surprising. You live in a culture where people watch an average of *over seven hours of television every day!!!* All that passive viewing does not allow much time for reading. Reading is a skill that must be actively practiced. The simple fact is that people who do not read very often are not likely to be strong readers.

• How much TV do you guess you watch on an average day? _____

Another reason besides TV for not reading much is that you may have a lot of responsibilities. You may be going to school and working at the same time, and you may have a lot of family duties as well. Given a hectic schedule, you're not going to have much time to read. When you have free time, you're exhausted, and it's easier to turn on the TV than to open up a book.

• Do you do any regular reading (for example, a daily newspaper, weekly

magazines, occasional novels)? _____

• When are you most likely to do your reading? _____

A third reason for not reading is that our public school system may have soured you on it. One government study after another has said that our schools have not done a good job of turning people on to the rewards of reading. If you had to read a lot of uninteresting and irrelevant material in grade and high school, you may have decided (mistakenly) that reading in general is not for you.

• Do you think that school made you dislike reading, rather than enjoy it?

_____

Here are three final questions to ask yourself.

- Do you feel that perhaps you don't need a reading course, since you "already know how to read"? _____

- If you had a choice, would you be taking a reading course? (It's OK to be honest.) _____

- Do you think that a bit of speed reading may be all you need? _____

Chances are that you don't need to read *faster* as much as you need to read *smarter*. And it's a safe bet that if you don't read much, you can benefit enormously from the reading course in which you are using this book.

One goal of the book is to help you become a better reader. You will learn and practice a number of key reading comprehension skills. As a result, you'll be able to better read and understand the many materials in your other college courses. The skills in this book have direct and practical value: they can help you perform better and more quickly—giving you an edge for success—in all of your college work.

The book is also concerned with helping you become a stronger thinker. Reading and thinking are closely related skills, and practice in thoughtful reading will also strengthen your ability to think clearly and logically. To find out just how the book will help you achieve these goals, read the next several pages and do the brief activities as well. The activities are easily completed and will give you a quick, helpful overview of the book.

HOW THE BOOK IS ORGANIZED

The book is organized into three parts:

Part I: Ten Steps to Building College Reading Skills (Pages 7–216)

To help you become a more effective reader and thinker, this book presents a series of ten key word and reading skills. They are listed in the table of contents on page v. Turn to that page to fill in the skills missing below:

1   Dictionary Use
2   *Vocabulary in Context* _____
3   Main Ideas
4   *Supporting Details* _____
5   Locations of Main Ideas
6   Implied Main Ideas
7   More About Supporting Details

8 *Transitions* _____

9 Patterns of Organization

10 *Inferences* _____

Each chapter is developed in the same way. First of all, clear explanations and examples help you *understand* each skill. Practices then give you the "hands-on" experience needed to *review* the skill.

- How many practices are there for the third skill, "Main Ideas" (pages 45–67)? __Six__

Closing each chapter are three review tests.

- On which pages are the first two review tests for "Main Ideas"? __60–62__

The third review test always consists of two parts: a review of the chapter and a reading selection that gives you a chance both to practice the skill learned in the chapter and to review skills learned in earlier chapters.

- How many questions are asked about the "Main Ideas" chapter (pages 62–63)? __Five__

- What is the title of the reading on page 63? __"Group Pressure"__

Part II: Mastery Tests (Pages 217–350)

This part of the book provides mastery tests for each of the ten skills in Part I.

- Look through pages 219–338. How many mastery tests are there for each skill? __Six__

The test pages are perforated and can be torn out and given to your instructor. There is a scorebox at the end of each test so you can track your progress. Your score can also be entered in the "Reading Performance Chart" at the back of the book.

- Exactly where is this chart located? __Inside back cover__

Part III: Ten Reading Selections (Pages 351–444)

The ten reading selections that make up Part III are followed by activities that give you practice in all of the skills studied in Parts I and II. Turn to the table of contents on page vi and answer the following question:

- Which selection is probably about developing good listening skills? _____
__"Are You a Good Listener?"__

Each reading begins in the same way. Look, for example, at "Disaster and Friendship" which starts on page 353. What are the headings of the two sections that come before the reading itself?

- *Preview* _____

- *Words to Watch* _____

Note that the vocabulary words in "Words to Watch" are followed by the numbers of the paragraphs in which the words appear. Now look at the first reading (353-361) and explain how each vocabulary word is marked in the reading itself:

- *It has a small circle after it.* _____

Activities Following Each Reading Selection

After each selection, there are four kinds of activities to improve your reading and thinking skills. Look at the activities following "Disaster and Friendship" (pages 353-361). Note that the first activity consists of **vocabulary questions**. The second consists of *(fill in the missing words)* _____
_____*reading comprehension questions*_____. The third activity involves **outlining** or **summarizing**. The fourth consists of *(fill in the missing words)* _____*discussion questions*_____.

- Look at the **vocabulary questions** for "Disaster and Friendship" on pages 357-358. The first five of these questions deal with vocabulary in context. The last five of the questions deal with words that are taken from the *(fill in the missing words)* ____*"Words to Watch"*____. These questions will help you improve your understanding of key words presented in the reading.

- Look at the **reading comprehension questions** for "Disaster and Friendship" on pages 358-360. You'll see that there are ten questions covering five basic skills. Note that there are always one to three questions for each skill. The questions give you a chance to practice the skills you learned in Part I and strengthened in Part II. How many questions deal with the skill of understanding transitions? ____*Two*____

- Look now at the activity titled **outlining** or **summarizing**. Either one of these will sharpen your ability to get to the heart of a piece and to think logically and clearly about what you read. What kind of activity is provided for "Disaster and Friendship"? ____*Outlining*____

· Write down how many **discussion questions** there are for "Disaster and Friendship" (page 361)—and for every other reading: _____*four*_____. The questions provide a chance for you to deepen your understanding of each selection.

HELPFUL FEATURES OF THE BOOK

1   The book centers on *what you really need to know* to become a better reader and thinker. It presents ten key comprehension skills, and it explains the most important points about each skill.

2   The book gives you *lots of practice*. We seldom learn a skill only by hearing or reading about it; we make it part of us by repeated practice. There are, then, numerous activities in the text. They are not "busy work," but carefully designed materials that should help you truly learn each skill.

 Notice that after you learn each skill in Part I, you read a selection in Review Test 3 that enables you to apply that skill. And as you move from one skill to the next, you continue to practice and reinforce the ones already learned.

3   The selections throughout the book are *lively and appealing*. Dull and unvaried readings work against learning, so subjects have been carefully chosen for their high interest level. Almost all of the selections here are excellent examples of how what we read can capture our attention. For example, take a look at the textbook selection "Dealing with Feelings" on page 426. It is full of helpful information about understanding and controlling one's feelings.

4   The readings include six *selections from college textbooks*. Therefore, you are practicing on materials very much like the ones in your other courses. Doing so will increase your chances of transferring what you learn in your reading class to your other college subjects.

HOW TO USE THE BOOK

1   A good way to proceed is to read and reread the explanations and examples in a given chapter in Part I until you feel you understand the ideas presented. Then carefully work through the practices. As you finish each one, check your answers with the "Limited Answer Key" that starts on page 445.

For your own sake, don't just copy in the answers without trying to do the practices! The only way to learn a skill is to practice it first and *then* use the answer key to give yourself feedback. Also, take whatever time is needed to figure out just why you got some answers wrong. By using the answer key to help teach yourself the skills, you will prepare yourself for the review tests at the end of each chapter as well as for the mastery tests and the reading selection tests in the book. Your instructor can supply you with answers to those tests.

If you have trouble catching on to a particular skill, stick with it. In time, you will learn each of the ten skills.

2   Read the selections with the intent of simply enjoying them. There will be time afterwards for rereading each selection and using it to develop your comprehension skills.

3   Keep track of your progress. In the "Reading Performance Chart" on the inside back cover, enter your scores for the mastery tests in Part II. In addition, fill in the "Check Your Performance" chart at the end of each reading in Part III. These scores can also be entered on the inside-back-cover chart, giving you a good view of your overall performance as you work through the book.

In summary, TEN STEPS TO BUILDING COLLEGE READING SKILLS has been designed to interest and benefit you as much as possible. Its format is straightforward, its explanations are clear, its readings are appealing, and its many practices will help you learn through doing. *It is a book that has been created to reward effort*, and if you provide that effort, you will make yourself a better reader and a stronger thinker. We wish you success.

John Langan
Bill Broderick

Part I

TEN STEPS TO BUILDING COLLEGE READING SKILLS

1

Dictionary Use

The dictionary contains a lot of useful information. But if you have trouble looking words up, that information won't do you much good. So this chapter begins with some helpful hints on how to look words up in the dictionary. Then the chapter will help you make sense of the information that a dictionary provides for each word.

OWNING A GOOD DICTIONARY

You can benefit greatly by owning two dictionaries. The first dictionary you should own is a paperback one you can carry with you. Any of the following would be an excellent choice:

The American Heritage Dictionary, Paperback Edition

The Random House College Dictionary, Paperback Edition

Webster's New World Dictionary, Paperback Edition

The second dictionary you should own is a desk-sized, hardcover edition which should be kept in the room where you study. All the above dictionaries come in hardbound versions, which contain a good deal more information than the paperback editions. And while they cost more, they are valuable study aids.

Dictionaries are often updated to reflect changes which occur in the language. New words come into use, and old words take on new meanings. Because of such changes, you should not use a dictionary which has been lying around the house for a number of years. Instead, invest in a new dictionary. It is easily among the best investments you may ever make.

FINDING WORDS IN THE DICTIONARY

This section describes how to use guide words and how to find words you can't spell.

Using Guide Words to Find a Word More Quickly

One way to find a given word in a dictionary is to use guide words—the pair of words at the top of each dictionary page. Reproduced below are the top and bottom parts of a page in *The American Heritage Dictionary*, Paperback Edition. The guide words are at the very top of the page.

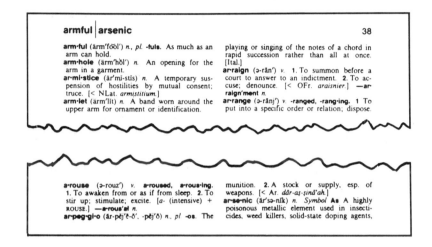

The first guide word tells what the first word is on that page; the second guide word tells what the last word is on the page. All of the other words on the page fall alphabetically between the two guide words.

Now see if you understand how to use guide words. Underline the three words below that would appear on the page with the guide words *armful / arsenic:*

art   aroma   army   arrest   ax   allow

The guide words *armful / arsenic* tell us right away that every word on the page will begin with *ar*. That immediately eliminates *ax* and *allow*. The words that would fall on the page with those guide words are *aroma*, *army*, and *arrest*. The word *art* also begins with *ar*, but alphabetically it comes after *arsenic*, the last word on the page.

➤ *Practice 1*

On the next page are five pairs of dictionary guide words followed by other words. Underline the three words in each series that would be found on the page with the guide words.

1. **fireside / fission**

   <u>fishbowl</u>   fireproof   <u>fiscal</u>   <u>firing squad</u>   fingerprint

2. **gloom / go**

   giant   <u>glow</u>   <u>gnaw</u>   <u>glue</u>   glitter

3. **litterbug / loathe**

   life   lover   <u>liver</u>   <u>load</u>   <u>lizard</u>

4. **dumbbell / dustpan**

   <u>during</u>   <u>duplicate</u>   dye   <u>dunk</u>   dull

5. **stuffed shirt / subconscious**

   <u>stumble</u>   sunstroke   <u>subcompact</u>   straw   <u>style</u>

Finding a Word You Can't Spell

Looking up the spelling of a word in the dictionary may seem frustrating. "If I can't spell a word," you might ask, "how can I find it in the dictionary?" The answer is that you have to guess what the letters might be.

Guessing is not too difficult with certain sounds, such as the sounds of *b* and *p*. But other sounds are more difficult to pin down because they can belong to more than one letter. And that's where the guessing comes in. Here are three hints to help in such cases:

Hints for Finding Words

Hint 1: If you're not sure about the vowels in a word, you will simply have to experiment. Vowels often sound the same. So try an *i* in place of an *a*, an *i* in place of an *e*, and so on. If, for example, you don't find a word that sounds like it begins with *pa*, try looking under *pe, pi, po, pu* or *py*.

Hint 2: Following are groups of letters or letter combinations that often sound alike. If your word isn't spelled with one of the letters in a pair or group shown below, it might be spelled with another in the same pair or group. For example, if it isn't spelled with a *k*, it may be spelled with a *c*.

c / k	**c / s**	**f / v / ph**	**g / j**	**qu / kw / k**	**s / c / z**
sch / sc / sk	**sh / ch**	**shun / tion / sion**		**w / wh**	**able / ible**
ai / ay	**al / el / le**	**ancy / ency**	**ate / ite**	**au / aw**	**ea / ee**
er / or	**ie / ei**	**ou / ow**	**oo / u**	**y / i / e**	

Hint 3: Consonants are sometimes doubled in a word. If you can't find your word with single consonants, try doubling them.

➤ *Practice 2*

For this practice you will need a dictionary. Try using your ear, the hints on the previous page, and guide words to help you find the correct spelling of the following words. Write each correct spelling in the answer space.

1. dicided _____*decided*_____
2. occazion _____*occasion*_____
3. dooty _____*duty*_____
4. aksident _____*accident*_____
5. nieghbor _____*neighbor*_____

6. experament _____*experiment*_____
7. rimember _____*remember*_____
8. attenshun _____*attention*_____
9. charicter _____*character*_____
10. fotocopy _____*photocopy*_____

LEARNING FROM A DICTIONARY ENTRY

The rest of this chapter will go over six common parts of dictionary word entries:

1 Spelling and syllables

2 Pronunciation

3 Parts of speech

4 Irregular spellings

5 Definitions

6 Synonyms

The entry below, from *The American Heritage Dictionary*, Paperback Edition (referred to from now on as the *AHD*), will be used as an example throughout.

Sample Dictionary Entry

> **in•sult** (ĭn-sŭlt′) *v.* To speak to or treat with disrespect or contempt. —*n.* (ĭn′sŭlt′). A disrespectful or contemptuous action or remark. [< Lat. *insultare*, to revile.]
>   **Syns.:** *insult, affront, offend, outrage v.*

1 SPELLING AND SYLLABLES

The dictionary first gives the correct spelling and syllable breakdown of a word. Dots separate the words into syllables. Each syllable is a separate sound, and each sound includes a vowel. In the entry shown above, *insult* is divided into two syllables.

How many syllables are in each of the following words?

dis·tinct   em·per·or   o·be·di·ent

If you answered two for *distinct*, three for *emperor*, and four for *obedient*, you were right.

⤜ *Practice 3*

Use your dictionary to separate the following words into syllables. Put a slash line (/) between each syllable. Then write down the number of syllables in each word. The first one is done for you as an example.

1. b i r t h/p l a c e   __2__ syllables
2. d i s p l e a s e   __2__ syllables   *dis/please*
3. h u r r i c a n e   __3__ syllables   *hur/ri/cane*
4. a s p a r a g u s   __4__ syllables   *as/par/a/gus*
5. s u f f i c i e n t   __3__ syllables   *suf/fi/cient*
6. i n h u m a n i t y   __5__ syllables   *in/hu/man/i/ty*

2   PRONUNCIATION SYMBOLS AND ACCENT MARKS

A dictionary entry word is followed by information in parentheses, as in the entry for *insult*:

> **in·sult** (ĭn-sŭlt') *v.* To speak to or treat with disrespect or contempt. —*n.* (ĭn'sŭlt'). A disrespectful or contemptuous action or remark. [< Lat. *insultare*, to revile.]
>
> **Syns:** *insult, affront, offend, outrage v.*

The information in parentheses shows you how to pronounce the word. It includes two kinds of symbols: pronunciation symbols and accent marks. Following are explanations of each.

Pronunciation Symbols

The pronunciation symbols tell the sounds of consonants and vowels in a word. The sounds of the consonants are probably familiar to you, but you may find it helpful to review the vowel sounds. Vowels are the letters *a, e, i, o,* and *u*. To know how to pronounce the vowel sounds, use the *pronunciation key* in your dictionary. Here is the key found on every other page of the *AHD*:

Pronunciation Key

ă pat	ā pay	â care	ä father	ĕ pet	ē be	ĭ pit
ī tie	î pier	ŏ pot	ō toe	ô paw, for		oi noise
ŏŏ took	ōō boot	ou out	th thin	*th* this		ŭ cut
û urge	yōō abuse	zh vision	ə about, item, edible, gallop, circus			

The key tells you, for instance, that the sound of the long *a* is pronounced like the *ay* in *pay*, the sound of the short *i* is pronounced like the *i* in *pit*, and so on. Note that long vowels have the sound of their own name.

To use the above key, first find the symbol of the sound you wish to pronounce. For example, suppose you want to pronounce the short *a* sound. Locate the short *a* in the key and note how the sound is pronounced in the short word (*pat*) that appears next to the short *a*. You'll see that the *a* has the sound of the *a* in the word "pat." The key also tells you, for instance, that the short *e* sound has the sound of the *e* in the word "pet"; that the short *o* has the sound of the *o* in the word "pot"; and so on.

Finally, note that the last pronunciation symbol in the key looks like an upside-down *e*: ə. This symbol is known as the *schwa*. As you can see by the words that follow it, the schwa has a very short sound that sounds much like "uh" (as in "about," "gallop," and "circus") or "ih" (as in "item" and "edible").

➤ *Practice 4*

Refer to the pronunciation key to answer the questions about the following ten words. Circle the letter of each of your answers.

1. **blos·som** (blŏs′əm)
   The first *o* in *blossom* sounds like the *o* in
   (a.) *pot.*
   b. *toe.*

2. **live·ly** (līv′lē)
   The *i* in *lively* sounds like the *i* in
   a. *pit.*
   (b.) *tie.*

3. **lum·ber** (lŭm′bər)
   The *u* in *lumber* sounds like the *u* in
   (a.) *cut.*
   b. *abuse.*

4. **gam·ble** (găm′bəl)
   The *a* in *gamble* sounds like the *a* in
   (a.) *pat.*
   b. *pay.*

5. **bla•tant** (blāt′nt)
   The first *a* in *blatant* sounds like the *a* in
   a. *pat.*
   (b.) *pay.*

6. **twin•kle** (twĭng′kəl)
   The *i* in *twinkle* sounds like the *i* in
   (a.) *pit.*
   b. *tie.*

7. **su•crose** (soo′krōs′)
   The *o* in *sucrose* sounds like the *o* in
   a. *pot.*
   (b.) *toe.*

8. **lu•cid** (loo′sĭd)
   The *u* in *lucid* sounds like the *oo* in
   a. *took.*
   (b.) *boot.*

9. **ve•he•ment** (vē′ə-mənt)
   The first *e* in *vehement* sounds like the *e* in
   a. *pet.*
   (b.) *be.*

10. **ter•res•tri•al** (tə-rĕs′trē-əl)
    The first *e* in *terrestrial* sounds like
    a. the *e* in *pet.*
    (b.) the schwa in the word *about.*

➤ *Practice 5*

A. Below are pronunciation symbols for five common words. Write in the word in each case and also the number of schwa sounds in each word. The first item has been done for you as an example.

Pronunciation symbols	Word itself	Number of schwas
1. (dĭs′ə-plĭn)	discipline	1
2. (ĕn-koun′tər)	encounter	1
3. (ar′tə-fĭsh′əl)	artificial	2
4. (mə-jôr′ĭ-tē)	majority	1
5. (năch′ər-əl)	natural	2

B. Use your dictionary to find and write in the pronunciation symbols for the following words. Make sure you can pronounce each word. The first word has been done for you as an example.

1. alleviate   ə-lē′vē-āt′

2. cynic   sĭn′ĭk

3. emanate   ĕm′ə-nāt′

4. feasible   fē′zə-bəl

5. prognosis   prŏg-nō′sĭs

Accent Marks

Notice the black marks in the pronunciation guide (the information shown in parentheses) for the verb and noun forms of *insult*. The marks look a little like apostrophes.

> **in·sult** (ĭn-sŭlt′) *v.* To speak to or treat with disrespect or contempt. —*n.* (ĭn′sŭlt′). A disrespectful or contemptuous action or remark. [< Lat. *insultare*, to revile.]
>   **Syns:** *insult, affront, offend, outrage v.*

The darker line (′) is a bold accent mark, and it shows which syllable has the stronger stress. That means the syllable is pronounced a little louder than the others. Syllables without an accent mark are unstressed. Some syllables—like the second one in the noun form of *insult*—are in between, and they are marked with a lighter accent mark (′).

The word *interview* is accented like this:

in·ter·view (ĭn′tər-vyo͞o′)

Say *interview* to yourself. Can you hear that the strongest accent is on *in*, the first syllable? Can you hear that the last syllable, *view*, is also accented but not as strongly? If not, say the word to yourself again until you hear the differences in accent sounds.

Below are some familiar words with syllable divisions and accent marks shown in parentheses. Use those guides to help you pronounce the words to yourself.

- ma·chine (mə-shēn′)
- de·ter·gent (dĭ-tûr′jənt)
- in·for·ma·tion (ĭn′fər-mā′shən)
- val·en·tine (văl′ən-tīn′)
- al·pha·bet·i·cal (ăl′fə-bĕt′ĭ-kəl)

Think for a moment of how each of these words would sound if you accented the wrong syllable.

➤ Practice 6

Answer the questions following each of the five words below.

1. **dis•a•gree** (dĭs′ə-grē′)

   a. How many syllables are in *disagree*? ___*three*___

   b. Which syllable is most strongly accented? ___*third*___

2. **mag•nif•i•cent** (măg-nĭf′ĭ-sənt)

   a. How many syllables are in *magnificent*? ___*four*___

   b. Which syllable is most strongly accented? ___*second*___

3. **tel•e•thon** (tĕl′ə-thŏn′)

   a. How many syllables are in *telethon*? ___*three*___

   b. Which syllable is most strongly accented? ___*first*___

4. **dis•til•la•tion** (dĭs-tə-lā′shən)

   a. How many syllables are in *distillation*? ___*four*___

   b. Which syllable is accented? ___*third*___

5. **ter•mi•nate** (tûr′mə-nāt′)

   a. How many syllables are in *terminate*? ___*three*___

   b. Which syllable is least strongly accented? ___*second*___

3 PARTS OF SPEECH

Every word in the dictionary is either a *noun*, a *verb*, an *adjective*, or another part of speech. In dictionary entries, the parts of speech are shown by letters in italics. In the entry for *insult*, for example, the abbreviations *v.* and *n.* tell us that *insult* is both a verb and a noun. The entry below for *flour* tells us that word is both a noun and verb. Another form of the word, *floury*, is identified as an adjective.

> **flour** (flour) *n.* **1.** A fine, powdery substance obtained by grinding grain, esp. wheat. **2.** Any similar soft, fine powder. —*v.* To cover or coat with flour. [ME.] —**flour′y** *adj.*

When a word is more than one part of speech, the dictionary gives the definitions for each part of speech separately. In the above entry for *flour*, the abbreviation telling us that *flour* is a noun comes right after the pronunciation symbols; the two noun definitions follow. When the noun meanings end, the abbreviation *v.* tells us that the verb definition will follow.

Parts of speech are abbreviated in order to save space. Following are the most common abbreviations for parts of speech:

n. — noun	*v.* — verb
pron. — pronoun	*conj.* — conjunction
adj. — adjective	*prep.* — preposition
adv. — adverb	*interj.* — interjection

Note: The abbreviations *tr.* and *intr.* in the *AHD* indicate two types of verbs, not other parts of speech. The abbreviation *tr.* stands for a transitive, or active verb; the abbreviation *intr.* stands for an intransitive, or passive verb. Some dictionaries indicate the two types of verbs with the abbreviations *vt* and *vi.*

➤ Practice 7

Use your dictionary to list the parts of speech for each of the following words. Each word has more than one part of speech.

Parts of speech:

1. incline   *verb, noun*

2. reverse   *adjective, noun, verb*

3. within   *adverb, preposition, noun*

4. bridge   *noun, verb*

5. level   *noun, adjective, verb, adverb*

4   IRREGULAR SPELLINGS

Look at the following two words and the forms that follow them in the *AHD*.

know (nō) *v.* **knew** (no͞o, nyo͞o), **known, know•ing.**

fun•ny (fŭn′ē) *adj.* **-ni•er, -ni•est.**

When other forms of a word are spelled in an irregular way, those forms are shown. As you can see in the examples above, those forms are given after the part of speech in an entry. With irregular verbs, the dictionary gives the past tense (*knew*), and the past participle (*known*), as well as the present participle (*knowing*). With adjectives, the dictionary gives the comparative (*funnier*) and superlative (*funniest*) forms.

Plural forms of irregular spellings are also included in this spot in an entry. For example, the entry for *country* begins:

coun•try (kŭn′trē) *n., pl.* **-tries.**

After the part of speech of *country* (*n.* for noun), the entry gives the irregular part of the plural (*pl.*) of *country*.

➤ *Practice 8*

Below are the beginnings of three dictionary entries. In the blanks, write in the part of speech and irregular or other troublesome spellings in full (not abbreviated).

1. **shake** (shāk) *v.* **shook** (sho͝ok), **shak•en** (shāk′ən), **shak•ing.**

   Part of speech: _____ *verb* _____

   Spelling of past tense: _____ *shook* _____

   Spelling of past participle: _____ *shaken* _____

   Spelling of present participle: _____ *shaking* _____

2. **live•ly** (līv′lē) *adj.* **-li•er, -li•est.**

   Part of speech: _____ *adjective* _____

   Spelling of form that means *most lively* (with *-est* ending): _____ *liveliest* _____

3. **qual•i•ty** (kwŏl′ĭ-tē) *n.* **-ties.**

   Part of speech: _____ *noun* _____

   Spelling of plural: _____ *qualities* _____

5   DEFINITIONS

Words often have more than one meaning. When they do, their definitions may be numbered in the dictionary. You can tell which definition of a word fits a given sentence by the meaning of the sentence. For example, the following are three of the definitions of the verb form of *revive* given in the *AHD*.

1. To bring back to life or consciousness.
2. To impart or regain health or vigor.
3. To restore to use.

Which of these definitions best fits the sentence below?

Modern technology can revive patients who have actually been considered medically dead.

The answer is definition 1: Modern technology can bring a patient back to life.

➤ *Practice 9*

Below are three words and their definitions from the *AHD*. A sentence using each word is also given. Choose the dictionary meaning that best fits each sentence.

1. **idle: 1.** Not working; inactive. **2.** Avoiding work; lazy.

   Which definition best fits the sentence below? _____1_____

   The streetcar tracks in our city have been *idle* since 1960, when the city switched from streetcars to buses.

2. **suspicion: 1.** The act of suspecting the existence of something, esp. of something wrong, with little evidence or proof. **2.** A faint trace; hint.

   Which definition fits the following sentence? _____2_____

   There was a *suspicion* of rum in the chocolate cake.

3. **sterile: 1.** Incapable of reproducing sexually. **2.** Producing little or no vegetation. **3.** Free from microorganisms.

   Which definition fits the following sentence? _____2_____

   The real estate agent had cheated young farmers by selling them *sterile* land.

6   SYNONYMS

A synonym is a word whose meaning is similar to that of another word. For instance, two synonyms for the word *fast* are *quick* and *speedy*.

Dictionary entries sometimes end with synonyms. Notice that the entry for *insult* ends with several synonyms:

> **in•sult** (ĭn-sŭlt′) *v.* To speak to or treat with disrespect or contempt. —*n.* (ĭn′sŭlt′). A disrespectful or contemptuous action or remark. [< Lat. *insultare*, to revile.]
> **Syns:** *insult, affront, offend, outrage v.*

A hardbound dictionary in particular will provide synonyms for a word and explain the differences in meaning among the various synonyms.

More information on synonyms as well as antonyms (words with opposite meanings) can be found in a *thesaurus* (thĭ-sôr′əs), which is a collection of synonyms and antonyms. A thesaurus can improve your writing by helping you to find the precise word needed to express your thoughts. A thesaurus works much like a dictionary. You look up a word and, instead of definitions, you get a list of synonyms and perhaps an antonym of the word. To help you find the right word when writing, a thesaurus is an important partner to your dictionary. Here are some good thesauruses, all of which are in paperback:

The New American Roget's College Thesaurus in Dictionary Form

The Random House Thesaurus

Roget's II: The New Thesaurus

Webster's New World Thesaurus

OTHER DICTIONARY INFORMATION: USAGE LABELS AND WORD ORIGINS

Usage Labels

In addition to listing definitions, a dictionary tells us if a meaning is considered something other than "Standard English." For example, the dictionary labels one meaning of the verb *ice*, "to kill," as *"Slang."* Other common labels include *"Colloquial"* (the word *pal* is labelled as colloquial) and *"Nonstandard"* (the word *ain't* is labelled as nonstandard). Such labels indicate language not considered appropriate in formal speech and writing.

In addition to usage labels, the dictionary provides field labels—special meanings of a word within a certain field. For instance, one dictionary definition of the word *farm* is labeled *"Baseball"* and is followed by a meaning that applies to the field of baseball: "assign to a minor-league baseball team."

Word Origins

The history of a word is called its *etymology*, which is shown in brackets at the end of some *AHD* entries. That information includes the language or languages the word came from and what it meant. Such information, which is more likely to appear in a hardbound dictionary than in a paperback one, may help you remember a word. For example, here is part of the entry in the hardbound *AHD* for the word *blunder*.

> **blun·der** (blŭn′dər) *n.* A stupid and serious mistake usually caused by ignorance, stupidity, or confusion. . . . . *v.* . . . **1.** To move awkwardly, or clumsily. **2.** To make a blunder. . . . [ME *blunderen*, to go blindly, prob. < ON *blunda*, to doze.]

From this we can see that *blunder* comes from words meaning *to doze* and *to go blindly*. Apparently the word is based on the idea that one who blunders is like someone who has fallen asleep on the job or someone who cannot see what he or she is doing. Making this connection between the word and its origins will help you better remember the meaning of *blunder.*

➤ *Review Test 1*

A. Where would you find the numbered words below—before, on, or following the page with the guide words? Fill in each blank with a **B** (for *before,*) an **O** (for *on*), or an **F** (for *following*).

Guide words: **mace / magazine**

1. machine _____ *O* _____

2. macaroni _____ *B* _____

3. moody _____ *A* _____

4. mailman _____ *A* _____

5. Mafia _____ *O* _____

B. Use your dictionary to find the correct spellings of the following words:

6. kabinit _____ *cabinet* _____

7. sircus _____ *circus* _____

8. dezign _____ *design* _____

9. jinjerbread _____ *gingerbread* _____

10. dinamite _____ *dynamite* _____

C. Answer the questions about the five words below. The pronunciation key on page 14 will help you answer some of the questions.

de•rive (dĭ-rīv′)	**trite** (trīt)
flu•ent (flōō′ənt)	**un•der•mine** (ŭn′dər-mīn)
ver•i•fy (vĕr′ə-fī′)	

11. Which word has the sound of the short *i*, as in *pit*? _____ *derive* _____

12-15. Which *four* words have the sound of the long *i*, as in *tie*? _____ *derive* _____
_____ *verify* _____   _____ *trite* _____   _____ *undermine* _____

16-18. Which *three* words have a schwa sound?
_____ *fluent* _____   _____ *verify* _____   _____ *undermine* _____

19. How many syllables are in the word *undermine*? _____ *three* _____

20. Which syllable is accented in the word *fluent*, the first or the second?
_____ *first* _____

► *Review Test 2*

Use your dictionary to do all of the following.

A. Place dots between the syllables in the following words. Then write the correct pronunciation symbols, including the accent marks.

1. s c r i b b l e ___scrib · ble___   ___skrĭb′əl___

2. e x h a u s t ___ex · haust___   ___ĭg-zôst′___

3. d e c i s i o n ___de · ci · sion___   ___dĭ-sĭzh′ən___

4. c e l e b r a t e ___cel · e · brate___   ___sĕl′ə-brāt′___

5. a v a l a n c h e ___av · a · lanche___   ___ăv′ə-lănch′___

B. List the parts of speech for each of the following words.

6. eclipse   *Parts of speech:* ___noun, verb___

7. green   *Parts of speech:* ___noun, adjective, verb___

C. Write the irregular plural form for the following word.

8. memory   *Irregular form:* ___memories___

D. What dictionary definition of *drown* fits the following sentence?

9. Elsie drowned her strawberry pancakes in strawberry syrup.

___to drench thoroughly or cover with or as if with a liquid___

_____

E. Write five synonyms given by the dictionary for the following word.

10. foolish   *Synonyms:* ___silly___

___absurd___

___preposterous___

___ridiculous___

___fatuous (or ludicrous)___

➤ *Review Test 3*

A. To review what you've learned in this chapter, answer each of the following questions by filling in the blank or circling the letter of the answer you think is correct.

1. Guide words can help you (*pronounce, find, define*) _____*find*_____ a word in the dictionary.

2. You can learn how to pronounce a word by using the pronunciation symbols and the
    a. part of speech.   b. synonyms.   c.) pronunciation key.

3. A schwa sounds like the *a* in the word
    a.) *about.*   b. *cake.*   c. *cat.*

4. The loudest syllable of a word is the one by the
    a.) bold accent mark.   b. schwa.   c. hyphen.

5. A thesaurus lists
    a. definitions.   b.) synonyms.   c. word origins.

B. Here is a chance to apply your understanding of the dictionary to a full-length selection. This reading is a true story about a relatively common event with an uncommon ending. Read the selection, and then answer the questions that follow.

Words to Watch

Following are some of the more difficult words that appear in the reading. Each word is followed by the number of the paragraph in which it appears and its meaning there. These words are indicated in the story by a small circle (°).

> *vulnerable* (2):   defenseless
> *confrontation* (6):   face-to-face meeting
> *heartening* (6):   encouraging

THE GENTLE GIANT AND THE RELUCTANT ROBBER

Tom Hinkle

Very often when a homeowner interrupts a robber in the course of   1
his work, injury or death is the result. A different ending occurred
recently at a home in a small New Jersey town. The figures in this true
drama were a small, slightly built thief who shall be called the

Reluctant Robber, and a largely built, tall homeowner who shall be known as the Gentle Giant.

The Giant awoke at 4 A.M. to the upsetting sound of glass shattering. He and his wife, Dorothea, thought at first their mischievous cat, Smokey, had done the deed. But just to be certain, since the couple's three children were fast asleep—and very vulnerable°—in the bedrooms upstairs, the Giant draped a bathrobe over his pajamas and crept silently downstairs to investigate.

"I was standing a short distance from the kitchen when I realized there was someone there, walking around in the darkness," he recalled. "I looked around for one of the children's baseball bats to use as a weapon." However, the Giant never found one—it was too dark. It was probably just as well, however, because the Giant, although an impressive physical figure, is by his own admission essentially a mild-mannered man with a marked dislike of violence.

Instead of finding a bat, the Giant suddenly found himself staring down directly into another man's eyeballs. His first impulse was simply to keep the guy calm. He saw that the intruder was unarmed and bleeding from cuts he sustained while breaking in the back door of the family's home. The Giant said, "Let's not kill ourselves over nothing. There's nothing in the house worth stealing and I know because I live here. Look, you're no threat to me and I'm no threat to you, so there's no use fighting. Besides, I can see you're bleeding pretty badly from the glass. Do you want to sit down?"

The robber replied, "You know, I think you've got a point. I am hurt. Would you mind if I lie down on your sofa for a bit?"

"No, go right ahead," the Giant answered. "I'll go tell my wife what's going on." The logic by both men during what could have been a dangerous confrontation° was heartening° and beautiful. "I'd have to live with it if I overreacted and blew him to kingdom come," the Giant said afterwards, during a police interview. "He stood there quietly and listened to everything I had to say. He was so polite, and I actually think the guy was only half-hearted about robbing the place anyway."

So, while the polite, bleeding, half-hearted Reluctant Robber rested on his couch—which was later badly stained with blood—the Giant tiptoed upstairs and asked Dorothea to phone the cops. Police from several towns responded to the call. The first patrol car whizzed right by the home while the Gentle Giant waved frantically for it to turn around. Then another police cruiser pulled up front. In the meantime, the other car had turned around and found the right address. A whole swarm of blue uniforms filed through the front door. At the same time the Giant greeted them, he pleaded with them to show some control. "I told them not to go in there with their guns drawn like gang-busters," he remarked. "I told them I'd talked to the man and he'd seemed cooperative and willing to give up. As soon as they walked in, the guy jumped up from the couch and looked startled."

The Reluctant Robber, whose mind was obviously fuzzy, told the   8 cops he was just dropping by for a visit. "Oh, really," the cops asked. "And just who is this man you're visiting at 4 A.M.? Tell us his name." Of course the Reluctant Robber had no idea who the Giant was. That made the cops laugh. Even the Giant laughed, and the robber himself managed a weak smile.

They took the Robber to a hospital where his wounds were   9 stitched. He is now being held on $5,000 bail for a charge of breaking and entering. The Giant, scratching his head, went back upstairs to go back to sleep.

A television police story? Never. The beauty of this encounter is   10 that it was real, not some make-believe cops-'n'-robbers script. Let's raise our glasses and toast both of these men. America needs level-headed folks like the Gentle Giant and the Reluctant Robber.

Dictionary Questions

Answer the questions that follow the two dictionary entries, both for words taken from the reading. The pronunciation key on page 14 will help you answer the pronunciation questions.

marked (märkt) *adj.* **1.** Having an identifying mark. **2.** Noticeable; distinctive. **—mark′ed•ly** (mär′kĭd-lē) *adv.*

1. The entry word would be found on the dictionary page with which guide words?
   a. manual alphabet / maraschino cherry
   b. maniac / manual
   c. marathon / markka
   d. marksman / marvelous

2. How many syllables are in the word *marked*?
   a. One
   b. Two
   c. Three
   d. Four

3. The *a* in *marked* sounds like the *a* in
   a. *pat.*
   b. *pay.*
   c. *care.*
   (d.) *father.*

4. The part of speech of *marked* is
   (a.) adjective.
   b. adverb.
   c. noun.
   d. verb.

5. Which definition of *marked* fits the sentence below?
   a. Definition 1
   (b.) Definition 2

   the Giant . . . is by his own admission essentially a mild-mannered man
   with a marked dislike of violence. (Paragraph 3)

sus•tain (sə-stān′) *v.* **1.** To maintain; prolong. **2.** To supply with necessities or
nourishment; provide for. **3.** To keep from falling or sinking. **4.** To support or
encourage. **5.** To endure or withstand. **6.** To suffer (loss or injury). **7.** To affirm the
validity or justice of. **8.** To prove or confirm. [< Lat. *sustinere,* to hold up.]
—sus•tain′a•ble *adj.*

6. *Sustain* would be found on the dictionary page with which guide words?
   a. sulfur dioxide / sunken
   b. Supreme Court / surprise
   (c.) surrealism / swab
   d. swaddle / sweat

7. The part of speech of *sustain* is
   (a.) verb.
   b. adverb.
   c. noun.
   d. adjective.

8. The *u* in *sustain* is pronounced like
   a. the *u* in *cut.*
   b. the *u* in *abuse.*
   c. the *a* in *father.*
   (d.) the *u* in *circus.*

9. The *ai* in *sustain* sounds like
   a. the *a* in *care.*
   b. the *a* in *pay.*
   c. the *a* in *about.*
   d. the *aw* in *paw.*

10. Which definition of *sustain* fits the sentence below?
    a. Definition 2
    b. Definition 3
    c. Definition 6
    d. Definition 8

> He saw that the intruder was unarmed and bleeding from cuts he sustained while breaking in the back door of the family's home. (Paragraph 4)

2

Vocabulary in Context

If you were asked to define the words *retain*, *forbearing*, and *bilingual*, you might have some difficulty. On the other hand, if you saw these words in the sentences below, chances are you could come up with quite accurate definitions:

Tina plans to *retain* her maiden name after she marries Phil. They have not decided what last name their children will have.

My parents are very different. My father, for example, is very *forbearing*, while my mother sometimes has no patience at all.

Rick is *bilingual*, speaking English almost as well as he speaks Spanish.

Now, see if you can choose the meaning of each word, based on the way each is used above. Circle the letter of the meaning you think is correct.

Definition of *retain*:

a. change   b. keep   c. remember

Definition of *forbearing*:

a. patient   b. strong   c. quiet

Definition of *bilingual*:

a. American   b. able to speak two languages   c. young

In the sentences above, the *context*—the words surrounding the unfamiliar word—provides clues to each word's meaning. You may have guessed from the context that *retain* means "keep," that *forbearing* means "patient," and that *bilingual* means "able to speak two languages."

Using **context clues** to understand new words will help you in a few important ways:

1   It will save you time when reading: you won't have to stop to look up words in the dictionary. (Of course, you won't always be able to understand a word from its context. You should always have a dictionary nearby to look up key words you cannot understand from context.)

2   It will improve your understanding of what you read because you will know more of the words.

3   It will expand your vocabulary. When you see a word more than once in context and guess its meaning, the chances increase that it will become part of your working vocabulary.

TYPES OF CONTEXT CLUES

There are four common types of context clues:

1   Examples

2   Synonyms

3   Antonyms

4   General Sense of the Sentence or Passage

In the following sections, you will learn about and practice each type. The practices will sharpen your skills in recognizing and using context clues. They will also help you add new words to your vocabulary.

1   Examples

Examples of an unknown word may reveal the word's meaning. To see how this works, read the sentences below. Using the boldfaced examples as clues, circle the letter of what you think is the definition for each word. Then read the explanations that follow.

Note: Examples may be introduced with such signal words as *for example, for instance, including,* and *such as.*

1.   In our house, hangers have various *functions*. For instance, in addition to **holding clothing**, they **scratch backs** and **hold up plants in the garden**.

Definition of *functions:*

a. shapes   b. problems   c. uses

2.   The relief pitcher had a few *eccentric* habits, such as **throwing exactly thirteen pitches when warming up** and **never wearing socks**.

Definition of *eccentric:*

a. normal   b. strange   c. messy

3. Throughout history, humans have built a wide variety of *dwellings*, from **tepees made of skin** to **mansions of stone**.

Definition of *dwellings:*

a. homes   b. stores   c. churches

Answers:

In each sentence, the examples probably helped you to figure out the meanings of the words in italics:

1. c   The *functions* named are "uses" of hangers.
2. b   The *eccentric* habits are "strange."
3. a   The *dwellings* are types of "homes."

➤ *Practice 1*

In each of the sentences below, underline the examples that are given of the italicized word. Then circle the letter of the definition of the italicized word.

1. The *debris* in the stadium stands included <u>numerous paper cups</u>, <u>ticket stubs</u>, and <u>cigarette butts</u>.

    a. products   b. papers   (c.) rubbish

2. For his weak stomach, Emilio ate a *bland* diet of <u>white bread</u>, <u>rice</u>, and <u>mashed potatoes</u>.

    a. spicy   b. varied   (c.) mild

3. After the terrorist was arrested, the FBI found in his apartment a large collection of *lethal* weapons, including <u>Uzi machine guns</u> and <u>plastic explosives</u>.

    (a.) deadly   b. harmless   c. noisy

4. My uncle often has embarrassing *mishaps*, such as <u>backing his car into the side of the boss's Cadillac</u> and <u>hurting himself while trying to walk through glass doors</u>.

    a. clever moves   (b.) accidents   c. projects

5. The Guinness Book of World Records tells many *bizarre* stories, such as those of <u>a man with 4,831 tattoos</u> and <u>a Chinese priest with twenty-two-inch fingernails</u>.

    a. untrue   (b.) odd   c. ordinary

2 Synonyms

Context clues are often found in the form of *synonyms*: words that mean the same, or almost the same, as the unknown word. Synonyms may be purposely included by an author to help readers understand a word. In such cases, the synonyms are often set off by commas, dashes, or parentheses. Also, they may be introduced by the words *or* ("Nuptials, or weddings, . . .") and *that is* ("an emetic, that is, a substance that causes vomiting. . . .").

A synonym may also appear anywhere in a sentence as a restatement of the meaning of the unknown word. Examples appear in the second and third sentences below.

In each of the following sentences, the word to be defined is italicized. Underline the synonym of each italicized word.

1. *Affluent*, or wealthy, Americans should be more concerned with the problems of the homeless.

2. My best friend *squandered* all his money; his drinking and gambling wasted his earnings.

3. Because my boss runs the toy store like a *despot*, all of the employees call her "the little dictator."

Answers:

In each sentence, the synonym given should have helped you understand the meaning of the word in italics:

1. People who are *affluent* are "wealthy."
2. *Squandered* means "wasted."
3. Someone who is a *despot* is a "dictator."

➤ *Practice 2*

Each item below includes a word or phrase that is a synonym of the italicized word. Underline the synonym of each italicized word.

1. With temperatures so cold this winter, the supply of natural gas for heating could be *depleted*, or used up, by spring.

2. After the heavy rains, the lake water became *murky*; in fact, the water was so cloudy you couldn't see to the bottom.

3. Some overweight people are called *furtive* eaters because they eat large quantities of food in secret.

4. What *criteria* should we use to judge the work of college professors? What standards can help us decide how effective they are?

5. The medicine Amy takes is very *potent*, so powerful, in fact, that she must not take it for more than a week.

3 Antonyms

Antonyms—words and phrases that mean the opposite of a word—are also useful context clues. Antonyms are often signaled by words and phrases such as *however, but, yet, on the other hand,* and *in contrast.*

In the sentences below, do two things:

(1) Find the words in each sentence that are the opposite of the italicized word. Underline those words.
(2) Then circle the letter of the definition of the italicized word.

1. The coach takes every opportunity to *censure* his players, yet he ignores every chance to praise them.

    Definition of *censure:*

    a. approve of   b. criticize   c. choose

2. "I am having *acute* pains in my chest now," said the patient, "but an hour ago all I felt was a mild pinch."

    Definition of *acute:*

    a. sharp   b. weak   c. no

3. Some teachers are too *lenient*—they have no rules in class and no real goals. I'd rather have a strict teacher who took class seriously.

    Definition of *lenient:*

    a. hard   b. easygoing   c. busy

Answers:

If you looked for the *antonyms* of the words in italics, you should have come up with these answers:

1. b   criticize   *Censure* is the opposite of "praise."
2. a   sharp   The opposite of *acute* is "mild."
3. b   easygoing   A *lenient* teacher is the opposite of a "strict" teacher.

➤ *Practice 3*

Antonyms provide context clues in the sentences below. Read each sentence and do two things:

(1) Underline the antonym for the word in italics. Each antonym may be one or more words.
(2) Circle the letter of the meaning of the word in italics.

1. Although Alex usually looked *unkempt*, he had a very <u>neat</u> appearance on his job interview.

    a. orderly   b. strange   (c.) messy

2. A <u>temporary</u> cough is nothing to worry about, but a *chronic* one can be a sign of a serious illness.

    (a.) continuing   b. brief   c. mild

3. When drinking was *prohibited* by the Nineteenth Amendment, alcohol became more popular with some people than it had been when <u>allowed</u>.

    a. permitted   b. defined   (c.) forbidden

4. "What we need is an *innovative* idea!" cried the chairman. "All I've heard so far are the same <u>old</u> ones."

    (a.) new   b. traditional   c. loud

5. The class was in *turmoil* when only the substitute teacher was there, but it quickly came to <u>order</u> once the principal entered the room.

    a. peace   (b.) confusion   c. gym

4   General Sense of the Sentence or Passage

Sometimes you can find a new word's meaning through the other ideas in a passage. Asking yourself questions about the passage may help.

Each sentence below is followed by a useful question. Thinking about the answers should help you define the italicized words. Circle the letters of the definitions you think are correct.

1. The newlyweds agreed to be very *frugal* in their shopping because they wanted to save enough money to buy a home.

    (*Hint:* How would people shop if they wanted to save money?)

    Definition of *frugal:*

    a. thrifty   b. wasteful   c. interested

2.   The owners *muted* the noises in their restaurant by installing special ceiling tiles and dividers between the booths.

(*Hint:* What would restaurant owners probably want to do about noise?)

Definition of *muted:*

a. increased   b. softened   c. created

3.   Friends tried to *dissuade* ninety-year-old Mrs. Kellen from attending her son's trial, but she went anyway, to show her support.

(*Hint:* What would the elderly woman's friends have tried to do if they didn't want her to go to her son's trial?)

Definition of *dissuade:*

a. question   b. describe   c. discourage

Answers:

Each sentence provides context clues that become clear if you read carefully.

1.   a   The sentence provides enough evidence for you to guess that *frugal* means "thrifty"—the newlyweds had to be thrifty if they wanted to save money.

2.   b   *Muted* means "softened"; a restaurant owner would probably want to cut down the noise.

3.   c   *Dissuade* means "discourage"—Mrs. Kellen went to the trial despite her friends' discouragement.

When you read, you may not hit on the exact dictionary definition of a word by using context clues, but you will often be accurate enough to make good sense of what you are reading.

➤ *Practice 4*

Try to answer the question that follows each of the items below. Then use your answer to help you choose the definition of the italicized word.

1.   Kelvin is very *humane*; yesterday he stopped his car on the highway to help an injured dog.

(*Hint:* How would we describe Kelvin's behavior?)

a. practical   b. uncaring   c. kind

2.   "Don't tell my sister where I'm going," Hong warned. "She loves to *divulge* secrets."

(*Hint:* What is Hong worried that his sister might do with a secret?)

a. reveal   b. hide   c. invent

3. Because the nicotine in cigarettes is addictive, many people favor *stringent* laws against their sale.

    (*Hint:* What type of laws would be favored by people concerned about the addictive nature of nicotine?)

    (a.) strict   b. weak   c. confusing

4. Taking the expression "raining cats and dogs" *literally*, the child looked for little animals on the ground after the storm.

    (*Hint:* In what way did the child interpret the phrase "raining cats and dogs"?)

    a. symbolically   b. musically   (c.) as the real facts

5. That old movie *evoked* many memories for my parents; they spent the rest of the evening recalling events from their childhoods.

    (*Hint:* How must the movie have affected the parents' memories?)

    (a.) brought to mind   b. confused   c. erased

A Note and Study Hint

You don't always have to use context clues or the dictionary to find definitions. Textbook authors usually give definitions of important terms. Here are three short excerpts from college texts. In each case, the term to be defined is set off in **boldface** type or *italic* type, and the definition then follows.

Excerpt from a psychology textbook:

Many children of normal intelligence have great difficulty learning how to read, write, or work with numbers. Often thought of as "underachievers," such children are said to have a **learning disability**, a disorder that interferes in some way with school achievement. The problem is common, affecting as many as 30 percent of all school children.

Excerpt from a business textbook:

DEF

EX

The changing work force has changed lifestyles and needs. No wonder many workers have found *flextime* a desirable option. Instead of working the standard nine-to-five day, five days a week, they choose their own hours within certain limits. For instance, a company may stipulate that everyone has to be at work between 10:00 A.M. and 2:00 P.M., but workers may arrive or depart whenever they want as long as they work a total of eight hours.

Excerpt from a sociology textbook:

Some older people respond to the fact of aging with **disengagement**—a retreat from relationships, organizations, and society. This behavior is considered normal and even satisying for the individual, because withdrawal brings a release from social pressures to compete and conform.

By using italic or boldface type, textbook authors are signaling to you that these terms are important to learn. Indeed, the first major step you should take to understand a textbook chapter is to mark off definitions and any examples in the text. Then write down those definitions and, if available, an example that makes the definition clear to you. Your focus on definitions and examples will help as you reread a chapter and work to increase your understanding of its content.

Which one of the three textbook excerpts shown above includes both a definition and an example? In the margin of that excerpt, write a "DEF" besides the definition and an "EX" besides the example. You will find it helpful to mark off definitions and examples in the same way when you are reading a textbook chapter.

➤ *Review Test 1*

Using context clues to help you, circle the letter of the best definition for the italicized word in each sentence.

1. The principal liked to *intimidate* students by walking through the halls with a baseball bat and shouting through a bullhorn.

   a. encourage   b. entertain   (c.) frighten

2. When the shoe popped up out of the lake, we were horrified to think what else might *emerge*.

   (a.) appear   b. go down   c. disappear

3. Some people work so non-stop that they accomplish a great deal but *forfeit* their health.

   a. strengthen   b. remember   (c.) lose

4. The crowd of protesters *dispersed* quickly when the police arrived with growling German shepherds.

   a. cheered   (b.) scattered   c. questioned

5. Paula was suspended from school because of several *infractions* of the rules, including smoking in the bathroom and dressing improperly.

   (a.) violations   b. observances   c. understandings

6. The students had *diverse* backgrounds, with many different nationalities and ethnic groups represented in the school.

    a. unknown   (b.) varied   c. similar

7. Just as water *erodes* riverbeds, constant criticism wears away self-confidence.

    (a.) eats away   b. builds up   c. reflects

8. While Louis is hardworking, his *indolent* brother spends most of his time watching TV or sitting around with friends.

    a. ambitious   b. energetic   (c.) lazy

9. We began the picnic in spite of such *ominous* signs as dark clouds and a falling temperature.

    a. welcome   b. cold   (c.) warning

10. Janice often asks *impertinent* questions such as "How did you get to be so fat?"; in contrast, her sister Samantha is always polite.

    a. clever   (b.) impolite   c. friendly

➤ *Review Test 2*

Using context clues to help you, write in the best definition for each italicized word. Choose from the meanings shown in the box. Each meaning should be used once.

force	shocked	sturdy
arrival	full of spirit	out of date
touching	interesting	disturb continuously
anger and disrespect		

1. The *advent* of spring is announced by the call "Play ball!" on sports fields across the country.

    Definition of *advent:* _____ *arrival* _____

2. Computers are now so common that typewriters are becoming *obsolete*, or old-fashioned.

    Definition of *obsolete:* _____ *out of date* _____

3. When Barbara's ex-boyfriend learned she was dating another guy, he started to *harass* her with threatening letters and obscene phone calls.

    Definition of *harass:* _____ *disturb continuously* _____

4. My sister is very *vivacious*; in fact, everyone at the party admired her lively personality.

    Definition of *vivacious*: _____ *full of spirit* _____

5. The story the former drug addict told was so *engrossing* to the students that they didn't move even when the bell rang.

    Definition of *engrossing*: _____ *interesting* _____

6. I have seen such *poignant* scenes as a homeless man caring for a little dog and a woman in a slum growing flowers in a patch of soil.

    Definition of *poignant*: _____ *touching* _____

7. The boys at the cafeteria table tried to *coerce* the shy new student into buying them ice cream.

    Definition of *coerce*: _____ *force* _____

8. I was *appalled* to learn that most chickens raised for food are put into such small cages that the birds are unable to spread their wings.

    Definition of *appalled*: _____ *shocked* _____

9. That baby needs a *durable* toy, not this fragile plastic one that could break and cause injury.

    Definition of *durable*: _____ *sturdy* _____

10. Most voters feel *contempt* for politicians who act as if they are above the law.

    Definition of *contempt*: _____ *anger and disrespect* _____

➤ Review Test 3

A. To review what you've learned in this chapter, answer each of the following questions. Fill in the blank or circle the letter of the answer you think is correct.

1. The context of a word is

    a. its meaning.   b. its opposite.   ⓒ the words around it.

2. One type of clue that helps readers figure out the meaning of a new word is the (*examples, synonyms, antonyms*) _____ *examples* _____ clue, which often follows such signal words as *including* or *such as*.

3. In the sentence below, which type of context clue is used for the italicized word?

   a. example   b. antonym   (c.) synonym

   I'm looking for a *unique* gift for my boyfriend; he appreciates unusual things.

4. In the sentence below, which type of context clue is used for the italicized word?

   a. example   (b.) antonym   c. synonym

   My dad's punishments tended to be mild; it was my mother who favored *stringent* penalties.

5. Often when textbook authors introduce a new word, they provide you with a _____*definition*_____ and follow it with _____*examples*_____ that help make the meaning of the word clear.

B. Here is a chance to apply the skill of understanding vocabulary in context to a full-length selection. The newspapers are filled with the stories of people who get pushed around by others, often for very little reason. The story below, from *The Philadelphia Inquirer*, is about someone who pushed back. After reading the selection, answer the vocabulary questions that follow.

Words to Watch

Following are some words in the reading that do not have strong context support. Each word is followed by the number of the paragraph in which it appears and its meaning there. These words are indicated in the story by a small circle (°).

oppressors:	those who use power unjustly
flushed (1):	reddened
simmering (2):	being filled with barely controlled emotion
riveting (7):	attention-demanding
obligatorily (9):	as expected, out of a sense of duty
predators (11):	those who abuse others for their own gains

VICTIMS VERSUS OPPRESSORS

Clark DeLeon

When I walked in the front door Sunday afternoon, Sara was   1
pacing back and forth like a caged lion. Her face was flushed°. She was
trembling from the waning effects of the adrenalin that had been

pumping through her body minutes before. I knew my first words should be more sensitive than, "Hi, honey, I'm home. What's for dinner?"

Sara had just returned from the supermarket at Sixth Street and Washington Avenue in South Philadelphia, where there had been another incident. There have been several of these incidents during the twelve years she has shopped there, but this was the worst. It started, as usual, in the checkout line. She was in the express line when a group of maybe five teenage boys walked up with some items and a couple of the teenagers pushed in front of her. Sara is one of those people who reacts to rudeness by speaking up rather than simmering° in silence and frustration. She told them that she was there first and they could get in line behind her. Big mistake.

The boys, in the 14–16 age range, began to make insulting remarks. "We can get in front of you if we want to," they muttered. Two of them pushed in front of her in line, and the other three were behind her. The remarks continued. Sara asked them to lay off, and they began mimicking her language: "Lay off, she wants us to lay off." Sara looked around. The cashier could easily see and hear what was going on, as could other customers. But no one wanted to do anything. This was her problem. She was invisible in a crowded place. Welcome to the New York subway.

They were waiting for her when she got outside. She figured she could leave the packages and get the car, in which case the food might be stolen, or she could walk to the car with her arms loaded and take that chance. She walked. They followed. They were punks, neighborhood toughs picking on a lone woman. What did they want? Maybe if she hadn't said anything. . . .

When Sara reached the car, they surrounded it. Then they sat on the hood. She asked them to get off, and they laughed at her. She put the packages inside the car. She asked them to get off the car again, and their taunts grew bolder. Then it happened.

Sara had been describing this to me in a trembling voice, and when she reached this part, she demonstrated what happened. "I slammed the door of the car, and I walked up to the one who had started it all and I went like this," she said, grabbing me hard by the lapels, pushing me against the wall at the same time she pulled my face close to her face, which was twisted in rage, "If you don't get off my car, you stupid . . . , you're dead!" she said.

Now to fully appreciate this, you'd have to know Sara. First of all, she is not a big woman, about 5-foot-6, and her face leans more to "sweet" than "tough." But I had no trouble believing she was capable of this display of imprudent temper (I call her an iron fist inside a velvet glove), and I also believed that this would have a riveting° effect on a 5-foot-10 teenager, considering that during the demonstration she almost lifted her 6-foot-3 husband off his feet.

The other thing you have to appreciate is that we don't use words like Sara used on these toughs. But here was Sara, surrounded by a gang, lunging at the ringleader, making Frank Sinatra threats and giving these kids a lecture in urban realities using urban "get out of my face" language. After she pushed off from the stunned teenager, she got in the car, started the engine, gunned the motor, put it in gear, and the kids scattered as she pulled away.

I looked at her in alarm and unbelievable pride. "That was a stupid thing to do," I said, obligatorily°. For the first time, she began to realize what she had done. She had been so caught up in the moment, she hadn't considered the extent of her action. Unarmed, unescorted women do not grab and threaten five menacing teenage boys. "Who do you think you are, Sara Goetz*?" I said. Then I laughed. We both laughed.

Sure it was a dumb thing to do, sure I could be writing a column with an entirely different ending right now. But I'm not, am I? If you choose to live in the city, you take your chances. To get all the good things that are to be had by city living, you run the risk of encountering the bad. There are many things Sara could have done to have avoided this situation—the first being nothing at all. But sometimes you get tired of being timid and you lash out at those who would take your city away from you. And sometimes that pure rush of righteous anger can stun those who would bully you, who would paralyze you through intimidation, who would make you feel small and powerless.

Are you wondering whether these boys were white or black? If so, ask yourself this: Does it matter? All race does is cloud the issue, and the issue here is victim versus oppressor. It's so rare when the victim turns the tables, and when that happens, we cheer. We see that, and we think to ourselves, let that be a lesson to the predators° of our cities.

As for you, Sara, don't you ever, ever, ever do something like that again.

*The reference here is to William Goetz, who shot several youths who threatened him on a New York City subway.

Vocabulary Questions

Use context clues in the reading to help you decide on the best definition for each italicized word. Then circle the letter of each choice.

1. The word *mimicking* in "Sara asked them to lay off, and they began mimicking her language: 'Lay off; she wants us to lay off'" (paragraph 3) means
   a. imitating.
   b. misunderstanding.
   c. avoiding.
   d. comparing.

2. In the sentence above, an example of *mimicking* is the words _____
   _____ *"Lay off; she wants us to lay off"* _____

3. The word *taunts* in "The boys, in the 14–16 age range, began to make insulting remarks. 'We can get in front of you if we want to'. . . . She asked them to get off the car again, and their taunts grew bolder" (paragraphs 3 and 5) means
   a. compliments.
   b. fears.
   c. insults.
   d. victims.

4. The word *imprudent* in "But I had no trouble believing she was capable of this display of imprudent temper (I call her an iron fist inside a velvet glove)" (paragraph 7) means
   a. angry.
   b. appropriate.
   c. rude.
   d. unwise.

5. The word *lunging* in "But here was Sara, surrounded by a gang, lunging at the ringleader, making Frank Sinatra threats" (paragraph 8) means
   a. moving forward forcefully.
   b. smiling quietly.
   c. avoiding.
   d. spying.

6. The word *menacing* in "Unarmed, unescorted women do not grab and threaten five menacing teenage boys" (paragraph 9) means
   a. armed.
   b. ordinary.
   c. threatening.
   d. energetic.

7. The word *timid* in "There are many things Sara could have done to have avoided this situation—the first being nothing at all. But sometimes you get tired of being timid and you lash out at those who would take your city away from you" (paragraph 10) means
   a. aggressive.
   b. fearful.
   c. avoided.
   d. prepared.

8. The word *encountering* in "To get all the good things that are to be had by city living, you run the risk of encountering the bad" (paragraph 10) means
   a. ignoring.
   b. giving in to.
   c. meeting unexpectedly.
   d. fighting against.

9. The word *intimidation* in "those who would bully you, who would paralyze you through intimidation, who would make you feel small and powerless" (paragraph 10) means
   a. threats.
   b. encouragement.
   c. illness.
   d. curiosity.

10. The words *turns the tables* in "It's so rare when the victim turns the tables, and when that happens, we cheer" (paragraph 11) mean
    a. protects oneself from an opponent with a table-like object.
    b. reverses a situation, gaining an advantage over an opponent.
    c. remains as calm as if sitting at a table.
    d. gets help from others.

3

Main Ideas

The most helpful reading skill is the ability to find an author's main idea. This chapter and Chapters 5 and 6 will develop your skill in recognizing main ideas.

UNDERSTANDING THE MAIN IDEA

The *main idea* is the central point of a passage. Very often the main idea of a paragraph appears in a sentence called the *topic sentence*. The rest of a paragraph consists of specific details that support and explain the main idea. You will find it helpful to remember that the main idea is a general idea compared to the specific ideas and details that support it.

You may also find it helpful to think of the main idea as an "umbrella" idea. Under the main idea, which is often expressed in a topic sentence, fits all the other material of the paragraph. The other material is specific details in the form of examples, reasons, facts, and other supporting evidence. The diagram below shows the relationship.

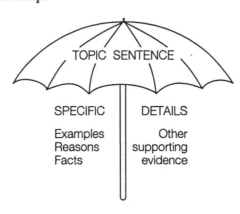

Now read the following paragraph and see if you can find the sentence that expresses the main idea.

As a rule, most of my dreams at night are pleasant ones. Recently, though, I had a really bad dream. I was in an alley dressed in light summer clothing. Coming out of the darkness at the end of the alley were hundreds of large gray rats. Their razor-sharp teeth glistened with saliva, and their eyes glowed red with a cold fury. I turned to run away, but attacking in the other direction were a dozen pit bulls. And these particular pit bulls were foaming at the mouth; they all had rabies. "Just my luck," I muttered, and did my best to wake up as quickly as possible.

Which of the following four sentences from the passage expresses the main idea of the paragraph? In other words, which is a general statement that is supported by most or all of the other material in the paragraph? Your choice will be the topic sentence of the passage. Write the letter of your choice in the blank below. Then read the explanation that follows.

Letter of the topic sentence: _____

a. I was in an alley dressed in light summer clothing.
b. Coming out of the darkness at the end of the alley were hundreds of large gray rats.
c. Recently, though, I had a really bad dream.
d. And these particular pit bulls were foaming at the mouth; they all had rabies.

Explanation:

Sentence a: This sentence is about only one narrow detail of the passage, the author's clothing. This sentence does not cover all of the other details that have nothing to do with what the author was wearing.

Sentence b: This sentence is also too narrow to be the main idea; it does not, for example, cover the attack by the pit bulls.

Sentence c: Is this sentence general or specific? The answer is that it is general. The words *really bad dream* are general enough to cover all of the specific details of the bad dream. Therefore, sentence *c* is the sentence with the main idea—it is the topic sentence.

Sentence d: This sentence is about another specific detail; it is thus too narrow to cover most or all of the specific details of the passage. For example, this sentence does not cover any of the details about the rats.

In summary, sentence *c* is the topic sentence—the sentence that expresses the main idea, and the other sentences are supporting details. Here is the umbrella diagram again. But this time it shows the relationship between the ideas in the paragraph about the bad dream.

RECENTLY I HAD A REALLY BAD DREAM

I was in an alley dressed in light summer clothing.
Hundreds of large gray rats came out of darkness.
Rats' razor-sharp teeth glistened with saliva.
Rats' eyes glowed red with a cold fury.
I turned to run away; a dozen pit bulls were attacking.
Pit bulls, foaming at the mouth, had rabies.
I did my best to wake up as quickly as possible.

In a nutshell, then, the main idea is a general idea that includes all or most of the material in a paragraph. The general idea is often stated in one sentence called the topic sentence. The other information is made up of specific details that support or explain the main idea.

GENERAL VERSUS SPECIFIC IDEAS

You have learned that the main idea in a paragraph is a *general* idea that is supported by *specific* ideas. To improve your skill at finding main ideas, then, it will be helpful for you to practice separating general from specific ideas.

You often use general and specific ideas without even realizing it. For example, in planning your food shopping you may think, "I need some vegetables. I guess I'll buy hot peppers, tomatoes, and onions." In such a case, "vegetables" is the general idea, and "hot peppers, tomatoes, and onions" are the specific ideas. General ideas (like vegetables) include many specific ideas (like hot peppers, tomatoes and onions).

Or if you are looking for a part-time job, you may think, "What features do I want for that job? I want at least $5 an hour, hours from 1 to 5 in the afternoon, and a travel time of no more than thirty minutes to the job." In this case, the *desired features of a part-time job* is the general idea, and *pay, hours,* and *travel time* are the specific ideas.

In other words, *general ideas* are broad, and *specific ideas* are narrower. *Animal*, for example, is a broad term that includes *tiger*, which is more narrow. *Feeling* is a broad term that includes specific terms like *depression* or *pity* or *happiness*, which are more narrow.

The practices that follow will give you experience in recognizing general-specific relationships.

➤ Practice 1

A. Each cluster of words below consists of one general idea and four specific ideas. The general idea includes all the specific ideas. Underline the general idea in each group. Before beginning, look at the examples:

Example   cotton   silk   <u>fabric</u>   rayon   velvet

(*Fabric* is the general idea; *cotton, silk, rayon,* and *velvet* are specific kinds of fabric.)

Example   fry   boil   steam   <u>cook</u>   bake

(*Cook* is the general idea; *fry, boil, steam,* and *bake* are specific kinds of cooking.)

1.   soup   water   <u>liquid</u>   gasoline   coffee

2.   potato chips   pretzels   salted nuts   <u>snacks</u>   dried fruit

3.   convertible   <u>car</u>   sedan   station wagon   hatch-back

4.   television   <u>entertainment</u> movies   concerts   card games

5.   bottles   cans   boxes   bags   <u>containers</u>

6.   rock   classical   country   jazz   <u>music</u>

7.   earrings   necklace   <u>jewelry</u>   ring   bracelet

8.   sundial   <u>timepiece</u>   digital clock travel alarm   wristwatch

9.   cough   sneeze   <u>symptoms</u>   sore throat   rash

10. talking   listening   yelling   whispering   <u>communicating</u>

B. In each pair below, one idea is general and the other is specific. The general idea includes the specific one. Do two things:

   (1) Underline the idea in each pair that you think is more general.

   (2) Then write in one more specific idea that is covered by the general idea. Look first at the examples.

Examples   maple   <u>tree</u>   _____*oak*_____

                     <u>command</u>   Stop!   ____*Come here.*____

1.   <u>insect</u>   cricket   *(Answers will vary.)*

2. <u>dessert</u>   ice cream   _____

3. <u>leader</u>   emperor   _____

4. wrench   <u>tool</u>   _____

5. <u>citrus fruit</u>   lemon   _____

6. <u>instrument</u>   piano   _____

7. <u>mathematics</u>   algebra   _____

8. coffee   <u>beverage</u>   _____

9. sapphire   <u>gem</u>   _____

10. squeak   <u>noise</u>   _____

Moving from General to Specific

Ideas can be arranged in order of how general or specific they are. For instance, *meal* is more general than *lunch* (lunch is one kind of meal), and *lunch* is more general than *sandwich* (sandwich is one type of lunch).

Try arranging the following three ideas in order of how specific they are. Put a *1* in front of the most general idea, a *2* in front of the less general idea, and a *3* in front of the most specific idea. Then read the explanation that follows.

_____ rock concert   _____ performance   _____ concert

The most general idea of the above three is *performance*, which can include types of performances other than concerts and rock concerts. There are, for example, performances at the circus. *Concert* is more specific than *performance* because a concert is a type of performance. *Concert*, however, is more general than *rock concert*, which is a specific type of concert. *Rock concert*, then, is the most specific of the three ideas. In summary, the correct answers are: 3 *rock concert*, 1 *performance*, and 2 *concert*.

➤ Practice 2

Put a *1* by the most general idea in each group, a *2* by the less general idea, and a *3* by the most specific idea.

1. __*2*__ rock singer   __*3*__ Bruce Springsteen   __*1*__ singer

2. __*1*__ animal   __*3*__ tiger   __*2*__ cat

3. __*2*__ board games   __*3*__ Monopoly   __*1*__ games

4. __*2*__ coin   __*1*__ money   __*3*__ quarter

5. __3__ microwave   __1__ appliance   __2__ kitchen appliance

6. __3__ *Newsweek*   __1__ publication   __2__ magazine

7. __1__ tools   __3__ circular saw   __2__ power tool

8. __1__ reading material   __3__ sports pages   __2__ newspaper

9. __2__ amusement-park rides   __3__ roller coasters   __1__ rides

10. __2__ parent   __3__ father   __1__ relative

TOPICS

Recognizing the topic of a selection can help you find the main idea. The *topic* is the subject that a selection is about. It is a general term that can usually be expressed in a few words. All of the sentences in a selection will be related to that topic. To find the topic of a selection, ask this simple question:

In general, who or what is the selection about?

Your answer should not be too broad or too narrow. Consider, for example, the following paragraph:

> Getting rid of garbage is an enormous problem in the United States. We must deal with over a billion pounds of garbage every day. That number is equal to about six to seven pounds of solid waste per person. A large amount of garbage is burned, but that creates air pollution. Ravines and swampy areas have been used for dumping garbage, but such locations near cities are fast being used up.

Now circle the letter of the item that you think is the topic of the paragraph. Then read the explanation below.

a. The world's garbage problem
b. Getting rid of garbage in the U.S.
c. U.S. dumping grounds

The topic of this paragraph is item *b*, "getting rid of garbage in the United States." We cannot say that the topic is "the world's garbage problem," for that is *too broad*—the paragraph is only about the U.S. We also cannot say that the topic is about "U.S. dumping grounds." That topic is *too narrow* because only one part of the paragraph is about U.S. dumping grounds.

Now try to find the topic of the paragraph below. One of the three subjects shown is too broad (that is, too general) to be the topic. One is too narrow (that is, too specific) to be the topic. A third subject is not too narrow or too broad—it is the topic of the paragraph.

Put a *B* by the subject that is too broad, an *N* by the subject that is too narrow, and a *T* by the subject that is the topic of the paragraph. Then read the explanation that follows and complete it by filling in the two words that are missing.

You may try harder to keep safe the body you have once you find out what it costs to replace body parts. One of the cheapest artificial body parts is the big toe, which can cost as little as $600, including surgery and hospital care. At the other end of the scale is the artificial heart, which costs as much as $90,000.

_____ Medical costs

_____ The cost of an artificial heart

_____ Costs of artificial body parts

Explanation:

"Medical costs" is not the topic of this paragraph, which discusses only

_____ type of medical cost. Thus "medical costs" is too broad. The one type of medical cost the paragraph does discuss is the "cost of artificial body parts," and that is the topic. "The cost of an artificial heart" is too narrow to be the topic—it is just an example of the topic. One other example is also given; that example is the cost of an artificial

_____ .

In summary, to decide if a particular subject is the topic of a passage, ask yourself these questions:

1 Does this subject include much more than what the passage is about? (If so, the subject is too broad to be the topic.)

2 Is there important information in the passage that isn't covered by this subject? (If so, the subject is too narrow to be the topic.)

➤ *Practice 3*

After each paragraph are three subjects. One is the topic, another is too broad to be the topic, and a third is too narrow to be the topic. Label each subject with one of the following:

>   *T*—for the topic of the paragraph
>   *B*—for the subject that is too broad
>   *N*—for the subject that is too narrow

Then try to fill in the missing words in the explanation that follows each paragraph.

1. There are a few steps you can take to improve your memory for names and faces. First of all, listen carefully for a person's name when he or she is introduced to you. Then repeat that name in responding to the introduction. If the name is unusual, ask how it is spelled. Then use the name again when you are saying goodbye. Finally, test your memory by repeating the name several times to yourself and by visualizing his or her face in the hour after you have met the person.

    _B_ Improving memory

    _N_ Improving memory for names

    _T_ Improving memory for names and faces

Explanation:

The best choice of topic for this paragraph is "Improving memory for names and faces." "Improving memory" is too broad—it covers memory for other things besides _____*names*_____ and faces. "Improving memory for names" is too narrow; it omits memory for _____*faces*_____, which is also part of the paragraph.

2. The sense of smell has two unappreciated roles. First, it is an important part of taste. Did you ever notice that when your nose is stuffed up with a cold, your food doesn't taste as good? Also, many of our memories are related to odors. The whiff of a scent as you pass a perfume counter, for example, can bring back memories of a whole summer you had long ago forgotten.

    _N_ The role of smell in tasting

    _T_ The sense of smell

    _B_ Our physical senses

Explanation:

"The role of smell in tasting" is just one part of this paragraph, so that subject is too narrow to be the topic. It does not account for the idea that odors can bring back _____*memories*_____. The topic is "The sense of smell," which covers all of the details in the paragraph. "Our physical senses" is much too broad to be the topic; a paragraph on that topic would have to include our other _____*senses*_____ as well as smell.

3.   Phobias are fears that are out of proportion to the actual dangers in given situations. For example, some people have a phobia about elevators. They worry that if they enter an elevator, the cable will break and they will fall hundreds of feet to their deaths. While such an accident can happen, it is extremely rare. Another instance of a phobia is a fear of medical needles. Some people will refuse to receive an injection, even if they are seriously ill. They fear the pain of the needle or the possibility that it might not be sterile, even in the doctor's office.

___B___ Fears

___T___ Phobias

___N___ Phobias about elevators

Explanation:

The topic of this paragraph is "phobias." "Fears" is too broad to be the topic—a paragraph on fears would include fears other than _____*phobias*_____. "Phobias about elevators" is too narrow to be the topic because the paragraph is about _____*phobias*_____ in general; the phobia about elevators is given only as an _____*example*_____. In addition, the paragraph gives a second example, the fear of _____*medical needles*_____.

➤ *Practice 4*

After each paragraph are three subjects. One is the topic, another is too broad to be the topic, and a third is too narrow to be the topic. Label each subject as follows:

> *T*—for the topic of the paragraph
> *B*—for the subject that is too broad
> *N*—for the subject that is too narrow

1. Mom was right about colds—the best cold remedies are simple ones. Resting, drinking hot liquids, and keeping warm are all useful, just as Mom said. Running a vaporizer or taking a hot shower helps relieve congestion. Sipping hot soup is also helpful, as is sucking on hard candies. Gargling with warm salt water is yet another simple but useful remedy.

    _B_   Remedies

    _T_   Cold remedies

    _N_   Treating a cold with liquids

2. If you smoke, your blood may be harmful to other people's health. According to one study, the blood donated by smokers contains high levels of pollutants that stay in the blood for up to thirty days. Someone receiving that blood may be deprived of oxygen and thus need another transfusion.

    _T_   The dangers of smokers' blood

    _B_   The dangers of smoking

    _N_   How long pollutants stay in smokers' blood

3. When video cassette recorders (VCRs) became popular in the early 1980s, many people thought the motion-picture industry would disappear. However, home movie rentals have caused a boom in the movie business. More films were released last year than in the previous ten years. And new movies are now being produced at a record pace.

    _B_   The movie industry

    _N_   The effect of VCRs on the movies last year

    _T_   The effect of VCRs on the movie industry

TOPIC SENTENCES

Finding the topic of a paragraph prepares you to find the topic sentence—the sentence that expresses the main idea of the paragraph. Once you have found the topic, you should ask yourself the question:

What is the author's main point about the topic?

For example, look again at the paragraph on garbage:

> Getting rid of garbage is an enormous problem in the United States. We must deal with over a billion pounds of garbage every day. That number is equal to about six to seven pounds of solid waste per person. A large amount of garbage is burned, but that creates air pollution. Ravines and swampy areas have been used for dumping garbage, but such locations near cities are fast being used up.

As you have seen, the *topic* of this paragraph is "Getting rid of garbage in the U.S." But what is the chief point the author is trying to make about that topic? Notice that each sentence after the first one discusses a specific part of that topic: 1) the problem of having to deal with huge amounts of garbage, 2) the problem of burning garbage creating air pollution, and 3) the problem of dumping garbage. The first sentence, however, is more general—it states that getting rid of garbage is an enormous problem in the U.S. It is this general idea that is the main idea. It is supported by the specific details in the rest of the paragraph.

To become skilled at finding main ideas, it can be helpful to distinguish between a passage's topic, main idea, and supporting details. Below is a group of four items. One is the topic, one is the main idea, and two are details that support the main idea. Label each item with one of the following:

> *T* —for the topic
> *MI*—for the main idea
> *SD*—for the supporting details

The topic will be the subject the items are about. The main idea will be the author's main point about the topic. And the supporting details will be specific ideas that help explain the main idea. After labeling each item, read the explanation that follows.

_____ a. Throwing toilet paper into tree branches is a common Halloween practice.

_____ b. Kids will often soap windows as they make their trick-or-trick rounds.

_____ c. Halloween pranks.

_____ d. There are certain traditional pranks associated with Halloween night.

Explanation:

All of the items are about Halloween tricks, or pranks. Thus item *c* is the topic (*T*). The main idea (*MI*) is item *d*—it gives the author's main point about Halloween pranks (that some of them are traditionally associated with Halloween night). Items *a* and *b* are specific details (*SD*); each supports the main idea by providing specific examples of traditional Halloween pranks.

The following exercise will give you more practice in distinguishing between the topic, main idea and supporting details of passages.

➤ *Practice 5*

Each group of items below includes one topic, one main idea (topic sentence), and two supporting details. In the space provided, label each item with one of the following:

> *T* —for the topic
> *MI*—for the main idea
> *SD*—for the supporting details

In addition, try to complete the explanation that follows the first group.

Group 1

_SD_ a. One pitcher smooths the dirt on the pitcher's mound before he throws each pitch.

_SD_ b. One infielder sits in the same spot on the dugout bench during every game.

_MI_ c. Some baseball players think that certain superstitious habits help them win games.

_T_ d. Superstitious baseball players.

Explanation:

Statements *a* and *b* each describe specific superstitious _____*habits*_____ of individual baseball players. Statement *c*, however, is more *(general or specific?)* _____*general*_____—it states that some players think certain superstitious habits help them win games. Statement *c* thus gives the main idea, and statements *a* and *b* are supporting details that explain that main idea. Item *d* is the topic.

Group 2

MI   a. During a night's sleep, you pass in and out of several stages of sleep.

T   b. Stages of sleep.

SD   c. At one point, you move into an especially deep sleep from which it is difficult to waken you.

SD   d. For about five minutes, the heart rate slows, breathing becomes uneven, and your body may twitch.

Group 3

MI   a. Some body fat is essential.

T   b. Body fat.

SD   c. Body fat insulates against the cold.

SD   d. Body fat protects organs from injury.

Group 4

T   a. Coconut oil.

MI   b. Coconut oil may be useful for food companies, but it is bad for the consumer.

SD   c. Coconut oil has a long shelf life.

SD   d. Coconut oil promotes heart disease more than other fats.

Group 5

MI   a. The safety of lawn pesticides is in doubt.

SD   b. Some people have had flu-like symptoms after their lawns were sprayed.

T   c. The safety of lawn pesticides.

SD   d. Some ingredients in lawn pesticides cause cancer in animals.

➤ *Practice 6*

Now that you've sharpened your skills in finding a topic and the main idea about that topic, use your skills on the following full paragraphs.

First, circle the letter of the correct topic of each paragraph. Then find the sentence in which the author states the main idea about that topic; put the number of that sentence in the space provided. In addition, complete the explanations after the first paragraph.

A.   ¹Marijuana is even worse for the body than tobacco. ²A joint does as much damage to the lungs as four tobacco cigarettes. ³One study showed that pot smokers absorb five times as much carbon monoxide into their blood streams and three to four times as much tar into their lungs as do cigarette smokers. ⁴Carbon monoxide is a known factor in coronary artery disease. ⁵And tar causes cancer.

1. The topic is
   a. addiction.
   b. consequences of inhaling tar.
   c. marijuana.

Explanation:

The subject of addiction is too (*broad or narrow?*) _____ broad _____ — it covers a great deal more than just an addiction to marijana, or to smoking. The subject of the consequences of inhaling tar is too (*broad or narrow?*)

_____ narrow _____; it does not cover the specific details about

carbon monoxide. Thus the topic is _____ marijuana _____, which is general enough to cover all the other material in the paragraph.

2. The author's main idea about that topic is expressed in sentence ___1___.

Explanation:

Sentences 2 through 5 list (*general or specific?*) _____ specific _____ ways in which marijuana is worse than tobacco. The first sentence, however,

makes the (*general or specific?*) _____ general _____ point that

marijuana is more harmful than tobacco. Thus sentence ___1___ is the umbrella statement that covers all the others—it is the topic sentence.

B. ¹The female black widow spider is not as terrible a killer as generally believed. ²While the creature is certainly poisonous, she is also very shy and will bite humans only when she feels cornered. ³Also, the idea that the black widow always kills the male after mating is untrue. ⁴The male is often spared—if he remembers to tap out a special signal as he ventures onto his mate's web. ⁵The vibrations on the web let her know he is one of her own kind, not an insect to be rushed at and killed.

1. The topic is
    (a.) the female black widow spider.
    b. poisonous spiders.
    c. the fate of the male black widow spider.

2. The author's main idea about that topic is expressed in sentence ___1___.

C. ¹When deciding on the timing of stoplights, traffic planners must consider a few factors. ²For instance, they must think about how fast traffic should move in a given area. ³In New York City, stoplights are usually set for traffic to move at twenty-three to thirty miles an hour. ⁴Traffic planners must also consider whether streets are one-way or two-way. ⁵On one-way streets, it is effective for a light on 10th Street, for example, to turn green a few seconds after the light on 9th Street. ⁶However, on two-way streets, several signals must all change at the same time.

1. The topic is
    (a.) the timing of stoplights.
    b. stoplights.
    c. the timing of stoplights on one-way streets.

2. The author's main idea about that topic is expressed in sentence ___1___.

IN CONCLUSION

In this chapter, you first worked on recognizing general-specific relationships. You then practiced distinguishing the topic of a paragraph from subjects that were too broad or too narrow. These activities prepared you for the main activity of this chapter—recognizing the main idea of a passage as expressed in its topic sentence.

Note that in longer selections made up of many paragraphs, such as articles or textbook chapters, there is an overall main idea called the *central point*. From now on, when you read longer selections in this text, you will be given practice in finding this central point, as well as in finding the main ideas of shorter passages within the reading.

The next chapter will sharpen your understanding of the specific details that authors use to support and develop their main ideas.

➤ *Review Test 1*

A. Each cluster below is made up of a general idea and four specific ideas that fit under it. Underline the general idea in each group.

1.	magician	<u>performer</u>	musician	actress	clown
2.	president	politician	<u>leader</u>	pope	general
3.	<u>housing</u>	tepee	condominium	palace	apartment
4.	hearing	smell	touch	<u>sense</u>	sight
5.	nicotine	alcohol	<u>drug</u>	cocaine	aspirin
6.	flour	<u>ingredient</u>	yeast	water	eggs
7.	tinsel	colored lights	<u>decorations</u>	streamers	wreath

B. In each pair below, one idea is general and the other is specific. The general idea includes the specific one. Do two things:

(1) Underline the idea in each pair that you think is more general.

(2) Then write in one more specific idea that is covered by the general idea.

8.	<u>clothing</u>	miniskirt	*(Answers will vary.)*
9.	Thanksgiving	<u>holiday</u>	_____
10.	measles	<u>illness</u>	_____
11.	<u>politician</u>	mayor	_____
12.	Dracula	<u>monster</u>	_____
13.	magazine	<u>publication</u>	_____
14.	<u>TV show</u>	situation comedy	_____

C. Each group of three items below contains three levels of ideas. Put a *1* by the most general idea in each group, a *2* by the less general idea, and a *3* by the most specific idea.

15.	_1_ plant	_3_ dandelion	_2_ weed
16.	_3_ poodle	_1_ pet	_2_ dog
17.	_2_ reference book	_3_ dictionary	_1_ book
18.	_3_ Martin Luther King	_1_ leader	_2_ civil-rights leader
19.	_1_ weapon	_3_ rifle	_2_ gun
20.	_2_ woman	_1_ human	_3_ Rita

➤ *Review Test 2*

A. After each paragraph are three subjects. One is the topic, another is too broad, and a third is too narrow. Label each subject with one of the following:

> *T*—for the topic of the paragraph
> *B*—for the subject that is too broad
> *N*—for the subject that is too narrow

1. For centuries people believed that sleepwalkers were possessed by evil spirits. These spirits forced them to wander throughout the night. Researchers today say that other, more worldly causes are behind sleepwalking. First of all, nighttime wandering may result from stresses and frustrations built up during the day. Also, the tendency to sleepwalk can be inherited. This was illustrated by the report of a patient at a California sleep disorder clinic. He once woke up in the dining room during a family reunion and found himself surrounded by sleepwalking relatives.

    __*B*__   sleep

    __*T*__   causes of sleepwalking

    __*N*__   the inherited tendency to sleepwalk

2. The teddy bear, one of the world's most popular toys, owes its existence to President Theodore Roosevelt. In 1902, President Roosevelt was on a trip to Mississippi. While there, he went on a hunting trip with his hosts. The hunting wasn't good that day, so his hosts, not wishing the President to return home empty-handed, trapped a bear cub for him to shoot. "Teddy" Roosevelt's refusal to shoot the little bear was reported on by newspapers around the world. A quick-thinking toy salesman in New York, realizing the value of publicity, made up a stuffed bear he named "Teddy's Bear." Orders for the bear poured in, and a classic toy was born.

    __*N*__   President Roosevelt's refusal to shoot a baby cub

    __*B*__   Unusual beginnings

    __*T*__   The teddy bear

B. Each group of four items includes one topic, one main idea (topic sentence), and two supporting ideas. Label each item with one of the following:

> *T* —for the topic
> *MI*—for the main idea
> *SD*—for the two supporting details

Group 1

_MI_   a. The human skeleton has certain important functions.

_SD_   b. The skeleton gives the body support and shape.

_SD_   c. The skeleton protects internal organs.

_T_   d. The human skeleton.

Group 2

_SD_   a. Native Americans have unusually high rates of alcoholism, homicide, and suicide.

_T_   b. Problems of American Indians.

_SD_   c. The unemployment rate of Native Americans stays around 50 percent.

_MI_   d. Statistics show that American Indians experience greater problems than any other minority.

C. Circle the letter of the correct topic of the following paragraph. Then find the sentence in which the author states the main idea about that topic, and write that number in the space provided.

> ¹The hedgehog, a spiny animal that lives in much of Europe and Africa, is a very effective snake-killer. ²First, the hedgehog sneaks up on the snake and bites its tail firmly. ³The hedgehog immediately curls up into a tight ball, still holding the snake's tail in its mouth. ⁴The snake then strikes the hedgehog again and again, but all it does is injure itself against the hedgehog's pointed spines. ⁵As the snake strikes, the hedgehog continues chewing until the snake is dead. ⁶Finally, the hedgehog uncurls and enjoys its meal.

   1. The topic is
     a. snake-killers.
     (b.) the hedgehog.
     c. the hedgehog's spines.

   2. The author's main idea about that topic is expressed in sentence __1__.

➤ Review Test 3

A. To review what you've learned in this chapter, answer each of the following questions by filling in the blank or circling the letter of the answer you think is correct.

   1. The supporting details are always more *(general or specific?)* ___specific___ than the main idea.

2. When the main idea is stated in one sentence of a paragraph, that sentence is called the
    a. topic. (b.) topic sentence. c. supporting detail.

3. The umbrella statement that covers all of the material in a paragraph is the
    a. topic. (b.) topic sentence. c. supporting detail.

4. To find the main idea of a passage, you may find it helpful to first decide on its
    (a.) topic. b. topic sentence. c. supporting details.

5. For selections made up of many paragraphs, the author's overall main point is called the
    a. central topic. (b.) central point. c. topic sentence.

B. Here is a chance to apply your understanding of main ideas to a full-length reading. First read the following selection from the college textbook *Sociology, Third Edition* (Wadsworth, 1989) by Rodney Stark—it will give you a fascinating view of the type of behavior we all witness every day. Then answer the questions that follow on topic, main idea, and central point. There are also vocabulary questions to help you continue practicing the skill of understanding vocabulary in context.

Words to Watch

Following are some words in the reading that do not have strong context support. Each word is followed by the number of the paragraph in which it appears and its meaning there. These words are indicated in the selection by a small circle (°).

conformity (2):	action in accordance with group ideas and customs
confirming (2):	proving true
perception (3:	observation
perceive (10):	observe through sight, sound, etc.
stakes (10):	something to be gained or lost

GROUP PRESSURE

Rodney Stark

It is <u>self-evident</u> that people tend to conform to the expectations   1
and reactions of others around them. But what are the limits of group
pressure? Can group pressure cause us to deny the obvious, even
physical evidence?

Over thirty-five years ago, Solomon Asch performed the most   2
famous experimental test of the power of group pressure to produce
conformity°. Since then his study has been repeated many times, with
many variations confirming° his original results. Perhaps the best way
to understand what Asch discovered is to pretend that you are a subject
in his experiment.

You have agreed to take part in an experiment on visual   3
perception°. Upon arriving at the laboratory, you are given the seventh
in a line of eight chairs. Other students taking part in the experiment sit
in each of the other chairs. At the front of the room the experimenter
stands by a covered easel. He explains that he wants you to judge the
length of lines in a series of comparisons. He will place two decks of
large cards upon the easel. One card will display a single vertical line.
The other card will display three vertical lines, each of a different
length. He wants each of you to decide which of the three lines on one
card is the same length as the single line on the other card. To prepare
you for the task, he displays a practice card. You see the correct line
easily, for the other lines are noticeably different from the comparison
line.

The experiment begins. The first comparison is just as easy as the   4
practice comparison. One of the three lines is obviously the same
length as the comparison line, while the other two are very different.
Each of the eight persons answers in turn, with you answering seventh.
Everyone answers correctly. On the second pair of cards, the right
answer is just as easy to spot, and again all eight subjects are correct.
You begin to suspect that the experiment is going to be a big bore.

Then comes the third pair. The judgment is just as easy as before.   5
But the first person somehow picks a line that is obviously wrong. You
smile. Then the second person also picks the same obviously wrong
line. What's going on? Then the third, fourth, fifth, and sixth subjects
answer the same way. It's your turn. You know without doubt that you
are right, yet six people have confidently given the wrong answer. You
are no longer bored. Instead, you are a bit confused, but you go ahead
and choose the line you are sure is right. Then the last person picks the
same wrong line everyone else has chosen.

A new pair is unveiled, and the same thing happens again. All the   6
others pick an obviously wrong line. The experimenter remains matter-
of-fact, not commenting on right or wrong answers but just marking
down what people pick. Should you stick it out? Should you go along?
Maybe something's wrong with the light or with your angle of vision.
Your difficulty lasts for eighteen pairs of cards. On twelve of them, all
the others picked a line you knew was incorrect.

When the experiment is over, the experimenter turns to you with a 7 smile and begins to explain. You were the only subject in the experiment. The other seven people were stooges paid by Professor Asch to answer exactly the way they did. The aim of the experiment was to see if social pressure could cause you to reject the evidence of your own eyes and conform.

In his first experiment, Asch tested fifty people in this situation. 8 Almost a third of them went along with the group and gave the wrong answer at least half of the time. Another 40 percent yielded to the group some of the time, but less than half of the time. Only 25 percent refused to yield at all. Those who yielded to group pressure were more likely to do so as the experiment progressed. Nearly everyone withstood the group the first several times, but as they continued to find themselves at odds with the group, most subjects began to weaken. Many shifted in their chairs, trying to get a different line of vision. Some blushed. Finally, 75 percent of them began to go along at least a few times.

The effects of group pressure were also revealed in the behavior 9 of those who steadfastly refused to accept the group's misjudgments. Some of these people became increasingly uneasy and apologetic. One subject began to whisper to his neighbor, "Can't help it, that's the one," and later, "I always disagree—darn it!" Other subjects who refused to yield dealt with the stress of the situation by giving each nonconforming response in a progressively louder voice and by casting challenging looks at the others. In a recent replication of the Asch study, one subject loudly insulted the other seven students whenever they made a wrong choice. One retort was "What funny farm did you turkeys grow up on, huh?"

The Asch experiment demonstrates that a high proportion of 10 people will conform even in a weak group situation. They were required merely to disagree with strangers, not with their friends, and the costs of deviance were limited to about half an hour of disapproval from people they hardly knew. Furthermore, subjects were not faced with a difficult judgment—they could easily perceive° the correct response. Little wonder, then, that we are inclined to go along with our friends when the stakes° are much higher and we cannot even be certain that we are right.

Reading Comprehension Questions

Vocabulary in Context

1. The word *stooges* in "The other seven people were stooges paid by Professor Asch to answer exactly the way they did" (paragraph 7) means
   a. comedians.
   b. people who played a role.
   c. true subjects in an experiment.
   d. educators.

2. The word *withstood* in "Nearly everyone withstood the group the first several times, but as they continued to find themselves at odds with the group, most subjects began to weaken" (paragraph 8) means
   a. recognized.
   b. agreed with.
   c. resisted.
   d. understood.

3. The word *steadfastly* in "The effects of group pressure were also revealed in the behavior of those who steadfastly refused to accept the group's misjudgments. Some of these people became increasingly uneasy and apologetic" (paragraph 9) means
   a. constantly.
   b. wrongly.
   c. helpfully.
   d. comfortably.

4. The word *replication* in "In a recent replication of the Asch study, one subject loudly insulted the other seven students" (paragraph 9) means
   a. memory.
   b. duplication.
   c. image.
   d. prediction.

5. The word *retort* in "one subject loudly insulted the other seven students whenever they made a wrong choice. One retort was 'What funny farm did you turkeys grow up on, huh?'" (paragraph 9) means
   a. genuine question.
   b. form of praise.
   c. choice.
   d. quick, sharp reply.

6. The word *deviance* in "they were required merely to disagree with strangers, not with their friends, and the costs of deviance were limited to about half an hour of disapproval from people they hardly knew" (paragraph 10) means
   a. going along with the crowd.
   b. an experimental test.
   c. differing from the normal group behavior.
   d. being a stranger.

Central Point

7. Which of the following is the topic of the whole selection?
   a. Visual perception
   b. Solomon Asch
   c. Asch's experimental test on group pressure
   d. Stooges in an experiment

8. Which sentence from the reading comes closest to expressing the central point of the whole selection?
   a. "Upon arriving at the laboratory, you are given the seventh in a line of eight chairs."
   b. "The experimenter remains matter-of-fact, not commenting on right or wrong answers but just marking down what people pick."
   c. "In his first experiment, Asch tested fifty people in this situation."
   d. "The Asch experiment demonstrates that a high proportion of people will conform even in a weak group situation."

Main Ideas

9. The topic of paragraph 9 is
   a. the behavior of subjects who refused to accept the group's misjudgments.
   b. subjects who became uneasy and apologetic.
   c. a duplication of the Asch study.
   d. subjects who insulted others.

10. The main idea of paragraph 9 is expressed in its
    a. first sentence.
    b. second sentence.
    c. next-to-the-last sentence.
    d. last sentence.

4

Supporting Details

You know from the previous chapter that the most important reading skill is the ability to find the main idea. Another key reading skill is the ability to locate *supporting details*. These details provide the added information that is needed to make sense of a main idea.

WHAT ARE SUPPORTING DETAILS?

Supporting details are reasons, examples, steps, or other kinds of factual evidence that explain main ideas. To see how details support a given main idea, it helps to contrast them with details that do not support that main idea.

For example, read the topic sentence below. (Remember, the topic sentence states the main idea.) Two of the three statements under it are **reasons** that support the main idea. One statement does not support the main idea. Circle the letter of the statement that *does not* support the main idea. Then read the explanation that follows.

Some students prefer going to school by means of a carpool.

a. Their gas and parking expenses are lower in a carpool.
b. Recent government regulations require some workers to use a carpool.
c. Students who are not driving can study or sleep on the way to school.

Which sentence does not support the main idea? The answer is sentence *b*. The other two sentences develop the main idea—they are **reasons** why some students prefer going to school with a carpool. Sentence *b,* however, is not such a reason—it concerns workers, and the main idea is about students.

Below is another topic sentence and another list. Two of the three statements in the list are **examples** that support the main idea. Circle the letter of the one statement that does not support the main idea.

Americans in the last century used different methods of oral hygiene than we do.

a. Nineteenth-century Americans purchased special powders that they mixed with honey to form a toothpaste.
b. The first tooth-cleaning device was the toothpick, which has been found in ancient ruins.
c. In the 1800s, a favorite American mouthwash was cologne.

Sentence *a* supports the main idea by giving us a specific example of an oral-hygiene method of the nineteenth century in America. Sentence *c* also supports the main idea with an example from nineteenth-century America. Sentence *b*, however, refers to oral hygiene in ancient days—not in America in the last century, so it does not support the main idea at all.

Here is a third topic sentence and another list. Two of the three statements in the list are **steps** in a process referred to generally in the main idea. Circle the letter of the one statement that does not support the main idea:

There are several steps to previewing a textbook chapter.

a. First of all, note carefully the title—it tells you the topic of the entire chapter.
b. Then read the first and last paragraphs, which often summarize the main ideas of the chapter.
c. Previewing, however, is not the way to read fiction.

Sentences *a* and *b* each support the main idea by providing a specific step in the process of previewing a textbook reading. Sentence *c* is also about previewing, but it is about reading fiction, not the textbook reading mentioned in the main idea. Thus sentence *c* does not support the main idea at all.

By now you probably have a better idea of how supporting details develop a main idea. They tell us more about the main idea—by proving it with reasons, by illustrating it, or by explaining it. The following practices will strengthen your sense of the relationship between a main idea and the details that support it.

Hint: To decide whether a sentence does or does not support a main idea, ask yourself, "Does this sentence give details that make the main idea clear? Or does it introduce a totally new point?" If the sentence clarifies the main idea, it is a supporting detail. If the sentence introduces a new point, it does not support the main idea.

➤ *Practice 1*

Each topic sentence below is followed by a list of three other sentences. Circle the letter of the one sentence that *does not* support the main idea.

1. People often wear symbols.
    a. A ring may symbolize that a person is engaged or married.
    b. Special clothing can symbolize that someone is a member of the clergy.
    (c.) Flags are symbols of countries.

2. Computers are greatly changing the workplace.
    a. Most company accounting systems have been computerized.
    (b.) Computers at home can be used for homework and tax returns.
    c. Computer systems can provide business with up-to-the-minute information.

3. Enjoying weekend nights at home has become popular for financial reasons.
    a. Renting a video is cheaper than going out to the movies.
    (b.) Saving a certain amount out of every paycheck is a good way to build savings.
    c. Eating take-out food at home, with your own beverages and no tips, is cheaper than eating out.

4. I had a hard time socially when I changed high schools in my junior year.
    (a.) My new high school didn't accept all my credits from my old high school.
    b. By junior year, my classmates were all set in their own circles of friends.
    c. Things were so bad that I ended up going to the prom with my cousin.

➤ *Practice 2*

The topic sentence of each of the following paragraphs is boldfaced. Locate and write down the number of the one sentence in each paragraph that *does not* support the main idea. Read the entire paragraph before making your decision.

1. ¹**In addition to routine jobs like doing taxes, computers can do some work usually associated with human thought.** ²Humans, however, are still more creative than computers. ³But computers can now be programmed to understand languages, a job once believed to need human thought. ⁴In addition, if computers are given all the factors involved in a situation, they can solve problems.

    The sentence that does *not* support the main idea: ___2___

2. ¹**Babies cry at different pitches and rhythms, depending on how distressed they are.** ²Low-pitched cries with a rhythmical "wah-wah" sound might mean only hunger or discomfort. ³You can often also tell when an adult is uncomfortable by the sound of his or her voice. ⁴A high-pitched cry

with a faster rhythm usually means that a baby is in real pain. [5]And then there's the very high-pitched cry, amounting to a screech, that often signals a problem requiring medical attention.

The sentence that does *not* support the main idea: _____3_____

3.   [1]**A research project showed that our work has a lot to do with how much we walk.** [2]For the project, people in various occupations wore pedometers (instruments that measure about how far one walks). [3]In that way, it was learned that hospital nurses walked the most on the job—over five miles a day. [4]Nursing is demanding in various other ways as well. [5]Walking between about three and four miles a day were security officers, city messengers, retail salespeople, and hotel servers. [6]Those who walked the least on the job—less than a mile each day—were dentists.

The sentence that does *not* support the main idea: _____4_____

4.   [1]**Experts have suggested several causes for the poor physical condition of our nation's children.** [2]For one thing, children watch too much television. [3]The more they watch, the more they are likely to be overweight. [4]Some blame also falls on the nation's schools. [5]Many schools fail to provide physical education classes on a daily basis. [6]Research has also revealed that parents are poor role models when it comes to physical exercise. [7]There is some evidence that the physical fitness of our children is less than it was ten years ago.

The sentence that does *not* support the main idea: _____7_____

READING CAREFULLY

In order to clearly understand the main idea of a selection, you need to carefully read the supporting details. If you read attentively, you are not likely to misinterpret what the author is saying. Your understanding will also be strengthened by noting the relationship of the main idea and its supporting details.

Read the following paragraph closely and answer the questions about it. The topic sentence (main idea) is boldfaced.

Explanations of the correct answers follow.

[1]**Elephants attracted to the odor of brewing beer have brought terror to some Indian villages.** [2]The beer is made from rice and is brewed after the rice harvest. [3]The smell of the brew in one remote village attracted thirteen elephants, who drank the town's beer. [4]Then they marched drunkenly through town searching for more. [5]In the process, they killed five people and injured twelve. [6]Two thousand residents were forced to flee. [7]Recently, similar disturbances by elephants have taken place in many villages, destroying more than fifteen thousand acres of rice paddies in one month.

1. _____ TRUE OR FALSE? The elephants get drunk from rice beer.

2. The answer to question 1 can be found in sentence
   a. 1.
   b. 3.
   c. 4.
   d. 7.

3. The idea below is
   a. true according to the paragraph.
   b. false according to the paragraph.
   c. not mentioned in the paragraph.

   Elephants have been causing destruction in Indian villages for years.

4. *Fill in the missing detail:* Elephants in search of rice beer have destroyed

   over _____ acres of rice paddies in one month.

5. Rice beer is brewed
   a. all year.
   b. before the rice harvest.
   c. after the rice harvest.

Explanations:

As you probably realize by now, answering the above questions involves reading the paragraph carefully. Here is an explanation of each answer:

1. A careful reading reveals that the answer to question 1 is *true*.

2. The answer is *c*—the answer to the first question can be found in sentence 4 in the words *they marched drunkenly*. Those words make it clear that elephants do, in fact, get drunk from the beer.

3. The answer is *c*, for the paragraph does not mention how long elephants have been causing the destruction.

4. The detail missing is *fifteen thousand*, which is given in sentence 7.

5. The answer to the final question is *c* because sentence 2 tells us that the beer "is brewed after the rice harvest."

> *Practice 3*

Answer the questions that follow the paragraphs. The topic sentence of each paragraph is boldfaced.

A. ¹**Some strange and disturbing events have happened around extra-high-voltage electrical lines.** ²The lines, for example, often glow a weird blue. ³Also, they can cause unconnected fluorescent bulbs to light up. ⁴Perhaps more scary, however, is that many people near the extra-high-voltage lines have gotten unexpected shocks. ⁵People living near such wires, for instance, have complained about getting shocks when touching wire fences or farm machines. ⁶Some have even complained of receiving shocks from damp clotheslines and even while sitting on the toilet.

1. The author feels that the most frightening of the types of events caused by the extra-high-voltage wires is probably
   a. the wires glowing blue.
   b. the disconnected fluorescent tubes lighting up.
   ⓒ people getting unexpected shocks.
   d. people getting shocks from touching farm machines.

2. The answer to question 1 can be found in sentence
   a. 2.
   b. 3.
   ⓒ 4.
   d. 6.

3. Near extra-high-voltage lines, people get shocks
   a. from touching fluorescent bulbs.
   b. only by touching metal objects.
   ⓒ by touching some metal and some non-metal objects.
   d. from the blue light.

4. The statement below is
   a. true according to the paragraph.
   b. false according to the paragraph.
   ⓒ not mentioned in the paragraph.

   There are numerous extra-high-voltage wires around the country.

5. __F__ TRUE OR FALSE? We can find an answer to the following question in the paragraph.

   What causes the electrical lines to glow blue?

B.   ¹**The negative effects of acid rain on soil have far-reaching consequences for humans.** ²First, acid rain dissolves and carries away valuable plant nutrients. ³This can damage farm soils, threatening our long-term food supply. ⁴Acid rain also converts harmless aluminum substances in the soil into harmful compounds. ⁵Those harmful forms of aluminum are causing forests to die. ⁶Also, the compounds have been washed into thousands of rivers and lakes, where they have killed off numerous fish.

1. __F__ TRUE OR FALSE? The one real problem with acid rain is that it causes forests to die.

2. Harmful aluminum substances
   a. are created by acid rain from plant nutrients.
   b. dissolve valuable plant nutrients.
   c. carry away plant nutrients.
   d. damage forests.

3. By damaging farm soils, acid rain threatens
   a. our food supply.
   b. aluminum compounds.
   c. rivers and lakes.
   d. fish.

4. *Fill in the missing word:* Having been washed into rivers and lakes, harmful aluminum compounds have killed many _____*fish*_____.

5. The answer to question 4 can be found in sentence
   a. 2.
   b. 4.
   c. 5.
   d. 6.

C.   ¹**There are several reasons why many homeless people resist being taken to city shelters, where they could get a hot meal and a bed for the night.** ²One is simple pride. ³If they remain on the street, they are their own bosses and do not feel humiliated by having to accept charity. ⁴In addition, many of the homeless are former mental patients who have difficulty getting along in society. ⁵For them, following shelter rules is next to impossible. ⁶Finally, conditions in the shelters are not always pleasant. ⁷They are noisy, and drug use and petty theft are common.

1. People who resist going to shelters because of pride
   a. do not like to accept charity.
   b. are former mental patients.
   c. cannot follow shelter rules.
   d. use drugs.

2. *(All, Many, A few)* _____Many_____ of the homeless are former mental patients.

3. *Fill in the missing word:* Shelter _____rules_____ are hard for former mental patients to follow.

4. The answer to question 3 can be found in sentence
   a. 2.
   b 3.
   c. 5.
   d. 6.

5. __T__ TRUE OR FALSE? We can find the answer to the following question in the paragraph.

   In what ways are shelters unpleasant?

IN CONCLUSION

The activities in this chapter help show that better reading depends upon an awareness of a main idea *and* its supporting details. You are now ready to go on, in the next two chapters, to deepen your understanding of main ideas. Those chapters will then be followed by one that will deepen your understanding of supporting details.

➤ *Review Test 1*

A. Each topic sentence below is followed by a list of three other sentences. Circle the letter of the one sentence that *does not* support the main idea.

1. There have been some strange beliefs about garlic.
   a. Ancient Egyptian priests, for instance, thought garlic was unclean.
   b. Today, garlic is widely used in cooking.
   c. In Europe, garlic has been thought to keep witches and vampires away.

2. Smoking is no longer as acceptable in our society as it once was.
   a. Smoking has been banned on certain commercial airline flights.
   b. Recently a woman in Southern California was refused a job because she smokes.
   c. Using drugs has also become less socially acceptable.

B. The topic sentence of each of the following paragraphs is boldfaced. Circle the number of the one sentence in each paragraph that *does not* support the main idea. Read the entire paragraph before making your decision.

3.   [1]**Among Thomas Jefferson's achievements were various inventions.** [2]For instance, he invented a revolving chair, a revolving music stand, and a pedometer for measuring the distance of his walks. [3]Many people today use a pedometer without realizing who invented it. [4]Jefferson also invented a walking stick that unfolded into a chair.

The sentence that does *not* support the main idea: ___3___

4.   [1]**Advertisers choose colors according to the emotional quality of each color.** [2]A sense of coolness and discipline is associated with blues and greens. [3]Heat and passion are found in the reds and oranges, which suggest fire and sun. [4]More in the middle is the warm (not hot) cheerfulness of yellow. [5]People also often consider these qualities when they choose colors for their homes.

The sentence that does *not* support the main idea: ___5___

5.   [1]**There are several ways in which managers can motivate workers by increasing their self-esteem.** [2]Managers can also motivate workers by setting a good example. [3]One way to build workers' self-esteem is to show interest in what they have to say. [4]It is very effective to write workers' ideas down and take them seriously. [5]Also, workers' self-esteem will grow if managers admit when they themselves are wrong, thus showing that everyone makes mistakes.

The sentence that does *not* support the main idea: ___2___

➤ *Review Test 2*

Answer the questions that follow the paragraphs. The topic sentence of each paragraph is boldfaced.

A.   [1]**Tranquilizers, though useful in helping people cope with their problems, can have very harmful side effects.** [2]First of all, tranquilizers can greatly affect a person's mental abilities. [3]For instance, memory and learning ability both decline. [4]A second damaging side effect is emotional. [5]People taking tranquilizers have been known to become confused and even see and hear things that aren't there. [6]The most dangerous side effect by far, however, is addiction. [7]Until the patient tries to stop taking the drug and develops withdrawal symptoms, he or she may be unaware of this side effect.

1.   ___T___ TRUE OR FALSE? Tranquilizers can weaken a person's memory.

2.   ___T___ TRUE OR FALSE? Tranquilizers can cause people to be confused.

3. *Fill in the missing word:* The author feels that the most dangerous side effect of tranquilizers is _____*addiction*_____.

4. The answer to question 3 can be found in sentence
   a. 2.
   b. 5.
   (c.) 6.
   d. 7.

5. People who take tranquilizers may not realize they are addicted until they
   a. remember.
   b. stop being confused.
   c. see and hear things that aren't there.
   (d.) have withdrawal symptoms.

B.   ¹**Various experiments reveal there are several factors involved in whether or not people help others.** ²One factor is how deserving the victim is thought to be. ³This was shown in an experiment in which people pretended to be in need of help. ⁴If they carried a cane, they were helped more promptly than if they carried a liquor bottle. ⁵Another factor is gender. ⁶Women tend to help both men and women equally. ⁷Men, on the other hand, are more likely to help women. ⁸Appearance also plays a part—people are more likely to help others who are dressed like themselves.

6. People are most willing to help those who
   a. are drunk.
   (b.) appear to deserve help.
   c. are in need of help.
   d. are male.

7. *Fill in the missing word:* _____*Men*_____ tend to help women in need more than men in need.

8. The answer to question 2 can be found in sentence
   a. 2.
   b. 4.
   c. 6.
   (d.) 7.

9. __*F*__ TRUE OR FALSE? Appearance has little to do with whether people do or don't help others.

10. __*F*__ TRUE OR FALSE? The paragraph answers the following question:

    How can we get people to be more helpful?

➤ Review Test 3

A. To review what you've learned in this chapter, answer each of the following
questions. Circle the letter of your answer or fill in the blank.

1.   Supporting details may
     a. explain main ideas.
     b. illustrate main ideas.
     c. prove main ideas.
     (d.) do all of the above.

2.   Supporting details are more *(general, specific)* _____*specific*_____ than
     main ideas.

3.   *Circle the letter of each of the three answers that apply:* Supporting details
     can be
     (a.) reasons.   d. main ideas.
     b. topics.   (e.) steps.
     (c.) examples.   f. central points.

4.   ____*T*____ TRUE OR FALSE? Noting the main idea and supporting details of a
     passage helps the reader to see the relationships between ideas.

B. Here is a chance to apply your understanding of supporting details to a magazine
article that appeared in the college textbook *Looking Out/Looking In* (Holt,
Rinehart and Winston, 1990) by Ronald B. Adler and Neil Towne. The author of
this article tells how she found a powerful way to communicate her love to her
children. Read the selection, and then answer the questions that follow on its
supporting details.

To help you continue to strengthen your work on skills taught in previous
chapters, there are also questions on vocabulary in context and and main ideas.

Words to Watch

Following are some words in the reading that do not have strong context support.
Each word is followed by the number of the paragraph in which it appears and its
meaning there. These words are indicated in the selection by a small circle (°).

exasperating (8):	very irritating
coaxed (9):	gently persuaded
to no avail (9):	without any benefit
chronic (10):	constant
incurring (13):	bringing about
compensate (14):	make up for
poignantly (18):	in a very touching manner
invoking (25):	calling forth
deride (32):	make fun of
crucial (40):	very important

TOUCH SPARKS LOVE

Phyllis Spangler

Our little girl was retreating into a walled-off world until we
found the key to unlock her love.   1

"Debbie, please brush that hair out of your face. It's even getting
into the food on your fork!"   2

It was suppertime; I had been late getting home from work, and I
was edgy. My irritation was apparent in my voice. Slowly,
mechanically, Debbie reached up and pushed her hair back. Then The
Look began to come over her face.   3

I had seen it before. She had been perhaps four years old when it
began. Her eyes became flat and expressionless, her face lost all
animation. Even her coloring seemed to fade, and with her pale lashes
and brows, she looked like an unpainted wooden doll. I knew that I
could pass my hand in front of her face and she wouldn't even see it.
Nor would she respond to anything that was said to her.   4

"There she goes again, feeling sorry for herself," commented
Don, her big brother.   5

And so it appeared. The middle child in a family of seven
children, it was understandable that she might feel sorry for herself.
The older children bossed her around, nagged her, and seemed to pick
on everything she said. The younger children demanded their own way,
and often got it through the privilege of their ages. Pushed from above,
threatened from below, Debbie didn't feel that she mattered to anyone.   6

The rest of the family continued with supper, ignoring Debbie.
From past experience, we knew that it was useless to try to bring her
back into the group. As the others were excused I led Debbie away
from her half-eaten dinner to the living room, where I sat her down in
front of the television set. Here she would gradually forget her
grievances and join in again.   7

I couldn't help but have mixed feelings, though. Poor little thing!
Six years old, and so unhappy! I wished desperately that I had more time
to spend with her as an individual. I knew I had nagged her again. But
why must she resort to that "Sorrowful Sal" act at every offense, either
real or imagined? It was positively exasperating° for her to tune us all out
when it was quite clear that she could see and hear everything around her.   8

When Debbie had first begun to get The Look, we thought she
was funny. "Isn't she cute when she's angry? See how she refuses to
pay any attention to you! But as time passed, it was no longer funny. It
was angering to be intentionally ignored. We coaxed°. We reasoned.
We scolded. We even spanked her for her stubbornness, all to no avail°.   9

But as long as it didn't happen often, we didn't pay much 10
attention to such behavior. In a large family, it's easy to put a problem
aside when a minor crisis has passed. Our older children were starting
school; we had one in the "terrible twos" and an infant, as well as a
chronic° invalid who required extensive home nursing care. Our hands
were full. The more urgent-appearing problems received our attention,
and Debbie's increasing needs went unrecognized.

Debbie was in the first grade when one of the older children said 11
to me one afternoon, "Mom, Debbie's teacher wants to talk to you."
The normal pangs of worry hit me that night. What trouble had Debbie
gotten herself into? I made an appointment for the next afternoon with
her teacher.

"I'm worried about Debbie," Mrs. Voorhees told me. "She's so . . . 12
alone. She craves attention and she desperately needs more of it from
you." She was telling me as gently as she could that I was failing my
daughter.

I turned the problem over and over in my mind. How could I give 13
Debbie more attention without incurring° the resentment of the other
children? Knowing that siblings in a large family are intensely
competitive, I decided it would be best to enlist their help. I called the
older children together and repeated what Mrs. Voorhees had told me.
"So I'm going to try to give Debbie what she needs. It means that she
has a greater need for attention at this time, and I'm trying to help her.
I'd do the same for any of you."

For a while this seemed to help. But as weeks went by, I found 14
that even the knowledge of reasons for my actions could not
compensate° for the unequal distribution of my attention. Don began to
take pokes and pinches at his little sister, or to kick her as she went by,
for no apparent reason.

Denise would keep track of every favor that I might give Debbie, 15
and accused me, "You've read to her four times in the past month, and
only once to me."

It was true. I was now working full time and trying to divide the 16
remaining time between the children. With the small amount of time
that there was to be divided, the inequality was obvious. The
resentment of the other children over the extra time given to Debbie
alone only made them more quarrelsome and belittling toward her. It
was defeating my original purpose.

Still, I wondered, what could I do? What should I do? Debbie was 17
getting good grades in school, so it didn't seem that she was too badly
in need of attention. I began to spend more time in group activities with
the family and less time with Debbie as an individual.

The Look returned more frequently, and Debbie ran away that 18 summer—several times. "Where will you live?" I asked her. "Under a bush," she would reply poignantly°. My heart ached for her.

Her comments began to reveal her feelings. "I wish I'd never 19
been born"; "I wish I was dead"; or "Some day I'm going to kill myself."

One afternoon she climbed up on the family car, and walked 20
around on it in her gritty shoes, scratching the paint. Her exasperated father spanked her vigorously. Afterward I sat down beside her at the foot of the stairway, where she sat sobbing. "Why ever did you do that, Debbie? You knew Daddy would get angry and spank you," I asked her.

"Because I don't like myself." 21

"Why don't you like yourself?" 22

"Because nobody likes me." Because nobody likes me. Oh, 23
Debbie!

"I like you, Debbie. I love you. You're my little girl." Words. Just 24
words. Again, The Look. She tuned me out. She didn't see or hear me.

What a desperate cry for help! A little girl, six years old, 25
invoking° the anger of her parents because she didn't think she was a person worth liking!

It took me a long time to acknowledge that Debbie—that WE— 26
needed help. "How could a six-year-old have any serious problems?" I would ask myself. "How could so young a child be too much for you to manage? Don't bring outsiders into it. We can handle our own problems if we work on them."

But we weren't handling them. By the time Debbie was seven 27
years old, The Look became a routine part of our daily life.

After a long inner struggle I finally decided to go to the county 28
mental-health center. "What if someone sees me there and thinks I'm a kook?" I wondered. But I swallowed my pride and went. It was the turning point in Debbie's life.

After I discussed the problem with the psychiatric social worker, 29
he set up an appointment for the entire family. "I want to see how they interact," he told me. After several such appointments, he began to see Debbie alone. A few weeks later he was able to give some help.

"She's a very unhappy little girl," he told me. "You must give her 30
the love and attention she needs. If you don't, her problems will probably come to a head when she is a teenager. Then there is a strong chance that she will either commit suicide, or turn for affection to the first fellow who will give her a little attention. And you know what that means. These girls often become unwed mothers in their teens."

"But how?" I asked. "I'm working full time; I must work. I've so 31
little time to give any of the children and when I try to give Debbie a little extra attention, the other children become jealous and are cruel to

her. And how do I cope with her when she tunes me out?"

"She's tuning you out to protect herself. Think about it," the ³² social worker said, "When does she do it? When you scold her or criticize her? When the other children argue with her or deride° her? These things hurt her so much that she can't cope with them. But if she can't see you or hear you, then you can't hurt her like that any more. So she withdraws. It's a defense mechanism she uses to keep from being hurt by other people."

He paused, then continued gently, "But you can reach her. There ³³ is one means you haven't tried yet. And that is—touch."

Touch? A strange thought. Communication without words. She ³⁴ could close her eyes and her ears, but she could still feel love.

"Touch her every chance you get. Ruffle her hair when you go by ³⁵ her. Pat her bottom. Touch her arm when you talk to her. Caress her. Put your hand on her shoulder, your arm around her. Pat her back. Hold her. Every chance you get. Every time you talk to her."

"Even when she refuses to see or hear you, she will feel you. And, ³⁶ incidently, this is something you can use to communicate with all your children. But pour it on Debbie."

Pour it on I did. And in a short time the results began to show ³⁷ noticeably. Debbie gradually became alive again. She smiled. She laughed. She had fun. She began to talk with me again. The Look became less and less frequent. And the other children never seemed to notice a thing, nor did they show any resentment of Debbie, possibly because I was touching them too.

Debbie is nine now, and she is like a different child. In addition to ³⁸ her new cheerful outlook on life, she has begun to discover some self-esteem. She stood in front of the mirror recently and told me, "I like my hair. It's pretty." What she was really telling me was that she has learned to like herself again. How far she has come! How far we all have come since I finally admitted that we needed professional help for a problem we hadn't been able to solve by ourselves.

The social worker's suggestion that I begin to communicate my ³⁹ love to my children by touching them was not guaranteed to be a miracle cure for Debbie's problems—or anyone else's. It did work for us, but not without a serious reevaluation of ourselves as individuals and as a family unit. We have had to learn a lot about ourselves, and we had to try hard to understand one another better, to accept one another as distinctly different human beings, each with intense feelings and needs.

I know the road ahead of us will have many rough spots and that ⁴⁰ the struggle to work out family difficulties is not an easy one. Debbie's problems are not over yet by any means. Strong rivalry remains among the children, and she is still right in the middle of it. She has many crucial° years in front of her, and we'll have to continue to boost her ego. We'll have to pay attention to her, give her the opportunity to express her feelings and listen to her when she does.

But no matter what the future holds, I have learned at least one   41 invaluable lesson: to let my children feel my love. Love can be shown in many ways—in facial expressions, in attitudes, in actions. Love can be heard. But—and perhaps this is most important of all—love can be felt, in one of the simplest means of communication there is: touch.

Reading Comprehension Questions

Vocabulary in Context

1. The word *retreating* in "Our little girl was retreating into a walled-off world until we found the key to unlock her love" (paragraph 1) means
   a. recognizing.
   b. withdrawing.
   c. playing.
   d. pushing others.

2. The word *animation* in "her eyes became flat and expressionless, her face lost all animation. . . . she looked like an unpainted wooden doll" (paragraph 4) means
   a. limits.
   b. livellness.
   c. cleanliness.
   d. silence.

3. The word *craves* in "She's so . . . alone. She craves attention and she desperately needs more of it from you" (paragraph 12) means
   a. greatly needs.
   b. provides a lot of.
   c. does not recognize.
   d. ignores.

4. The word *enlist* in "Knowing that siblings in a large family are intensely competitive, I decided it would be best to enlist their help. I called the older children together and repeated what Mrs. Voorhees had told me" (paragraph 13) means
   a. avoid.
   b. imitate.
   c. forget.
   d. get.

5. The word *acknowledge* in "It took me a long time to acknowledge that Debbie—that WE—needed help" (paragraph 26) means
   a. deny.
   b. remember.
   c. forget.
   d. admit.

Central Point

6. Which sentence best expresses the central point of the selection?
   a. The author's little girl withdrew more and more into the protection of "The Look."
   b. The author learned that touch is a very effective means of communicating love.
   c. Even though Debbie's siblings understood why their mother was giving special attention to Debbie, they still resented Debbie and took out their feelings on her.
   d. There are many ways to communicate love and affection.

Main Ideas

7. The main idea of paragraph 35 is best expressed in the paragraph's
   a. first sentence.
   b. second sentence.
   c. third sentence.
   d. fourth sentence.

Supporting Details

8. According to the reading, Debbie's "Look" angered her family because
   a. it meant she had a mind of her own.
   b. they didn't like being intentionally ignored.
   c. it meant she had to be spanked.
   d. her siblings did not like to be imitated.

9. The author eventually realized that
   a. Debbie was not doing well in school.
   b. she and her family could not solve Debbie's problem by herself.
   c. unlike Debbie, the other children didn't need attention.
   d. it was unlikely that Debbie would ever really run away or commit suicide.

10. According to the social worker, Debbie used "The Look"
    a. to protect herself.
    b. to hurt others.
    c. until she was seven.
    d. from infancy.

5

Locations of Main Ideas

In the chapters you have already worked on, most of the main ideas were in the first sentence of each paragraph. But the main idea may appear elsewhere in the paragraph as well. This chapter begins by describing common locations of topic sentences. It then provides practice in finding the topic sentence in a series of paragraphs. By the end of the chapter, you should have a solid sense of how to locate the main idea.

TOPIC SENTENCE FIRST IN A PARAGRAPH

Topic Sentence
Supporting Detail
Supporting Detail
Supporting Detail
Supporting Detail

Authors often begin a paragraph with the main idea. The rest of the paragraph then supports the main idea with details. Here is an example:

> Pain can cause aggression. When two rats in the same cage were given foot shocks, they attacked each other immediately. In addition, stronger shocks resulted in more violent aggression. Pairs of various other animals reacted similarly. A stubbed toe or a headache has been known to cause similar responses in humans.

The author's main idea is presented in the first sentence and explained with examples in the rest of the paragraph.

TOPIC SENTENCE WITHIN A PARAGRAPH

Introductory Detail
Topic Sentence
Supporting Detail
Supporting Detail
Supporting Detail

The topic sentence often follows one or more introductory sentences. These opening sentences may catch the reader's interest, relate the main idea to a previous paragraph, or give background for the main idea. The paragraph about the bad dream began with an introductory sentence following by the topic sentence:

> As a general rule, most of my dreams at night are pleasant ones. Recently, though, I had a really bad dream. . . .

Here is another example of a paragraph with such an introduction. Try to find the topic sentence, and write its number in the space provided. Then read the explanation that follows.

Topic sentence: _____

¹Why aren't the letters on a typewriter keyboard in alphabetical order? ²The odd letter arrangement on the keyboard was developed over a hundred years ago to solve a problem. ³The mechanical parts of early typewriters were too slow to keep up with fast typing, which would result in jammed keys. ⁴As a result, the designers chose an awkward arrangement of letters for the keyboard. ⁵The typist was thus forced to slow down, and the keys didn't jam.

If you thought the second sentence gives the main idea, you were correct. The first sentence introduces the question of why the letters are arranged as they are on a typewriter keyboard. The topic sentence then gives the writer's main idea—that the odd letter arrangement was used to solve a problem. The rest of the paragraph explains the problem and the solution.

It is fairly common for the topic sentence to appear in the second or third sentence of a paragraph. But the topic sentence may appear at times anywhere within a paragraph. See if you can find the topic sentence in the following paragraph. Then write its number in the space provided.

Topic sentence: _____

¹Everyone has heard of accountants, salespeople, and lawyers. ²But have you ever heard of a kiss mixer or a belly builder? ³Most jobs have common titles, but there are also many unusual position titles. ⁴A kiss mixer, for instance, is the person who mixes the ingredients for candy kisses. ⁵And

a belly builder is the individual who assembles and fits the inside parts of pianos.

Did you guess that the topic sentence is the third sentence? If so, you were correct. The first two sentences introduce the subject of the commonness of job titles by contrasting common job titles with uncommon ones. Then sentence 3 states the umbrella statement: while most jobs have common titles, there are many unusual titles as well. The supporting details in the last two sentences are specific examples of uncommon job titles.

TOPIC SENTENCE AT THE END OF A PARAGRAPH

Supporting Detail
Supporting Detail
Supporting Detail
Supporting Detail
Topic Sentence

When the topic sentence comes at the *end* of a paragraph, the previous sentences build up to the main idea. Here is an example of a paragraph in which the topic sentence comes last.

A couple's daughter had just graduated from college. So they were not surprised when a florist's truck pulled in front of their house. However, they were surprised when they saw that the dozen red roses were addressed to them. The card read, "Thanks, Mom and Dad, for making this day possible. I could not have done it without your love and support." In an unusual switch, the graduate had given her parents a graduation gift.

TWO TOPIC SENTENCES: FIRST AND LAST

Topic Sentence
Supporting Detail
Supporting Detail
Supporting Detail
Topic Sentence

When there are two topic sentences in a paragraph, they are often at *the beginning and the end*. In such cases, the author has chosen to introduce the main idea at the start of the paragraph and then emphasize it by restating it in other words at the end. Such is the case in the following paragraph:

Dental research on rats may lead to chocolate that's good for you. In one study, researchers found that rats who ate chocolate candy high in fat and casein got 71 percent fewer cavities than those who ate sugar or fudge alone. In a follow-up study, rats were fed chocolate candy that had an even greater amount of casein, a milk protein. The rats then got almost no cavities at all. Because of this research, one company may develop a chocolate candy that's healthy for your teeth.

As you can see, the main idea in the first sentence of the paragraph is restated in other words in the final sentence.

TOPIC SENTENCE IMPLIED

```
+--------------------------+
|   Supporting Detail      |
|   Supporting Detail      |
|   Supporting Detail      |
|   Supporting Detail      |
+--------------------------+
```

Sometimes a paragraph will lack a topic sentence, but that does not mean it lacks a main idea. The author may have decided to let details of the selection suggest the main idea. Such suggested or implied main ideas will be the concern of the next chapter.

➤ *Practice*

The topic sentence appears in different locations in the following five paragraphs. Identify each topic sentence by filling in the correct sentence number in the space provided. In the one case where there are two topic sentences, write in both numbers.

To find each topic sentence, you should do the following:

   a Look for a general statement.
   b Then ask yourself, "Is this general statement supported by all or most of the details in the paragraph?"

1.   ¹In the past, America's homeless made important contributions to society. ²Homeless scouts blazed the trails for the first pioneers. ³Later, hobos cut timber, worked in mines, did farm work, laid railroad tracks, and built towns. ⁴Traveling freely from town to town, they made up a flexible work force, one available to do whatever work was needed at any particular time.

   Topic sentence(s): _____1_____

2.   [1]People have bombarded fleas with all types of chemicals. [2]The surviving fleas are superfleas—harder to kill than ever. [3]Similarly, the overuse of antibiotics has led to bacteria that resist all medicines. [4]Obviously, in the effort to get rid of some of our tiny enemies, we have created even worse ones.

Topic sentence(s): _____4_____

3.   [1]Occasionally someone will act in a most unexpected way, like the woman who walked down a busy Chicago street with no clothes on. [2]But usually social behavior is quite predictable. [3]You can generally assume your English teacher will come to class instead of going swimming. [4]You can also expect to find groceries at the grocery and most drivers stopping at red lights.

Topic sentence(s): _____2_____

4.   [1]Unfortunately, great artists do not always live long enough to know how successful they'll be. [2]The painting "Irises" by the nineteenth-century Dutch painter Vincent Van Gogh recently sold at an auction for more than $30 million. [3]Yet during his own lifetime, Van Gogh sold only one of his paintings. [4]He died ignored and poor. [5]The seventeenth-century Dutch painter Vermeer sold few of his paintings and died in debt. [6]Today, his works also sell for millions. [7]Van Gogh and Vermeer illustrate the sad truth that great artists are often appreciated only long after they are dead.

Topic sentence(s): _____1, 7_____

5.   [1]The yo-yo is, of course, a harmless toy. [2]Children spend hours perfecting their skill at making the wheel-like body descend the string and rebound smoothly into the hand. [3]Early yo-yos were not used as toys, however, but as deadly weapons. [4]The typical hunting yo-yo was made of a four-pound stone tied to a twenty-foot vine. [5]From his hiding place in a tree, a hunter would hurl the heavy stone at his prey or enemy. [6]Then he would quickly draw the weapon back up for a second blow.

Topic sentence(s): _____3_____

MAIN IDEAS ON INCREASING LEVELS OF DIFFICULTY

As has already been said, finding the main idea is the most important of all reading skills. To give you practice in finding the main idea, the rest of this chapter presents a series of paragraphs. They are grouped into three levels of increasing difficulty, with the topic sentence appearing at varying places. By working with care, you will gradually strengthen your ability to find the topic sentence.

Don't skip any levels. Doing the easier ones will prepare you for the more difficult ones. The principle that applies here applies to the book in general: one becomes better at a skill by practicing it in a series of steps, each a bit more difficult than the one before.

As you work on the practices, remember the guidelines for finding the main idea:

a The topic sentence is a general statement.

b That general statement is supported by all or most of the specific material in the paragraph.

➤ Practice: Level 1

Write the number of each topic sentence in the space provided.

1. ¹For one study, twenty-six retarded one-year-olds were divided between two types of care. ²Half were cared for by retarded women. ³The rest were given routine care in an institution. ⁴After three years, the IQ of those mothered by retarded women went up 29 points. ⁵The babies in institutions lost about 26 points. ⁶This study suggests that home-like care is much better than institutional care.

   Topic sentence: _____6_____

2. ¹Several products are available to help people stop smoking. ²Audio and video tapes use suggestion to encourage people to quit. ³Gum containing nicotine allows quitters to gradually cut down on the nicotine they got from cigarettes. ⁴There are also special cigarette filters that reduce the amount of smoke and nicotine that get to the smoker's mouth. ⁵And recently a patch has been put on the market that releases nicotine gradually. ⁶Like the gum and filters, the patch allows people to continue to get nicotine while eliminating cigarettes.

   Topic sentence: _____1_____

3. ¹You've heard of acupuncture for weight loss and for pain. ²Now there's acupuncture for your pet. ³Over two hundred vets are already certified in acupuncture. ⁴One Colorado vet claims success for acupuncture in fighting arthritis. ⁵For example, one of his patients is a German shepherd who could hardly walk. ⁶After three treatments, that dog is active again. ⁷A session once or twice a month keeps him that way.

   Topic sentence: _____2_____

4. ¹One problem busy people face is getting their laundry done. ²Another equally frustrating problem for many is setting aside time to exercise. ³A California company called "Clean and Lean" offers a time-saving service for people: it lets them work out while their clothes get clean. ⁴Clean and Lean centers have exercise bikes, space for jogging, and a dozen weight machines. ⁵Of course, they also have washers and dryers.

    Topic sentence: _____3_____

5. ¹One family saved money on groceries by stocking up on often-used items when the price was right. ²In fact, over a year, this family saved three thousand dollars on groceries by using several methods. ³Another method was to sit down together on Sunday and look over supermarket ads for the best buys. ⁴Also, the family was careful to wrap and date leftovers for use in soups, casseroles, and sandwiches.

    Topic sentence: _____2_____

➤ *Practice: Level 2*

Write the number of each topic sentence in the space provided. For the one case in which there are two topic sentences, write in both numbers.

1. ¹Conservationists are concerned about Mount Everest for a couple of reasons. ²First of all, people are leaving old boots, axes, and other old gear at the top of the mountain. ³If this continues, Mount Everest will be the world's highest junk pile. ⁴Also, the forest at the base of the mountain is rapidly being cut down. ⁵Natives are selling it to tourists and mountaineers to use as firewood.

    Topic sentence(s): _____1_____

2. ¹The creation of the ice-cream cone goes back to the Louisiana Purchase Exposition in St. Louis, in 1904. ²It was there that an ice-cream salesman brought his date two gifts—an ice-cream sandwich and a bouquet of flowers. ³The lady had trouble holding both at the same time. ⁴So she took one cookie wafer from the sandwich and wrapped it around the flowers like a vase. ⁵She used the other wafer to wrap around the ice cream to keep it from dripping. ⁶The ice-cream cone was born, then, because of a date at the 1904 Exposition.

    Topic sentence(s): _____1, 6_____

3.   ¹Eskimos begin building an igloo by cutting blocks of ice from well-packed snow. ²The tops are cut at a slight angle, so when they are piled in a circle, they curve inward and form a dome. ³When the igloo is completed, a door is carved out. ⁴The final step is to cut a tunnel entrance, with a slight bend to reduce the flow of cold air. ⁵In this simple manner, Eskimos build igloos from solid ice.

Topic sentence(s): _____5_____

4.   ¹Generally people with higher status are given more space and privacy. ²We knock before entering our boss's office, but we walk into the office work area without hesitating. ³In many schools, teachers have offices, dining rooms, and even toilets that are private, but students do not have such special places. ⁴Among the military, greater space and privacy usually come with rank: privates sleep forty to a barracks, sergeants have their own rooms, and generals have government-provided houses.

Topic sentence(s): _____1_____

5.   ¹On the one hand, people hunger for relationships. ²They want the support and release that come from opening up, from sharing thoughts and feelings with others. ³But people also fear and avoid contact. ⁴They are afraid to reveal themselves for fear of looking foolish, of being hurt. ⁵They like the privacy that comes from keeping thoughts to themselves and from not having to explain or justify their actions. ⁶People are, clearly, both drawn toward relationships and pushed away from them.

Topic sentence(s): _____6_____

➤ Practice: Level 3

Write the number of each topic sentence in the space provided. In the one case in which there are two topic sentences, write in both numbers.

1.   ¹Today we view childhood as a long and gradual road to adulthood. ²However, after the West became industrialized, children were cruelly forced into adulthood at an early age. ³Many worked full-time in mines and factories. ⁴Some worked up to fourteen hours a day for low pay under terrible working conditions. ⁵There were even cases of children being chained to their beds at night, so that they would be there for work the next day. ⁶Then, to be sure they kept working, some were chained to their machines during the day.

Topic sentence(s): _____2_____

2.   [1]Our nonverbal communications can often be as important as or more important than what we say. [2]For instance, body language—how we stand, sit, and move—carries messages. [3]If you went to a job interview, for instance, would you put your feet up on the desk? [4]We also send messages by how close or far we stand from a person we're talking to. [5]If a person is standing too close to you, chances are he or she is being aggressive and/or wants to become intimate with you. [6]The way we dress communicates too. [7]A person who wears gym clothes to a wedding, for example, is sending a message to everyone else there.

Topic sentence(s): _____*1*_____

3.   [1]Several recent studies indicate that we could learn a lot about diet from our Stone Age ancestors. [2]According to recent research, cave dwellers ate about three times as much protein as we do today and only half as much fat. [3]Their diet consisted of about 65 percent fruits and vegetables and 35 percent meat. [4]But the wild animals they ate were far leaner than today's grain-fed beef. [5]And Stone Age people also ate twice as much fiber and calcium and four times as much vitamin C as we do. [6]These findings suggest that the diet of our distant ancestors could be a model for protecting ourselves against the diseases of civilization.

Topic sentence(s): _____*1, 6*_____

4.   [1]In 1983, Kool cigarettes were advertised in over three thousand movie theaters. [2]Many of those theaters were running movies rated PG and G. [3]Also, Philip Morris paid to have Marlboro cigarettes featured in *Superman*. [4]The Marlboro logo appears about two dozen times in that movie. [5]In publicity photos for the movie, Lois Lane is smoking Marlboros. [6]Philip Morris also allows the Marlboro trademark to be used on candy cigarettes. [7]Clearly, cigarette companies don't mind aiming their advertising at young people.

Topic sentence(s): _____*7*_____

5.   [1]Shanghai, one of China's busy cities, is so thickly populated that each person's living space amounts to roughly the size of a king-sized bed. [2]As this suggests, the *population density*—that is, the number of people who live in a given area—varies greatly throughout the world. [3]The overall density of the United States in 1985 was 67 people for every square mile of land. [4]But residents of New Jersey felt far more crowded with 1,013 people per square mile. [5]Montana, meanwhile, had only 6.

Topic sentence(s): _____*2*_____

➤ *Review Test 1*

Identify each topic sentence by filling in the correct sentence number in the space provided. In the one case where there are two topic sentences, write in both numbers.

1. ¹Americans are not very honest about money that belongs to corporations. ²For example, of the $765,000 that fell out of an armored truck in San Francisco, only about $400 was ever returned. ³The people who did return money received some praise. ⁴But they also received much criticism from their families and co-workers. ⁵Similar stories can be told across the country.

    Topic sentence(s): _____1_____

2. ¹Does this sound like science fiction? ²A couple has a new low-maintenance dock built which is guaranteed to be splinterless. ³No, it is not made of wood, but from recycled plastics, and it's not science fiction. ⁴Workmen install wall-to-wall carpet with rich color and soft, plush pile. ⁵It, too, is made from recycled plastics. ⁶A skier keeps warm on the slopes wearing an attractive pair of bib-front pants and matching parka made with fiberfill from recycled plastics. ⁷Yes, today more and more products are being made from recycled plastics.

    Topic sentence(s): _____7_____

3. ¹Speaking before a group is more frightening to many than almost anything else. ²But there are ways to overcome the fear of speaking and become an effective speaker. ³The first step is to think positively. ⁴Replace thoughts of failure with statements such as, "I am interested in my topic, and I expect my listeners to be interested too." ⁵It also helps to plan a speech with only two or three major points and to try to speak naturally. ⁶Finally, visualize yourself standing in front of your audience feeling comfortable and relaxed.

    Topic sentence(s): _____2_____

4. ¹While plants often provide food for animals, some plants turn the tables and dine on smaller members of the animal kingdom. ²One, the Venus's-fly-trap, uses its leaves like a steel trap. ³It attracts small insects with its sweet perfume, and then clamps down its "jaws" so it can digest the insects at its leisure. ⁴Another leafy hunter is the pitcher plant, whose sweet juices tempt insects to explore the plant. ⁵Once deep within the plant, the insect meets a watery death. ⁶Plants are essential for animal life, but for members of the insect community, they can also be a health hazard.

    Topic sentence(s): _____1, 6_____

5. ¹Some television ads scare you into buying products, others make you feel homey, and still others promise you popularity. ²You can probably think of some mildly fearful ads: commercials for deodorants, soaps, mouthwash, denture adhesive, and radial tires usually begin with someone suffering rejection or facing a problem. ³Other ads are more pleasant, with products associated with a warm, loving, old-fashioned atmosphere. ⁴For example, you may be told about cookies, breads, or spaghetti sauce such as Grandmother used to make. ⁵And some ads appeal to our need for popularity. ⁶They imply, for instance, that if you wear the right type of jeans or use the right perfume or drink the right kind of beer, you will win intimate friendships.

Topic sentence(s): _____1_____

➤ *Review Test 2*

Identify each topic sentence by filling in the correct sentence number in the space provided. In the one case where there are two topic sentences, write in both numbers.

1. ¹According to one study, sounds influence how well we remember. ²Researchers asked students to try to memorize nine-digit numbers under different circumstances. ³When students studied around noises like those on a subway, they remembered as many numbers as when they studied in silence. ⁴In contrast, when students studied while someone read a book out loud, they remembered about 10 percent less.

Topic sentence(s): _____1_____

2. ¹There are various steps a parent can take to protect children when they're alone in the house. ²If children are sometimes home alone when the telephone rings, they should be told not to tell the caller their parents are away. ³Instead, they should say, "My parents can't come to the phone now." ⁴They should also lock the doors and not open them to a stranger for any reason. ⁵And the phone number of a trusted neighbor should be handy, so a child can call if he or she needs help. ⁶Preventive measures like these will help protect children when parents aren't home.

Topic sentence(s): _____1, 6_____

3. ¹Feeling chilly? ²Understanding how clothing keeps you comfortable is the secret to fighting the cold. ³Because heat rises, one of the best ways to keep your whole body warm is to wear a hat or cap. ⁴Dressing in layers is another useful tip, since air trapped between layers stays warm. ⁵This principle also applies when choosing gloves. ⁶Loose-fitting gloves trap warm air near your

skin. ⁷On the other hand, because gloves that fit snugly do not have that layer, they are less likely to keep you warm.

Topic sentence(s): _____2_____

4.   ¹Studies of men's speech show it is typically direct and positive. ²Women's speech, on the other hand, tends to be less bold and more hesitant. ³While a man is likely to state, "It's cold in here," a woman is more likely to ask, "Is it cold here, or is it just me?" ⁴Similar studies show that men interrupt women far more often than the reverse happens. ⁵And in listening to couples' conversations, researchers have found that topics that succeed (those that are pursued in the conversation) are usually introduced by the man. ⁶Apparently, men's greater social power influences how men and women speak.

Topic sentence(s): _____6_____

5.   ¹Suppose someone asked you to sit on top of a flagpole for twelve hours and promised you a reward. ²The reward was a stick of gum. ³Would you be likely to repeat the flagpole-sitting behavior? ⁴Chances are you would not unless there was a severe gum shortage and you craved gum. ⁵Although the gum was a reward, it would not serve as a positive reinforcement that would encourage more of the same behavior. ⁶What would it take to make you climb up and sit on top of the flagpole again? ⁷Perhaps a good positive reinforcer for you would be a new car, a screen test from a movie studio, or a free vacation to Hawaii. ⁸For a positive reinforcement to be effective enough to shape behavior, it must be appropriate.

Topic sentence(s): _____8_____

➤ Review Test 3

A. To review what you've learned so far about main ideas, complete each of the following sentences.

1.   The topic sentence states the (*supporting details, introductory details, main idea*) _____*main idea*_____ of a passage.

2.   To find the topic sentence of a passage, look for a (*general, specific*) _____*general*_____ statement.

3.   The supporting details of a passage are more (*general, specific*) _____*specific*_____ than the main idea.

4.   The topic sentence may appear in a paragraph (*only once, more than once*) _____*more than once*_____.

5.   When the main idea is expressed in the second or third sentence, the paragraph may begin with (*the main idea, background for the main idea, the implied main idea*) _____*background for the main idea*_____.

B. Here is a chance to apply your understanding of topic sentences to a full-length selection. Read the following article and then answer the questions that follow on the central point and main ideas. There are also vocabulary questions to help you continue practicing the skill of understanding vocabularly in context.

This selection tells what it might mean when your boss pats you on the back, when men and women run their hands through their hair, and more. The selection may convince you that no matter how quiet you are, your body has been speaking loudly and clearly.

Words to Watch

Following are some words in the reading that do not have strong context support. Each word is followed by the number of the paragraph in which it appears and its meaning there. These words are indicated in the article by a small circle (°).

gestures (2):	motions made which express thought or emphasize speech
context (2):	overall situation
abrupt (10):	rudely sudden
staging (11):	performing
meek (15):	willing to yield to the power of another

BODY LANGUAGE

Beth Johnson Ruth

Imagine yourself in the following situation: You're a young   1
woman interviewing for a new job. You have been talking for about half an hour with the interviewer, a pleasant man slightly older than yourself. You feel the interview has gone well, but you're not sure what he's thinking. Suddenly the mood in the room changes. Your interviewer sits back in his chair, crosses one ankle over his knee and begins tapping his pen against his shoe. Should you:
    (a) Forget about the job?
    (b) Congratulate yourself?
    (c) Tell him you're not that kind of girl?
The answer is *b*—you're probably going to be hired, says Dr. Robert Rosenthal of Harvard University. Dr. Rosenthal, a clinical psychologist, is a pioneer in the study of how people send and receive non-verbal messages—in other words, in "body language."

Researchers say body language sends out messages far more 2
powerful than we're generally aware of. At the same time, they warn
that nonverbal communication—which involves gestures°, posture,
tone of voice and eye contact—is more complicated than the drugstore-
type books on the subject suggest. Body language can only be
explained within its context°, they say; you shouldn't expect to find a
"dictionary" for reliable definitions of crossed arms, sideways glances
and tapping toes.

Still, those that study the field agree that a better awareness of 3
nonverbal communication makes you a more sensitive observer of any
situation. Such awareness can also help you understand how people
perceive you.

Let's take an example: How would a student of body language 4
explain the interview story told above? What in the world does
touching a shoe have to do with making a favorable hiring decision?
Dr. Rosenthal admits he doesn't know for sure. But after watching
many job interviews, he is certain that the foot-touching gesture means
the interview subject has made a good impression. This is his theory:
an interview is likely to make both persons involved feel uneasy. Both
will probably sit stiffly in their chairs. But once the interviewer
decided, "Yes. I'm going to hire this person," he relaxes. At that point,
he's apt to shift into a more comfortable position, often bringing his
foot within easy touching distance.

Status differences on the job offer other interesting examples, 5
points out Allan Mazur, professor of sociology at Syracuse University.
When a respected executive talks with a lower-ranking employee, for
example, the employee usually keeps his eyes glued to the boss's face.
But when the employee is talking, the executive feels free to glance
around the room. Another example is the manager who shows his
superiority by patting a worker on the back—something the employee
would never do to the manager. In an office, the person with the most
status even established how a conversation will take place: If he stands,
the lower-ranking person remains standing as well. If the lower-status
person violates any of these rules, he risks looking disrespectful.

Of course, the working world is not the only place where body 6
language is used. Every would-be Romeo or Juliet knows that the
language of courtship goes far beyond words. Much of our flirtatious
behavior is instinctive, not consciously thought out. But if you can get
them to admit it, many expert flirts are aware of their seductive use of
body language.

"I've got my tricks," admits Patti, 22, a college student who 7
spends many evenings out dancing with a group of friends. Patti is not

a beauty, but she always attracts men at the clubs she goes to.

"I don't know why some things work the way they do, but certain 8 gestures make men feel more confident about coming up to me," she says. When asked to describe those gestures, she laughs nervously. "That's kind of embarrassing . . . It's just little things like glancing sideways at a guy with a little smile. Then you look away as if you didn't do it. But a minute later you sort of let your eyes slide back to meet his while you're talking to someone else. After that, he'll usually get up and come over."

When you spend an hour observing Patti in action, you see other 9 "tricks" she uses while talking to men she's attracted to. She lightly draws her finger across her lip as she listens to a man. She plays with her hair. She tilts her head and gazes upward into his eyes. She lazily shrugs her shoulders. It's no wonder Patti gains all the attention she can handle, according to Dr. David Givens, a University of Washington anthropologist. Her "vocabulary" of body language sends out a strong signal: "I'm friendly. I'm approachable."

Taken a step further, the message becomes "I'm sexually 10 available." Patti admits that the men she enjoys flirting and dancing with often read that message in her behavior. So she has become equally expert at "freezing" a too-insistent man with a nonverbal vocabulary of rejection: a stiff posture, expressionless face, and abrupt° gestures. Patti is a pro with body language, and as she says, "You can say about anything you want without words."

Where does nonverbal communication come from? Researchers 11 trace various kinds of body language back to our roots in the animal world. Courtship practices such as marking out one's territory, staging° battles before the object of one's affection, or grooming onself in front of a would-be mate are all common animal behaviors that humans use as well.

An evening of observation at a singles bar demonstrates the links 12 between animal and human body language. Si and Mark are a couple of factory workers in their early 20's out for an evening at Lights, their favorite hangout. As they settle at the bar, they automatically scatter their jackets, Si's car keys, and a cigarette lighter across the bar in front of them. They're marking out their territory—warning other men to stay away.

Before long they have spotted several women that they 13 particularly like. As those women move into hearing range, Si and Mark's casual, low-volume conversation changes noticeably. Their voices rise and take on a challenging, though still good-humored, quality. They begin to argue: "You're crazy!" "You're outta your mind!" "I can't believe this guy." They are laughing, but their voices are loud and rough. They glance around, hoping to include the women in their conversation. But they are passed by, and Si and Mark's conversation quickly returns to a lower tone.

Later in the evening, however, Si has better luck with a second 14 target. As she approaches, he and Mark go into their "arguing" routine. She pauses. Catching Si's eyes, she leans against the wall and begins running her fingers through her already well-combed hair. Si slowly makes his way across the room to speak to her. The message of her preening in response to his masculine display is one he quickly recognizes—as would any animal scientist.

Animal behavior, however, is not the only source of nonverbal 15 communication. As Dr. Givens points out, another rich source of nonverbal vocabulary is our childhoods. When we want to seem meek° and friendly—which in the case of women often translates into "romantically available"—we may borrow gestures from as far back as babyhood. An infant scared by a loud noise will respond with the "startle reflex": a combination of lifting its shoulders, lowering its head and pulling in its chin. An older child will use the same gestures when he's being scolded, making the child seem cute and meek. But when used by Patti upon meeting new dance partners, the same moves seem less childish than seductive and feminine.

Dr. Givens further demonstrates this point by putting together 16 photographs of children looking adorable and adult female fashion models looking sexy: the poses are identical.

Everyone uses body language. Because nonverbal communication, 17 based in our animal roots and childhoods, is universal, it is useful to become more aware of it. What we and others "say" when we're not saying anything can richen and entertain us as we spend each day in the human "laboratory."

Reading Comprehension Questions

Vocabulary in Context

1. The word *apt* in "once the interviewer decides, 'Yes. I'm going to hire this person,' he relaxes. At that point, he's apt to shift into a more comfortable position" (paragraph 4) means
   a. unlikely.
   b. likely.
   c. unable.
   d. not ready.

2. The word *instinctive* in "Much of our flirtatious behavior is instinctive, not consciously thought out" (paragraph 6) means
   a. planned.
   b. natural.
   c. strange.
   d. poor.

3. The word *seductive* in "Every would be Romeo or Juliet knows that the language of courtship goes far beyond words. . . . many expert flirts are aware of their seductive body language" (paragraph 6) means
   a. tempting.
   b. insulting.
   c. unattractive.
   d. fearful.

4. The word *links* in "Researchers trace various kinds of body language back to our roots in the animal world. . . . An evening of observation at a singles bar demonstrates the links between animal and human body language" (paragraphs 11–12) means
   a. differences.
   b. questions.
   c. friendship.
   d. connections.

5. The word *preening* in "she . . . begins running her fingers through her already well-combed hair. . . .The message of her preening. . . is one he quickly recognizes" (paragraph 14) means
   a. exercising.
   b. grooming.
   c. messiness.
   d. avoidance.

Central Point

6. Which of the following sentences from the reading best expresses the central point of the selection?
   a. "Dr. Rosenthal, a clinical psychologist, is a pioneer in the study of how people send and receive non-verbal messages—in other words, in 'body language.'"
   b. "Every would-be Romeo or Juliet knows that the language of courtship goes far beyond words."
   c. "Researchers trace various kinds of body language back to our roots in the animal world."
   d. "Because nonverbal communication, based in our animal roots and childhoods, is universal, it is useful to become more aware of it."

Main Ideas

7. The topic sentence of paragraph 5 is its
   a. first sentence.
   b. second sentence.
   c. third sentence.
   d. last sentence.

8. The main idea of paragraph 9 is best expressed in its
   a. first sentence.
   b. second sentence.
   c. third sentence.
   d. fourth sentence.

9. A topic sentence sometimes provides the main idea for more than one paragraph. The first sentence of paragraph 12 expresses the main idea for paragraphs
   a. 10–12.
   b. 11–13.
   c. 12–13.
   d. 12–14.

10. The main idea of paragraph 15 is best expressed in its
    a. first sentence.
    b. second sentence.
    c. next-to-last sentence.
    d. last sentence.

6

Implied Main Ideas

Following is a paragraph considered in earlier chapters except that the introductory sentence and the topic sentence are missing.

I was in an alley dressed in light summer clothing. Coming out of the darkness at the end of the alley were hundreds of large gray rats. Their razor-sharp teeth glistened with saliva, and their eyes glowed red with a cold fury. I turned to run away, but attacking in the other direction were a dozen pit bulls. And these particular pit bulls were foaming at the mouth; they all had rabies. "Just my luck," I muttered and did my best to wake up as quickly as possible.

What is the main idea of this paragraph? You may remember it from earlier chapters. But even if you did not, you could figure out the main idea. It gradually becomes clear that the terrible details add up to the main idea that "I really had a bad dream." All the details combine to imply the main idea of the paragraph.

Paragraphs often lack a topic sentence, but that does not mean they lack a main idea. In this chapter, you will learn how to figure out the main ideas in paragraphs that have no topic sentence.

IMPLIED MAIN IDEAS

When paragraphs have no topic sentence, it means that the author has simply decided to let the supporting details suggest the main idea. The main idea is *unstated*, or *implied*, and you must figure it out by deciding upon the point of the supporting details.

For example, read the following paragraph. Pay special attention to what each sentence says. Is one sentence general enough to include all of the others?

One odd suggestion for curing hiccups is to cut some holes in a paper bag, put the bag over your head, and breathe deeply. Another is to put a teaspoon of sugar on your tongue; by the time the sugar has disappeared, some claim, so have the hiccups. Some people feel that the way to get rid of hiccups is to cover a glass of water with a clean handkerchief and then drink the water through the hankie. If none of these methods works, you might try yet another odd cure for hiccups: stand on your head, close your eyes tightly, take a deep breath, and recite "Mary Had a Little Lamb."

You can see that no sentence in the paragraph is a good "umbrella" statement that covers all the others. You can, though, decide on the author's main idea by asking two questions:

1 What is the topic, or subject, of the paragraph? In other words, what is the whole paragraph about?

2 What is the main point being made about that topic?

To find the answer to the first question, you must see what subject is constantly being referred to. In this case, the subject that comes up repeatedly is cures for hiccups, and so that is the topic of the paragraph.

Once you have found the topic, finding the answer to the second question is easier. To do so, ask yourself, "What main point is being made about the topic?" The answer is: "There are some odd cures for hiccups." This idea is general enough to include all the specific material in the paragraph.

Now read the paragraph below. See if you can pick out the topic and the unstated main idea. Circle the letters of your answers, and then read the explanation that follows.

A Washington, D.C., student was shot to death two weeks before Christmas. Police believe he was shot by teenagers who were stealing his radio. An eighth grader in Pasadena, Texas, held an assistant principal hostage with a pistol. The boy was upset over his parents' recent separation. Two brothers who obtained guns through their gang terrorized members of their own family. And a survey of a Baltimore high school shows that well over half of the students polled knew someone who had carried a handgun within the last six months.

The topic of this paragraph is

a. teenagers who use guns for theft.
b. violence.
c. teenagers and violence.
d. teenagers having guns.

The unstated main idea of this paragraph is:

a. Violence is a growing problem among teenagers.
b. According to one survey, many high-school students have carried a handgun recently.
c. Teens having guns are a major problem.
d. Teens may use guns against educators.

Explanations:

What is the *topic*, or *subject*, of the paragraph? Let's consider the four choices given above:

a. teenagers who use guns for theft	This is too narrow to be the topic—the paragraph is about more than just teenagers who use guns for theft. For example, one teen used a gun to hold someone hostage.
b. violence	This answer is too broad. It covers more kinds of details than are in the paragraph. If this were the topic, the paragraph would also include details about violence that did not involve teenagers at all.
c. teenagers and violence	This answer is also too broad. If teenagers and violence were the topic, the paragraph would include violent details about teenagers without guns. For example, it might mention teens who use knives.
d. teenagers having guns	Every sentence in the paragraph discusses teenagers having guns. Thus *d* is the correct answer.

Now that we have the topic of the paragraph, what is the author's *main point* about the topic? In other words, what is the author suggesting or implying *about* teenagers having guns? The answer must be an idea that covers the supporting details in the paragraph. Again, let's consider the four answer choices:

a. Violence is a growing problem among teenagers.

This answer is too broad. The paragraph discusses only teens and guns; other types of violence and the idea that violence is growing among teens are not mentioned.

b. According to one survey, many high-school students have carried a handgun recently.

This answer is too narrow—only one supporting detail in the paragraph is about the survey.

c. Teens having guns are a major problem.

A careful reading tells us that every sentence discusses a problem with one or more teenagers who have guns. Thus this is the main idea of the paragraph.

d. Teens may use guns against educators.

This answer is also too narrow. Only one example in the paragraph mentions a teen who used a gun against an educator.

By now you probably see that to find an unstated main idea, you have to be a bit of a detective. You must use all of the evidence in a paragraph to figure out the topic and the author's main point about that topic.

This chapter provides a careful sequence of activities to help you develop skill at finding implied main ideas. Do not skip any of these activities. They will help you learn, in a step-by-step way, what you need to know about this challenging skill.

Step 1: Recognizing Implied General Ideas

Learning how to find unstated *general* ideas is a helpful step in finding unstated *main* ideas. Read the following list of specific ideas, and then circle the letter of the general idea that best covers the specifics. The answer will be the general idea that tells what all of the specific ideas have in common.

Specific ideas: baseball cap, football helmet, Easter bonnet

The general idea is
a. sports hats.
b. clothing.
c. hats.

Since an Easter bonnet is not a sports hat, answer *a* is wrong—it is too narrow to cover all the specific ideas. It is true that all the specific ideas can be considered items of clothing, but they have more in common than that—they are only items of clothing worn on the head. Thus answer *b* is much more broad than necessary, and answer *c* is the correct choice.

When you are looking for the general idea, remember these points:

1. The general idea must cover all of the specific ideas. (*Hats* covers *baseball cap, football helmet,* and *Easter bonnet.*)
2. The general idea must not be so narrow that it excludes any of the specific ideas. (*Sports hats* is too narrow—it does not cover *Easter bonnet.*)
3. A general idea that covers many kinds of specific ideas other than those on the list is too broad. (*Clothing* is too broad—it covers specific ideas other than *hats*, such as *shoes* and *pajamas.*)

Here is another example:

Specific ideas: "I couldn't take the final because my grandmother died."
"I couldn't come in to work because I had a migraine headache."
"I couldn't study because I forgot to bring my book home."

The general idea is
a. common remarks.
b. common excuses.
c. common student excuses.

The specific ideas are common remarks. Yet *common remarks* covers various types of remarks—common compliments, common greetings, common excuses, and so on. But all of the specific ideas above are one type of common remark—common excuses. Thus answer *a* is too broad, and answer *b* is the correct answer. Answer c is too narrow because only two of the three specific ideas are student excuses; one is a worker excuse.

➤ *Practice 1*

Read each group of specific ideas. Then circle the letter of the general idea that tells what the specific ideas have in common. Keep in mind that the correct general idea will not be too narrow or too broad.

1. *Specific ideas:* poodle, spaniel, German shepherd, terrier

   The general idea is
   a. pets.
   (b.) dogs.
   c. dogs that help the blind.

2. *Specific ideas:* mosquito, butterfly, gnat, wasp

   The general idea is
   a. living creatures.
   b. pests.
   (c.) insects.

3.   *Specific ideas:* Superman, Batman, Wonder Woman

   The general idea is
   (a.) comic-book heroes.
   b. comic-book characters.
   c. fictional characters.

4.   *Specific ideas:* spaghetti and meatballs, pizza, eggplant Parmesan

   The general idea is
   a. food.
   b. main dishes.
   (c.) Italian main dishes.

5.   *Specific ideas:* Martha Washington, Jacqueline Kennedy, Hillary Clinton

   The general idea is
   a. famous women.
   b. famous American women.
   (c.) wives of American presidents.

6.   *Specific ideas:* combs, brushes, razors

   The general idea is
   (a.) items for grooming.
   b. women's items for grooming.
   c. men's items for grooming.

7.   *Specific ideas:* stealing, lying, cheating during a test

   The general idea is
   (a.) dishonest acts.
   b. illegal acts.
   c. acts.

8.   *Specific ideas*: count to ten, take a deep breath, go for a walk

   The general idea is
   a. actions.
   (b.) ways to calm down.
   c. ways to calm down before a test.

9.   *Specific ideas:* putting sticky tape on someone's chair, putting a "kick me"
   sign on someone's back, putting hot pepper in someone's cereal

   The general idea is:
   a. jokes.
   (b.) practical jokes.
   c. practical jokes played on teachers.

10. *Specific ideas:* "I like your dress"; "Your new haircut looks terrific"; "You look great in red"; "You did a fine job on last week's theme."

The general idea is:
a. comments.
b. judgments.
c. compliments.

Step 2: Putting Implied General Ideas in Your Own Words

Now that you have practiced recognizing general ideas, you are ready to practice stating such ideas on your own. Below is an example. Consider the four specific ideas, and then decide on a general idea that is neither too broad nor too narrow.

General idea: _____

Specific ideas: juice
 blood
 water
 milk

At first glance it might seem that the general idea of these specific ideas is *beverages*. But blood does not fall into that category (except for Dracula). So you must broaden the general idea to include blood. Thus the general idea here is *liquids*.

➤ Practice 2

In the following lists, the specific ideas are given, but the general ideas are unstated. Fill in the blanks with the unstated general ideas.

1. *General idea:* _____ hair colors _____

 Specific ideas: red
 gray
 brown
 strawberry blonde

2. *General idea:* _____ containers _____

 Specific ideas: box
 jar
 can
 bag

3. *General idea:* _____ cold symptoms _____

    Specific ideas: sniffles
    sore throat
    coughs
    sneezes

4. *General idea:* _____ building materials _____

    Specific ideas: cement
    bricks
    nails
    lumber

5. *General idea:* _____ types of music _____

    Specific ideas: pop
    hard rock
    classical
    soul

6. *General idea:* _____ furniture for seating _____

    Specific ideas: rocker
    sofa
    love seat
    recliner

7. *General idea:* _____ people who work at a restaurant _____

    Specific ideas: chef
    waitress
    cashier
    bus boy

8. *General idea:* _____ household chores _____

    Specific ideas: making the beds
    washing the dishes
    drying the dishes
    dusting the furniture

9. *General idea:* _____ insults _____

    Specific ideas: "Your mother stinks."
    "You look like an ape."
    "Your father's a bum."
    "Your car is a real junk heap."

10. *General idea:* _____ *steps in making pizza* _____

    Specific ideas: Roll the dough out in a circle.
                    Cover the dough with tomato sauce.
                    Cover the sauce with mushrooms and onions.
                    Then add grated mozzarella cheese.

Step 3: Recognizing Implied Main Ideas

Just as with unstated *general* ideas, your choices of unstated *main* ideas must not be too broad or too narrow. You must select a general statement that includes all or most of the specific ideas in a paragraph.

The following exercises will give you lots of help and practice in finding unstated main ideas. By the time you have finished this chapter, you will be writing out full unstated main ideas in your own words.

Begin by reading the follow group of statements. Then circle the letter of its unstated main idea. Finally, read the explanation that follows.

1. Men accuse women of not trusting them.

2. Men complain that women tell their secrets to friends.

3. Men say that women change the subject when they're losing an argument.

4. According to men, women talk too much.

The statement that best expresses the implied main idea is:
a. Men think women don't trust them.
b. Men have various complaints about women.
c. Men accuse women of talking too much.
d. Men have strong views about women.

Explanation:

a. Item *a* is too narrow to be the unstated main idea. It mentions a specific detail that is included in only one statement.
b. In contrast to item *a*, item *b* mentions men's "complaints about women" in general. Each of the four statements is about such a complaint. So item *b* is the main idea—it covers all of the statements in the group.
c. Like item *a*, item *c* is a specific detail that appears only once, so it is also too narrow to be the main idea.
d. Item *d* is incorrect, too. The idea that "men have strong views about women" is too broad to be the main idea—it includes views about women other than just complaints.

➤ *Practice 3*

Read each group of four sentences. Then circle the letter of the answer that best states the implied main idea.

Group 1

1. The average part-timer earns more than three dollars an hour less than the average full-time worker.
2. Part-time workers are easily laid off.
3. Most part-time workers get no fringe benefits.
4. Few part-timers are protected by unions.

   Which statement best expresses the unstated main idea of these sentences?
   a. Part-time workers have second-class status.
   b. Part-timers get paid lower salaries.
   c. Workers have numerous problems.
   d. Part-timers make up a significant part of our working population.

Group 2

1. The science fiction writer Robert A. Heinlein predicted a manned rocket to the moon.
2. Jules Verne included a submarine in an 1873 novel.
3. In the same book, Verne also predicted electrical stoves.
4. In a novel published in 1899, H. G. Wells wrote about portable TV sets and air conditioning.

   The unstated main idea of these sentences is:
   a. Through the years, people have made many predictions.
   b. Jules Verne predicted the submarine and electrical stoves.
   c. Science fiction writers have made correct predictions.
   d. Science fiction writers make the best predictors.

Group 3

1. Of thirteen traits, the majority of parents chose honesty as most important for children to have.
2. The second most-desirable trait for children was "good sense and sound judgment."
3. Obedience to parents came in third.
4. Being considerate and being responsible came in fourth and fifth, but far behind the first three.

   The unstated main idea of these sentences is:
   a. For a survey, parents chose the traits they felt were most important for children.
   b. Parents feel it is more important for children to be honest than obedient.

c. The trait most parents agree children should have is honesty.

d. A survey shows that most people feel honesty is the most important human trait.

Step 4: Recognizing Implied Main Ideas in Paragraphs

You have practiced finding unstated main ideas for a group of statements. The next step is to work at finding unstated main ideas in paragraphs. Read the following passage and see if you can choose the statement that best expresses its main idea.

> If people stop to think about the plots in children's stories, they may be surprised. Hansel and Gretel, for example, were abandoned by their father and stepmother and left to wander in a dark forest. Cinderella was treated like a slave by her stepmother and stepsisters. Little Red Riding Hood was eaten by a wild animal, and the three blind mice had their tails cut off by the farmer's wife.

The unstated main idea is:

a. Children's stories are about stepfamilies.

b. Cinderella was treated like a slave.

c. Animals and children are important characters in children's stories.

d. Children's stories often deal with evil and violence.

Explanation:

An important clue to the main idea of this paragraph is the first sentence: "If people stop to think about the plots in children's stories, they may be surprised." From this we see that the main idea must do two things: it must 1) cover most or all of the details and 2) refer to something about those stories that could be surprising.

With these ideas in mind, let's examine the four answer options:

a. Children's stories are about stepfamilies.

Only two of the details of the paragraph are about stepfamilies, so answer *a* is too narrow to be the main idea. Also, it is not surprising.

b. Cinderella was treated like a slave.

Only one of the details in the paragraph is about Cinderella, so answer *b* is much too narrow to be the main idea.

c. Animals and children are important characters in children's stories.

The detail about Cinderella has nothing to do with animals and children. Also, this answer is not surprising—most people would expect animals and children to be common characters in children's stories.

d. Children's stories often deal with evil and violence.

The fact that children's stories deal with very mean and violent behavior *could* surprise people since many think such themes are not suited to children. And all of the examples in the paragraph *are* about children's stories that include evil and violence. Thus statement *d* expresses the implied main idea of the paragraph.

The best way to strengthen your skill in figuring out implied main ideas is with practice. The rest of this chapter will give you practice in recognizing and then stating implied main ideas of paragraphs.

➤ Practice 4

Circle the letter of the answer that best states the implied main idea of each paragraph.

1. The Roman emperor Nero was probably behind some of the earliest frozen desserts. He had snow brought to him from nearby mountains to cool his wine cellar. Historians believe that the snow was also mixed with fruit, juices and honey. It wasn't until the 1200s, however, that the first frozen dessert made with milk reached Europe. It was introduced by Marco Polo, who brought the recipe from the Orient.

   The unstated main idea is:
   a. Some of the earliest known frozen desserts were made for Nero.
   b. The history of frozen desserts was influenced by Nero and Marco Polo.
   c. A frozen dessert in ancient Rome consisted of snow, fruit, juices, and honey.
   d. There are many delicious and healthful frozen desserts.

2. Personality plays a big role in who is chosen to be a TV game-show contestant. Producers of *The Price Is Right*, for instance, like contestants who almost jump onto the stage. Of course, contestants must also be good game players. The way game-show producers find out just how good candidates are is through tryouts. Would-be contestants should live in the Los Angeles area. Except for a few shows that sponsor auditions around the country, most tryouts take place in Los Angeles.

   The unstated main idea is:
   a. Producers of *The Price is Right* like very energetic contestants.
   b. Game-show contestants must have the right type of personality.
   c. There are several factors involved in selecting TV game-show contestants.
   d. Producing television shows is a very complicated process.

3. According to psychiatrist Richard Moscotti, the ability to work well is one key to a balanced life. He feels both underworking and overworking are to be avoided. A second key is the ability to love, which requires a certain amount of openness. The ability to be loved is the third key to a balanced life. This is difficult for those who feel unworthy of love. The last key, according to Moscotti, is the ability to play, which involves knowing how to relax.

The unstated main idea is:
a. The first key to a balanced life, according to Moscotti, is the ability to work well.
b. According to Moscotti, some people have trouble receiving love.
c. Psychiatrists have specific ideas on what makes up a balanced life.
d. According to Moscotti, there are four keys to a balanced life.

Step 5: Putting Implied Main Ideas into Your Own Words

You are now ready to try putting into your own words the unstated main ideas of paragraphs. To do so, remember that you should first look for a topic. Then decide on what point the author is making about that topic.

➤ Practice 5

After reading each paragraph below, write what you think is its unstated main idea. For help in figuring out the main idea, complete the hint that follows each paragraph.

1. The factor most often named by workers as being important to job satisfaction is a feeling of accomplishment. The opportunity for advancement is the next most popular factor. Close behind that is pay. Next come job security and shorter hours at work.

What is the unstated main idea of this paragraph? _____ *There are several*
factors that workers feel are most important to job satisfaction.

Hint: The author's primary point is that there are several _____ *factors* _____
that workers feel are most _____ *important* _____ to satisfaction at work.

2. Videotape recorders (VCRs) enable people to enjoy blockbuster movies soon after they are seen in theaters. VCRs also help people manage their TV viewing time. For example, instead of fighting to stay awake to catch their favorite late-night show, VCR owners can program their machines to stay up for them. Then the show can be watched later at a more convenient time.

Also, VCRs offer another, even more attractive benefit—they allow the user to fast-forward through the commercials of recorded programs.

What is the unstated main idea of this paragraph? _____
VCRs have several advantages.

Hint: The topic of this paragraph is VCRs. The author's point about VCRs is

that they have _____ *several advantages.* _____.

3. Lonnie had to work every night the week of finals. He barely had time to study or sleep. He got home every night at midnight, and some of his finals began first thing in the morning. Because he was so tired, his concentration was weak. Even when he knew a subject well, he couldn't think clearly during the test. As a result, he got poorer grades than he expected in most of his classes.

    What is the unstated main idea of this paragraph? _____
    Lonnie's grades suffered because of his heavy work schedule.

    Hint: The topic of this paragraph is how Lonnie's ___ *work schedule* ___
    affected his grades.

➤ *Review Test 1*

A. In each item below, the specific ideas are given, but the general idea is unstated. Circle the letter of the general idea that tells what the specific ideas have in common. Remember that the correct general idea *will not be too narrow or too broad.*

1. *Specific ideas:* Persian cats, cocker spaniels, elephants, canaries

    The general idea is:
    (a.) animals.
    b. household pets.
    c. endangered animals.

2. *Specific ideas:* alcohol, tobacco, heroin

    The general idea is
    a. substances.
    (b.) addictive substances.
    c. illegal substances.

3. *Specific ideas:* for better health, for vanity, to fit into old clothes

    The general idea is
    a. reasons to eat healthy foods.

b. reasons to take vitamins.
ⓒ reasons to go on a diet.

B. Read each group of four sentences. Then circle the letter of the answer that best states the implied main idea.

Group 1

1. The average debt per American today is around $30,125, including mortgages.
2. Some people owe thousands of dollars on their credit cards.
3. The Treasury Department accepts credit cards for some payments.
4. Hospitals, taxi drivers, and prostitutes take credit-card payments.

The unstated main idea of these sentences is
a. Americans owe a lot on their mortgages.
b. People ought to use their credit cards to pay their mortgages.
c. The Treasury department accepts credit cards.
ⓓ Credit and debt are a way of life in America.

Group 2

1. Try substituting pinto beans for the beef in Mexican foods.
2. Instead of a meat sauce, make a tomato and bean sauce for spaghetti.
3. Make a stew with such beans as lentils or split peas.
4. You can make a salad out of two or three kinds of beans mixed with chopped onions, olive oil, and lemon juice.

The unstated main idea of these sentences is
a. Mexican foods can be made with pinto beans instead of beef.
b. There are easy ways to add pinto beans to your diet.
ⓒ There are easy ways to add beans to your diet.
d. Mexican foods can be very enjoyable.

➤ *Review Test 2*

A. In the following lists, the specific ideas are given but the general ideas are unstated. Fill in the blanks with the unstated general ideas.

1. *General idea:* _____ *test items* _____

   Specific ideas: multiple choice
   essay
   true-false
   fill in the blank

2. *General idea:* _____ directions _____

    Specific ideas: up
                       down
                       northwest
                       south

3. *General idea:* _____ greetings _____

    Specific ideas: a handshake
                       "Hi."
                       "Welcome."
                       "Glad to meet you."

B. Circle the letter of the answer that best states the implied main idea in each paragraph.

4. Through the years, farmers around the world have used much land that once was wilderness. Logging, mining, and oil development in many countries have also used up wilderness lands. Huge blocks of wilderness have almost totally disappeared in Europe and the United States. Of U.S. land, only about 3 percent is wilderness, and almost all of that is in Alaska.

    The unstated main idea is:
    a. Wilderness lands have been lost to farming.
    b. Wilderness lands have been lost to logging, mining, and oil development.
    c. Changes have occurred in the world's wilderness.
    d. The wilderness in the U.S. has shrunk greatly.

5. The novel *Lord of the Flies* begins with a group of schoolboys being left on an island by a plane crash. At first the group is cooperative, helping one another to find food and shelter. Then it divides into two camps. One is led by a peaceful boy named Ralph; the other by a violent one named Jack. Jack's group becomes more and more powerful until Ralph is the only "civilized" person left on the island. He is nearly killed by the other boys before, finally, a rescue ship arrives.

    The unstated main idea is:
    a. *Lord of the Flies* is a fictional view of how young people interact with each other in various circumstances.
    b. *Lord of the Flies* is a fictional view of what can happen when young people are alone and removed from civilization.
    c. The author of *Lord of the Flies* feels that boys are basically more uncivilized than girls.
    d. *Lord of the Flies* is a story about a rescue ship.

C. Read each paragraph below. Then write what you think is the unstated main idea of the paragraph.

6. To avoid an accident with your lawn mower, always keep your hands away from the moving blades. Also, make sure that children and pets are kept a safe distance away. Never use an electric mower if the grass is wet or if it's raining. Wear sturdy shoes that cover the toes. And finally, clear all sticks, rocks, and other objects from the mower's path.

What is the unstated main idea of this paragraph? _____

To avoid an accident with a lawnmower, take some simple precautions.

7. One big advantage of speaking is that it gives you a chance to influence others' thoughts and actions. Whatever your goal—for example, to get your boss to give you a raise, or to get a teacher to change a grade—a key to success is your ability to speak well. Another advantage of speaking is the chance to gain the admiration and respect of others. People often respond positively to a person who talks well. Finally, talking gives you a chance to release energy. Whether you are frustrated or excited about something, it often helps to talk about it rather than keep it inside.

What is the unstated main idea of this paragraph? _____

There are several advantages to talking.

➤ *Review Test 3*

A. To review what you've learned in this chapter, answer each of the following questions.

1. __T__ TRUE OR FALSE? A paragraph without a topic sentence may have an implied main idea.

2. __T__ TRUE OR FALSE? A paragraph without a topic sentence may have supporting details.

3. Another name for an unstated idea is
    a. a general idea.   ⓑ an implied idea.   c. a stated idea.

4. To find the unstated main idea of a passage, you may find it helpful to first decide on its
    ⓐ topic.   b. length.   c. topic sentence.

5. To find the unstated main idea of a passage, you must use
    a. a dictionary.   ⓑ reasoning.   c. topic sentences.

B. Here is a chance to apply your understanding of implied main ideas to a selection from the "My Turn" column of *Newsweek* magazine. The author tells in touching detail about her difficulties as a single mother on welfare.

Read the article and then answer the questions that follow on the central point and main ideas. There are also vocabulary questions to help you continue practicing the skill of understanding vocabulary in context.

Words to Watch

Following are some words in the reading that do not have strong context support. Each word is followed by the number of the paragraph in which it appears and its meaning there. These words are indicated in the article by a small circle (°).

snickering (2):	laughing a nasty, slightly hidden laugh
hysterectomy (6):	surgery in which the uterus is removed, either totally or partially
tactics (6):	methods
extractions (6):	removals
soaring (8):	rising very high

MESSAGES FROM A WELFARE MOM

Ramona Parish

Like many other single mothers, I am on welfare. I have received   1
Aid to Families with Dependent Children ever since I divorced my husband six years ago. Living on government aid does several things to people. It destroys their pride and dignity; it makes them dependent on a system that penalizes them for being willing to work. I am not lazy and I want to work. But at this time the best I can hope for is a minimum-wage job that would only undermine my attempts to get ahead. Instead of just being poor, I would become one of the nation's working poor. I cannot survive on $3.35 per hour with three children, without regular child-support payments or health insurance. So I live on AFDC and often feel guilty because I take advantage of this system and its services. But I'm also made to feel ashamed because I cannot pay for things with my own hard-earned money.

To the people behind me on the grocery-store line: You have   2
helped me feel guilty. You chip away at what little pride I have left by snickering° to others when I use my food stamps, at the same time commenting loudly about an abuse of taxpayers' dollars. It is because of such comments that I shop in a town fifteen miles away, and even

there my face reddens with shame.

To all landlords: Some of you believe that because I receive welfare I have no pride in my home or my surroundings. Many times I've called on the phone to ask about a rental and, sight unseen, been turned down when I mention I receive AFDC. I know you have heard that most welfare people will destroy your home and are completely unreliable in paying the rent on time. It doesn't matter if I have excellent references from previous landlords or that I can have the rent payments sent directly to you. On the other hand, there are some of you who will rent *only* to welfare. You like having the money sent to you from social services. You don't care what condition your apartment is in because if I complain about needed repairs (windows that won't open, doors with broken locks), you tell me: "So? Move out." Because there are only a few of you who will rent to AFDC, your apartment will not be empty long.

To my ex-husband: In the past six years I have asked very little from you. Although I appreciate the bags of used clothing you sent when I asked if you could help with school clothes, I would have preferred if you had sent child support. Why should I have been the one who was embarrassed when your father stopped by and gave our son a pair of tennis shoes and each of our two daughters ten dollars? You should be the one who is embarrassed—more help from you could make a difference in the way our children live. I make sure they have all their basic needs met, but I get tired of telling them, no, they can't have things they want because I don't have the money.

To my children: I did not intend to raise you on welfare. Bear with me a few more years, for I am trying to make a bad situation better. All of you kids have complained about having to apply for the free-lunch program. I know how ashamed you must feel when you're singled out in the classroom as a free-luncher, and the hurt caused by whispers among your friends that you're poor and your mother is on welfare. I'm sorry for the things I can't afford. But my biggest apology is for the groceries and boxes of toys you saw delivered to the house four years ago by the Old Newsboys organization. Tears still come to my eyes when I think of the question you each asked so innocently, "Mom, I thought people collected these for the poor who can't afford food and toys for the holidays." Little did you know, we were one of the poor. Since that day my pride has not allowed me to accept any more gift baskets.

To all doctors and dentists: Would my hysterectomy° which was done three years ago when I was only twenty-eight have been so urgent if I hadn't had Medicaid to pay for it? Could I have avoided having to take estrogen every day for the rest of my life? Although I

3

4

5

6

had a choice of whether to have the surgery or not, I believe scare tactics° were used. I wonder if some professionals take advantage of Medicaid recipients because women on AFDC are seen as uneducated and are expected to believe what they are told? And would that explain why so many AFDC women have lost all their teeth? After several extractions°—six teeth lost in the six years on AFDC with three more to go soon—I find it difficult to chew my food properly. It's a standard joke now that I'm always the last one to leave the table; in reality, I'm too embarrassed to tell people that dentists suggest pulling teeth because Medicaid won't pay for root canals and crowns.

To all pharmacists: When there is a long line of customers   7
waiting to have their prescriptions filled and I hand you mine, do not shout, "Do you have your current Medicaid card?" Because the shouting is an advertisement that I am on welfare, I will walk around the store until the line is gone. Welfare moms do have some dignity.

To all social-service case workers: When I am willing to help   8
myself and work, why do you take everything away? Can't you at least let me keep the food stamps and medical insurance until I'm above the poverty level? Without these benefits I cannot make it, so I stay on the soaring° welfare rolls. I don't want a free ride, but I do need a lift.

To whom it may concern: Do not feel pity for me. I don't want   9
it. I have been given an abundance of self-worth these past two years. Enrolling in college and getting an education is my key to a future without AFDC. Managing a full-time class load, twenty hours a week on a work-study program, and being a mother hasn't been easy, but I've survived. Every time I cash my work-study check, I get back a piece of my pride. I still use my food stamps in another town, but at the same time I use dollar bills that I have earned myself. With each passing semester my head lifts a little higher. What I could use is a smile of understanding and words of encouragement and support. With help, not hindrance, I will make it.

Reading Comprehension Questions

Vocabulary in Context

1. The word *penalizes* in "it makes them dependent on a system that penalizes them for being willing to work" (paragraph 1) means
   a. praises.
   b. punishes.
   c. forgives.
   d. aids.

2. The word *undermine* in "a minimum-wage job . . . would only undermine my attempts to get ahead" (paragraph 1) means
   a. weaken.
   b. help.
   c. begin.
   d. balance.

3. The word *abuse* in "To the people behind me on the grocery-store line: You have helped me feel guilty. . . . commenting loudly about an abuse of taxpayers' dollars" (paragraph 2) means
   a. misuse.
   b. collection.
   c. aid.
   d. growth.

4. The word *abundance* in "Do not feel pity for me. . . . I have been given an abundance of self-worth these past two years" (paragraph 9) means
   a. lack.
   b. definition.
   c. plentiful amount.
   d. waste.

5. The word *hindrance* in "With help, not hindrance, I will make it" (paragraph 9) means
   a. assistance.
   b. interference.
   c. education.
   d. dignity.

Central Point

6. Which sentence best expresses the implied central point of the selection?
   a. People often feel guilty about taking help.
   b. Living on welfare makes people feel guilty and ashamed and discourages independence.
   c. People on welfare are not encouraged to work.
   d. The author has not asked her ex-husband for much help.

Main Ideas

7. Which sentence best expresses the implied main idea of paragraph 2?
   a. The author feels guilty.
   b. The author has no pride.
   c. People make the author feel guilty and hurt her pride by looking down on her for using food stamps.
   d. The author prefers to do her grocery shopping in a town fifteen miles from where she lives.

8. Which sentence best expresses the implied main idea of paragraph 3?

    Some landlords believe that welfare recipients take no pride in their home.

    Landlords should not be allowed to make a profit from welfare tenants.

    Being on welfare has made it difficult for the author to rent a decent apartment.

    Only a few landlords will rent apartments to women who receive Aid to Families with Dependent Children.

9. Which sentence best expresses the implied main idea of paragraph 6?

    The author feels she should not have had a hysterectomy at such a young age.

    The rules of Medicaid and, possibly, the poor ethics of health-care professionals have resulted in poor health care for the author.

    Like many women receiving Aid to Families with Dependent Children, the author has had several teeth extracted.

    Being on welfare can be extremely difficult, especially for single mothers of young children.

10. Which sentence best expresses the implied main idea of paragraph 8?

    Welfare rules discourage the author from helping herself more and getting off welfare.

    More and more people are on welfare.

    The author is willing to work.

    The author does not want a free ride.

7

More About Supporting Details

An earlier chapter explained supporting details and gave you practice with the careful reading needed to understand those details. This chapter will explain the difference between two levels of supporting details: major and minor. It will also describe a helpful way to locate both kinds of supporting details.

UNDERSTANDING MAJOR AND MINOR SUPPORTING DETAILS

Suppose the passage that began an earlier chapter consisted of just a main idea:

Main Idea

Recently I had a really bad dream.

How much do we learn from that sentence? Not much. We need more information about the dream to know just what it was about and how bad it really was. Suppose instead of writing just one sentence, the author had introduced a few important details about the dream. Those points would be the major supporting details. *Major supporting details* are the separate, primary points that support the main idea. This is how a paragraph on the bad dream would look if it included both the main idea and the major supporting details:

Main Idea and Major Details

Recently I had a really bad dream. Coming out of the darkness were hundreds of large gray rats. Coming at me in the other direction were a dozen angry pit bulls. I did my best to wake up as quickly as possible.

Now there is some meat on the bare bone of the main idea. The author has provided the major supporting details about his dream. Those supporting details help us understand the main idea and convince us of its truth. Together, the main idea and the major supporting details form the basic framework of paragraphs.

Often, however, the major details themselves can be explained in more detail, and that's where minor supporting details come in. Major details provide more information about the main idea, and *minor supporting details* provide more information about the major details.

Imagine now that the author had further fleshed out his dream experience by adding minor details as well. The result would be the passage discussed in an earlier chapter.

Main Idea and Major and Minor Details

As a rule, most of my dreams at night are pleasant ones. Recently, though, I had a really bad dream. I was in an alley dressed in light summer clothing. Coming out of the darkness at the end of the alley were hundreds of large gray rats. Their razor-sharp teeth glistened with saliva. Their eyes glowed red with a cold, murderous fury. I turned to run away, but coming at me in the other direction were a dozen angry pit bulls. And these particular pit bulls were foaming at the mouth; they all had rabies. "Just my luck," I muttered and did my best to wake up as quickly as possible.

Just as the major details gave body to the main idea, the minor details have filled out the major details. Now the main idea is clear, and the paragraph is convincing. Now we clearly and fully understand what the author meant by the statement: "Recently I had a really bad dream." Remember, then, that the major details in any well-written paragraph will help you make sense of the main idea.

A Model Paragraph

Try your hand at separating major from minor support in the paragraph below. The first sentence gives the main idea. Then the paragraph goes on to present two major details in support of the main idea. The rest of the specifics are minor details. See if you can put a *1* in front of the first major detail and a *2* in front of the second one.

As you read, watch for words that commonly introduce new points, such as *first, secondly, next, also,* and *in addition.* Such words are sometimes called "addition words."

Some colleges today offer two active learning programs for students. First, students can do independent research. For example, one senior did a traffic and parking study for a small town. And an art major did research towards cataloging the works of a well-known painter. Secondly, students can serve in any of various internships. A major in agriculture, for instance, held an internship with a grain company, and a journalism student was an intern with a public-television station.

Now see if you correctly marked the two major supporting details. You'll find them after the main idea in the following outline of the paragraph:

Main idea: Some colleges today offer two active learning programs for students.

1. Students can do independent research.

   a. _____

   b. _____

2. Students can serve in various internships.

   a. _____

   b. _____

Notice that the first major detail in the paragraph was introduced by the word *first,* and the second major detail was introduced with the word *secondly*.

The other details in the paragraph are the minor ones. Take a minute now to fill in the blanks with the missing minor details. Then read the explanation that follows.

Explanation:

The minor details clarify the major details by illustrating them. The first two missing minor details are examples of students doing independent research: a) a senior did a traffic and parking study and b) an art major cataloged the works of a well-known painter. The second two missing minor details are examples of students serving in internships: a) an agriculture major was an intern with a grain company and b) a journalism student was a public-television intern.

➤ *Practice 1*

Major and minor supporting details are mixed together in the three lists that follow. The details of each list support a given main idea.

Separate the major, more general details from the minor ones by filling in the outlines. You may find this easier to do if you begin with the major details; once they are filled in, add the minor details. Some details have been filled in for you.

List 1

Main idea: My mother loves to cook from scratch, but my aunt uses shortcuts.
- Uses only frozen and canned vegetables
- My mother's longer methods
- Makes chicken broth for cream soups
- My aunt's shortcut methods

Major detail: **1.** *My mother's longer methods*

Minor details: a. *Makes chicken broth for cream soups*

   b. Uses only fresh vegetables

   c. Takes hours to finish spaghetti sauce

Major detail: **2.** *My aunt's shortcut methods*

Minor details: a. Adds spices to a can of soup

   b. *Uses only frozen and canned vegetables*

   c. Makes spaghetti in fifteen minutes with a bottled sauce

List 2

Main idea: There are several types of job-related factors to consider in choosing a job.

- Is there room to advance?
- Some factors have to do with the environment.
- Is the work interesting?
- Is the workplace safe?

Major detail: **1.** Some factors have to do with the work itself.

Minor details: a. *Is the work interesting?*

   b. Is the work challenging?

Major detail: **2.** *Some factors have to do with the environment.*

Minor details: a. Is the workplace pleasant?

   b. *Is the workplace safe?*

Major detail: **3.** Some factors have to do with the future.

Minor details: a. Will the company continue to need you?

   b. *Is there room to advance?*

List 3

Main idea: There are advantages to television.

> • It's possible to learn about law from shows like *People's Court.*
> • It is educational.
> • Watching TV movies is cheaper for us than going to the movies.
> • It allows me to be antisocial.
> • It is useful for dates with my girlfriend.

Major detail: 1. *It allows me to be antisocial.*

Minor details: a. When I watch TV during dinner, my family doesn't expect me to tell them about my day.

b. My parents' friends don't expect me to converse with them if I'm watching TV.

Major detail: 2. *It is useful for dates with my girlfriend.*

Minor details: a. *Watching TV movies is cheaper for us than going to the movies.*

b. If we watch television instead of talking, we don't fight.

Major detail: 3. *It is educational.*

Minor details: a. Shows like *60 Minutes* inform me about important issues.

b. *It's possible to learn about law from shows like* <u>People's Court</u>.

TWO HELPFUL WAYS TO FIND MAJOR DETAILS

Two common ways in which authors alert you to the major details of a passage are by using:

1 An opening phrase

2 Addition words, such as *first, second, next*

An *opening phrase* often tells you that a series of details is coming. And *addition words* often introduce each of the details. You can use each of these clues to help you find the major details of a passage. Often a passage contains both an opening phrase and one or more addition words.

Opening Phrases

Paragraphs often contain a main idea and a list of supporting details—a list of reasons, examples, steps, and so on. Opening phrases can often alert you to what type of detail to watch for. Here are some typical opening phrases:

Typical Opening Phrases

several kinds of	a few causes	a few reasons
two advantages	several characteristics	three factors
four steps	among the results	

When you see phrases like the above, you can expect a list of major details to follow. In addition, you will also know at times *how many* major details to expect. For example, you may look for *two* advantages or *three* factors or *four* steps.

Such phrases are generally part of the topic sentence. For example, here are two topic sentences that include opening phrases:

• Humor performs certain key functions in our lives.

(The opening phrase *key functions in our lives* suggests that a list of those functions will follow.)

• There are three basic forces pushing up health costs.

(The opening phrase *three basic forces pushing up health costs* suggests that the author will name those three forces.)

You may have noticed that each of the opening phrases listed above includes a word that ends in *s*. These are plurals that refer to the types of details being listed, such as advantage*s*, reason*s*, characteristic*s*, cause*s*, and step*s*. These plurals will help you identify the major details being listed.

Now read the paragraph below, and number each of the major details—*1, 2,* and so on. Then, in the spaces provided, take study notes on the paragraph by creating an outline:

• First complete the heading, including the word that ends in *s*.
• Then fill in the major details briefly.

When you are finished, read the explanation that follows the outline.

There are several popular solutions to the problem of child care for working couples. The most popular is to leave children with relatives. Another common solution is for each parent to work different hours so that either the mother or father is home to care for the children. Also, many parents take their children to day-care centers.

Heading: _____s to Problems of Child Care for
     Working Couples

List of major details:

1. _____

2. _____

3. _____

Explanation:

As the topic sentence indicates, the type of major detail being listed is
"popular solutions to the problem of child care for working couples." Three
major details are listed: 1) leaving children with relatives, 2) each parent
working different hours, and 3) taking the children to day-care centers.

Addition Words

Here are common addition words that may introduce major details:

Addition Words

one	first of all	in addition	furthermore
first	also	next	last of all
second	another	moreover	finally

In the paragraph above on the problem of child care for working couples, the
two last major details are introduced with addition words ("*Another* popular
solution is for each parent to work different hours. . . . *Also*, many parents take
their children to day-care centers").

In the paragraph below, all of the three major details are introduced by one
of the words in the above list. Read the paragraph, and use the addition words
(and the opening phrase) to help you put a *1*, a *2*, or a *3* before each of the three
major details.

¹Several kinds of voice-operated robots may soon be available to help
the disabled. ²One such robot, already developed, is a desktop machine. ³It
can do various chores, including brushing teeth and serving a can of soup.
⁴Also, a robot that can move from one location to another is now being built
for the handicapped. ⁵It will be able to do such jobs as getting the mail and
answering the door. ⁶Another type of robot for the disabled will be useful in
offices. ⁷This type would do such office work as opening file cabinets and
putting disks in a computer.

Explanation:

The main idea of this paragraph is in the first sentence: "Several kinds of voice-operated robots may soon be available to help the disabled." Notice that the opening phrase "Several kinds of . . . " suggests that a list of kinds of voice-operated robots is coming.

Sentence 2 begins with the addition word *one*, which introduces the first major supporting detail: a desktop robot. Sentence 3 then gives minor details that explain that first major detail.

Sentence 4 begins with the addition word *also*, which alerts us that a new point is being introduced. The new point is that a moving robot for the disabled is being produced. This is another major detail in support of the main idea. Sentence 5 gives minor details that explain the moving robot.

The signal word *another* in sentence 6 tells us that yet another major detail is being introduced. This last major detail is that another robot being planned for the disabled is for the office. The last sentence of the paragraph expands on that point about robots for the office.

Be on the lookout, then, for opening phrases that tell you a list of major details may appear in a paragraph. And look for addition words that will often help you locate some or all of the major details. (While addition words do not always indicate major details, they often do.)

➤ Practice 2

This practice will help you develop a thinking process to use in finding major and minor supporting details. Each paragraph is followed by an explanation that includes blanks. Read the paragraph and explanation and fill in the blanks.

1. ¹Birds communicate with two different types of sounds. ²One type is the song. ³Bird songs can be defined as groups of sounds that are repeated in patterns. ⁴Such sounds do not need to be vocal. ⁵The sounds of wings drumming, feathers vibrating, or a woodpecker's beak tapping are also songs if they have meaningful, repeated patterns. ⁶Songs are used to attract females and warn off competing males. ⁷The second type of sound birds make to communicate is the call. ⁸Calls are sharp, short sounds. ⁹Calls have various functions, including warning birds of an enemy or calling the young to eat.

Explanation:

The main idea of this paragraph is given in the first sentence. That sentence suggests that ____*two*____ *(how many?)* major details will follow. The first point about the main idea is introduced in sentence 2 by the addition word "____*one*____." The first major detail is: One kind of sound birds use to communicate is the _____*song*_____. Sentences 3 through __6__ expand on the first major detail. Those sentences thus give minor details.

The second major detail is introduced in sentence __7_. The addition word that introduces a new point in that sentence is "_____*second*_____." The second major detail in support of the main idea is: Another type of sound birds use to _____*communicate*_____ is the _____*call*_____. The sentences that expand on the second major detail are sentences _8__ through 9. They therefore give _____*minor*_____ details.

2. ¹Lyme disease and Rocky Mountain spotted fever are potentially dangerous diseases carried by ticks. ²It's important to take steps to avoid tick bites, especially when you're walking in underbrush or tall grass. ³First, you should be sure to dress carefully. ⁴Pull socks up over your pants, tuck in your long-sleeved shirt, and wear a hat. ⁵Next, put on insect repellent. ⁶Spray not only your exposed skin, but also your clothing and shoes. ⁷Finally, shower as soon as you return from a tick-infested area. ⁸Be especially careful to scrub your scalp and around your hairline.

Explanation:

The main idea of this paragraph is in the second sentence: It's important to take _____*steps*_____ to avoid tick bites.

Sentence 3 begins with the addition word "_____*first*_____," which introduces the first _____*major*_____ supporting detail. This detail is that you should be sure to _____*dress carefully*_____. Sentence 4 then gives some minor details that develop the first major detail.

The addition word "_____*next*_____" is a clue that the second major detail is being given in sentence ___5___. The second major detail is: _____*Put on insect repellent*_____. The following sentence gives minor details to expand upon the second major detail.

Sentence 7 then begins with the addition word "_____*finally*_____," which marks the last major detail. The last major detail is: _____*Shower as soon as you return from a tick-infested area*_____. Sentence 8 then gives (*major or minor?*) _____*minor*_____ details to explain the last major detail.

3.   ¹According to its inventor, Rich Hall, a "sniglet" is "any word that doesn't appear in the dictionary, but should." ²Some sniglets describe useless objects. ³For example, *flopcorn* is the name for those kernels of corn that refuse to pop. ⁴*Spirobits* are the pieces of paper that are left behind after a page is torn out of a notebook. ⁵Other sniglets are names for certain frustrating actions. ⁶*Gladhandling*, for instance, is the attempt to find and separate the two ends of a plastic food bag. ⁷And people who dial a telephone number and then forget whom they've called suffer from *phonesia*.

Explanation:

The main idea of this paragraph—the concept of the "sniglet"—is given in the first sentence. The first major detail is that some sniglets *describe useless objects*; this major detail is given in sentence _2_. Sentences _3_ – _4_ are minor details; those minor details are examples of the first type of sniglet. The two examples are the words "_flopcorn_" and "_spirobits_."

The second major detail, given in sentence _5_, is that other sniglets are _names for frustrating actions_.

The minor details supporting the second major detail are given in the last (how many?) _two_ sentences. Those minor details are two _examples_ of that type of sniglet.

➤ *Practice 3*

Number with a *1* and 2 or a *1, 2,* and *3* the major details in each of the paragraphs that follow. (Remember that addition words can often help you identify supporting details.)

Next, complete the heading by writing in the word that ends in *s*. Then fill in the major details.

A.   There are a couple of ways you can protect yourself from skin cancer. First of all, use a sunscreen with a sun-protection factor of fifteen or more. Also, try not to get much exposure at the time of day when the sun's rays are strongest, which is between 10 A.M. and 3 P.M.

Heading: _____Way_____s to Protect Yourself from Skin Cancer

List of major details:

1. *Use a sunscreen with a sun-protection factor of fifteen or more.*

2. *Limit your exposure when the sun's rays are strongest (10 a.m. to 3 p.m.).*

B.   While Freud greatly influenced other psychologists, some of his followers ended up breaking away from him. For example, Carl Jung, once a close associate of Freud, differed from him in many ways. Unlike Freud, Jung believed there were two separate levels of the unconscious: a personal unconscious and a collective unconscious. Alfred Adler broke with Freud and founded his own school. Among the differences between the two is that Adler emphasized the ego more.

Heading: _____ *Follower* _____ s Who Broke Away from Freud

List of major details:

1. *Carl Jung, who believed there were two levels of the unconscious*

2. *Alfred Adler, who emphasized the ego more*

C.   Some of our more interesting words have come from people's names. One such word is *guillotine*, which is a machine with a heavy blade used to behead people. It was named for a Dr. Guillotin, who, during the French Revolution, pleaded for a kinder way than hanging to execute criminals. Another word based on a person's name is *sandwich*. It comes from John Montagu, the 4th Earl of Sandwich. Montagu was a gambler known for all-day sessions. At 5 A.M. one day in 1762, he became hungry. Unwilling to leave the card table, he told his servant to bring some roast beef between two pieces of toasted bread. Thus the modern sandwich was born. Finally, *nicotine* is named for Jean Nicot. In the sixteenth century, Nicot introduced tobacco into France.

Heading: _____ *Word* _____ s Based on People's Names

List of major details:

1. *Guillotine was named for Dr. Guillotin, who wanted a kinder method of executing criminals.*

2. *Sandwich comes from the Earl of Sandwich, who invented the sandwich.*

3. *Nicotine is named for Jean Nicot, who introduced tobacco into France.*

➤ *Practice 4*

Answer the questions that follow the paragraphs. The topic sentence of each paragraph is set off in boldface.

A.   [1]**There are various types of cures for snoring for those who wake up others or themselves with their nighttime noises.** [2]First, the most common are the various gadgets designed to keep people from sleeping on their backs, the most common position for snoring. [3]They include things like the "snore ball whistle," a rubber ball clipped to the seat of the snorer's pajamas that shrieks when he rolls onto his back. [4]There are also various anti-snoring chin straps. [5]They work on the principle that people can't snore if they don't open their mouths. [6]Occasionally people will even have surgery in their quest to stop snoring. [7]But that works only in the rare cases where the snoring is caused by growths of tissue in the sinus area.

1. The opening phrase that signals the list of major details is
   a. *types of cures for snoring.*
   b. *those who wake up others.*
   c. *nighttime noises.*

2. The major details of this paragraph are
   a. 1) gadgets and 2) surgery.
   b. 1) gadgets to keep people from sleeping on their backs, 2) anti-snoring chin straps, and 3) surgery.
   c. 1) gadgets, 2) the "snore ball whistle," 3) surgery.

3. The second major detail is introduced with the addition word
   a. *first.*
   b. *also.*
   c. *finally.*

4. *Complete the sentence:* The reason anti-snoring chin straps are supposed to

   work is that   __people can't snore if they don't open their mouths.__

   _____.

5. *Fill in the number:* The answer to question 4 can be found in sentence __5__.

B. How close is too close? **According to one social scientist, we choose different comfort zones for different people and social settings.** First, the space within about a foot from us is "intimate" space. We share it willingly only with loved ones. If forced to share it with strangers (in a crowded elevator, for instance) we feel uncomfortable. Between one and four feet away from us is our "personal" space, which we share with friends. This is about how far apart we sit at a restaurant table, for example. Beyond this, between about four and ten feet, is "social" space. This is about the distance we keep from strangers at a party or other gathering, for example. Finally, the space more than about ten feet away is "public" space—a distance at which we can pretty much ignore other people.

1. In general, the major details of this paragraph are
   a. social settings.
   b. comfort zones.
   c. different people.

2. Specifically, the major details of this paragraph are
   a. 1) a foot, 2) intimate space, and 3) personal space.
   (b.) 1) intimate space, 2) personal space, 3) social space, and 4) public space.
   c. 1) loved ones, 2) strangers, and 3) friends.

3. *Fill in the addition word:* The last major detail is introduced with the
   addition word "_____*finally*_____."

4. "Personal space" is the
   a. space we share with loved ones.
   (b.) space we share with friends.
   c. distance between us and strangers.
   d. distance at which we can ignore others.

5. At a party, we are likely to put a distance between ourselves and strangers of
   about
   a. a foot.
   b. between one and four feet.
   (c.) between four and ten feet.
   d. ten feet and more.

➤ *Review Test 1*

A. Major and minor supporting details are mixed together in the list that follows. The
   details of each list support a given main idea. Separate the major, more general
   details from the minor ones by filling in the outline. Some details have been filled
   in for you.

   - Hang gliding   • Those that depend on gravity
   - Those that use mechanical power   • Skateboarding
   - Amusement park rides

Main idea: Some means of transportation are more fun than efficient.

Major detail: 1. Those that use body power

Minor details: a. Roller skating

                b. *Skateboarding*

Major detail: 2. *Those that depend on gravity*

Minor details: a. *Hang gliding*

                b. Parachuting

Major detail: 3. *Those that use mechanical power*

Minor details: a. Motorized skates

                b. *Amusement park rides*

B. Number with a *1* and *2* the major details in each of the paragraphs that follow. Remember that addition words can often help you identify supporting details.

Then, in the spaces provided, complete the notes on each paragraph: First complete the headings, being sure to include the word that ends in *s*. Then fill in the missing major details.

1.   Florida has more than its share of odd creatures. For example, it is the home of a walking catfish, which can be out of water for as long as eighty days. Another resident of Florida is a toad that can get as large as a football. It likes to eat food left outdoors in bowls for pets.

Heading: _____ Odd Creature _____s That Live in Florida

List of major details:

1. _A walking catfish which can be out of water for as long as eighty days_

2. _A toad that can get as large as a football_

2.   There are certain techniques that help older people find work. One of these is self-advertisement. Older job-hunters should let as many people as possible know they are interested in a job. Even their children's friends and local tradespeople should be told, since they may have contacts that could yield job leads. Also, when they do have interviews, older job-seekers should accent the positive. They should list all their skills and emphasize their years of experience.

Heading: _____ Technique _____s _____ That Help Older People

_____ Find Work _____

List of major details:

1. Self-advertisement

2. _During interviews, accent the positive_

➤ *Review Test 2*

Answer the questions that follow the paragraphs. The topic sentence of each paragraph is set off in boldface.

A.   [1]**Certain stages of family reactions are predictable when a loved one becomes seriously ill.** [2]First, the family goes through denial, a natural defense against emotional pain and conflict. [3]After denial comes disorganization. [4]In this stage, family members become more demanding and irrational. [5]Next, family members become too anxious and overwhelmed to make any decision. [6]Finally, the family reaches the stage of acceptance. [7]By this time the family is adjusted to the loved one's illness.

1. In general, the major details of this paragraph are
    a. types of serious illness.
    (b.) stages of family reactions to a loved one being seriously ill.
    c. natural defenses against emotional pain and conflict.

2. Specifically, the major details of the paragraph are
    a. 1) denial, 2) disorganization, and 3) becoming more demanding and irrational.
    b. 1) a family member becomes seriously ill and 2) the family finally becomes adjusted to the illness.
    (c.) 1) denial, 2) disorganization, 3) inability to make a decision because of anxiety and being overwhelmed, and 4) acceptance.

3. According to the passage, denial that a family member is seriously ill is the way the family protects itself from _____ *emotional pain and conflict* _____.

4. Sentence 4 provides
    a. a major detail.
    (b.) minor details.

B. ¹Americans who complain about their car problems are not as badly off as they think. **²In Japan, the problems of automobile ownership are even greater.** ³Japanese drivers must deal with traffic jams that add hours to every trip. ⁴To pass time during these delays, they stock their cars with comic books and tape cassettes. ⁵Another source of frustration is the high cost of driving. ⁶Fuel costs up to $3.60 a gallon there, and tolls for the trip from downtown Tokyo to the airport—only forty miles—add up to $16. ⁷Finally, parking is a constant problem in Japan's overcrowded, narrow streets. ⁸A car buyer must have proof, including maps and diagrams, that he or she has a parking place before being allowed to purchase a car.

1. In general, the major details of this paragraph are
    a. car problems that Americans have.
    b. ways of coping with traffic jams in Japan.
    (c.) problems of car ownership in Japan.

2. Specifically, the major details of the paragraph are
    a. 1) car problems in America and 2) car problems in Japan.
    (b.) 1) terrible traffic jams, 2) high driving costs, and 3) parking problems.
    c. 1) problems of car ownership, 2) ways to pass time during traffic jams, and 3) problems with parking.

3. The addition word that introduces the second major detail of the paragraph is
    (a.) *another.*
    b. *only.*
    c. *add up to.*

4. *Complete the sentence:* Japanese drivers stock their cars with comic books and tape cassettes in order to _____*pass time during long traffic jams*_____

_____.

5. The answer to question 4 can be found in sentences
   a. 2 and 3.
   b. 3 and 4.
   c. 4 and 5.

➤ *Review Test 3*

A. To review what you've learned in this chapter, answer each of these questions about supporting details.

1. *Fill in the blank:* Minor supporting details are more *(general, specific)*
   _____*specific*_____ than major details.

2. Opening phrases can tell us
   a. that a list of some type will follow.
   b. how many major details will be listed.
   c. both of the above.

3. An addition word can tell us
   a. how many major details to expect.
   b. that a new major detail is being introduced.
   c. both of the above.

4. Label each part of the outline form below with one of the following:

   • Main Idea
   • Major Supporting Detail
   • Minor Supporting Detail

   _____*Main Idea*_____

   1. _____*Major Supporting Detail*_____

      a. _____*Minor Supporting Detail*_____

      b. _____*Minor Supporting Detail*_____

   2. _____*Major Supporting Detail*_____

B. Here is a chance to apply your understanding of supporting details to a reading on a troubling aspect of family life. The selection is from the college textbook *Sociology,* Fourth Edition (Random House, 1991). Read the selection and then answer the questions that follow on supporting details.

To help you continue to strengthen your work on the skills taught in previous chapters, there are also questions on vocabulary in context and the central point and main ideas.

Words to Watch

Following are some words in the reading that do not have strong context support. Each word is followed by the number of the paragraph in which it appears and its meaning there. These words are indicated in the article by a small circle (°).

unique (2):	unusual
resolved (3):	settled
virtually (3):	almost entirely
brutalized (5):	cruelly treated
stakes (6):	benefits that can be gained and lost
appalled (6):	horrified
intensity (6):	great strength of feeling
restraints (7):	controls
intercede (7):	become involved in order to bring about agreement
constitute (8):	make up, form

BEHIND CLOSED DOORS: VIOLENCE IN THE FAMILY

Michael S. Bassis
Richard J. Gelles
Ann Levine

"And they lived happily ever after." Hundreds of stories about   1
marriages and families end with this line. Typically, loved ones are reunited; obstacles to marriage overcome; problems with children resolved. Indeed, the very idea of living happily ever after is linked, in our minds, with the special warmth of the family. Yet if we look behind the closed doors of many American households, we discover that all is not peace and harmony.

Some Myths and Realities

With the exception of the police and the military, the family is the most violent social group in our society. The home is a more dangerous place than a dark alley. A person is more likely to be murdered in his or her home, by a member of the family, than by anyone else, anywhere else, in society. One in every four murders in the United States is committed by a member of the victim's family. Our country is not unique° in this respect.

Fifteen or twenty years ago, few Americans would have believed these statements. Then, in 1975, the sociologists Murray Straus, Richard Gelles, and Barbara Steinmetz conducted a national survey on family violence. Rather than relying on official statistics (incidents of physical abuse known to the police and other social agencies), the researchers asked a representative sample of Americans how they resolved° family conflicts, whether they had hit, spanked, punched, or otherwise assaulted a family member, and how often. The results of this survey exploded a number of myths about violence in the home. The first myth was that incidents of family violence are rare. They are not. In 1975–1976, nearly two million children, two million wives, and two million husbands (yes, husbands) had been punched, kicked, beaten up, or injured with a knife or gun by a member of their own family. Sixteen percent of couples reported at least one incident of violence in the year of the survey, and nearly a third had experienced violence at some point in their marriage. Two-thirds reported that they had hit a child at least once. In most cases, child abuse was not an isolated incident: if a child was assaulted once, he or she was usually assaulted several times. A second myth suggested that violence occurs only in poor, uneducated families. This, too, proved false. Economic stress does make family violence more likely. But someone had been slapped (or worse) in virtually° every household in the United States, regardless of family income. One reason for the belief that only poor families are violent is that the wealthy take their injuries to private doctors, who were more likely to treat the problem as a private matter than to report family violence to authorities.

As for educational level and family violence, 16 percent of college students in one survey knew of at least one physical fight between their parents during the preceding year. Nearly 50 percent of the students had been hit by their parents during their senior year of high school, and 8 percent had been injured severely enough to require first aid or medical attention.

Most of us assume that anyone who brutalized° a loved one is "sick"—mentally ill. This is also a myth. The proportion of violent family members who are psychologically disturbed, in the clinical sense, is no higher than the proportion in the population as a whole.

Sociological Explanations

How do sociologists explain the high levels of violence in the family? A number of factors seem to be at work. The first is *intimacy*. Family members are intensely involved with one another. They have deep emotional investments in one another. When quarrels break out or problems arise, the stakes° are higher than in other social groups. A man who is amused by the behavior of a female colleague who is drunk may become enraged if his wife has a little too much to drink. A politician who has been an active supporter of gay rights, at some risk to her career, may be appalled° to discover that her own child is homosexual. Why? Because the behavior of a member of our family is a direct reflection on ourselves. The intensity° of family relationships tends to magnify the most trivial things, such as a burned dinner or a whining child. When did you last hear of someone beating up the cook in a restaurant for preparing an unacceptable meal? But such minor offenses and small oversights often spark violent family fights.

A second factor contributing to violence in the home is *privacy*: because family affairs are regarded as private, there are few outside restraints° on violence. When a family quarrel threatens to become a fight, there are no bystanders to break it up, as there might be on the street or in some other public place. Police are reluctant to intercede° in family quarrels—for good reason. More police are killed responding to calls about domestic disturbances than arc killcd chasing armed robbers. Neighbors may know that a parent is abusing a child but resist "getting involved." The family, after all, has a right to privacy. Victims may be too ashamed to report family violence to the police. Indeed, a small child may not know something is wrong or unusual when mother holds his or her hand in a flame as punishment.

Third, and perhaps most disturbing, there is a good deal of *social and cultural support* for the use of physical force in the family. Parents are allowed—indeed, encouraged—to spank their children. "Spare the rod and spoil the child," the old saying goes. Most people do not think of spanking a child as violence. But suppose a total stranger in the supermarket smacked your daughter because he disapproved of something she said? Suppose a teacher hit her across the face? Either would constitute° assault and battery in a court of law. What makes parents different? In effect, parenthood confers a "license for hitting" in our society. So, according to some, does marriage. In one survey, one out of four people agreed that it is sometimes justifiable for a husband

6

7

8

to hit his wife. Battered wives often say (and believe), "I asked for it" or "I had it coming." (Imagine if the attacker had been her boss, another "authority" figure, but one whose authority is limited. Because it was her husband who beat her, the situation is viewed quite differently.)

Finally, in the process of *socialization* we learn to associate   9
violence with the family. Our first experience of force nearly always takes place at home. Most of our parents use physical punishment on occasion—for our own good, of course, and because they love us. (The child is told, "This hurts me more than it hurts you.") From here it is only a small step to the conclusion that the use of violence is legitimate whenever something is really important. And the things that are most important to us are often family matters. In addition, we learn *how* to be violent from our families. (It takes observation and practice, perhaps with siblings, to learn how to beat up another person.) Study after study has shown that the more violence an individual experiences as a child, the more violent he or she will be as a parent. Brutality breeds brutality.

Reading Comprehension Questions

Vocabulary in Context

1. The word *trivial* in "the intensity of family relationships tends to magnify the most trivial things, such as a burned dinner or a whining child" (paragraph 6) means
   a. rare.
   b. colorful.
   c. pleasant.
   (d.) unimportant.

2. The word *confers* in "parents are allowed—indeed, encouraged—to spank their children. . . . In effect, parenthood confers a 'license for hitting'" (paragraph 8) means
   a. denies.
   (b.) gives.
   c. repeats.
   d. destroys.

Central Point and Main Ideas

3. Which sentence best expresses the central point of the selection?
   a. Numerous murders take place at home.

(b.) The American family is more violent than previously thought, a situation for which several causes have been identified.

c. According to sociologists, there are a number of factors that explain family violence.

d. Because family affairs are considered private, there are few outside controls on violence in the home.

4. The main idea of paragraph 7 is best expressed in its
   (a.) first sentence.
   b. second sentence.
   c. third sentence.
   d. last sentence.

Supporting Details

5. __F__ TRUE OR FALSE? People who experience violence as children are more likely to avoid violence toward their own children.

6. The major details of paragraphs 3–5 are
   (a.) myths about family violence.
   b. steps to take to counteract family violence.
   c. factors that explain the high levels of violence in the family.
   d. types of family conflicts.

7. The major details of paragraphs 6–9 are
   a. myths about family violence.
   b. steps to take to counteract family violence.
   (c.) factors that explain the high levels of violence in the family.
   d. the effects of family intimacy.

8-10. Complete the following outline of the reading by filling in the blanks.

   Main idea: Research shows that violence is more common among all American families than once thought, a situation for which there seem to be several causes.

   A. A sociological survey discovered that there are several myths about violence.

      1. First myth: Incidents of family violence are rare.

      2. *Second myth: Violence occurs only in poor, uneducated families.*
      _____

      3. Third myth: People who brutalize a loved one are mentally ill.

   B. Sociologists have identified several factors *to explain the high levels of violence in the family.*

1. Intimacy magnifies the importance of unimportant things, sparking family fights.

2. The view that family affairs are private has resulted in few outside restraints on family violence.

3. There is much social and cultural support for the use of physical force in the family.

4. *In the process of socialization, we learn to associate violence with the family.*

8

Transitions

I like my psychology teacher. She is short on patience.

Does the writer like his teacher *because* she is short on patience? We're not sure because the above sentences are unclear. To make it clear, a transition is needed. *Transitions* are words and phrases that show the connections between ideas. They are like signposts that inform travelers. To see how transitions guide us, look at the same two ideas, but this time with a transition:

I like my psychology teacher *even though* she is short on patience.

Now we know that the writer likes his teacher *despite* her impatience. The relationship between the two ideas is clear. A transition has bridged the gap from one idea to the other. In Latin, *trans* means "across," and transitions live up to their name—they carry the reader "across" from one thought to another.

There are a number of ways in which transitions connect ideas and show relationships. Here is a list of the major types of transitions:

1   Words that show addition

2   Words that show time

3   Words that show contrast

4   Words that show comparison

5   Words that show illustration

6   Words that show cause and effect

Each of these kinds of transitions will be explained in the pages that follow.

1   WORDS THAT SHOW ADDITION

Put a check beside the item that is easier to read and understand:

_____   Paperback books take up less shelf space than hardcover books. They are less expensive.

_____   Paperback books take up less shelf space than hardcover books. They are also less expensive.

The word *also* in the second item makes the relationship between the sentences clear. The author is discussing the advantages of paperback books. One advantage is that the books take up less space. An *additional* advantage is that they are less expensive. *Also* and words like it are known as addition words.

Addition words tell us that one or more ideas continue in the same line of thought as a previous idea. They introduce ideas that *add to* what has already been mentioned. Here are some common addition words:

Addition Words

one	first of all	in addition	furthermore
first	also	next	last of all
second	another	moreover	finally

Examples:

One reason people have dogs is for companionship; *another* reason is for protection.

Why do I prefer organic vegetables? Well, *first of all*, they taste better.

My father dislikes being interrupted at home by telephone salespeople. *Moreover*, he hates when they become rude after he won't purchase their products.

➤ *Practice 1*

Insert an appropriate addition word or phrase from the list above into each of the following items. Try to use a variety of transitions.

1.   One good way to lose friends is to talk constantly and never listen. _____*Another*_____ way is to buy yourself a fine shirt before paying back money you borrowed.

2. "This class has done so well," said the teacher, "that you are excused early. _____*In addition*_____, you have no homework tonight."

3. The basketball team's long hours of practice paid off—the team won many of their games this year. _____*Also*_____, they set a record for season attendance.

4. I have a few problems with my research paper. _____*First of all*_____, I have trouble getting to the library when it's open.

5. A drinking problem can destroy an individual's life; _____*furthermore*_____, it can tear a family apart.

2 WORDS THAT SHOW TIME

Put a check beside the item that is easier to read and understand:

_____ The bee seemed to sting me for no reason. I let it land on my hand.

_____ The bee seemed to sting me for no reason after I let it land on my hand.

The word *after* in the second item makes the relationship between the sentences clear. The bee stung the author for no reason *after* he let it land on his hand. *After* and words like it are known as time words.

These transitions indicate **time relationships**. They tell us *when* something happened in relation to something else. Here are some common time words:

Time Words

first	before	when
next	during	then
often	after	now

Examples:

When I take my morning shower, there is usually no hot water left.

It used to take me thirty-five minutes to get to school. *Now*, due to the subway strike, that time has nearly doubled.

I begin my "Things To Do" list by writing down everything I need to do the next day. *Then* I label each item A (very important), B (important), or C (not important).

Helpful Points About Transitions

Here are two helpful points to keep in mind about transitions:

1   Certain words within a group mean very much the same thing.

For example, *also* and *moreover* both mean "in addition." Authors often use different transitions simply for the sake of variety.

2   In some cases, the same word can serve as two different types of transitions, depending on how it is used.

For example, the word *first* may be an *addition* word, as in the following sentence:

> My brother has some strange kitchen habits. *First*, he loves to cook with the radio on full blast. *Moreover*, ...

First may also be used to signal a *time* sequence, as in this sentence:

> Our English class had several interruptions this morning. *First*, the radiator began squeaking. *Then*, ...

➤ *Practice 2*

Insert an appropriate time word from the list on the previous page into each of the following sentences. Try to use a variety of transitions.

1.   Carlos _____*often*_____ falls asleep while watching television.

2.   First, my uncle studies the food ads to see which stores have the best specials. _____*Then*_____ he clips all the cents-off coupons.

3.   Our counselors try to help students _____*before*_____ the students' problems get very big.

4.   _____*When*_____ I was in the shower, a hairy spider crept out of the drain.

5.   Jenelle did her math homework _____*during*_____ English class.

3   WORDS THAT SHOW CONTRAST

Put a check beside the item that is easier to read and understand:

_____   The weather in Florida is usually wonderful, but the summers are hot and humid.

_____   The weather in Florida is usually wonderful. The summers are hot and humid.

In the second item, we're not sure if the author feels that the weather in Florida is wonderful *because of* or *despite* the hot and humid summers. The transition *but* in the first item makes the relationship clear: the weather in Florida is wonderful *despite* the summer heat and humidity. *But* and words like it are known as contrast words.

Contrast words show that two things *differ* in one or more ways. Here are some common contrast words.

Contrast Words

but	in contrast	on the other hand
however	instead	even though
yet	still	although

Examples:

There are advantages to getting my own apartment; *on the other hand*, living at home is much cheaper.

Even though the calf fell down three times in a row, she kept trying to stand up and walk by herself.

Only 10 percent of the population is left-handed. *In contrast*, among babies that are born more than two months prematurely, 54 percent are left-handed.

➤ *Practice 3*

Insert an appropriate contrast word from the above list into each of the following sentences. Try to use a variety of transitions.

1. Our Toyota is ten years old, _____*but*_____ it still runs perfectly.

2. Surprisingly, our exercise instructor has flabby arms _____*even though*_____ she teaches a class every day.

3. American women have been dyeing their hair for years. American men, _____*on the other hand*_____, only recently started coloring theirs.

4. _____*Although*_____ it was only forty degrees outside, Bill was determined to have a barbecue.

5. "We tend to think famous authors like Shakespeare were starving and ignored in their own times," said the teacher. "_____*However*_____, Shakespeare was a success and lived very well."

4 WORDS THAT SHOW COMPARISON

Put a check beside the item that is easier to read and understand:

_____   Mickey Mouse has been a favorite of several generations of children. Bugs Bunny has been beloved for many years.

_____   Mickey Mouse has been a favorite of several generations of children. Bugs Bunny has been equally beloved for many years.

The first item makes us wonder if the author is discussing what's different about Bugs Bunny and Mickey Mouse—or what's alike about them. The word *equally* in the second version makes it clear that the author is discussing one way in which the cartoon characters are alike. *Equally* and words like it are known as comparison words.

These **comparison words** signal that the author is pointing out a similarity between two subjects. The words tell us that the second subject is *like* the first one in some way. Here are some common comparison words:

Comparison Words

like	just as	in like manner	as if
as	likewise	in the same way	equally
just like	similarly	as well	

Examples:

The carpet was so old and faded it looked *like* a gray shadow.

Parents today often dislike the music their children listen to, *just as* their own parents disliked the Beatles or the Rolling Stones.

Cabbage is a vegetable that can be grown in cold weather. *Likewise*, turnips can survive in a garden well into the winter.

➤ *Practice 4*

Complete each sentence with a suitable transition from the above box. Try to use a variety of transitions.

1. Mrs. Potts cooks chicken and noodles every Saturday, _____*just as*_____ her mother always did.

2. Many Hispanic girls have a special party for their fifteenth birthday. _____*Similarly*_____, Anglo girls often celebrate their sixteenth birthday in a special way.

3. Good teachers are _____*as*_____ skilled in praising what students have accomplished as they are in challenging them to do more.

4. One cleaning expert says that vinegar can do many cleaning tasks around the home. _____*In like manner*_____, she advises using ammonia in place of many store-bought cleansers.

5. The bright rainbow over the gentle hill made the scene look _____*as if*_____ it belonged in a fairytale.

5 WORDS THAT SHOW ILLUSTRATION

Put a check beside the item that is easier to read and understand:

_____ Getting organized is not that difficult. Important dates can be routinely marked on a large calendar.

_____ Getting organized is not that difficult. For example, important dates can be routinely marked on a large calendar.

The first item leads us to believe that marking important dates on a monthly calendar is all that is needed for getting organized. But the words *for example* in the second item make it clear that marking dates on a calendar is only *one illustration* of how to get organized. *For example* and words like it are known as illustration words.

Illustration words point out that one or more examples will be used to explain a given idea. They tell us that a specific detail is being provided as *an example*. Here are some common illustration words:

Illustration Words

for example	to illustrate	once
for instance	such as	including

Examples:

Robert is late for everything. *For instance*, he doesn't make his New Year's resolutions until January 2.

My mother's love of chocolate has led to some pretty weird combinations. *Once* she put Hershey's syrup on a cheese sandwich.

Uncle Arthur has several annoying habits, *such as* flicking cigar ashes onto the tablecloth and picking his teeth with a fork.

➤ *Practice 5*

Insert an appropriate illustration word from the box on the previous page into each of the following sentences. Try to use a variety of transitions.

1.   Loni hates to miss an important concert. _____*For instance*_____, she waited in line fifteen hours to buy tickets to see the Grateful Dead.

2.   There have been many famous only children, _____*including*_____ actress Marilyn Monroe and astronaut Frank Borman.

3.   When we were young, my older brother liked to tease me. _____*Once*_____ he put raisins in my cereal and told me they were roaches.

4.   Colonists came to America for many reasons. The Puritans, _____*for example*_____, came in 1620 seeking religious freedom.

5.   A large part of what seems to be taste is really smell. _____*To illustrate*_____, try eating some bread while holding a banana or piece of onion near your nose.

6   WORDS THAT SHOW CAUSE AND EFFECT

Put a check beside the item that is easier to read and understand:

_____   Because Elena cares for her elderly parents, she has very little free time.

_____   Elena cares for her elderly parents. She has very little free time.

In the second item, we are not sure of the relationship between the two sentences. Does Elena have little free time *with which* to care for her parents? Or does she have little free time *because* she cares for her parents? The word *because* in the first item shows the connection between the two ideas. *Because* and words like it are known as cause-and-effect words.

Cause-and-effect words show that the author is discussing the *reason or reasons* why something happened. One event *caused* another to happen. Here are some common cause-and-effect words:

Cause-and-Effect Words

because	the result was	therefore
since	if . . . then	thus
reason	so	as a result

Examples:

Because Sunday night is the most popular night for watching TV, miniseries always begin then.

One father discovered that his baby quieted down when riding in a car. *As a result*, he invented a gadget for the crib that sounds and feels like a moving car.

If you don't prick an eggplant before baking it, *then* it may explode in the oven.

➤ Practice 6

Insert an appropriate cause-and-effect transition from the above list into each of the following sentences. Try to use a variety of transitions.

1. _____*Because*_____ there's no room in your mouth for your wisdom teeth, they will have to be removed.

2. Nikki wanted a large wedding reception. _____*As a result*_____, her parents had to rent a hall.

3. _____*Since*_____ my roommate has never applied for a full-time job before, he needed help in writing a résumé.

4. A survey of customers showed that many of them lived or worked within five miles of Westbridge. _____*Therefore*_____, the bank opened a branch office there.

5. The _____*reason*_____ our skin wrinkles when we're in the water a long time is that the top layer of skin absorbs much more water than the bottom one.

USING A VARIETY OF TRANSITIONS

It is important to keep in mind that transitions provide logical connections between sentences. For example, look at the following three sentences. Each needs a short transitional word to logically connect the two ideas that are present.

See if you can fill in the correct transition in each case. Choose from *and*, which means "in addition"; *but*, which means "however"; or *so*, which means "as a result."

1. The couple wanted to buy the house, _____ they didn't qualify for a mortgage.

2. We washed the car in the morning, _____ we cleaned the garage in the afternoon.

3. A baby elephant has no thumbs, _____ it sucks its trunk.

Explanations:

1. The couple wanted to buy the house, but (meaning *however*) they didn't qualify for a mortgage.

2. We washed the car in the morning, and (meaning *in addition*) we cleaned the garage in the afternoon.

3. A baby elephant has so thumbs, so (meaning *as a result*) it sucks its trunk.

   In each case, only one of the words logically expresses the relationship between the ideas in the sentence. It would not make sense, for example, to say "The couple wanted to buy the house, *and* they didn't qualify for a mortgage." Nor would it make sense to say, "The couple wanted to buy the house, *so* they didn't qualify for a mortgage."

Now see if you can fill in a correct longer transition in each case. Choose from *moreover*, which means "in addition"; *however*, which means "but"; or *therefore*, which means "as a result."

1. Our class wanted to do something for the hurricane victims;
    _____, we sent a donation to the Red Cross.

2. The boss wants us to work four hours without a break; _____,
    he slips away to the vending machine area at least once an hour.

3. I hate commercials that glamorize smoking; _____, I despise
    commercials that glamorize drinking.

Explanations:

1. The answer that logically connects the two parts of the sentence is *therefore*. Our class wanted to do something; therefore (meaning *as a result*), we sent a donation.

2. The answer that logically connects the two parts of the sentence is *however.* The boss wants us to work four hours without a break; however (meaning *but*), he slips aways for snacks at least once an hour.

3. The answer that logically connects the two parts of the sentence is *moreover.* I hate commercials that glamorize smoking; moreover (meaning *in addition*), I despise commericals that glamorize drinking.

Remember, then, that transitions show the logical relationship between two ideas. On the next page is a chart of some of the most common transition words, with brief meanings.

Common Transitions and Their Meanings

Transition Word	Meaning	Transition Word	Meaning
and	in addition	on the other hand	however
also	in addition	nevertheless	however
moreover	in addition	so	as a result
furthermore	in addition	therefore	as a result
but	however	thus	as a result
yet	however	consequently	as a result

> *Practice 7*

Insert the transition that logically fits in each of the following items. Read carefully to make sure you understand the logical relationship between ideas.

1. The restaurant was beautiful, _____*but*_____ the food was overpriced.

   and   but   so

2. My instructor is allergic to chalk dust, _____*so*_____ she has students write the assignment for the day on the blackboard.

   so   but   and

3. The shutters on that house are falling down, _____*and*_____ the paint is peeling.

   and   so   but

4. Carla wants to go dancing at the local club, _____*but*_____ her friends want to go bowling.

   but   so   and

5. A short nap late in the afternoon relaxes me. _____*Moreover*_____, it gives me the energy to spend evenings on my homework.

   Yet   Moreover   However

6. My neighbor has been in three car accidents in the last year; _____*consequently*_____, his auto insurance rates have doubled.

   consequently   nevertheless   furthermore

7. Going grocery shopping is one of my least favorite tasks on the weekend; _____*on the other hand*_____, I would rather shop for groceries than wash the kitchen floor.

    consequently   on the other hand   moreover

8. The Erie Canal opened up the Great Lakes region to commerce; _____*consequently*_____, the canal provided a first important link between the East and the West.

    consequently   yet   on the other hand

9. Taking a night class is a good way to develop a new interest or hobby; _____*furthermore*_____, it's a great way to meet people with similar interests.

    furthermore   consequently   therefore

10. Many people view football as a modern game, _____*but*_____ the sport is actually descended from a Middle Ages game in which villagers kicked, threw, or carried a ball across fields to another village.

    but   and   so

➤ Practice 8

Insert the transition that logically fits in each of the following items. Read carefully to make sure you understand the logical relationship between ideas.

1. I thought I had planned the date perfectly, _____*but*_____ I forgot my wallet.

    and   but   so

2. The air in the apartment was very dry, _____*and*_____ the heat was up to eighty degrees.

    and   but   so

3. The day was cold and rainy, _____*so*_____ we decided not to go shopping.

    and   but   so

4.   The business letter was beautifully written and typed on expensive stationery, _____ *but* _____ the recipient's name was misspelled.

but   consequently   in addition

5.   The traveler was exhausted and mentally drained after the long flight; _____ *nevertheless* _____, he walked the five blocks to his hotel instead of taking a cab.

therefore   nevertheless   furthermore

6.   I like the new store because it has a play area for small children; _____ *also* _____, its dressing rooms are always clean and brightly lit.

also   on the other hand   thus

7.   In 1891, James Naismith wanted to improve YMCA attendance during cold weather. _____ *Therefore* _____, he invented a game to be played indoors using two peach baskets and a round ball—and basketball was born.

Therefore   Moreover   Yet

8.   Millions of children die every year in underdeveloped countries because of infection, _____ *but* _____ many of these deaths could be prevented through inexpensive medical treatments and relatively basic medical knowledge.

but   consequently   moreover

9.   Where we sit or stand in relation to other people generally signals certain attitudes about our willingness to cooperate. _____ *Furthermore* _____, the way that we walk, sit, and stand often indicates our emotional state.

Furthermore   Yet   Thus

10. Millions of people watch the Super Bowl each year. _____ *Therefore* _____, advertisers are willing to pay very high rates to have their commercials aired during this popular event.

Furthermore   Therefore   But

➤ *Review Test 1*

In the spaces provided, add logical transitions to tie together the sentences and ideas in the following paragraph. Use the five transitions shown in the box below.

Note: You may find it helpful to check (✓) each transition after you insert it into the passage.

before	in addition	result
for example	instead	

There are several good reasons to shop by mail-order catalog _____ *instead* _____ of shopping at the mall or downtown. First, catalog shopping is easy. By using several catalogs, you can compare prices without leaving home. _____ *In addition* _____, you can learn a lot about products sold through catalogs. Catalogs provide information that a busy salesclerk may not know or have time to tell you. Many go into great detail about the construction, fit, or workmanship of the products offered. You may read, _____ *for example* _____, that the blue checkered shirt you like is "100% long staple Egyptian cotton that can be machine washed at warm temperature." Third, catalog shopping gives you access to unusual items. You can find gifts that are unavailable in your area and clothing not carried by local retailers. So _____ *before* _____ running out to do your shopping, check those catalogs you've been getting in the mail. The _____ *result* _____ may be a change in your shopping habits.

➤ *Review Test 2*

Complete each sentence with the appropriate transition word or phrase. Then circle the kind of transition you have used.

1. a. Taking large doses of vitamin C can cause the body to absorb too much iron. _____ *Likewise* _____, too much vitamin D can lead to too much calcium in the blood.

   Likewise
   Because
   For example

   b. The transition indicates:
      illustration ⟨comparison⟩ cause and effect

2. a. Of all kitchen appliances, the upright freezer uses the most energy. Refrigerators with automatic defrost _____also_____ use up a lot.

   in contrast
   also
   for instance

   b. The transition indicates:

   (addition)   contrast   illustration

3. a. First the disappointed batter threw down his bat; _____then_____ he yanked off his batting helmet and drop-kicked it into the dugout.

   then
   instead
   thus

   b. The transition indicates:

   (time)   contrast   cause and effect

4. a. Clothes reflect society's values. _____For example_____, in Victorian times, when women were expected to be inactive, they wore clothing that limited their movements.

   Soon
   For example
   However

   b. The transition indicates:

   (illustration)   contrast   time

5. a. Movies shown on TV often have original scenes removed. _____In addition_____, they are frequently interrupted for commercials.

   Therefore
   But
   In addition

   b. The transition indicates:

   contrast   (addition)   cause and effect

6. a. The United States has had a two-party system _____since_____ 1800.

   therefore
   since
   even though

   b. The transition indicates:

   contrast   (time)   cause and effect

7. a. Sports injuries can sideline even a champion. _____Thus_____, experts urge every athlete to do warm-up exercises.

   Soon
   Thus
   On the other hand

   b. The transition indicates:

   time   contrast   (cause and effect)

8. a. In 1965, the average American ate only 0.3 pounds of
broccoli; in 1985, _____*in contrast*_____, the average
American ate 2.6 pounds of that nutritious vegetable.

   b. The transition indicates:

   (contrast)   cause and effect   illustration

thus
in contrast
for instance

9. a. More Americans than ever are keeping their own teeth,
thanks to preventive measures, _____*including*_____
fluoridated water and toothpaste.

   b. The transition indicates:

   contrast   addition   (illustration)

but
including
also

10. a. A year usually has 365 days; _____*however*_____,
every fourth year, one day is added to the calendar.

    b. The transition indicates:

    (contrast)   addition   cause and effect

however
because
for example

➤ *Review Test 3*

A. To review what you've learned in this chapter, complete each of the following
sentences about transitions.

1. Transitions are words that signal *(main ideas in, relationships between, the
importance of)* _____*relationships between*_____ ideas.

2. A(n) _____*addition*_____ transition means that the writer is adding to
an idea or ideas already mentioned.

3. A(n) _____*time*_____ transition tells us *when* something is happening
in relation to something else.

4. The transitions *but* and *however* signal a _____*contrast*_____ relationship.

5. The transitions *so* and *therefore* signal a _____*cause-and-effect*_____ relationship.

B. Here is a chance to apply your understanding of transitions to an excerpt from the
longtime bestselling book *The Road Less Traveled*. The author, M. Scott Peck, a
psychiatrist, explains a useful first step in solving your problems.

   Following the reading are questions on transitions and the relationships they
signal. To help you continue reinforcing the skills taught in previous chapters,
there are also questions on the following:

- vocabulary in context
- central point and main ideas
- supporting details.

Words to Watch

Following are some words in the reading that do not have strong context support. Each word is followed by the number of the paragraph in which it appears and its meaning there. These words are indicated in the article by a small circle (°).

self-evident (1):	not requiring any explanation
ludicrous (2):	laughable because of being obviously ridiculous
clarified (19):	made clear
whining (29):	childish complaining
glared (37):	stared angrily

RESPONSIBILITY

M. Scott Peck

We cannot solve life's problems except by solving them. This statement may seem idiotically self-evident°, yet it is seemingly beyond the comprehension of much of the human race. This is because we must accept responsibility for a problem before we can solve it. We cannot solve a problem by saying "It's not my problem." We cannot solve a problem by hoping that someone else will solve it for us. I can solve a problem only when I say, "This is my problem and it's up to me to solve it." But many, so many, seek to avoid the pain of their problems by saying to themselves: "This problem was caused by other people, or by social circumstances beyond my control, and therefore it is up to other people or society to solve this problem for me. It is not really my personal problem." 1

The extent to which people will go psychologically to avoid assuming responsibility for personal problems, while always sad, is sometimes almost ludicrous°. A career sergeant in the army, stationed in Okinawa and in serious trouble because of his excessive drinking, was referred for psychiatric evaluation and, if possible, assistance. He denied that he was an alcoholic, or even that his use of alcohol was a personal problem, saying, "There's nothing else to do in the evenings in Okinawa except drink." 2

"Do you like to read?" I asked. 3

"Oh yes, I like to read, sure." 4

"Then why don't you read in the evening instead of drinking?"   5

"It's too noisy to read in the barracks."   6

"Well, then, why don't you go to the library?"   7

"The library is too far away."   8

"Is the library farther away than the bar you go to?"   9

"Well, I'm not much of a reader. That's not where my interests lie."   10

"Do you like to fish?" I then inquired.   11

"Sure, I love to fish."   12

"Why not go fishing instead of drinking?"   13

"Because I have to work all day long."   14

"Can't you go fishing at night?"   15

"No, there isn't any night fishing in Okinawa."   16

"But there is," I said. "I know several organizations that fish at night here. Would you like me to put you in touch with them?"   17

"Well, I really don't like to fish."   18

"What I hear you saying," I clarified°, "is that there are other things to do in Okinawa except drink, but the thing you like to do most in Okinawa is drink."   19

"Yeah, I guess so."   20

"But your drinking is getting you in trouble, so you're faced with a real problem, aren't you?"   21

"This damn island would drive anyone to drink."   22

I kept trying for a while, but the sergeant was not the least bit interested in seeing his drinking as a personal problem which he could solve either with or without help, and I regretfully told his commander that he was not amenable to assistance. His drinking continued, and he was separated from the service in mid-career.   23

A young wife, also in Okinawa, cut her wrist lightly with a razor blade and was brought to the emergency room, where I saw her. I asked her why she had done this to herself.   24

"To kill myself, of course."   25

"Why do you want to kill yourself?"   26

"Because I can't stand it on this dumb island. You have to send me back to the States. I'm going to kill myself if I have to stay here any longer."   27

"What is it about living on Okinawa that's so painful for you?" I asked.   28

She began to cry in a whining° sort of way. "I don't have any friends here, and I'm alone all the time."   29

"That's too bad. How come you haven't been able to make any friends?"   30

"Because I have to live in a stupid Okinawan housing area, and none of my neighbors speak English." 31

"Why don't you drive over to the American housing area or to the wives' club during the day so you can make some friends?" 32

"Because my husband has to drive the car to work." 33

"Can't you drive him to work, since you're alone and bored all day?" I asked. 34

"No. It's a stick-shift car, and I don't know how to drive a stick-shift car, only an automatic." 35

"Why don't you learn how to drive a stick-shift car?" 36

She glared° at me. "On these roads? You must be crazy." 37

Reading Comprehension Questions

Vocabulary in Context

1. The word *inquired* in "'Do you like to fish?' I then inquired" (paragraph 11) means
   a. joked.
   b. stuttered.
   c. thought.
   d. asked.

2. The word *amenable* in "but the sergeant was not the least bit interested in seeing his drinking as a personal problem which he could solve either with or without help, and I regretfully told his commander that he was not amenable to assistance" (paragraph 23) means
   a. opposed.
   b. lost.
   c. agreeable.
   d. transported.

Central Point and Main Ideas

3. Which sentence best expresses the central point of the selection?
   a. People often blame others for their own problems.
   b. Americans in Okinawa had many problems.
   c. A young army wife who refused to help make her life on Okinawa better wanted someone else to solve her problem.
   d. Before a problem can be solved, a person must take responsibility for it, which many refuse to do.

4. Which sentence best expresses the main idea of paragraphs 2–23?
   a. The sergeant said that the only thing there was to do in Okinawa was drink.
   b. People will go to ridiculous extremes to avoid taking responsibility for their own problems.
   c. The sergeant's drinking problem had gotten him in serious trouble with the army.
   d. The sergeant was referred to the author for psychiatric evaluation.

Supporting Details

5. According to the author, many people see their problems as being
   a. beyond their control.
   b. easy to solve.
   c. caused by drinking.
   d. caused by loneliness.

6. The young wife
   a. couldn't speak English.
   b. couldn't drive a car.
   c. was lonely.
   d. lived in the American housing area.

7. Which of the following best outlines the reading?
   a. Although we cannot solve our problems without facing them, many people will go to extremes to avoid facing their problems.
      1. There are common problems people refuse to face.
         a. Alcoholism
         b. Loneliness
      2. The author saw how people go to great extremes to avoid assuming responsibility for their own problems.

   b. Although many people blame others for their problems, we must take responsibility for our own problems if we wish to solve them.
      1. An army career sergeant was unable to overcome his drinking problem because he refused to face it.
      2. A young army wife was unable to overcome her loneliness because she refused to do what was necessary to meet people.

Transitions

8. Fill in the blanks with two contrast transitions from paragraph 1.

   _____*yet*_____   _____*But*_____

9. The statement below expresses a relationship of
   a. time.
   b. addition.
   c. illustration.
   (d.) cause and effect.

   > A career sergeant in the army . . . [was] in serious trouble because of his excessive drinking. . . . (Paragraph 2)

10. The relationship between the two parts of the sentence below is one of
    a. addition.
    b. illustration.
    c. comparison.
    (d.) contrast.

    > I kept trying for a while, but the sergeant was not the least bit interested in seeing his drinking as a personal problem which he could solve. . . . (Paragraph 23)

9

Patterns of Organization

To help readers understand their main ideas, authors try to present supporting details in a clearly organized way. Details might be arranged in any of several common patterns. Sometimes authors may build a paragraph or longer passage entirely on one pattern; more often, the patterns are mixed. By recognizing the patterns, you will be better able to make sense of what you read.

UNDERSTANDING THE FIVE BASIC PATTERNS

There are five basic patterns of organization:

1 Time order
2 List of Items
3 Comparison and/or Contrast
4 Cause and Effect
5 Definition and Example

How the Patterns of Organization Use Transitions

All five of the patterns are based on relationships you learned about in the chapter on transitions. All five, then, involve transition words you may now recognize. The time order pattern, for example, is marked by transitions that show time (*first, then, next, after,* and so on). The list on the next page shows some of the transitions used with each pattern.

Pattern	Transitions Used
Time order	Words that show time (*then, next, after . . .*)
List of items	Words that show addition (*also, another, moreover . . .*)
Comparison and/or contrast	Words that show comparison or contrast (*like, just as, however, in contrast . . .*)
Cause and effect	Words that show cause and effect (*because, as a result, since . . .*)
Definition and example	Words that show illustration (*for example, to illustrate . . .*)

The following pages provide explanations and examples of each pattern.

1 TIME ORDER

Arrange the following group of sentences into an order that makes sense. Put a *1* in front of the sentence that should come first, a *2* in front of the sentence that comes next, and a *3* in front of the sentence that should be last. Then read the explanation that follows.

_____ According to one Holmes scholar, Holmes died in 1951, from a bee sting.

_____ In 1912, Sherlock Holmes retired to a farm, where he took up beekeeping.

_____ He later came out of retirement long enough to break up a World War I spy ring.

Events are usually presented in the order in which they happened, which results in the **time order** pattern of organization. Clues to the pattern of the above sentences include the dates (1912 and 1951) and the time transition *later*. Logically arranged, the sentences form the following paragraph:

> In 1912, Sherlock Holmes retired to a farm, where he took up beekeeping. He later came out of retirement long enough to break up a World War I spy ring. According to one Holmes scholar, Holmes died in 1951, from a bee sting.

As a student, you will see time order used frequently. Textbooks in all fields describe various events and processes, such as the events leading to the Boston Tea Party, how a bill travels through Congress, or the stages in a butterfly's life. Also, time order may be involved in the directions teachers give you.

Transitions like the following often signal that a paragraph or selection is organized according to *time order*.

Time Transitions

first	next	as	while
second	before	now	during
then	after	until	when
since	soon	later	finally

(Other signals for this pattern are dates, times, and such words as *years, stages, series, steps,* and *process.*)

Time order can be divided into two types: a *series of events or stages* and a *series of steps (directions)*. Each is discussed below.

Series of Events or Stages

Following is a paragraph in which stages in a process are organized in the order in which they happen—in other words, according to time order. Note that the author uses several time transitions: *first, second,* and *finally.*

In the spaces provided, complete the outline of the paragraph by listing the stages in the order in which they happen. One point has already been done for you, and a second has been started.

Children go through three social stages between the ages of one and three. First is the object-oriented stage. In this stage, they are more interested in objects of play than in each other. Their interaction with each other may be simply to organize play with an object. Second is the simple interactive stage, in which children relate to each other in simple ways for short periods. A child, for instance, might ask for a piece of candy by making a noise and putting out a hand. Finally, children reach the mutual interactions stage. In this stage interactions that often involve language take place. Children now imitate each other and take on roles in simple games, such as hide and seek.

Main idea: Children go through three social stages between the ages of one and three.

1. Object-oriented stage: greater interest in objects than in each other

2. Simple interactive stage: _____

_____

3. _____

_____

You should have completed the second point of the outline by writing something like "simple, short interactions with each other." The third point in your outline should be similar to "Mutual interactions stage: frequent interactions involving language."

➤ *Practice 1a*

The following two passages describe a sequence of events or stages. Complete the outline that comes after each passage.

A.   There are four initial stages in the life of a newborn baby kangaroo, called a joey. First, the joey must find its way from the mother's birth canal to her pouch. Since the tiny joey is both deaf and blind, it probably finds its way to the pouch by smell. Once in the pouch, it grasps one of the mother's teats and drinks a concentrated milk solution. When it is a little larger, the baby can drink more at a time and "graduates" to a more diluted form of milk. Finally, when it is almost ready to give up its mother's milk, the joey is able to come and go from the pouch as it pleases.

Main idea: There are four initial stages in a joey's life.

1. Finds way from birth canal to ___*pouch.*_____

2. Grasps one of mother's teats and ___*drinks concentrated milk solution.*___

_____

3. When large enough, drinks _____*a more diluted form of milk.*____

4. *When almost ready to give up mother's milk, the joey leaves pouch as it*

*pleases.*_____

B.   Advertising has been around for centuries. Probably the first ads were called out loud by town criers or carried on handwritten signs. The signs gave the locations of inns and shops. Both types of ads were found in ancient Egypt, Rome, and Greece. In 1440, movable type was invented, and soon after came the first printed English ad. Hung on church doors, it advertised a prayerbook. The next big event for advertising came soon after the newspaper was born in the early 1600s. A London newspaper carried the first newspaper ad. It offered a reward for the return of some stolen horses. By the end of the 1800s, magazines became yet another place for ads. In this century, ads on radio and television provided a hugely popular source for advertising.

Implied main idea: The history of advertising is related to developments in technology and publishing.

1. Ancient advertising consisted of speech and handwritten signs.

2. After _____ *movable type was invented* _____, ads were printed.

3. In the 1600s, *after the newspaper was born, the first newspaper ad was published in London.*

4. *By the end of the 1800s, magazines became another place for ads.*

5. *In the 20th century, radio and TV ads are common.*

Series of Steps (Directions)

Directions use time order to explain a series of steps towards a specific goal. The ability to follow directions carefully will help you succeed in many activities at school and throughout life. Here is a paragraph in which directions are given. Read it and then number in correct order the steps listed below.

An easy procedure will help you improve your memory for names. First, as you are introduced to someone, pay close attention to the name being given. If you did not hear the name clearly, ask the person to repeat it. Next, repeat the name with your greeting: "Nice to meet you, Ms. Baron." Then take a good look at the person and concentrate on matching the face with the name. Finally, repeat the name again when you are leaving that person: "Good meeting you, Ms. Baron."

Type of directions: How to remember a person's name

___4___ Concentrate on matching the name with the face.

___1___ Pay attention to the name during an introduction.

___5___ When you leave the person, repeat his or her name.

___2___ If you missed the name, ask the person to repeat it.

___3___ Repeat the name as you greet the person.

This is the order in which you should have put the points: 1) Pay attention to the name during an introduction. 2) If you missed the name, ask the person to repeat it. 3) Repeat the name as you greet the person. 4) Concentrate on matching the name with the face. 5) When you leave the person, repeat his or her name.

➤ *Practice 1b*

The following two passages give directions that involve several steps that must be done in order. Number in correct order the steps listed below each passage.

A.   To massage away the tension in someone's forehead, have the person lie on his or her back on a firm surface. Then line up your index and middle fingers across both sides of the bridge of the nose. Next, slowly run your fingers up across the forehead; press gently as you do so. Continue pressing your fingers up into the scalp until you reach the middle of the head. Then pause and repeat.

Type of directions: Steps to massaging away the tension in someone's forehead

   2   Place index and middle fingers on both sides of the bridge of the person's nose.

   5   Pause and repeat.

   3   Pressing gently, run your fingers up across the forehead.

   4   Press your fingers up into the scalp to the middle of the head.

   1   Have the person lie face up on a firm surface.

B.   Don't assume you are safe after hiking near poisonous plants. Instead, take preventive measures to avoid or overcome their effects. First, rinse off your shoes, which are most likely to have come in contact with poisonous plants. Then rinse your body with cold water or alcohol to remove invisible poisons. If you still develop swollen red patches, apply calamine lotion to them. Later relieve any itching by lying in bath water with a cup of cornstarch or oatmeal in it. Finally, if redness and itching persist, see a doctor.

Type of directions: Measures to avoid or overcome the effects of poisonous plants

   5   See a doctor if redness and itching continue.

   1   Rinse off your shoes.

   4   Later, relieve any itching by lying in water to which a cup of cornstarch or oatmeal has been added.

   2   Rinse your body with cold water or alcohol.

   3   Apply calamine lotion to any swollen red patches.

2   LIST OF ITEMS

Arrange the following group of sentences in an order that makes sense. Put a *1* in front of the sentence that should come first, a *2* in front of the sentence that comes second, and a *3* in front of the sentence that should be last. Then read the explanation that follows.

_____ Another treatment, behavior therapy, is often used to help children stop such behaviors as temper tantrums.

_____ Psychological treatment can take several forms.

_____ One form of treatment is family therapy, which allows the therapist to help members of a family relate more effectively to one another.

_____ A third treatment, cognitive therapy, helps individuals control their feelings by learning how to think more clearly.

This paragraph should begin with the statement that introduces the main idea: "Psychological treatment can take several forms." The three sentences that follow list three of those forms, resulting in a **list of items** pattern of organization. The transition words *one, another,* and *a third* introduce each of the forms of treatment: "*One* form of treatment is family therapy, which allows the therapist to help members of a family relate more effectively to one another. *Another* treatment, behavior therapy, is often used to help children stop such behaviors as temper tantrums. *A third* treatment, cognitive therapy, helps individuals control their feelings by learning how to think more clearly."

A *list of items* refers to a series of details, such as reasons or examples, that support a point. The items have no time order, so they are listed in the order the author prefers. The transitions used in lists tell us that another supporting detail is being added to one or more already mentioned. Following are some transitions that show addition and that often signal a listing pattern of organization.

Addition Transitions

one	first of all	in addition	furthermore
first	also	next	last of all
second	another	moreover	finally

A List of Items Paragraph

The paragraph below provides a list of items. Read it and then answer the questions that follow. You may find it helpful to check the major details as you read. An explanation follows the questions.

Several factors about the environment influence our behavior. First of all, temperature can influence us greatly. We seem to feel best when the temperature is in the seventies. If it is too hot or too cold, we have trouble concentrating. Have you ever tried to concentrate in a class when it was very hot? Also, lighting influences how we function. A dark lecture hall may interfere with a lecture, or a bright nightclub might spoil romantic conversation. Finally, our behavior is affected by color. Some colors make us feel peaceful, while others stimulate us. If you wanted a quiet room in which to study, for example, you would not paint it bright orange or red.

1. How many items are listed?
   a. Two
   b. Three
   c. Four
   d. Five

2. What type of item is listed?
   a. Weather conditions that influence us
   b. Parts of the environment that influence our behavior
   c. The best environmental factors for study
   d. The worst environmental factors for study

This paragraph consists of a main idea, stated in the topic sentence (the first one), followed by a list of three items. As it happens, each item is introduced by a transition, and each item takes up a few sentences. The type of item listed is *parts of the environment that influence our behavior* (temperature, lighting, and color). Notice that the items could have been listed in any order without affecting the main idea of the paragraph.

As you've already seen, outlines are often a good way of organizing the supporting details of a passage. An outline often allows you to quickly see (and review) the major details that are listed as well as the minor supporting details. Below is an outline of the above passage. The heading, based on the "opening phrase," tells the type of major detail being listed.

Factors About the Environment That Influence Our Behavior

1. Temperature
   a. Best temperatures in the seventies
   b. Concentration affected by extremes in temperature

2. Lighting
   a. Dark hall may harm lecture
   b. Brightness may spoil romantic mood

3. Color
   a. Stimulating colors
   b. Peaceful colors

➤ *Practice 2*

The following two passages use a listing pattern. Underline each main idea. Then number each new item, which may or may not be introduced with a transition. (Some, but not all, of the listed items are introduced with an addition transition.) Finally, answer the questions that follow each passage.

A. <u>It is possible to raise your low self-esteem.</u> One way is to improve yourself so that your self-image will come closer to your ideal self. Another is to question whether or not this ideal self is realistic. If you have set your standards unreasonably high, you cannot hope to meet them, and you might thus ignore your genuine accomplishments. Also, you can stress the positive: decide that the areas in which you are not successful are less important than those in which you are. Finally, avoid associating with people who are overly critical. Such people lower the self-esteem of others in order to raise their own.

What type of item is listed? <u>*Ways to raise your self-esteem*</u>

How many items are listed? <u>*four*</u>

B. <u>There are a few defense methods that opossums use to cope with danger.</u> The best known defense is "playing dead." An opossum using this defense goes into a coma. In that state, it appears dead and can be dropped, kicked, or even cut without responding. This may seem to be a foolish method of defense, for it leaves the animal open to attack. But many predators will not eat what they haven't killed, and others won't attack something that doesn't run away from them. However, most opossums—over 90 percent—never use this defense. Some, instead, simply flee danger immediately. Others use the method of trying to scare off enemies—they hiss, salivate, bare their teeth, excrete wastes, or release a terrible odor.

What type of item is listed? <u>*Defense methods used by opossums*</u>

How many items are listed? <u>*three*</u>

Which of the following best outlines the material in the paragraph, *a* or *b*?
<u> *b* </u>

a. Dangers Faced by Opossums
   1. Attack
   2. Being kicked or cut
   3. Being eaten

b. Defense Methods Used by Opossums
   1. Playing dead
   2. Fleeing danger
   3. Trying to scare off enemies

3 COMPARISON AND/OR CONTRAST

Arrange the following group of sentences in an order that makes sense. Put a *1* in front of the sentence that should come first, a *2* in front of the sentence that comes second, and a *3* in front of the sentence that should be last. Then read the explanation that follows.

_____ Men tend not to reveal intimate information about themselves.

_____ Men and women communicate about themselves differently.

_____ On the other hand, women frequently express their inner feelings.

The first sentence in this paragraph is the general one: "Men and women communicate about themselves differently." The sentence suggests a **comparison and/or contrast** pattern of organization. As the contrast phrase *on the other hand* suggests, the other two sentences, in fact, do contrast two things: "Men tend not to reveal intimate information about themselves. *On the other hand*, women frequently express their inner feelings."

The *comparison-contrast* pattern shows how two things are alike or how they are different, or both. When things are *compared*, their similarities are pointed out; when they are *contrasted*, their differences are discussed.

We often compare and contrast, whether we are aware of it or not. For example, a simple decision such as whether to make a hamburger or a Swiss-cheese sandwich for lunch requires us to compare and contrast the two choices. We may consider them both because of their similarities—both taste good and are filling. We may, however, choose one over the other because of how they differ— a hamburger needs cooking while a cheese sandwich can be put together quickly. If we are in a rush, we will probably choose the sandwich. If not, we may cook a hamburger.

Here are some common transitions showing comparison and contrast:

Comparison Transitions

like	likewise	similarly
just like	equally	similarities
just as	resembles	same
alike	also	similar

Contrast Transitions

however	on the other hand	different
in contrast	as opposed to	differently
instead	unlike	differs from

A Comparison/Contrast Paragraph

In the following paragraph, the main idea is stated in the first sentence. As is often the case, the main idea indicates a paragraph's pattern of organization. Here the transition *difference* is a hint that the paragraph may be organized in a comparison or contrast pattern. Read the paragraph, and answer the questions below.

There can be a big difference between what people say they will do and what they really do. For example, researchers once did a revealing experiment with nurses. The researchers asked what the nurses would do if a doctor they didn't know asked them to give what was an obvious overdose of a drug to a patient. Almost all of the nurses said they would not have followed that doctor's orders. In contrast, another group of nurses was actually given such an order over the phone. All but one of those twenty-two nurses proceeded to follow the orders—until someone stopped them on their way to the patients.

1.   Is this paragraph comparing, contrasting, or both? _____

2.   What two things are being compared and/or contrasted?_____
_____

3.   Which two comparison and/or contrast signal words or phrases are used in
the paragraph? _____

The paragraph is only contrasting, not comparing—it discusses only differences, not similarities. There are two things contrasted here—1) what people say is contrasted with 2) what they do. The words used to indicate contrast are *difference* and *in contrast.*

➤ Practice 3

The following passages use the pattern of comparison and/or contrast. Answer the questions after each.

A.   Many students find it difficult to make the transition from high school to college. This is because the two are very different. In high school, teachers often treat students like children. For instance, teachers may require homework to be done in a certain color ink, or they may call parents when children misbehave. On the other hand, college teachers treat students as adults. No one other than the students themselves is expected to take responsibility for learning. Also, adjusting to greater independence can be a challenge for many college freshmen. While in high school, students usually live at home. In college, however, many students live on their own and have no one to answer to or depend on but themselves.

1. Is this paragraph comparing, contrasting, or both? _____*contrasting*_____

2. What two things are being compared and/or contrasted?_____

   _____*high school and college*_____

B. Because goat's milk is becoming more popular, consumers should know how it stacks up to cow's milk. In many ways, the two milks are very similar. They are nearly identical when it comes to how much protein, fat, and carbohydrate they contain. And they are both excellent sources of calcium and riboflavin. Cow's milk, however, is a good source of vitamin D and folic acid, and goat's milk is a poor source for those essential nutrients.

1. Is this paragraph comparing, contrasting, or both? _____*both*_____

2. What two things are being compared and/or contrasted?_____

   _____*goat's milk and cow's milk*_____

4   CAUSE AND EFFECT

Arrange the following group of sentences in an order that makes sense. Put a *1* in front of the sentence that should come first, a *2* in front of the sentence that comes second, and a *3* in front of the sentence that should be last. Then read the explanation that follows.

_____ The earthquakes that follow can cause great loss of life and millions of dollars of damage.

_____ Earthquakes are caused by sudden slips of rock along breaks in the earth's crust.

_____ Such breaks result when the pressure on rock layers becomes too great.

As the words *cause, caused,* and *result* suggest, this paragraph discusses the causes and effects of earthquakes. In paragraph form, those sentences would read as follows:

> Earthquakes are *caused* by sudden slips of rock along a break in the earth's crust. Such breaks *result* when the pressure on rock layers becomes too great. The earthquakes that follow can *cause* great loss of life and millions of dollars of damage.

Cause-effect paragraphs answer such questions as "What are the *causes* of an event?" or "What are the *effects* of an event?"

Authors usually explore events by using a cause-and-effect approach. In other words, they don't just tell *what* happened; they explain *why* as well. A textbook section on the sinking of the ship *Titanic*, for example, would be incomplete if it did not include the cause of the disaster. (The cause was that, going at a high speed, the ship collided with an iceberg.) An important part of understanding events and processes includes learning about cause-effect relationships.

Explanations of cause and effects very often use transitions such as the following:

Cause-and-Effect Transitions

because	causes	results
lead to	reasons	therefore
bring about	effects	thus

A Cause-and-Effect Paragraph

Read the paragraph below, and see if you can answer the questions about cause and effect that follow. Then read the explanation to see how you did.

> Child abuse can lead to serious physical and emotional results. Abused children may show delays in speech. They are also more likely to become hyperactive or physically handicapped. Abused children will probably be more aggressive themselves in adult life than nonabused children. Sexually abused girls are more likely to be concerned with sex and to have behavior problems in school than nonabused girls. Finally, adults who were abused as children often suffer from low self-esteem and feelings of isolation.

1. What is the one *cause* described in this paragraph? _____

   _____

2. What are the two general *effects*?

   a. _____

   b. _____

3. What two cause-effect signal words or phrases are used?

   _____

The *cause* discussed in this paragraph is child abuse. One *effect* is the physical problems that result from child abuse, such as delays in speech. The second effect is the emotional problems that result from child abuse, such as aggression in adult life and low self-esteem. The two cause-effect signals are *lead to* and *results*.

The three activities that follow will give you a sharper sense of cause-and-effect relationships.

➤ *Practice 4a*

The following sentences all describe cause-and-effect relationships. Identify the cause and the effect in each sentence. One is done for you as an example.

1. I put a casserole in the oven and then forgot about it; as a result, the family went out for pizza that night.

    Cause: ___*Left a casserole in the oven too long*___

    Effect: ___*Family ate out*___

2. Because of the dog's barking, the family woke up in time to escape the burning house.

    Cause: ___*Dog's barking*___

    Effect: ___*Family awoke in time to escape fire*___

3. I worked in the garden for three hours yesterday, and today my back is killing me.

    Cause: ___*Worked in garden for three hours*___

    Effect: ___*Back pain*___

4. The jury did not believe the witness's testimony because he was constantly contradicting himself.

    Cause: ___*Witness kept contradicting himself*___

    Effect: ___*Jury didn't believe the witness*___

5. Taking large amounts of carotene (a form of vitamin A) can turn the skin orange.

    Cause: ___*Taking large amounts of carotene*___

    Effect: ___*Skin turns orange*___

➤ *Practice 4b*

The following sentences all list either two causes leading to the same effect or two effects resulting from a single cause. Identify the causes and effects in each sentence. One has been done for you as an example.

1. High winds and hailstones as big as golf balls resulted in $10,000 worth of property damage.

    High winds: ___*cause*___

    Hailstones: ___*cause*___

    Property damage: ___*effect*___

2. Some students drop out of school as a result of a shortage of money or problems with personal relationships.

    Students dropping out of school: _____ *effect* _____

    Shortage of money: _____ *cause* _____

    Problems with personal relationships: _____ *cause* _____

3. Eating cheese or chewing sugarless gum after a sugary meal reduces cavities.

    Eating cheese after a sugary meal: _____ *cause* _____

    Chewing sugarless gum after a sugary meal: _____ *cause* _____

    Fewer cavities: _____ *effect* _____

4. Plants that produce more blossoms and that resist infection result from good breeding.

    More blossoms: _____ *effect* _____

    Resistance to infection: _____ *effect* _____

    Good breeding: _____ *cause* _____

5. Because there were so few parking spaces downtown, shoppers avoided downtown and went to the mall instead.

    The low number of parking spaces downtown: _____ *cause* _____

    Avoidance of downtown by shoppers: _____ *effect* _____

    Shoppers going to the mall: _____ *effect* _____

➤ *Practice 4c*

The following passages list either several causes leading to the same effect or several effects resulting from a single cause. In the space provided, label each item as either a cause or an effect.

1. Tight neckties and collars hurt vision. This is the conclusion of some researchers at a university textiles and clothing department. They suspected that tight ties and collars could harm sight by cutting down the blood supply to the retina. So they gave eye tests to men wearing both loose and tight ties and collars. The test showed their suspicions were correct—men could see better with loose ties.

    Tight neckties: _____ *cause* _____

    Tight collars: _____ *cause* _____

    Weaker vision: _____ *effect* _____

2. A traveler to India noticed a curious thing: the wild animals and birds he saw were not afraid of human beings. They did not run away when he approached them. In fact, they seemed entirely comfortable with his presence. The reason for this behavior, he concluded, was the fact that Indians are respectful and considerate of non-human life. The members of one Indian religious sect in particular, the Jains, hold all life sacred and are forbidden to harm any living creature.

Animals staying in presence of traveler: _____ *effect* _____

Animals' comfort with traveler's presence: _____ *effect* _____

Respect of Indians for animals: _____ *cause* _____

5   DEFINITION AND EXAMPLE

Arrange the following group of sentences in an order that makes sense. Put a *1* in front of the sentence that should come first, a *2* in front of the sentence that comes second, and a *3* in front of the sentence that should be last. Then read the explanation that follows.

_____   When acupuncture is used to kill pain, needles are inserted far from the area of pain.

_____   Acupuncture is a Chinese therapy technique that involves inserting special needles in certain places in the body.

_____   In one stomach operation, for instance, four needles in the patient's outer ears eliminated pain.

This paragraph begins with a definition: "Acupuncture is a Chinese therapy technique that involves inserting special needles in certain places in the body." The second sentence further explains acupuncture by discussing a special use: "When acupuncture is used to kill pain, needles are inserted far from the area of pain." Finally, an example of the use of acupuncture for pain is given: "In one stomach operation, for instance, four needles in the patient's outer ears eliminated pain." As you can now see, the **definition and example** pattern of organization includes (as its name implies) a definition and an example.

Textbook authors often help readers understand the words and ideas they use. If a word or term is likely to be new to readers, the author may include a *definition*. Then, to make sure that definition is clear, the author may explain it with one or more *examples*.

Examples are often introduced by transitions like the following:

Example Transitions

for example	to illustrate	one
for instance	such as	specifically
as an illustration	to be specific	including

A Definition and Example Paragraph

The paragraph below defines a term, explains it a bit, and then gives examples of it. After reading the paragraph, see if you can answer the questions that follow. Finally, read the explanation that follows.

> [1]*Emblems* are gestures or body motions that mean the same as words or phrases. [2]Just as we learn the meanings of words, we learn the meanings of emblems in our society. [3]One common emblem in many places is the thumbs-up signal, which often expresses success or hope. [4]Other emblems are shrugging of the shoulders, which can mean "I don't know," and nodding the head to communicate "yes."

What term is being defined? _____

Which sentence gives the definition? _____

Which sentence explains something about the term? _____

In which sentence does the first example appear? _____

How many examples are given in all? _____

The term *emblem* is defined in sentence 1. It is further explained in sentence 2. The first example—"the thumbs-up signal"—is given in sentence 3. A second and third example—"shrugging of the shoulders" and "nodding the head"—are also given in sentence 4. By illustrating the new term with familiar examples, the author helps the reader better understand what *emblem* means.

➤ *Practice 5*

The following two passages each include a definition and one or more examples. In the spaces provided, write the number of the definition sentence and the number of the sentence where each example begins.

A.   [1]Chronic suicide is the attempt to escape stress by using means that in the long run are fatal. [2]This contrasts with the more well-known type of suicide in which people attempt to end their lives immediately. [3]Alcoholism is one common form of chronic suicide; drug abuse is another. [4]They each eventually cause enough damage to the body to cause death.

Definition: ___1___   Example 1: ___3___   Example 2: ___3___

B.   ¹One common method of solving problems is hill-climbing, in which every step moves us progressively closer to the final goal. ²Along the way, we evaluate how far "up the hill" we have come and how far we still have to go. ³On a multiple-choice test, for example, one useful strategy is to omit the obviously incorrect answers, bringing us closer to the final answer. ⁴Another instance of hill-climbing is trying to balance a budget by gradually reducing one expense after another.

Definition: ___1___   Example 1: ___3___   Example 2: ___4___

TOPIC SENTENCES AND PATTERNS OF ORGANIZATION

A paragraph's topic sentence often suggests its pattern of organization. For example, the topic sentence of a paragraph you worked on earlier is: *There are four initial stages in the life of a newborn baby kangaroo, called a joey.* This sentence strongly suggests that the paragraph will go on to list those four stages. Even before reading the paragraph, you can expect that it will be organized according to time order (a series of steps).

Here are two more topic sentences from paragraphs you read earlier:

Several factors about the environment influence our behavior.

There can be a big difference between what people say they will do and what they really do.

The first sentence suggests that a series of factors will follow; you can thus guess that the paragraph will be organized as a list of items. The second sentence suggests that the paragraph will contrast what people say versus what they do; you can guess that it will be a contrast paragraph.

Keep in mind, then, that the topic sentence may help you quickly recognize a paragraph's pattern of organization. The final practice that follows will help you look closely at topic sentences for clues about the patterns of organization.

➤ Practice 6

Circle the letter of the pattern of organization that each topic sentence suggests.

1.   In nature, many young animals follow their mothers around because they have imprinted on them: that is, they have formed a strong bond to the first moving object to which they have come into contact.

   a. Time order   ⓑ Definition and example   c. List of items

2.   Throughout the course of history, people have relied on drugs to treat both physical ailments and unhappiness.

   a. Definition and example   (b.) Time order   c. Comparison/contrast

3.   The students who are most likely to drop out of school share a number of family characteristics.

   (a.) List of items   b. Cause and effect   c. Time order

4.   Childhood dental problems in the United States have decreased significantly because of the widespread use of fluoride in drinking water and toothpaste.

   a. Definition and example   b. Time order   (c.) Cause and effect

5.   The eyes of newborns differ in two important ways from those of adults.

   a. Definition and example   b. Time order   (c.) Comparison/contrast

➤ Review Test 1

Identify the pattern used in each item below by writing in the letter of one of the following:

a   Time order
b   List of items
c   Comparison and/or contrast
d   Cause and effect
e   Definition and example

Each pattern is used twice.

   _d_   1. Because Lee came to the interview in jeans, he wasn't even considered for the job.

   _e_   2. Cardiovascular exercise is physical activity that burns calories while increasing the breathing and pulse rate. Swimming is an excellent form of cardiovascular exercise.

   _c_   3. Being married to someone is different in some ways from living with someone. Marriage, for example, has certain legal characteristics that living together does not.

   _b_   4. Orangutans in the wild eat numerous types of fruit, including wild plum, breadfruit, and strangling fig. They also eat leaves and bark.

   _a_   5. To give a cat a pill, first hold the cat firmly and pull back its head. Then gently press behind its jaw to open its mouth. While the mouth is open, pop in the pill.

_d_ 6. Rain forests are a major source of oxygen for the atmosphere. Thus when rain forests are chopped down, the oxygen supply is also cut down.

_b_ 7. One of the basic values and goals of American society is freedom. Another is equality. And a third is democracy.

_e_ 8. Snap judgments are opinions formed on the spot, often on little evidence. One instance of such a judgment is deciding that Perry is a jerk after meeting him briefly at a party.

_a_ 9. Benjamin Franklin served as an apprentice for five years in his brother's print shop. Then, at the age of seventeen, Franklin went to New York. Failing to find work there, he soon went on to Philadelphia.

_c_ 10. Both diet soft drinks and seltzer water are low in calories. However, diet soft drinks contain artificial sweeteners and are not really thirst-quenching, while seltzer water refreshes without being sickeningly sweet.

➤ *Review Test 2*

A. Circle the letter that correctly identifies the pattern of organization in each of the following passages.

1. Recent studies indicate that male and female babies act very differently after only a few months of life. Baby girls seem to be more interested in people. They can distinguish between individual faces and voices at four months, well before baby boys can. In addition, they begin to smile and speak earlier than boys, and their vocabularies are larger. In contrast, baby boys react to objects with as much interest as they react to human beings. They will try to talk to the brightly colored toys that hang over their cribs just as often as they will try to talk to a parent. And before long, they will attempt to take these objects apart.

    a. cause and effect   (b.) contrast   c. time order

2. Events leading to alcohol abuse in the United States took place in the eighteenth century. That's when developments in agriculture led to a surplus of grain. Farmers in the Midwest wanted to sell their surplus grain on the East Coast, which was more heavily populated. The cheapest way to do this was to transport the grain in the form of whiskey. As a result, whiskey production rose. And the increase in whiskey led to an increase in its use. Before long, alcohol consumption in the country rose to alarming proportions.

    a. list of items   b. comparison   (c.) cause and effect

3.   Hysterical amnesia is an amnesia for which there is no apparent physical cause. A person with this type of amnesia generally has experienced something very frightening. Rather than remember this experience, he or she has smothered all personal memories. Movies have portrayed a typical example of someone with hysterical amnesia: A man awakens in a strange town. He remembers such impersonal information as the alphabet and how to drive. But he cannot remember his name or where he came from.

a. time order   b. list of items   ⓒ definition and example

B. Read each of the following two paragraphs. Then answer the pattern-of-organization question and complete the outline that follows.

Paragraph 1

There are several signs that often indicate someone has a serious problem with marijuana. One sign is daily or almost daily use over a long period. Another is the decline of someone's performance, either socially or at work. Other signs are the use of other drugs with marijuana, apathy, an inability to feel pleasure, and memory problems.

1. The main pattern of organization of the paragraph is
   a. time order   ⓑ list of items   c. definition and example

2. Complete the outline of the paragraph by finishing the heading and writing in the missing major details.

Heading: Several signs that often indicate _____*a serious problem with*_____
  marijuana

   1. *Daily or almost daily use over a long period*

   2. Decline of social or work performance

   3. Use of other drugs with marijuana

   4. *Apathy*

   5. An inability to feel pleasure

   6. *Memory problems*

Paragraph 2

To remove an object from someone's throat, follow the steps of the Heimlich maneuver. First, stand behind the choking victim. Then wrap your arms around his or her waist. Place your fist, thumbside in, against the victim's abdomen, slightly above the navel and below the rib cage. Grasp your fist with your other hand. Then press into his or her abdomen with a quick upward thrust. Repeat the upward thrust until the victim can breathe.

1. The main pattern of organization of the paragraph is
   (a.) time order   b. list of items   c. contrast

2. Complete the outline of the paragraph by finishing the heading and writing in the missing major details.

   Heading (implied): Steps to ___*performing the Heimlich maneuver*___

   1. Stand behind the choking victim.
   2. *Wrap your arms around the victim's waist.*

   3. Press your fist, thumbside in, above the victim's navel and below the rib cage.
   4. *Grasp your fist with your other hand.*

   5. Press into victim's abdomen with a quick upward thrust.
   6. *Repeat the thrust until the victim can breathe.*

➤ Review Test 3

A. To review what you've learned in this chapter, complete each of the following sentences about patterns of organization.

1. A paragraph's pattern of organization is the pattern in which its (*supporting details, main idea, causes and effects*) ___*supporting*___ ___*details*___ is or are organized.

2. The pattern in which a series of details are presented in any order the author considers best is called a ___*list of items*___.

3. The pattern in which the details discuss how two or more things are alike or different is a pattern of ___*comparison/contrast*___.

4. When a passage provides a series of directions, it uses a ___*time*___ order.

5. When textbook authors provide a definition of a term, they are likely to also provide one or more ___*examples*___ to help make that definition clear.

B. Here is a chance to apply your understanding of patterns of organization to a selection aimed at college students. It offers practical advice to students who are trying to juggle family, friends, a job, and school. And to help you continue to strengthen your work on the skills taught in previous chapters, there are also questions on

- vocabulary in context
- central point and main ideas
- supporting details
- transitions.

Words to Watch

Following are some words in the reading that do not have strong context support. Each word is followed by the number of the paragraph in which it appears and its meaning there. These words are indicated in the article by a small circle (°).

queasy (3):	sick
distracted (4):	sidetracked
plod (7):	labor
hermit (13):	one who lives alone, apart from others
overwhelming (21):	overpowering
compatible (22):	able to get along with others

HOW TO MAKE IT IN COLLEGE, NOW THAT YOU'RE HERE

Brian O'Keeney

Today is your first day on campus. You were a high school senior three months ago. Or maybe you've been at home with your children for the last ten years. Or maybe you work full-time and you're coming to school to start the process that leads to a better job. Whatever your background is, you're probably not too concerned today with staying in college. After all, you just got over the hurdle (and the paperwork) of applying to this place and organizing your life so that you could attend. And today, you're confused and tired. Everything is a hassle, from finding the classrooms to standing in line at the bookstore. But read my advice anyway. And if you don't read it today, save this article. You might want to look at it a little further down the road. 1

By the way, if this isn't your first day, don't skip this article. Maybe you haven't been doing as well in your studies as you'd hoped. 2

Or perhaps you've had problems juggling your work schedule, your class schedule, and your social life. If so, read on. You're about to get the inside story on making it in college. Based on my own experience as a final-year student, and on dozens of interviews with successful students, I've worked out the no-fail system for coping with college. These are the inside tips every student needs to do well in school. I've put myself in your place, and I'm going to answer the questions that will cross (or have already crossed) your mind during your stay here.

What's the Secret to Getting Good Grades?

It all comes down to getting those grades, doesn't it? After all, you came here for some reason, and you're going to need passing grades to get the credits or degree you want. Many of us never did much studying in high school; most of the learning we did took place in the classroom. College, however, is a lot different. You're really on your own when it comes to passing courses. In fact, sometimes you'll feel as if nobody cares if you make it or not. Therefore, you've got to figure out a study system that gets results. Sooner or later, you'll be alone with those books. After that, you'll be sitting in a classroom with an exam sheet on your desk. Whether you stare at that exam with a queasy° stomach, or whip through it fairly confidently, depends on your study techniques. Most of the successful students I talked to agreed that the following eight study tips deliver solid results:

1. *Set up a study place.* Those students you see "studying" in the cafeteria or game room aren't learning much. You just can't learn when you're distracted° by people and noise. Even the library can be a bad place to study if you constantly find yourself watching the clouds outside or the students walking through the stacks. It takes guts to sit, alone, in a quiet place in order to study. But you have to do it. Find a room at home or a spot in the library that's relatively quiet—and boring. When you sit there, you won't have much to do except study.

2. *Get into a study frame of mind.* When you sit down, do it with the attitude that you're really going to get this studying done. You're not going to doodle on your notebook or make a list for the supermarket. Decide that you're going to study and learn now, so that you can move on to more interesting things as soon as possible.

3. *Give yourself rewards.* If you sweat out a block of study time, and do a good job on it, treat yourself. You deserve it. You can

"psych" yourself up for studying by promising to reward yourself afterwards. A present for yourself can be anything from a favorite TV show to a relaxing bath to a dish of double-chocolate ice cream.

4. *Skim the textbook first.*   Lots of students sit down with an   7
assignment like "read chapter five, pages 125–150" and do just that. They turn to page 125 and start to read. After a while, they find that they have no idea what they just read. For the last ten minutes, they've been thinking about their five-year-old or what they're going to eat for dinner. Eventually, they plod° through all the pages but don't remember much afterwards.

   In order to prevent this problem, skim the textbook   8
chapter first. This means: look at the title, the subtitles, the headings, the pictures, the first and last paragraphs. Try to find out what the person who wrote the book had in mind when he or she organized the chapter. What was important enough to set off as a title or in bold type? After skimming, you should be able to explain to yourself what the main points of the chapter are. Unless you're the kind of person who would step into an empty elevator shaft without looking first, you'll soon discover the value of skimming.

5. *Take notes on what you're studying.*   This sounds like a hassle,   9
but it works. Go back over the material after you've read it, and jot down key words and phrases in the margins. When you review the chapter for a test, you'll have handy little things like "definition of rationalization" or "example of regression" in the margins. If the material is especially tough, organize a separate sheet of notes. Write down definitions, examples, lists, and main ideas. The idea is to have a single sheet that boils the entire chapter down to a digestible lump.

6. *Review after you've read and taken notes.*   Some people swear   10
that talking to yourself works. Tell yourself about the most important points in the chapter. Once you've said them out loud, they seem to stick better in your mind. If you can't talk to yourself about the material after reading it, that's a sure sign you don't really know it.

7. *Give up.*   This may sound contradictory, but give up when   11
you've had enough. You should try to make it through at least an hour, though. Ten minutes here and there are useless. When your head starts to pound and your eyes develop spidery red

lines, quit. Rest for a bit with a short nap and go back later.

8. *Take the college skills course if you need it.* Don't hesitate or feel embarrassed about enrolling in a study skills course. Many students say they wouldn't have made it without one.   12

How Can I Keep Up with All My Responsibilities Without Going Crazy?

You've got a class schedule. You're supposed to study. You've got a family. You've got a husband, wife, boyfriend, child. You've got a job. How are you possibly going to cover all the bases in your life and maintain your sanity? This is one of the toughest problems students face. Even if they start the semester with the best of intentions, they eventually find themselves tearing their hair out trying to do everything they're supposed to do. Believe it or not, though, it is possible to meet all your responsibilities. And you don't have to turn into a hermit° or give up your loved ones to do it.   13

The secret here is to organize your time. But don't just sit around half the semester planning to get everything together soon. Before you know it, you'll be confronted with midterms, papers, family, and work all at once. Don't let yourself reach that breaking point. Instead, try these three tactics: 14

1. *Prepare a monthly calendar:* Get one of those calendars with big blocks around the dates. Give yourself an overview of the whole term by marking down the due dates for papers and projects. Circle test and exam days. This way those days don't sneak up on you unexpectedly.   15

2. *Make up a study schedule:* Sit down during the first few days of this semester and make up a sheet listing the days and hours of the week. Fill in your work and class hours first. Then try to block out some study hours. It's better to study a little every day than to create a huge once-or-twice-a-week marathon session. Schedule study hours for your hardest classes for the times when you feel most energetic. For example, I battled my tax law textbook in the mornings; when I looked at it after 7:00 P.M., I may as well have been reading Chinese. The usual proportion, by the way, is one hour of study time for every class hour.   16

In case you're one of those people who get carried away, remember to leave blocks of free time, too. You won't be any good to yourself or anyone else if you don't relax and pack in the studying once in a while.   17

3. *Use "to-do" lists:* This is the secret that singlehandedly got me through college. Once a week (or every day if you want to), write a list of what you have to do. Write down everything from "write English paper" to "buy cold cuts for lunches." The best thing about a "to-do" list is that it seems to tame all those stray "I have to" thoughts that nag at your mind. After you finish something on the list, cross it off. Don't be compulsive about finishing everything; you're not Superman or Wonder Woman. Get the important things done first. The secondary things you don't finish can simply be moved to your next "to-do" list.   18

What Can I Do If Personal Problems Get in the Way of My Studies?

One student, Roger, told me this story: 19

Everything was going okay for me until the middle of the spring semester. I went through a terrible time when I broke up with my girlfriend and started seeing her best friend. I was trying to deal with my ex-girlfriend's hurt and anger, my new girlfriend's guilt, and my own worries and anxieties at the same time. In addition to this, my mother was sick and on a medication that made her really irritable. I hated to go home because the atmosphere was so uncomfortable. Soon, I started missing classes because I couldn't deal with the academic pressures as well as my own personal problems. It seemed easier to hang around my girlfriend's apartment than to face all my problems at home and at school.

Another student, Marian, told me: 20

I'd been married for eight years and the relationship wasn't going too well. I saw the handwriting on the wall, and I decided to prepare for the future. I enrolled in college because I knew I'd need a decent job to support myself. Well, my husband had a fit because I was going to school. We were arguing a lot anyway, and he made it almost impossible for me to study at home. I think he was angry and almost jealous because I was drawing away from him. It got so bad that I thought about quitting college for a while. I wasn't getting any support at home and it was just too hard to go on.

Personal troubles like these are overwhelming° when you're going through them. School seems like the least important thing in your life. The two students above are perfect examples of this. But if you think about it, quitting or failing school would be the worst thing for these two students. Roger's problems, at least with his girlfriends, would simmer down eventually, and then he'd regret having left school.   21

Marian had to finish college if she wanted to be able to live independently. Sometimes, you've just got to hang tough.

But what do you do while you're trying to live through a lousy time? First of all, do something difficult. Ask yourself, honestly, if you're exaggerating small problems as an excuse to avoid classes and studying. It takes strength to admit this, but there's no sense in kidding yourself. If your problems are serious, and real, try to make some human contacts at school. Lots of students hide inside a miserable shell made of their own troubles and feel isolated and lonely. Believe me, there are plenty of students with problems. Not everyone is getting A's and having a fabulous social and home life at the same time. As you go through the term, you'll pick up some vibrations about the students in your classes. Perhaps someone strikes you as a compatible° person. Why not speak to that person after class? Share a cup of coffee in the cafeteria or walk to the parking lot together. You're not looking for a best friend or the love of your life. You just want to build a little network of support for yourself. Sharing your difficulties, questions, and complaints with a friendly person on campus can make a world of difference in how you feel. 22

Finally, if your problems are overwhelming, get some professional help. Why do you think colleges spend countless dollars on counseling departments and campus psychiatric services? More than ever, students all over the country are taking advantage of the help offered by support groups and therapy sessions. There's no shame attached to asking for help, either. In fact, almost 40 percent of college students (according to one survey) will use counseling services during their time in school. Just walk into a student center or counseling office and ask for an appointment. You wouldn't think twice about asking a dentist to help you get rid of your toothache. Counselors are paid—and want—to help you with your problems. 23

Why Do Some People Make It and Some People Drop Out?

Anyone who spends at least one semester in college notices that some students give up on their classes. The person who sits behind you in accounting, for example, begins to miss a lot of class meetings and eventually vanishes. Or another student comes to class without the assignment, doodles in his notebook during the lecture, and leaves during the break. What's the difference between students like this and the ones who succeed in school? My survey may be non-scientific, but everyone I asked said the same thing: attitude. A positive attitude is the key to everything else—good study habits, smart time scheduling, and coping with personal difficulties. 24

What does "a positive attitude" mean? Well, for one thing, it 25 means not acting like a zombie. It means not only showing up for your classes, but also doing something while you're there. Really listen. Take notes. Ask a question if you want to. Don't just walk into a class, put your mind in neutral, and drift away to never-never land.

Having a positive attitude goes deeper than this, though. It means 26 being mature about college as an institution. Too many students approach college classes like six-year-olds who expect first grade to be as much fun as *Sesame Street*. First grade, as we all know, isn't as much fun as *Sesame Street*. And college classes can sometimes be downright dull and boring. If you let a boring class discourage you so much that you want to leave school, you'll lose in the long run. Look at your priorities. You want a degree, or a certificate, or a career. If you have to, you can make it through a less-than-interesting class in order to achieve what you want. Get whatever you can out of every class. But if you simply can't stand a certain class, be determined to fulfill its requirements and be done with it once and for all.

After the initial high of starting school, you have to settle in for 27 the long haul. If you follow the advice here, you'll be prepared to face the academic crunch. You'll also live through the semester without giving up your family, your job, or Monday Night Football. Finally, going to college can be an exciting time. As you learn things, the world truly becomes a more interesting place.

VOCABULARY QUESTIONS

Use context clues to help you decide on the best definition for each italicized word. Then circle the letter of each choice.

1. The word *hurdle* in "you just got over the hurdle . . . of applying to this place. . . . And today, you're confused and tired" (paragraph 1) means
   a. easy task.
   b. difficulty.
   c. entertainment.
   d. example.

2. The word *tactics* in "The secret here is to organize your time. . . . try these three tactics. 1. Prepare a monthly calendar. . . . 2. Make up a study schedule. . . . 3. Use 'to-do' lists" (paragraphs 14–18) means
   a. methods.
   b. reasons.
   c. requirements.
   d. scenes.

3. The word *confronted* in "don't just sit around half the semester planning to get everything together soon. Before you know it, you'll be confronted with midterms, papers, family, and work all at once" (paragraph 14) means
    a. delighted.
    (b.) faced.
    c. finished.
    d. forgotten.

4. The word *compulsive* in "Don't be compulsive about finishing everything; you're not Superman or Wonder Woman" (paragraph 18) means
    a. overly relaxed.
    b. dishonest.
    (c.) overly concerned.
    d. happy.

5. The words *simmer down* in "Roger's problems, at least with his girlfriends, would simmer down eventually, and then he'd regret having left school" (paragraph 21) mean
    (a.) calm down.
    b. increase.
    c. become interesting.
    d. worsen.

READING COMPREHENSION QUESTIONS

Central Point and Main Ideas

1. Which sentence best expresses the central point of the selection?
    a. Going to college is exciting.
    (b.) There are ways to succeed in college and stay in control of your life.
    c. Most students are not concerned about staying in college.
    d. College can be confusing and tiring.

2. Which sentence best expresses the main idea of paragraph 26?
    a. First grade is less fun than kindergarten.
    b. College classes are sometimes quite boring.
    (c.) Students should be mature enough to tackle a class even when it's boring.
    d. A boring class encourages some to leave school.

Supporting Details

3. Which of the following is a poor study technique?
    (a.) Never give up, no matter how tired you get.
    b. Take a study skills course if you need it.
    c. Sit alone in a quiet place, skim the material, take notes, and review.
    d. Reward yourself for studying well.

4. Complete the following outline of paragraphs 3–12 by filling in the missing detail.

   Eight Study Tips
   1. Set up a study place.
   2. Get into a study frame of mind.
   3. Give yourself rewards.
   4. Skim the textbook first.
   5. Take notes on what you're studying.
   6. *Review after you've read and taken notes.*
   7. Give up.
   8. Take a college skills course if you need it.

5. Complete the following outline of paragraphs 14–18 by finishing the heading and filling in the missing detail.

   Ways to *Organize Your Time*
   1. Fill out a monthly calendar.
   2. Make up a study schedule.
   3. *Use "to-do" lists.*

Transitions

6. In the third sentence of paragraph 26, the author compares some students to six-year-olds with the transition word _____*like*_____.

7. The author introduces his last point in paragraph 27 with the addition transition word _____*finally*_____.

Patterns of Organization

8. Just as paragraphs are organized according to patterns, so are entire selections. What is the main pattern of organization of this selection?
   (a.) list of items.
   b. comparison and contrast.
   c. time order.
   d. definition and example.

9. Paragraph 19 combines the patterns of
   a. list of items and contrast.
   (b.) time order and cause-effect.
   c. definition/example and time order.
   d. definition/example and comparison.

10. __T__ TRUE OR FALSE? Paragraphs 24–26 contrast a positive attitude with a poor one.

10

Inferences

You have probably heard the expression "to read between the lines." When you "read between the lines," you pick up ideas that are not directly stated in what you are reading. These implied ideas are usually important for a full understanding of what an author means. Discovering the ideas that are not stated directly is called *making inferences,* or *drawing conclusions.*

AN INTRODUCTION TO INFERENCES

You have already practiced making inferences in this book. Do you remember the following sentence from the second chapter?

> My parents are very different: my father, for example, is very *forbearing,* while my mother sometimes has no patience at all.

That sentence does not tell us the meaning of *forbearing,* but it does suggest that *forbearing* means the opposite of having "no patience at all." Thus we can infer in this sentence that *forbearing* means "patient."

You also made inferences in the chapter on implied main ideas. Implied ideas, by definition, are never stated directly. Instead, you must find them through inference. Just as you used evidence in a sentence to infer the meaning of a vocabulary word, so you used evidence in a paragraph to infer a main idea.

In this chapter, you will get more practice in drawing inferences. Read again the passage about an author's bad dream and then answer the question on inferences that follows.

> As a rule, most of my dreams at night are pleasant ones. Recently, though, I had a really bad dream. I was in an alley dressed in light summer clothing. Coming out of the darkness at the end of the alley were hundreds of large gray rats. Their razor-sharp teeth glistened with saliva. Their eyes glowed red with a cold, murderous fury. I turned to run away, but coming at me in the other direction were a dozen pit bulls. And these particular pit bulls were foaming at the mouth; they all had rabies. "Just my luck," I muttered and did my best to wake up as quickly as possible.

Which one of the following inferences is most soundly supported by the evidence in the passage? Remember that an inference is a reasonable guess or logical conclusion that we make based on the evidence presented.

    a. This was the worst dream the author ever had.
    b. The author did not sleep the rest of the night.
    c. The author hates animals.
    d. The author had a dramatic dream.

Explanation:

- The statement in answer *a* is not supported. The passage doesn't compare the dream about the rats and pit bulls with any other dreams.
- Answer *b* is also poorly supported. While the author probably woke up from his dream, that does not mean that he stayed up all night.
- The author clearly fears the rats and pit bulls in the dream, but there is no support for the idea in statement *c* that the author hates animals.
- Answer *d* is most soundly supported by the passage. The frightening details about the rats and pit bulls were certainly dramatic.

Take a moment now to look at the following *New Yorker* cartoon. How well a cartoon works often depends on the reader's inference skills. What can you infer about this cartoon?

Now put a check by the **two** inferences that are most logically based on the information given in the cartoon.

____ 1. The book is meant to look like a crook.

____ 2. The book is meant to look like a superhero.

____ 3. The book wants to enjoy watching videos with the children.

____ 4. The book wants to "save" the children from watching too many videos and too much TV—and not reading enough.

____ 5. The children are watching Batman or Superman movies.

Explanation:

Here are comments on the five items:

1-2. It's true that the book, like some crooks, is wearing a mask, but it is also wearing a cape, long gloves and tall boots—none of which are typically worn by crooks. They are, however, part of the typical superhero costume. Thus you should have checked item 2, not item 1.

3-4. Since the book is a "superhero," it must have come to help the children with some problem. And from the videos on the floor and the fact that the children are in front of the TV, we can infer that the children's problem is watching too many videos and too much TV. Moreover, since the superhero is a book, we can assume the children's problem also includes not reading enough. So you should have checked item 4, but not 3.

5. If the cartoonist had wished to show Batman or Superman, he would have drawn those characters, not a book. And if the book were meant to be a character from a show the children were watching, then the cartoonist would have made it coming from the TV, not from the other direction. So you should not have checked this item.

INFERENCES IN EVERYDAY READING

In our everyday reading, we make logical leaps from the information given directly on the page to ideas that are not stated directly. To draw such inferences, we use all the clues provided by the writer, by our own experience, and by logic.

Read the passage on the next page. Then answer the questions that follow it by circling the letters of the logical inferences. Hints are provided to help you think through the choices for each question.

A twenty-eight-year-old woman named Catherine Genovese was returning home from work one day. Kitty, as she was called by almost everyone in her Queens neighborhood, had just parked her car. Then a man with a knife grabbed her. She screamed, "Oh my God, he stabbed me! Please help me! Please help me!"

For more than half an hour, thirty-eight neighbors watched the killer stalk Kitty. The last time he stabbed her, she was slumped on the foot of the stairs to her apartment. Not one person telephoned the police during the fatal attack. Later, the police gathered statements from the witnesses. Among their comments were, "I didn't want to get involved," "We thought it was a lovers' quarrel," and "I was tired. I went back to bed."

1. We can infer that Kitty was attacked
   a. while she was on vacation.
   b. in her own neighborhood.
   c. on her way from work to her car.

   Hints: The passage tells us that Genovese "was returning home from work" and that she "had just parked her car."

2. We can conclude that the man who stabbed Genovese
   a. was someone she knew.
   b. intended to kill her.
   c. was a convicted criminal.

   Hints: Where is evidence that Genovese knew her killer or that he was a convicted criminal? Also, Genovese's killer stabbed her even after he was sure she was wounded and weak.

3. We can infer that the witnesses
   a. might have stopped the attack by calling the police.
   b. wanted the man to kill Genovese.
   c. would not want others to get involved if they were being attacked.

   Hints: First, the crime took at least half an hour. Also, knowledge of human nature tells us how the witnesses must have felt about Genovese being killed and themselves being attacked.

Explanations:

Here is an explanation of each item:

1. The answer to the first question is *b*. We have solid evidence to conclude that Genovese was attacked in her neighborhood: she was returning home from work and had parked her car. Since she was returning home from work, she was not on vacation. Also, if she had just parked her car after coming home from work, the attack could not have taken place before she got into the car to go home.

2. The answer to the second question is *b*. We can conclude that Genovese's attacker wanted to kill her. If his goal was to rob or rape her, he could have done so long before the last time he stabbed her. And no evidence in the passage indicates that Genovese knew her attacker. In fact, because he is simply referred to as "a man with a knife," we have some evidence that she did not know him. Had she called out his name, he probably would have been identified more specifically in the passage. Finally, although we cannot be sure the attacker was never convicted of a crime, there is absolutely no evidence in the passage to support that conclusion—his past is not referred to at all.

3. The answer to the third question is *a*. The crime took at least a half hour; thus we can conclude that if the police had been called, there is a chance they would have arrived in time to save Genovese. We, however, have no reason to believe the witnesses actually wanted the man to kill Genovese. Most people, in fact, would be horrified to see someone stabbed to death. And based on our knowledge of human nature, we can be pretty sure the witnesses would have wanted others to get involved if they were victims.

➤ *Practice 1*

Read the following passage. Then circle the letter of the most logical answer to each question, based on the information given in the passage. Use the hints provided to help you answer each question.

Have you ever seen one of the *Friday the 13th* movies? This bloody R-rated series of movies has been a box-office smash for almost ten years. The plots involve teens having sex and then getting sliced and diced. The chopping is done by a zombie named Jason who wears a hockey mask. Such movies offer date-night appeal. People tend to hold, squeeze, and grab onto each other when they're scared. They also offer some privacy to teenagers intent on making out. Any sensible adult wouldn't be caught dead at one of these movies.

1. We can conclude that *Friday the 13th* movies
   a. attract many adults.
   b. are uninteresting to teens.
   (c.) attract teens.

   Hints: The passage says that the movies have been "a box-office smash for almost ten years" and that they "offer some privacy to teenagers."

2. We can infer that the author of the passage feels that teens who go to *Friday the 13th* movies
   (a.) like to be scared by those movies.
   b. do not like to be scared by those movies.
   c. are never scared by those movies.

   Hints: The passage says that the movies have "date-night appeal" and that people tend to "grab onto each other when they're scared."

3. We can infer that the author of the passage feels that the plots of *Friday the 13th* movies
   a. differ greatly from one another.
   (b.) are all similar.
   c. are rich in meaning.

   Hint: The author describes the plots of all of the *Friday the 13th* movies with the same words.

➢ Practice 2

Read the following passage. Then circle the letter of the most logical answer to each question, based on the information given.

> British prime minister Winston Churchill was a master of the elegant put-down. At one fancy dinner party, he was seated next to a favorite target—a woman whose political views were the opposite of his own. The two argued more or less continually throughout the meal. Totally annoyed, the lady said, "Sir Winston, if you were my husband, I'd put poison in your coffee!" "Madam," replied Churchill, "if you were my wife, I'd drink it."

1. We can conclude that Churchill
   a. constantly put people down.
   (b.) liked to put down his political opponents.
   c. preferred to put down women, rather than men.

2. When Churchill said, "If you were my wife, I'd drink it," he meant to imply that
   a. he admired the woman so much he would do whatever she said.
   b. he would never insult the woman by refusing her coffee.
   c. if she were his wife, he would prefer to die.

3. We can conclude that the author of the passage admires
   a. Churchill's politics.
   b. the woman's politics.
   c. Churchill's wit.

➤ *Practice 3*

Read the following passage. Then circle the letter of the most logical answer to each question, based on the given information.

> The real heroes of the fight against drugs are the teenagers who resist the ghetto's fast track—those who live at home, stay in school and juggle their studies with a low-paying job. The wonder is that there are so many of them. "Most of our youngsters are not involved in crack," says the chief judge of one juvenile court in Michigan. "Most are not running around with guns. Most aren't killing people. Most are doing very well—against great odds." These are the youngsters who fit Jesse Jackson's words: "You were born in the slum, but the slum wasn't born in you."

1. We can conclude that the author's attitude toward ghetto teenagers who live at home, stay in school, and work is
   a. disapproving.
   b. admiring.
   c. neutral.

2. We can infer that the author believes that resisting crime in the ghetto
   a. is difficult.
   b. is easy.
   c. is impossible.

3. When Jackson says, ". . . but the slum wasn't born in you," he implies that
   a. being born in the slums is good.
   b. people can rise above their slum environment.
   c. people can never escape the worst fate of the slums.

➢ *Practice 4*

The ability to make inferences will help you in all kinds of reading, including textbook material. After reading the following textbook passage, put a check by the **three** inferences that are most firmly based on the given information.

> A question that interests many is why a woman will remain with a husband who abuses her. Interviews with violent families revealed that the decision is related to three major factors. First, the more severe and more frequent the violence, the more a woman is likely to end her marriage or to seek help from social agencies or police. The second factor has to do with how much violence she experienced as a child. The more she was struck by her own parents, the more inclined she is to stay with an abusive husband. Third, wives who have not completed high school and those who are unemployed are less likely to leave their husbands. It appears that the fewer resources a woman has, the fewer alternatives she sees and the more trapped in her marriage she feels.

____ 1. The same three factors listed here influence husbands to stay with wives who are abusive.

✓ 2. People who were beaten as children learn to tolerate being abused.

✓ 3. Women who are dependent on their husbands economically are more likely to stay in an abusive marriage.

____ 4. Employed women who are well educated are never abused by their husbands.

____ 5. Most women who leave abusive husbands have been beaten only once.

✓ 6. A woman who needs to be hospitalized because of an attack by her abusive husband is more likely to divorce her spouse than one who is not severely injured.

➢ *Practice 5*

After reading the following textbook passage, put a check by the **three** inferences that are most firmly based on the given information.

> In the mid-1980s *teleshopping* developed as a new method of selling consumer goods in the American culture. Unlike regular commercials that attempt to create interest in a product, teleshopping is designed to create instant sales. Products are shown on the screen with a discount price. Viewers are urged to call in their charge-card numbers immediately before the limited number of products are sold. These programs sell everything

from cubic zirconia "diamonds" to fur coats and computers. Many of them broadcast twenty-four hours a day. Some viewers admit to watching these marketing channels more than twelve hours a day. All a viewer needs is a TV set, telephone, and credit card to make numerous purchases. It is estimated that in 1992 sales figures from these shows approached three billion dollars. Teleshopping began with the Home Shopping Network in 1982. By the late 1980s there were over a dozen such operations.

___ 1. Initial sales were disappointing for the Home Shopping Network.

✓ 2. Impulse buying is the force that makes teleshopping successful.

✓ 3. The fact that a product is available in limited quantities makes it more attractive to teleshoppers.

___ 4. People who buy items through teleshopping shows frequently return them for refunds.

✓ 5. People who spend a lot of time in their homes are teleshopping's best customers.

___ 6. By the time customers pay to ship the products they buy on teleshopping networks, they often find purchasing the products in their local stores would have been cheaper.

➤ Review Test 1

After reading each short passage, put a check by the **two** inferences that are most firmly based on the given information.

1. Although the company has a large cafeteria, most offices have their own coffeemakers.

    ✓ a. Making coffee in the office is more convenient.

    ___ b. The coffee in the cafeteria is terrible.

    ✓ c. Many people in the company drink coffee.

2. A retired widower spends some time each day sitting on a bench in a shopping mall. He frequently starts conversations with people who sit near him.

    ✓ a. The man is lonely and goes to the mall to be around people.

    ___ b. The man is mentally disturbed.

    ✓ c. One of the man's favorite places is the mall.

3.   The four girls sat in a corner booth in the diner, giggling and looking around self-consciously. Every few minutes they glanced over at a group of boys and whispered excitedly to each other.

   ✓ a. The girls would like the boys to notice them.

   ___ b. The boys are teasing the girls.

   ✓ c. The girls are attracted to the boys.

4.   The teenage boy tiptoed into the kitchen and selected a gin bottle from under the sink. He poured out a glass and then added tap water to the gin bottle. Then he hurried back to his bedroom.

   ✓ a. The boy did not want anyone to know he had taken the gin.

   ✓ b. The family keeps their liquor supply under the kitchen sink.

   ___ c. Several people in his family have drinking problems.

5.   As her father let go of the bike, Robin pedaled another ten feet before falling. "I was flying!" whooped Robin.

   ✓ a. Robin is learning to ride a two-wheeler.

   ___ b. She was badly hurt when she fell.

   ✓ c. Robin is thrilled with her own progress.

6.   For her birthday, Kate received a kitten that she named "Purrfect." She put a basket in her bedroom so the kitten could sleep there. About a week later, Kate began to sneeze a lot.

   ___ a. Kate must be allergic to the kitten.

   ✓ b. She likes the kitten.

   ✓ c. She may have a cold.

7.   Several police cars with their lights whirling zipped up the highway ahead of us. An ambulance also passed us. All this happened after traffic ahead of us came to a dead halt.

   ✓ a. An accident was blocking traffic on the speaker's side of the road.

   ✓ b. Someone had gotten hurt in the accident.

   ___ c. The police would give someone a ticket.

8.   The old man bent over and put a piece of paper on the floor. Then he brushed the ant onto the paper, lifted it, walked to the open window, and flipped the ant outside.

   ✓   a. The man wasn't afraid of ants.

   ✓   b. He preferred not to kill ants.

        c. He was a vegetarian.

9.   Mark walked into the high-school office and said to the secretary, "I'm supposed to see the principal." "Dr. Edgar is expecting you, Mark," she answered. "Please go in."

   ✓   a. The secretary knew Mark.

        b. Mark's teacher did not like the way he behaved in class.

   ✓   c. The meeting with the principal had been prearranged.

10.   The restaurant often has a long line of people waiting to be seated. On nights when there are plays at the theatre next door, it is especially busy at that restaurant.

        a. The restaurant has a very varied menu.

   ✓   b. Some people eat at that restaurant when they attend plays at the theatre next door.

   ✓   c. The restaurant is popular.

➤ *Review Test 2*

A. After reading the passage, put a check by the **two** inferences that are most firmly based on the given information.

> I once hired a roofer to repair the roof of my home. He quoted me a price of $1,000. I agreed. He tore the old roof off, then came down. He had a smirk on his face. "Sorry," he said, "it's gonna cost you $1,800. I didn't know it needed so much work." "No way," I said. "Whatever you say," the roofer said. "Looks like rain." I sighed and said, "Finish the job."

   ✓   1. At first, the author did not want to spend the extra $800.

        2. The author's old roof would have held up for another year or two.

   ✓   3. The roofer may have planned all along to raise the price after the old roof was torn off.

        4. The author is a man.

        5. The roofer had been recommended to the author.

B. After reading the passage, put a check by the **three** inferences that are most firmly based on the given information.

> About two million dollars fell onto the highway in downtown Columbus, Ohio, from an armored truck. By the time the police came and closed the area off, most of that money had already been taken by motorists. One man, a farmer, returned the bag of money he found to the police right away. A policeman's comment was, "Are you nuts?" Then it became known that someone had taken pictures of the scene of motorists rushing to grab money. After that, many more began to return the money they found. However, well over one million dollars was never returned.

_____ 1. Most of those who found the money gave it to charity.

__✓__ 2. The policeman assumed that people who found money would keep it.

__✓__ 3. Many people will steal money if they think they won't get caught.

_____ 4. People in Columbus are less honest than people in other towns.

__✓__ 5. The police intended to gather the money after they had closed off that area of the highway.

➤ *Review Test 3*

A. To review what you've learned in this chapter, complete each of the following sentences about inferences.

1. An inference is a conclusion that is *(directly stated, suggested)* _____ suggested _____ by the author.

2. When making inferences, it is *(a mistake, useful)* _____ useful _____ to use our own experience as well as the author's clues.

3. When making inferences, it is *(a mistake, useful)* _____ useful _____ to use our sense of logic as well as the author's clues.

B. Here is a chance to apply your understanding of inferences to a reading taken from the textbook *Psychology: An Introduction*, Seventh Edition (Prentice Hall, 1990). If you have found that college tests are a source of stress, you're certainly not alone. In fact, this selection reports on how test stress affects even the health of students' grandmothers. It also tells how one teacher helps his students reduce test stress.

Following the reading are questions on inferences. To help you continue reinforcing the skills taught in previous chapters, there are also questions on:

- vocabulary in context
- central point and main ideas
- supporting details
- transitions
- patterns of organization.

Words to Watch

Following are some words in the reading that do not have strong context support. Each word is followed by the number of the paragraph in which it appears and its meaning there. These words are indicated in the article by a small circle (°).

onset (2):	start
provoke (2):	cause
marked (2):	noticeable
hypersensitive (9):	overly sensitive
syllabus (10):	course outline
incidence (10):	rate
mortality (10):	death
spectacular (11):	very impressive
refined (11):	improved
longevity (11):	long life
scope (11):	the area covered by something
provisions (11):	arrangements

EXAM ANXIETY AND GRANDMA'S HEALTH

Charles G. Morris and John J. Chiodo

Every student knows that examination time can be a source of 1 great stress. In the following article, Professor John J. Chiodo of Clarion University describes some truly extraordinary effects of exam-related stress and suggests a variety of ways in which faculty members can help to alleviate the problem.

I entered the academic world as well prepared as the next fellow, 2 but I was still unaware of the threat that midterm exams posed to the health and welfare of students and their relatives. It didn't take long, however, for me to realize that a real problem existed. The onset° of midterms seemed to provoke° not only a marked° increase in the family problems, illnesses, and accidents experienced by my students, but also above-normal death rates among their grandmothers.

In my first semester of teaching, during the week before the 3 midterm exam, I got numerous phone calls and visits from the roommates of many of my students, reporting a series of problems. Mononucleosis seemed to have struck a sizable portion of my class, along with the more common colds and flu.

A call from one young woman awakened me with the news that her 4 roommate's grandmother had died, so she (my student) would be unable to take the exam. I expressed my condolences, and assured the caller that her roommate would not be penalized for such an unexpected tragedy.

Over the next few days I received many more calls—informing me of sickness, family problems, and even the death of a beloved cat. But the thought of three grandmothers passing away, all within the short exam period, caused me a good deal of remorse. But the term soon ended and, with the Christmas break and preparations for the new semester, I forgot all about the midterm problem.   5

Eight weeks into the second semester, however, I was once again faced with a succession of visits or phone calls from roommates about sick students, family problems, and, yes, the deaths of more grandmothers. I was shaken. I could understand that dorm meals and late nights, along with "exam anxiety," might well make some students sick, but what could account for the grandmothers? Once again, though, other things occupied my mind, and before long I had stopped thinking about it.   6

I moved that summer to a large Midwestern university, where I had to reconstruct my teaching plans to fit the quarter system. I taught three classes. By the end of the first midterm exams two of my student's grandmothers had died; by the time the year was over, a total of five had gone to their reward.   7

I began to realize the situation was serious. In the two years I had been teaching, 12 grandmothers had passed away; on that basis, if I taught for 30 years 180 grandmothers would no longer be with us. I hated to think what the university wide number would be.   8

I tried to figure out the connection. Was it because grandmothers are hypersensitive° to a grandchild's problems? When they see their grandchildren suffering from exam anxiety, do they become anxious too? Does the increased stress then cause stroke or heart failure? It seemed possible; so it followed that if grandmothers' anxiety levels could be lowered, a good number of their lives might be prolonged. I didn't have much direct contact with grandmothers, but I reasoned that by moderating the anxiety of my students, I could help reduce stress on their grandmothers.   9

With that in mind, I began my next year of teaching. On the first day of class, while passing out the syllabus°, I told my students how concerned I was about the high incidence° of grandmother mortality°. I also told them what I thought we could do about it.   10

To make a long story short, the results of my plan to reduce student anxiety were spectacular°. At the end of the quarter there had not been one test-related death of a grandmother. In addition, the amount of sickness and family strife had decreased dramatically. The next two   11 quarters proved to be even better. Since then, I have refined° my anxiety-reduction system and, in the interest of grandmotherly longevity°, would like to share it with my teaching colleagues. Here are the basic rules:

- Review the scope° of the exam.
- Use practice tests.
- Be clear about time limits.
- Announce what materials will be needed and what aids will be permitted.
- Review the grading procedure.
- Provide study help.
- Make provisions° for last-minute questions.
- Allow for breaks during long exams.
- Coach students on test-taking techniques.

I have been following these rules for thirteen years now, and during that time have heard of only an occasional midterm-related death of a grandmother. Such results lead me to believe that if all faculty members did likewise, the health and welfare of students—and their grandmothers—would surely benefit. 12

Vocabulary Questions

Use context clues to help you decide on the best definition for each italicized word. Then circle the letter of each choice.

1. The word *alleviate* in "Professor John J. Chiodo . . . describes some truly extraordinary effects of exam-related stress and suggests a variety of ways in which faculty members can help to alleviate the problem" (paragraph 1) means
   a. enlarge.
   (b.) relieve.
   c. start.
   d. deny.

2. The word *remorse* in "the thought of three grandmothers passing away, all within the short exam period, caused me a good deal of remorse" (paragraph 5) means
   (a.) deep guilt.
   b. boredom.
   c. satisfaction.
   d. unexpected results.

3. The word *succession* in "Eight weeks into the second semester, however, I was once again faced with a succession of visits or phone calls from roommates about sick students, family problems, and, yes, the deaths of more grandmothers" (paragraph 6) means
   a. absence.
   b. series.
   c. memory.
   d. success.

4. The word *prolonged* in "it followed that if grandmothers' anxiety levels could be lowered, a good number of their lives might be prolonged" (paragraph 9) means
   a. good examples.
   b. educated.
   c. made longer.
   d. overstressed.

5. The word *moderating* in "I reasoned that by moderating the anxiety of my students, I could help reduce the stress on their grandmothers" (paragraph 9) means
   a. noticing.
   b. imitating.
   c. taking advantage of.
   d. lessening.

Reading Comprehension Questions

Central Point and Main Ideas

1. Which sentence best expresses the central point of the selection?
   a. Students do not like midterm exams.
   b. Exam anxiety can be reduced if teachers tell students what is expected of them and give them study and test aids.
   c. An unusually high number of students' and their roommates' grandmothers die during midterms and finals.
   d. Teachers should have a variety of rules for their classrooms.

2. Which sentence best expresses the main idea of paragraph 9?
   a. Grandmothers are overly sensitive to their grandchildren's problems.
   b. Increased stress may cause stroke or heart failure.
   c. The author realized he could reduce students' midterm excuses by lessening their exam anxiety.
   d. The author didn't have much direct contact with grandmothers.

3. Which sentence best expresses the main idea of paragraph 11?
   a. By following a few basic rules, Professor Chiodo was able to greatly reduce students' excuses at exam time.
   b. Practice tests reduced students' stress over midterms.
   c. Reviewing the grading procedure reduced student stress over midterms.
   d. Teaching is more successful if various rules are followed.

Supporting Details

4. Professor Chiodo's preparation for teaching had not prepared him for
   a. writing tests.
   b. grading tests.
   c. the extent of student anxiety over tests.
   d. teaching in the Midwest.

Transitions

5. The relationship of the second part of the sentence below to the first is one of
   a. time.
   b. addition.
   c. comparison.
   d. contrast.

   I entered the academic world as well prepared as the next fellow, but I was still unaware of the threat that midterm exams posed to the health and welfare of students and their relatives. (Paragraph 2)

Patterns of Organization

6. Paragraphs 2–10 are organized mainly according to the pattern of
   a. time order.
   b. list of items.
   c. comparison and/or contrast.
   d. definition and example.

7. In paragraph 9, the author playfully
   a. narrates a series of events in his classes.
   b. lists a number of ways to reduce test anxiety.
   c. discusses possible cause-effect relationships.
   d. defines and illustrates a term.

Inferences

8. Professor Chiodo implies that students
   a. take too many courses.
   b. have no feeling for their grandmothers.
   c. sometimes lie and make excuses in order to avoid taking midterms.
   d. are more likely to be sick if they live in dormitories.

9. From the selection, we can conclude that Professor Chiodo
    a. is unpopular with his students.
    b. wants to eliminate midterm exams.
    c. has a good sense of humor.
    d. all of the above.

10. We can infer that for classes in which teachers do not follow Professor Chiodo's rules, students can help themselves by
    a. finding out the scope of upcoming exams.
    b. getting study help.
    c. learning test-taking techniques.
    d. all of the above.

Part II

MASTERY TESTS

DICTIONARY USE: Test 1

A. Answer the following questions about the dictionary entry for *eminent*. The pronunciation guide below will help you answer two of the questions.

Pronunciation Key

ă pat	ā pay	â care	ä father	ě pet	ē be	ĭ pit
ī tie	î pier	ŏ pot	ō toe	ô paw, for		oi noise
ŏŏ took	ōō boot	ou out	th thin	*th* this		ŭ cut
û urge	yōō abuse	zh vision	ə about, item, edible, gallop, circus			

em•i•nent (ĕm′ə-nənt) *adj.*   **1.** Outstanding, as in reputation; distinguished. **2.** Towering above others; projecting. [< Lat. *eminere*, to stand out.] **—em′i•nent•ly** *adv.*

1. *Eminent* would be found on the dictionary page with which guide words?
   a. elsewhere / embryo   c. emporium / encumber
   (b.) embryology / employment   d. eject / electrocute

2. How many syllables are in the word *eminent*? _____*three*_____

3. Which syllable is accented?
   (a.) the first   c. the third
   b. the second   d. the fourth

4. The first *e* in *eminent* is pronounced like the *e* in which word in the pronunciation key? _____*pet*_____

5. The *i* in *eminent* is pronounced like
   a. the *e* in *pet*.   c. the *i* in *tie*.
   b. the *i* in *pit*.   (d.) the *e* in *item*.

6. What part of speech is *eminent*? _____*adjective*_____.

7. Which definition of *eminent* best fits the sentence below, 1 or 2? ___*1*___

   Dr. Bones is an *eminent* chiropractor.

8. Which definition of *eminent* best fits the sentence below, 1 or 2? ___*2*___

   Eminent among the structures in town was the new fifty-floor office building. The next tallest building is forty floors.

(Continues on next page)

9. Which definition of *eminent* best fits the sentence below, 1 or 2? ___*1*___

   Vincent van Gogh, the *eminent* Dutch painter, never achieved great success during his lifetime.

10. *Eminent* comes from a Latin word that means _____*"to stand out"*_____.

B. Use your dictionary to find the correct spelling of the following words. (Feel free to use the spelling hints on page 11.)

11. pasport _____*passport*_____

12. sieze _____*seize*_____

13. docter _____*doctor*_____

14. jelatin _____*gelatin*_____

15. breaze _____*breeze*_____

C. Use your dictionary to put dots between the syllables in each word. Then write out the word with the correct pronunciation symbols, including the accent marks.

16. c o m p l y _____*com·ply*   *kəm-plī′*_____

17. e l a p s e _____*e·lapse*   *ĭ-lăps′*_____

18. d u b i o u s _____*du·bi·ous*   *doō′bē-əs*_____

19. a n t i d o t e _____*an·ti·dote*   *ăn′tĭ-dōt′*_____

20. c o h e r e n t _____*co·her·ent*   *kō-hîr′ənt or kō-hĕr′ənt*_____

DICTIONARY USE: Test 2

Use your dictionary to find the information needed for sections A-D of this test.

A. List the parts of speech given for the following words.

    1. pocket   *adjective, verb, noun*

    2. blue   *adjective, verb, noun*

    3. wild   *adjective, adverb, noun*

B. Write the irregular plural forms for the following words.

    4. wife   *wives*

    5. penny   *pennies*

    6. hero   *heroes*

C. Write in the dictionary definition of *pest* that fits each of the following sentences.

    7. Ragweed is the *pest* whose pollen is one of the main causes of hay fever.

          an injurious plant or animal

    8. Some businessmen consider the homeless who hang around their stores to be *pests*. Mr. Green, however, has given several of the homeless near his store part-time jobs.

          an annoying person or thing; a nuisance

D. Write four synonyms given by your dictionary for each of the following words.

    9. decrease   *diminish, ebb, lessen, reduce (Other answers are possible.)*

    10. honor   *dignity, prestige, reputation, status (Other answers are possible.)*

(Continues on next page)

E. Answer the questions that follow the dictionary entries. The pronunciation guide below will help you answer the pronunciation questions.

Pronunciation Key

ă pat	ā pay	â care	ä father	ĕ pet	ē be	ĭ pit
ī tie	î pier	ŏ pot	ō toe	ô paw, for		oi noise
ŏŏ took	ōō boot	ou out	th thin	*th* this		ŭ cut
û urge	yōō abuse	zh vision	ə about, item, edible, gallop, circus			

a•vert (ə-vûrt′) *v.* **1.** To turn away: *avert one's eyes.*   **2.** To ward off; prevent. [< Lat. *avertere.*] —**a•vert′i•ble** or **a•vert′a•ble** *adj.*

11. The *e* in *avert* sounds like the *u* in
    a. *cut.*   ⓑ *urge.*

12. *Avert* is accented on the
    a. first syllable.   ⓑ second syllable.

13. What part of speech is *avert*? _____*verb*_____

14. Which definition of *avert* best fits the sentence below—1 or 2? __*1*__

    Gene preferred to *avert* his thoughts from the topic of taxes.

15. Which definition of *avert* best fits the sentence below—1 or 2? __*1*__

    The chef *averted* her face to avoid the heat from the fire.

e•merge (ĭ-mûrj′) *v.* **e•merged, e•merg•ing. 1.** To rise up or come forth into view; appear. **2.** To come into existence. **3.** To become known or evident. [< Lat. *emergere.*] —**e•mer′gence** *n.* —**e•mer′gent** *adj.*

16. The first *e* in *emerge* sounds like the
    a. *e* in *pet.*   ⓑ *i* in *pit.*

17. The part of speech of *emergent* is
    a. verb.   ⓑ adjective.

18. The number of syllables in *emerging* is ___*3*___.

19. Which definition of *emerge* best fits the sentence below—1, 2, or 3? __*1*__

    The sun *emerged* from behind the clouds.

20. Which definition of *emerge* best fits the sentence below—1, 2, or 3? __*3*__

    The fact that the defendant was once a prison guard *emerged* in court last week.

DICTIONARY USE: Test 3

Use your dictionary to find the information needed for parts A and B of this test.

A. Find the correct spelling of the following words. (Feel free to use the spelling hints on page 11.)

1. comfortible   *comfortable*

2. suceed   *succeed*

3. counseler   *counselor*

4. recieve   *receive*

5. wherewolf   *werewolf*

B. Put dots between the syllables in each word. Then write out the word with the correct pronunciation symbols, including the accent marks.

6. p r e v a i l   *pre· vail*   prĭ-vāl′

7. i n n a t e   *in· nate*   ĭ-nāt′

8. r e c i p i e n t   *re· cip· i· ent*   rĭ-sĭp′ē-ənt

9. v i t a l i z e   *vi· tal· ize*   vīt′l-īz′

10. p r o c r a s t i n a t e   *pro· cras· ti· nate*   prō-krăs′tə-nāt′

C. Answer the questions that follow the dictionary entries. The pronunciation guide below will help you answer the pronunciation questions.

Pronunciation Key

ă pat	ā pay	â care	ä father	ĕ pet	ē be	ĭ pit
ī tie	î pier	ŏ pot	ō toe	ô paw, for		oi noise
ŏŏ took	ōō boot	ou out	th thin	*th* this		ŭ cut
û urge	yōō abuse	zh vision	ə about, item, edible, gallop, circus			

(Continues on next page)

trans•mit (trăns-mĭt′, trănz-) *v.* **-mit•ted, -mit•ting. 1.** To send from one person, thing, or place to another. **2.** To cause to spread, as an infection. **3.** To impart by heredity. **4.** To send (a signal), as by radio. **5.** To convey (force or energy) from one part of a mechanism to another. [< Lat. *transmittere.*] —**trans•mis′si•ble** or **trans•mit′ta•ble** *adj.* —**trans•mit′tal** *n.*

11. *Transmit* would be found on the dictionary page with which guide words?
    a. transliterate / trappings   c. trade-in / trance
    b. tranquil / translate   d. trying / tumble

12. The *a* in *transmit* sounds like the *a* in
    a. *pay.*
    b. *pat.*

13. The accent in *transmit* is on the (*first or second?*) ____second____ syllable.

14. Which definition of *transmit* best fits the sentence below—1, 2, 3, 4, or 5?
    ___2___

    AIDS can be *transmitted* by bodily fluids, especially blood and semen.

15. Which definition of *transmit* best fits the sentence below—1, 2, 3, 4, or 5?
    ___3___

    The tendency to have twins is *transmitted* genetically.

in•cline (ĭn-klīn′) *v.* **-clined, -clin•ing. 1.** To lean; slant; slope. **2.** To lower or bend (the head or body) in a nod or bow. **3.** To influence (someone or something) to have a certain preference; dispose. **4.** To tend toward a particular state or condition. —*n.* (ĭn′klīn′). An inclined surface; a slope. [< L. *inclinare.*]

16. What parts of speech is *incline*? ____verb and noun____

17. How many syllables are in *inclined*? ___2___

18. The second *i* in *incline* sounds like
    a. the *a* in *pat.*   c. the *i* in *tie.*
    b. the *i* in *pit.*   d. the *u* in *urge.*

19. Which definition of *incline* best fits the sentence below—1, 2, 3, 4, or the last one? ___4___

    My sister is *inclined* to be overly thin, while I tend to be chubby.

20. Which definition of *incline* best fits the sentence below—1, 2, 3, 4, or the last one? ___last___

    The basketball rolled down the concrete *incline* and into the street.

DICTIONARY USE: Test 4

Use your dictionary to find the information needed for parts A–D of this test.

A. List the parts of speech given for the following words.

1. muzzle _____ *verb, noun* _____

2. cold _____ *adjective, noun* _____

3. off _____ *adjective, adverb, preposition* _____

B. Write the irregular plural forms for the following words.

4. cry _____ *cries* _____

5. potato _____ *potatoes* _____

6. mother-in-law _____ *mothers-in-law* _____

C. Write in the dictionary definition of *mild* that fits each of the following sentences.

7. Fran will eat only very *mild* cheeses; anything stronger than American cheese nauseates her.

   _____ *not sharp or strong in taste or odor* _____

8. Our dog is as big as a small pony, but as *mild* as a baby lamb. He even lets our little son ride on his back.

   _____ *gentle or meek in disposition or behavior* _____

D. Write four synonyms given by your dictionary for each of the following words.

9. raise _____ *increase, advance, grow, cultivate (Other answers are possible.)* _____

10. rude _____ *discourteous, ill-mannered, impolite, unmannerly (Other answers are possible.)* _____

E. Answer the questions that follow the dictionary entries. The pronunciation guide below will help you answer the pronunciation questions.

Pronunciation Key

ă pat	ā **pay**	â care	ä father	ĕ pet	ē be	ĭ pit
ī tie	î **pier**	ŏ pot	ō toe	ô paw, for		oi noise
ŏŏ **took**	ōō **boot**	ou **out**	th thin	*th* this		ŭ cut
û **urge**	yōō abuse	zh vision	ə about, item, edible, gallop, circus			

(Continues on next page)

sus•pend (sə-spĕnd′) *v.* **1.** To bar for a period from a privilege, office, or position. **2.** To cause to stop for a period; interrupt. **3. a.** To hold in abeyance; defer: *suspend judgment.* **b.** To render ineffective temporarily: *suspend parking regulations.* **4.** To hang so as to allow free movement. **5.** To support or keep from falling without apparent attachment. [< Lat. *suspendere,* to hang up.]

11. The *u* in *suspend* sounds like the *u* in
    a. *circus.*   b. *cut.*

12. The *e* in *suspend* sounds like the *e* in
    a. *pet.*   b. *be.*

13. Which definition of *suspend* best fits the sentence below—1, 2, 3, 4, or 5?
    __2__

    The parade was *suspended* for a while on Broad Street while the police pushed back the crowds.

14. Which definition of *suspend* best fits the sentence below—1, 2, 3, 4, or 5?
    __1__

    The conductor of the train was *suspended* until it could be determined if he had used marijuana.

15. *Suspend* comes from a Latin word that means _____*"to hang up"*_____.

u•ni•ver•sal (yo͞o′nə-vûr′səl) *adj.* **1.** Extending to or affecting the entire world; worldwide. **2.** Including or affecting all members of a class or group. **3.** Of or pertaining to the universe or cosmos; cosmic. [< Lat. *universus,* whole, entire.]

16. The *u* in *universal* is pronounced like
    a. the *u* in *abuse.*   b. the *u* in *cut.*

17. The *e* and *a* in *universal* are pronounced like
    a. the *u* in *urge* and the *a* in *about.*   b. the *e* in *pet* and the *a* in *father.*

18. The stronger accent in *universal* is on the
    a. first syllable.   b. third syllable.

19. Which definition of *universal* best fits the sentence below—1, 2, or 3? __3__

    The subject matter in an astronomy class is truly *universal,* taking into account galaxies far beyond our own solar system.

20. Which definition of *universal* best fits the sentence below—1, 2, or 3? __2__

    The *universal* opinion of the teachers was that a strike was necessary.

DICTIONARY USE: Test 5

Use your dictionary to find the information needed for parts A and B of this test.

A. Find the correct spelling of the following words. (Feel free to use the spelling hints on page 11.)

1. begining _____ *beginning* _____

2. toona _____ *tuna* _____

3. freaze _____ *freeze* _____

4. tendancy _____ *tendency* _____

5. tention _____ *tension* _____

B. Put dots between the syllables in each word. Then write out the word with the correct pronunciation symbols, including the accent marks.

6. o v e r t _____ *o · vert* _____ *ō-vûrt′* _____

7. f i n i t e _____ *fi · nite* _____ *fī′nīt′* _____

8. l i a b l e _____ *li · a · ble* _____ *lī′ə-bəl* _____

9. a p p r e h e n s i v e _____ *ap · pre · hen · sive* _____ *ăp′rĭ-hĕn′sĭv* _____

10. s i m u l t a n e o u s _____ *si · mul · ta · ne · ous* _____ *sī′məl-tā′nē-əs* _____

C. Answer the questions that follow the dictionary entries. The pronunciation guide below will help you answer the pronunciation questions.

Pronunciation Key

ă pat	ā pay	â care	ä father	ĕ pet	ē be	ĭ pit
ī tie	î pier	ŏ pot	ō toe	ô paw, for		oi noise
ŏŏ took	ōō boot	ou out	th thin	*th* this		ŭ cut
û urge	yōō abuse	zh vision	ə about, item, edible, gallop, circus			

(Continues on next page)

le·git·i·mate (lə-jĭt′ə-mĭt) *adj.* **1.** Lawful. **2.** In accordance with accepted standards. **3.** Reasonable: a *legitimate solution.* **4.** Authentic; genuine. **5.** Born in wedlock. —*v.* (lə-jĭt′ə-māt′) **-mat·ed, -mat·ing.** To justify as legitimate. [< Lat. *legitimus.*] —**le·git′i·ma·cy** (-mə-sē) *n.* —**le·git′i·mate·ly** *adv.*

11. The vowels in *legitimate* are pronounced like
    a. the *e* in *pet* and the schwa.   (b.) the schwa and the *i* in *pit.*

12. The number of syllables in *legitimated* is
    a. four.   (b.) five.

13. How many definitions are given for the verb form of *legitimate*?
    a. Five   (b.) One

14. Which definition of *legitimate* best fits the sentence below—1, 2, 3, 4, or 5?
    _____1_____

    Ever since Keith got out of jail, he has worked at *legitimate* jobs.

15. Which definition of *legitimate* best fits the sentence below—1, 2, 3, 4, or 5?
    _____4_____

    The researchers hoped they had found a *legitimate* example of cave art.

fra·ter·ni·ty (frə-tûr′nĭ-tē) *n., pl.* **-ties. 1.** A body of men linked together by similar interests or professions. **2.** A chiefly social organization of male college students. **3.** Brotherhood; brotherliness. [< Lat. *frater,* brother.]

16. The *e* in *fraternity* sounds like
    a. the *e* in *pet.*   (b.) the *u* in *urge.*

17. The *y* in *fraternity* sounds like
    a. the *i* in *tie.*   (b.) the *e* in *be.*

18. Which syllable does the accent in *fraternity* fall on—the first, second, third, or fourth? _____second_____

19. Which definition of *fraternity* best fits the sentence below—1, 2, or 3? _____1_____

    The *fraternity* of firefighters is so strong that Captain Akins could walk into any firehouse in the country and be assured of a welcome.

20. Which definition of *fraternity* best fits the sentence below—1, 2, or 3? _____2_____

    Some *fraternity* members on this campus spend more time drinking than studying.

DICTIONARY USE: Test 6

Use your dictionary to find the information needed for parts A-D of this test.

A. List the parts of speech given for the following words.

1. yellow _____*noun, adjective, verb*_____

2. goggle _____*verb, noun*_____

3. zero _____*noun, adjective, verb*_____

B. Write the irregular plural forms for the following words.

4. moose _____*moose*_____

5. crisis _____*crises*_____

6. passerby _____*passersby*_____

C. Write in the dictionary definition of *boost* that fits each of the following sentences.

7. Almost anybody can have hard luck and need a *boost* from society.

_____*a lift or help*_____

8. I had forgotten my key, so my friend *boosted* me up to my bedroom window, which was partially open.

_____*to lift by or as if by pushing up from behind or below*_____

D. Write four synonyms given by your dictionary for each of the following words.

9. defeat _____*conquer, overcome, subdue, vanquish (Other answers are possible.)*_____

10. yield _____*capitulate, submit, succumb, surrender (Other answers are possible.)*_____

E. Answer the questions that follow the dictionary entries. The pronunciation guide below will help you answer the pronunciation questions.

Pronunciation Key

ă pat	ā pay	â care	ä father	ĕ pet	ē be	ĭ pit
ī tie	î pier	ŏ pot	ō toe	ô paw, for		oi noise
ŏŏ took	ōō boot	ou out	th thin	*th* this		ŭ cut
û urge	yōō abuse	zh vision	ə about, item, edible, gallop, circus			

(Continues on next page)

sat•el•lite (săt′l-īt′) *n*. **1.** A relatively small body, natural or artificial, orbiting a planet. **2.** One who attends a dignitary. **3.** A nation dominated politically by another. [< Lat. *satelles*, an attendant, escort.]

11. The *a* in *satellite* sounds like the *a* in
    (a.) *pat*.   b. *care*.

12. The *i* in *satellite* sounds like the *i* in
    a. *pit*.   (b.) *tie*.

13. Which definition of *satellite* best fits the sentence below—1, 2, or 3? __3__

    Before the Soviet Union fell apart, Poland was one of its *satellites*.

14. Which definition of *satellite* best fits the sentence below—1, 2, or 3? __1__

    Scientists were puzzled by what appeared to be a new *satellite* circling Saturn.

15. *Satellite* comes from a Latin word that means __*"an attendant or escort"*__.

cul•ti•vate (kŭl′tə-vāt′) *v*. **-vat•ed, -vat•ing. 1.** To improve and prepare (land) for raising crops. **2.** To grow or tend, as a plant or crop. **3.** To form and refine, as by education. **4.** To seek the acquaintance or good will of. [< Lat. *cultus*, pp of *colere*, to till, cultivate.] **—cul′ti•va′tion** *n*. **—cul′ti•va′tor** *n*.

16. The *a* in *cultivate* sounds like the *a* in
    a. *father*.   (b.) *pay*.

17. The part of speech of *cultivate* is
    a. noun.   (b.) verb.

18. The number of syllables in *cultivate* is
    (a.) three.   b. four.

19. Which definition of *cultivate* best fits the sentence below—1, 2, 3, or 4?
    __4__

    The would-be actress *cultivated* the directors she met in hopes of being given a movie part.

20. Which definition of *cultivate* best fits the sentence below—1, 2, 3, or 4?
    __3__

    Brad *cultivates* his knowledge of gardening through taking classes and reading on his own.

VOCABULARY IN CONTEXT: Test 1

Try to figure out the meanings of the following five words by studying how each is used in context. Then complete the matching and fill-in sections of the test.

1 **delete**
(dĭ-lēt′)

The television censor told the director to *delete* the offensive language from the film.

Because the essay was a little longer than the five-page limit, Jeff decided to *delete* an interesting but unnecessary passage.

2 **obstinate**
(ŏb′stə-nĭt)

My boss is so *obstinate* that once she makes up her mind, nothing any of her salespeople say can change it.

The *obstinate* three-year-old continued to refuse to take his bath, despite his father's efforts to reason with him.

3 **self-evident**
(sĕlf′ĕv′ĭ-dənt)

Nobody needs proof to know that conflict is part of life—it is *self-evident.*

"I came to find out why you didn't come to work today," said Beth, looking at the red dots all over Myrna's face. "But there's no need to explain—the reason is *self-evident.*"

4 **tedious**
(tē′dē-əs)

The awards show was so *tedious* that my grandfather fell asleep and my mother kept yawning.

I find typing to be *tedious*; I type so slowly that I lose all interest.

5 **wary**
(wâr′ē)

The wolf was *wary*, circling around the camp until he felt sure that all the hikers were asleep.

Because Nora's father is so violent, she is *wary* about all men.

Note: A key to pronunciation is on page 14.

A. Match each word with its definition.

1. delete   __2__   stubborn, unwilling to give in

2. obstinate   __5__   on one's guard

3. self-evident   __4__   uninteresting; tiresome; boring

4. tedious   __3__   clear; obvious without any explanation or proof

5. wary   __1__   to take out; to omit

(Continues on next page)

B. Fill in each blank with one of the words in the box. Use each word once.

delete	obstinate	self-evident
tedious	wary	

6. It is _____*self-evident*_____ that humans benefit greatly from peace, yet we seem to make war at every chance we get.

7. Sometimes it is useful to be _____*obstinate*_____. For example, it's usually the person who stubbornly works toward a goal that achieves it.

8. The history teacher's lectures were so _____*tedious*_____ that by the end of the semester very few students attended.

9. Barbra Streisand decided to _____*delete*_____ the second *a* in her first name, which was originally "Barbara."

10. Because the puppy had been treated badly by his previous owner, he was _____*wary*_____ when well-meaning strangers took him home from the animal shelter.

VOCABULARY IN CONTEXT: Test 2

Try to figure out the meanings of the following five words by studying how each is used in context. Then complete the matching and fill-in sections of the test.

1 **compatible**
(kəm-păt′ə-bəl)

Bonita and her roommate are always quarreling; they certainly aren't *compatible.*

To be successful and happy on the job, you should be *compatible* with your fellow workers.

2 **imprudent**
(ĭm-prōōd′nt)

It's usually *imprudent* to make important decisions while you're angry.

When I couldn't fall asleep last night, I realized I had been *imprudent* to drink so much coffee after dinner.

3 **patron**
(pā′trən)

The waitress was surprised because a *patron* who usually left a large tip left nothing today.

The prices at the corner grocery got so high that even its oldest and most regular *patrons* began to shop elsewhere for groceries.

4 **retreat**
(rĭ-trēt′)

"It is better to *retreat* to safety," said the general, "than to go forward foolishly."

As a child, I was shy. Whenever my parents had company, I *retreated* to my room.

5 **valid**
(văl′ĭd)

The teacher decided that the test results were not *valid* because some students had gotten hold of the questions before the test.

It is a *valid* judgment that a student is irresponsible if he or she does not hand in even one assignment all semester.

Note: A key to pronunciation is on page 14.

A. Match each word with its definition.

1. compatible   __4__   to remove oneself from participation or involvement; to move back or withdraw

2. imprudent   __5__   well-grounded; having a logical basis

3. patron   __3__   regular customer

4. retreat   __2__   unwise

5. valid   __1__   capable of getting along with others or each other

(Continues on next page)

B. Fill in each blank with one of the words in the box. Use each word once.

compatible	imprudent	patron
retreat	valid	

6. My old girlfriend and I weren't very _____*compatible*_____; whenever she wasn't angry with me, I was angry with her.

7. The owner of the Italian restaurant knew all her _____*patron*_____s by their first names.

8. It was very _____*imprudent*_____ of Matt to put ketchup in the class bully's gym shoes.

9. The driver claimed that the drunkenness test was not _____*valid*_____ because the equipment was known to be unreliable.

10. We started to leave the cabin, but _____*retreat*_____ed when we saw the swarm of bees on the porch.

VOCABULARY IN CONTEXT: Test 3

Try to figure out the meanings of the following five words by studying how each is used in context. Then complete the matching and fill-in sections of the test.

1 **ambiguous**
(ăm-bĭg′yōo-əs)

The phone message was *ambiguous*: Did Ken intend to meet Al at school or after school at football practice?

How you interpret the *ambiguous* sentence "Visiting relatives can be boring" may depend on which you find annoying—relatives who visit or visits to relatives.

2 **apathy**
(ăp′ə-thē)

One advantage of a poor economy is that people have less *apathy* about politics and voting.

After Gino broke up with Meg, his *apathy* towards social activities worried his parents—he wasn't even interested in a night out with the boys.

3 **flaunt**
(flônt)

Lola has a good figure, which she likes to *flaunt* by wearing snug clothing.

The old saying "If you've got it, *flaunt* it" means you should display your good qualities.

4 **inevitable**
(ĭn-ĕv′ĭ-tə-bəl)

A fight between the two brothers seemed *inevitable* that rainy Saturday; they had been teasing each other all morning.

It was *inevitable* that Polly and Gerald would break up; Polly's dad got a new job, and the entire family was moving out of the state.

5 **vital**
(vīt′l)

Water is *vital* to the survival of all living things.

Because Mac had left out a *vital* ingredient, the apple cake came out looking like a pancake.

Note: A key to pronunciation is on page 14.

A. Match each word with its definition.

1. ambiguous   __4__ unavoidable

2. apathy   __3__ to show off

3. flaunt   __5__ essential

4. inevitable   __1__ able to be interpreted in more than one way

5. vital   __2__ lack of interest

(Continues on next page)

235

B. Fill in each blank with one of the words in the box. Use each word once.

ambiguous	apathy	flaunt
inevitable	vital	

6. It is _____*inevitable*_____ that couples will have disagreements from time to time.

7. Rich people who _____*flaunt*_____ their wealth may be more likely to be robbed.

8. If parents show _____*apathy*_____ towards their children's education, how can we expect the students to show interest?

9. For Zena to pass her biology course, it is _____*vital*_____ that she pass the final exam.

10. The teacher decided to regrade the exams after several students pointed out that one question was _____*ambiguous*_____ and thus could be answered in more than one way.

VOCABULARY IN CONTEXT: Test 4

Try to figure out the meanings of the following five words by studying how each is used in context. Then complete the matching and fill-in sections of the test.

1 **adverse**
   (ăd-vûrs′)

The baby food company settled the case out of court because it did not want any *adverse* publicity.

Carol survived her freshman year despite such *adverse* events as missing two weeks of class because of a strep throat and having all her books stolen just before finals.

2 **clarify**
   (klăr′ə-fī′)

Textbook authors often *clarify* general statements with specific examples; the illustrations make the general point more clear.

The directions for making a gingerbread house were *clarified* by illustrations of all the major steps.

3 **immaculate**
   (ĭ-măk′yə-lĭt)

Contrary to what you might expect, Judy's room is always *immaculate*, but her mother's room is usually a mess.

Although the dog had run merrily through the mud earlier that morning, a walk in the warm rain with Luis left his coat *immaculate*.

4 **phenomenon**
   (fĭ-nŏm′ə-nŏn′)

The deadly *phenomenon* known as the Black Death killed much of England's population in the fourteenth century.

An interesting *phenomenon* exists near Alaska, where the United States and Russia are just two miles apart.

5 **proficient**
   (prə-fĭsh′ənt)

Bill wanted to become *proficient* on the saxophone, so he practiced every day for several hours.

The basketball team worked on the complicated play until the coach felt they were *proficient* enough to use it in the next game.

Note: A key to pronunciation is on page 14.

A. Match each word with its definition.

1. adverse   __4__ an unusual or significant happening, situation, or fact

2. clarify   __5__ highly skilled

3. immaculate   __1__ unfavorable

4. phenomenon   __3__ spotless

5. proficient   __2__ to make clear   *(Continues on next page)*

B. Fill in each blank with one of the words in the box. Use each word once.

adverse	clarify	immaculate
phenomenon	proficient	

6. My son was a(n) _____*proficient*_____ speaker at the age of four months; unfortunately, he was the only one who could understand what he meant.

7. If the kitchen isn't _____*immaculate*_____ at the end of a day, the head chef insists that someone stay late to finish cleaning.

8. Dishonesty usually has _____*adverse*_____ effects upon a relationship.

9. AIDS is an especially important _____*phenomenon*_____ because it has had many medical, social, and financial effects on society.

10. To _____*clarify*_____ to students how the heart works, teachers often compare it to a pump.

VOCABULARY IN CONTEXT: Test 5

Try to figure out the meanings of the following five words by studying how each is used in context. Then complete the matching and fill-in sections of the test.

1 **dilemma**
(dĭ-lĕm′ə)

The settlers faced a *dilemma*: should they stay in their town for another harsh winter or return to civilization?

What a *dilemma*! I have to choose between completing my English paper and studying for my biology exam.

2 **gregarious**
(grĭ-gâr′ē-əs)

"Elena is too *gregarious*," complained Craig. "She is always surrounded by friends, so I can never be alone with her."

Wolves, being *gregarious* creatures, travel in packs.

3 **morose**
(mə-rōs′)

Before the game, the locker room had been cheerful; now the players were *morose*.

Jill glanced at her report card full of C's and D's, and a *morose* expression crossed her face.

4 **regress**
(rĭ-grĕs′)

For a short time after his baby sister was born, seven-year-old Ryan *regressed* to sucking his thumb again.

Norma had come a long way in her fight against alcohol abuse, but when her husband left her, she *regressed* to overdrinking.

5 **sound**
(sound)

Writing a research paper gives students experience developing *sound* support for a point.

Many businesses fail because their owners did not develop *sound* plans, plans firmly based on facts and other people's experience.

Note: A key to pronunciation is on page 14.

A. Match each word with its definition.

1. dilemma   _3_   gloomy; sad

2. gregarious   _5_   logical; based on experience or knowledge

3. morose   _4_   to move backward, especially to a former worse condition

4. regress   _1_   a situation forcing a choice between unpleasant alternatives

5. sound   _2_   fond of the company of others; tending to move in a group

(Continues on next page)

239

B. Fill in each blank with one of the words in the box. Use each word once.

dilemma	gregarious	morose
regress	sound	

6. Teenagers are often _____*gregarious*_____, for they find status and a sense of identity by hanging out with a particular group.

7. When my twelve-year-old neighbor Eddie doesn't get his way, he will _____*regress*_____ to the temper tantrums of a baby.

8. When the news of the popular teacher's accident reached school, the entire student body was _____*morose*_____.

9. To reach a _____*sound*_____ conclusion about an issue, you must carefully consider all the facts involved.

10. Otis was faced with the _____*dilemma*_____ of sinking more money into his ancient Chevy or doing without a car.

VOCABULARY IN CONTEXT: Test 6

Try to figure out the meanings of the following five words by studying how each is used in context. Then complete the matching and fill-in sections of the test.

1 **empathy**
   (ĕm′pə-thē)

My aunt has little *empathy* when it comes to other people's problems. She thinks only one person really has troubles, and that's herself.

Because of Dee's *empathy* for others, she always gives beggars a few coins when she passes them.

2 **overwhelming**
   (ō-vər-hwĕl′mĭng)

The town found the hurricane *overwhelming*; residents could not have rebuilt their lives without outside help.

There was so much to learn on my new job that it was *overwhelming* for me at first.

3 **provoke**
   (prə-vōk′)

Our children are so afraid of snakes that even a toy rubber snake *provokes* panic in them.

Certain comedians can *provoke* laughter without even opening their mouths.

4 **subside**
   (səb-sīd′)

Gale makes a good first impression, but once people know her, their admiration begins to *subside*.

The comedian waited for the laughter to *subside* before going on with his next joke.

5 **unprecedented**
   (ŭn-prĕs′ĭ-dĕn′tĭd)

The move was *unprecedented*—never before had the student body elected a pig to student council.

It was *unprecedented* for a ten-year-old to enroll in any college; previously, the youngest student had been eleven.

Note: A key to pronunciation is on page 14.

A. Match each word with its definition.

1. empathy   ___4___ to lessen

2. overwhelming   ___3___ to bring on

3. provoke   ___5___ without a previous similar case

4. subside   ___1___ identification with and understanding of
                             another's situation

5. unprecedented   ___2___ overpowering, physically and/or mentally

(Continues on next page)

241

B. Fill in each blank with one of the words in the box. Use each word once.

empathy	overwhelming	provoke
subside	unprecedented	

6. The politician could only hope that the untrue rumors would _____*subside*_____ before the next election.

7. Since the smoke from the fire was _____*overwhelming*_____, the firefighters had to put on masks before going inside the building.

8. In an _____*unprecedented*_____ move, the governor suggested returning unneeded money to every taxpayer in the state.

9. The sight of the Statue of Liberty _____*provoke*_____d tears of joy in the immigrants on the ship.

10. A therapist without _____*empathy*_____ is like a dancer without rhythm.

MAIN IDEAS: Test 1

A. Each cluster of words below is made up of a general idea and four specific ideas. The general idea includes all of the specific ideas. Underline the general idea in each group.

1.	ivy	<u>plant</u>	cactus	rosebush	fern
2.	harmonica	piano	<u>instrument</u>	drum	guitar
3.	wool	nylon	linen	cotton	<u>cloth</u>
4.	<u>reference book</u>	thesaurus	encyclopedia	atlas	dictionary
5.	<u>breakfast food</u>	waffles	French toast	scrambled eggs	bagel
6.	cancer	diabetes	emphysema	bronchitis	<u>disease</u>
7.	copying machine	word processor	fax machine	<u>office equipment</u>	computer terminal

B. In each pair below, one idea is general and the other is specific. The general idea includes the specific one. Do two things:

    a Underline the idea in each pair that you think is more general.

    b Then write in one more specific idea that is covered by the general idea.

Example	<u>greeting</u>	"How are you?"	*"Hi there"*
8.	<u>emotion</u>	anger	*(Answers will vary.)*
9.	square	<u>shape</u>	_____
10.	<u>seafood</u>	clams	_____
11.	poker	<u>card game</u>	_____
12.	sweater	<u>clothing</u>	_____
13.	<u>coin</u>	nickel	_____
14.	<u>toy</u>	pogo stick	_____
15.	<u>novel</u>	mystery	_____
16.	college	<u>school</u>	_____
17.	<u>life stage</u>	middle age	_____
18.	<u>personal quality</u>	patience	_____

(Continues on next page)

C. Each group of three items below contains three levels of ideas. Write a *1* by the most general idea in each group, a *2* by the less general idea, and a *3* by the most specific idea.

19. __*1*__ entertainer   __*2*__ magician   __*3*__ Houdini

20. __*2*__ physician   __*1*__ health professional   __*3*__ cardiologist

21. __*3*__ Paris   __*1*__ Europe   __*2*__ France

22. __*1*__ criminal   __*2*__ thief   __*3*__ bank robber

23. __*2*__ state capital   __*1*__ city   __*3*__ Atlanta

24. __*3*__ Girl Scouts   __*1*__ club   __*2*__ girls' club

25. __*2*__ aerobic exercise   __*1*__ exercise   __*3*__ jogging

MAIN IDEAS: Test 2

A. Each cluster of words below is made up of a general idea and four specific ideas. The general idea includes all of the specific ideas. Underline the general idea in each group.

1.	cut	scrape	<u>injury</u>	fracture	bruise
2.	vacuuming	dusting	cooking	washing dishes	<u>chores</u>
3.	comic strip	pun	<u>humor</u>	practical joke	cartoon
4.	bobcat	lion	<u>cat</u>	tiger	panther
5.	spatula	<u>kitchen utensil</u>	egg timer	knife	saucepan
6.	sun	Earth	<u>solar system</u>	moon	Mars
7.	junk mail	long lines	stuck doors	<u>annoyances</u>	slow waiters
8.	rape	<u>crime</u>	arson	robbery	murder

B. After each paragraph are three subjects. Label each subject with one of the following:

> *T*—for the topic of the paragraph
> *B*—for the subject that is too broad
> *N*—for the subject that is too narrow

9–11. There are several ways to spend less at the movies. First of all, go in the afternoons, when prices are lower. That can save as much as two dollars a ticket. You can save even more by bringing your own refreshments. Buy candy at the grocery store instead of the theater, where it is much more expensive. Or make popcorn at home and take it to the theater. It costs pennies to make popcorn at home, while a large tub at the theater can cost a few dollars.

   _*B*_ Spending less on recreation

   _*T*_ Spending less at the movies

   _*N*_ Spending less on movie refreshments

(Continues on next page)

12-14. By the year 2010, the world's population may have doubled. Such a huge population in the next century may cause many problems. For example, underdeveloped nations may suffer great food shortages. Natural resources like petroleum and iron ore may be used up entirely. In addition, garbage may compete with people for space.

   _T_ Overpopulation in the next century

   _N_ Food shortages in an overpopulated future

   _B_ The future

15-17. Graffiti are found almost everywhere, from bathrooms to skyscrapers. Who is mostly responsible for them, men or women? It turns out that both men and women must share the blame for graffiti. A recent study found that females produce most of the graffiti on the bathroom walls. In contrast, males are responsible for most of the graffiti done on outdoor walls.

   _B_ Environmental problems

   _N_ Bathroom graffiti-makers

   _T_ Makers of graffiti

18-20. The hospice movement has helped to restore dignity to the dying. Hospices provide homelike rooms as well as medical and emotional support for people with terminal illnesses. A hospice is a place where people can die without pain, among loved ones. More recently, hospice programs have also started providing support for the dying patients who want to be at home.

   _T_ Hospice programs

   _N_ Home hospice programs

   _B_ Programs for the dying

MAIN IDEAS: Test 3

A. In each pair below, one idea is general and the other is specific. The general idea includes the specific one. Do two things:

    a Underline the idea in each pair that you think is more general.

    b Then write in one more specific idea that is covered by the general idea.

			(Answers will vary.)
1.	<u>dance</u>	polka	_____
2.	<u>subject</u>	biology	_____
3.	aluminum	<u>metal</u>	_____
4.	<u>symptom</u>	cough	_____
5.	tuition	<u>expense</u>	_____
6.	<u>music</u>	classical	_____

B. After each paragraph are three subjects. Label each subject with one of the following:

        T—for the topic of the paragraph
        B—for the subject that is too broad
        N—for the subject that is too narrow

7-9. If you have to give a speech, don't wait for the last minute. A successful speech requires careful preparation. Begin by writing a speech that has a clear beginning, middle, and end. Be certain that the speech has humor, covers one or more specific points, and is not too complicated. Know how much time you have to speak and stay within the limit. Then practice your speech over and over again so you can spend time looking at the audience rather than the text.

    __*N*__ Humor in a speech

    __*T*__ A successful speech

    __*B*__ Effective communication

(Continues on next page)

10-12. Most famous inventions are the result of endless thought and experimentation. The invention of Ivory Soap, one of the world's most popular brands, was an accident. Manufacturer Procter & Gamble had begun making a product called White Soap in 1878. The soap was selling well. But one day a factory worker went to lunch, forgetting to turn off the mixing machine that was whipping the liquid White Soap mixture. As a result, far more air than usual was added to the soap. Rather than wasting the batch, the man poured it into the soap molds. When the air-filled product was unmolded, Procter & Gamble had produced the world's first floating soap. Customers loved the soap because it could not be lost at the bottom of a tub. Realizing they had a winner on their hands, Procter & Gamble named the new soap Ivory.

___B___ Famous inventions

___T___ The invention of Ivory soap

___N___ A mixing machine that ran too long

C. 13-20. Each group of items below includes one topic, one main idea (topic sentence), and two supporting details. In the space provided, label each item with one of the following:

> T —for the topic
> MI—for the main idea
> SD—for the supporting details

Group 1

___SD___ The first stage people usually go through when told they are dying is denial.

___MI___ Most people go through five stages after learning they will die soon.

___SD___ The last four stages are anger, bargaining with God, depression, and peaceful acceptance.

___T___ Stages in accepting death.

Group 2

___T___ Construction of the Egyptian pyramids.

___SD___ Foreign slaves lived and died building the pyramids.

___MI___ The Egyptian pyramids were built with manpower and skill, not secret engineering.

___SD___ Pyramid builders used ropes, wooden levers, and muscle power to move giant stones.

MAIN IDEAS: Test 4

A. Each group of three items contains three levels of ideas. Write a *1* by the most general idea in each group, a *2* by the less general idea, and a *3* by the most specific idea.

1. __2__ beverage   __3__ iced tea   __1__ liquid

2. __3__ IRS   __2__ government agency   __1__ agency

3. __1__ leisure activities   __2__ hobbies   __3__ gardening

4. __1__ beachwear   __3__ bikini   __2__ bathing suit

5. __1__ games   __2__ ball games   __3__ soccer

6. __2__ cartoon character   __1__ fictional character   __3__ Popeye

B. After each paragraph are three subjects. Label each subject with one of the following:

> *T*—for the topic of the paragraph
> *B*—for the subject that is too broad
> *N*—for the subject that is too narrow

7-9. Baseball was introduced into Japan by American soldiers after World War II and has since become enormously popular there. A decade after the war, there were a dozen Japanese teams playing in stadiums as big as those in Los Angeles and New York. On Saturday afternoons, Japanese fans rush to the ball park to hear the umpire call "Dao hai!"—"Play ball!" And Japanese players are national heroes who appear on TV in commercials for everything from motorcycles to tea.

__B__ Baseball

__T__ Baseball in Japan

__N__ Japanese baseball stadiums

(Continues on next page)

10-12. Would you take an airplane trip sitting in the thirteenth row of seats? Go to a doctor on the thirteenth floor of the medical center? Of all superstitions, few are as widely believed as the one saying the number thirteen is unlucky. So many people are uncomfortable with thirteen that the number is eliminated from most airline seating charts. Many high-rise apartment and office buildings have a twelfth floor and a fourteenth floor—but nothing in between. In France, houses are never numbered thirteen. And the national lottery in Italy doesn't use the number.

   _T_   The superstition about the number thirteen

   _N_   Buildings without a thirteenth floor

   _B_   Superstitions

C. 13-20. Each group of items below includes one topic, one main idea (topic sentence), and two supporting details. In the space provided, label each item with one of the following:

> _T_ —for the topic
> _MI_—for the main idea
> _SD_—for the supporting details

Group 1

   _SD_   The creakings of a house settling may sound like a monster coming out of a grave.

   _MI_   Nighttime noises can be frightening to children.

   _SD_   Gusts of wind rattling windows could sound like invaders about to come in.

   _T_   Noises at night.

Group 2

   _SD_   Some stations that once played rock-and-roll now play only "golden oldies."

   _T_   Radio programming.

   _MI_   To attract listeners, many radio stations have changed their programming.

   _SD_   Some former classical music stations now offer many hours of "talk radio."

MAIN IDEAS: Test 5

A. Each group of items below includes one topic, one main idea (topic sentence), and one supporting detail. In the space provided, label each item with one of the following:

> *T* —for the topic
> *MI*—for the main idea
> *SD*—for the supporting detail

Group 1

__SD__ 1. Calls to emergency 911 numbers are the basis for a popular TV show.

__MI__ 2. Today's culture often blurs the line between entertainment and reality.

__T__ 3. Entertainment and reality.

Group 2

__T__ 4. Childhood safety and the law.

__SD__ 5. Federal law requires "child-proof" caps on certain kinds of medication.

__MI__ 6. An increasing number of state and federal laws have been passed in the interests of children's safety.

B. Circle the letter of the correct topic of each of the following paragraphs. Then find the sentence in which the author states the main idea about that topic, and write that number in the space provided.

> [1]The effects of poverty upon physical health are many. [2]Poverty means inadequate nourishment and unsanitary, poorly heated housing. [3]It means postponing trips to the doctor to treat minor ailments until they become major ones. [4]Living in poverty may increase one's exposure to stress and violence. [5]Furthermore, the frustrations of poverty may lead to self-destructive behavior such as alcoholism, smoking, drug abuse, and other behaviors that weaken the body's natural resistance to disease.

7. The topic is
   a. poverty and self-destructive behaviors.
   (b.) poverty's effects upon health.
   c. poverty's effects.

8. The main idea is stated in sentence __1__.

(Continues on next page)

¹Poodles' fashionable appearance stems from their earlier role as tough hunting dogs. ²They were bred to serve as gun dogs for European hunters. ³The hunters clipped the poodles' thick coats so they could swim faster and run more quickly through underbrush. ⁴To provide the dogs with warmth, however, the hunters left long hair around their chests, ankles, and hips. ⁵Hunters tied different colored ribbons around the dogs' topknots to identify which dogs belonged to which man. ⁶As poodles became popular as pets, owners borrowed these hunters' practices to dress up their dogs.

9. The topic of the paragraph is
   a. poodles' ribbons.
   b. poodles' fashionable appearance.
   c. dogs and their roles.

10. The main idea is stated in sentence ___1___.

MAIN IDEAS: Test 6

A. Each group of items below includes one topic, one main idea (topic sentence), and one supporting detail. In the space provided, label each item with one of the following:

> *T* —for the topic
> *MI*—for the main idea
> *SD*—for the supporting detail

Group 1

___T___ 1. Older and newer homes.

___MI___ 2. Older houses have several advantages over newer ones.

___SD___ 3. Older houses have more one-of-a-kind features than newer ones, which all tend to look alike.

Group 2

___SD___ 4. The roads over the mountains were in terrible condition.

___T___ 5. Traveling westward in a covered wagon.

___MI___ 6. Traveling westward in a covered wagon was difficult and uncomfortable.

B. Circle the letter of the correct topic of each of the following paragraphs. Then find the sentence in which the author states the main idea about that topic, and write that number in the space provided.

> [1]Whether ruffled or ridged, potato chips all began because of a hard-to-please restaurant customer in 1853. [2]In that year, George Crum was working as a chef at an elegant resort in Saratoga Springs, New York. [3]He prepared thick-cut French-fried potatoes for diners there. [4]But one diner kept sending his potatoes back to the kitchen, complaining that they were too thick for his taste. [5]Crum cut the potatoes thinner and thinner and finally, very annoyed, made a serving of potatoes too thin and crisp to eat with a fork. [6]To his surprise, the guest loved them. [7]Other guests demanded a taste. [8]Soon "Saratoga Chips" were the most popular item on the menu.

7. The topic is
   a. ruffled potato chips.
   b. the origins of foods.
   (c.) potato chips.

8. The main idea is stated in sentence ___1___.

(Continues on next page)

[1]Violence is common in American families and is increased by stressful conditions. [2]The study of 2,143 couples showed that in any one year 1.8 million wives are beaten two or more times a year. [3]Child and wife abuse occurs in families of every financial status. [4]Research suggests, however, that it is most common among poorer families. [5]In part, the higher prevalence of violence in these households is caused by the more stressful situations that are present. [6]For instance, unemployment or part-time employment of males increases the incidence of violence. [7]Child abuse also happens more often in single-parent than in two-parent families.

9. The topic is
   a. violence in the American family.
   b. child abuse in single-parent households.
   c. violence in America.

10. The main idea is stated in sentence ___1___.

SUPPORTING DETAILS: Test 1

A. Each topic sentence below is followed by a list of three other sentences. Circle the letter of the one sentence that *does not* support the main idea.

1. Per ounce, chicken is a better buy than pork.
   - (a.) Both chicken and pork can be used in a wide variety of recipes.
   - b. While 100 grams of chicken meat contain about 150 calories, a like amount of pork contains 450 calories.
   - c. Chicken has double the protein of pork.

2. Through biofeedback, people have learned to control some activities of the body.
   - a. For example, they have learned to control muscle tension that may lead to headache pain.
   - b. People have even learned to control their heart rate and blood pressure through biofeedback.
   - (c.) A few people have learned to control their heart rate without biofeedback.

B. The main idea of each of the following paragraphs is boldfaced. Locate and write down the number of the one sentence in each paragraph that *does not* support the main idea. Read the entire paragraph before making your decision.

3. [1]**Diamonds are usually thought of as gems, but they have many more practical uses.** [2]Because of their hardness, they are used in metal working, stone-cutting, grinding, polishing and sharpening. [3]They are also used for phonograph needles and drill bits, including the kind used by dentists. [4]It is interesting to note that diamonds come in many colors, including black and pale blue.

   The sentence that does *not* support the main idea: ___4___

4. [1]**If you have trouble falling asleep at times, there are some simple precautions you can take.** [2]Avoid drinks with caffeine after about 6 or 7 p.m. [3]Caffeine can also be bad for those with stomach and heart problems. [4]Getting in the habit of going to bed at the same time every night will also help you fall asleep. [5]In addition, get a moderate amount of exercise regularly. [6]And finally, because alcohol interferes with sound sleep, don't drink any after dinner.

   The sentence that does *not* support the main idea: ___3___

(Continues on next page)

5.   [1]**Every twenty-four seconds in America, a major crime occurs.** [2]The most common crimes are rape (once every six seconds), burglary (once every eight seconds), and auto theft (once every thirty-nine seconds). [3]There is a murder once every twenty-three minutes. [4]Obviously, people who commit murder should get the death penalty.

The sentence that does *not* support the main idea: ___4___

SUPPORTING DETAILS: Test 2

A. Each topic sentence below is followed by a list of three other sentences. Circle the letter of the one sentence that *does not* support the main idea.

1. Dorothea Dix devoted her life to improving the care of the insane.
   a. She traveled to every state in the Union inspecting asylums.
   b. She reported after one trip that insane people in Massachusetts were being kept in cages, "chained, naked, beaten with rods, and lashed into obedience."
   c. Mentally ill people were punished in the belief that they could behave normally if they so chose.

2. There is good reason to believe that vitamin C can prevent colds, or at least make them less severe.
   a. Some scientists also believe that vitamin C can help prevent certain types of cancer.
   b. Studies have indicated that people who take vitamin C catch fewer colds per year than others.
   c. Similar studies show that the colds the vitamin C group catches last a shorter time than other people's colds.

B. The main idea of each of the following paragraphs is boldfaced. Locate and write down the number of the one sentence in each paragraph that *does not* support the main idea. Read the entire paragraph before making your decision.

3. [1]**Studies of facial expressions show that some emotions are experienced by all humans and are expressed by the same facial muscles.** [2]These emotions include anger, disgust, fear, joy, sadness, and surprise. [3]Animals do not seem to experience all of these emotions. [4]Other emotions scientists believe are common to all people and expressed in like ways are guilt and shame.

   The sentence that does *not* support the main idea: ___3___

(Continues on next page)

4. [1]**Our nation's high pregnancy rate among teenagers has many unpleasant results.** [2]Adolescent pregnancy increases the health risks of both the child and the mother. [3]But more and more, girls are less likely to give up their babies for adoption. [4]Infants born to adolescent mothers are more likely to have low birth weights, as well as childhood problems and illnesses. [5]Adolescent mothers often drop out of school, fail to gain employment, and become dependent on welfare. [6]And adolescent parents are more likely than those who delay childbearing to have low-paying, low-status jobs or to be unemployed.

    The sentence that does *not* support the main idea: _3_

5. [1]**Sara Josepha Hale, editor of the early women's magazine *Godey's Lady's Book*, is responsible for Americans celebrating the holiday of Thanksgiving.** [2]She was also the author of a novel, *Northwood*. [3]A native of New Hampshire, Mrs. Hale felt strongly that the anniversary of the first Thanksgiving meal shared by the Pilgrims and Indians should be observed as a national holiday. [4]Every fall Mrs. Hale would run editorials in her magazine, encouraging readers to support the idea of an annual Thanksgiving. [5]Finally, due to Mrs. Hale's efforts, Abraham Lincoln set aside the last Thursday of November as the official holiday.

    The sentence that does *not* support the main idea: _2_

SUPPORTING DETAILS: Test 3

Answer the questions that follow the paragraphs. The main idea of the first paragraph is boldfaced.

A. **¹The image of Superman was greatly influenced by his radio show.** ²Because he could not actually be seen flying, some now immortal lines were written: "Faster than a speeding bullet! More powerful than a locomotive! Able to leap tall buildings in a single bound! Look! Up in the sky! It's a bird! It's a plane! It's Superman!" ³In addition, it was because Superman was played by a real person that Kryptonite was invented. ⁴This happened because the actor who played Superman, Bud Collyer, wanted to go on vacation. ⁵Kryptonite's main quality was that it weakened Superman. ⁶By creating something that Superman had to avoid, the writers could keep him in a closet while the actor was gone. ⁷Only soft sounds from the closet were heard from Superman until the actor got back from vacation.

1. __*T*__ TRUE OR FALSE? Special lines were written for Superman's radio show to help listeners imagine his flying.

2. *Fill in the missing word:* Kryptonite _____*weakened*_____ Superman.

3. The answer to question 2 can be found in sentence
    a. 3.
    (b.) 5.
    c. 6.
    d. 7.

4. The writers invented Kryptonite to
    a. add some spice to their plots.
    b. make Superman less perfect.
    c. give Superman's enemies a new weapon.
    (d.) allow the actor who played Superman to take a vacation.

5. *Fill in the missing words:* When Bud Collyer was on vacation, Superman would be _____*in a closet*_____ during the entire show.

(Continues on next page)

B. [1]"If I take my hand out of my pocket, someone in the room might die." [2]This concern is an example of a delusion. [3]Delusions are beliefs that have no basis in reality but that are very strongly held by an individual. [4]A delusion is just one of several symptoms of many serious mental disorders. [5]For the delusional person, life can be very frightening. [6]Imagine honestly believing you have the power to kill by moving your hand—even by accident. [7]Fortunately, like many other symptoms of mental illnesses, delusions can often be reduced or eliminated through medication.

Implied main idea: There are several important general facts about delusions.

6. *Fill in the missing word:* Delusions are beliefs that are not grounded in
   _____reality_____ but that are strongly held by an individual.

7. The answer to question 6 can be found in sentence.
   a. 2.
   (b.) 3.
   c. 4.
   d. 7.

8. An example of a delusion is given in sentence
   (a.) 1.
   b. 3.
   c. 4.
   d. 5.

9. Delusions are one of several symptoms of
   a. fears.
   b. beliefs.
   (c.) mental disorders.
   d. depression.

10. ___F___ TRUE OR FALSE? Delusions cannot be influenced by medication.

SUPPORTING DETAILS: Test 4

A. The main idea of each of the following paragraphs is boldfaced. Locate and write down the number of the one sentence in each paragraph that *does not* support the main idea. Read the entire paragraph before making your decision.

1. **¹In recent years there has been a trend toward more time at work and less time for leisure.** ²One reason is the growing number of women who are working. ³Unfortunately, many women are paid less than men working at the same jobs. ⁴With both spouses on the job, there is less time for leisure. ⁵Another reason for the trend is the decline in jobs for laborers and the rise in jobs for office workers. ⁶While hours for laborers have either stayed the same or gone down, work hours for office workers have increased.

   The sentence that does *not* support the main idea: ___3___

2. **¹The disease of smallpox, which ravaged Europe during the 1600s, introduced an interesting fashion.** ²Fortunately, in 1796 a vaccine for smallpox was developed. ³The people who survived the dreaded disease usually carried facial scars, a reminder of their illness. ⁴To disguise their facial scars, women and men both took to wearing tiny black "beauty patches," cut in the shapes of stars, moons, and hearts. ⁵The patches were made of silk or velvet.

   The sentence that does *not* support the main idea: ___2___

3. **¹There are interesting stories behind the names of some products.** ²The naming of the first synthetic fiber at Du Pont is an example. ³One suggestion for the fiber was *klis—silk* spelled backwards. ⁴The product was finally named *nylon*, simply because it sounded good to the naming committee. ⁵Nylon is sometimes used to give strength to other fibers. ⁶Another interesting story involves lollipops, which were created in the early 1900s. ⁷They were named for one of the most famous race horses at the time—Lolly Pop.

   The sentence that does *not* support the main idea: ___5___

(Continues on next page)

B. Answer the questions that follow the paragraph.

> [1]Experts were doubtful when Wilhelm von Osten claimed his horse Hans understood math and language. [2]Zoologists and psychologists took turns asking Hans questions like "How much are three plus seven?" and "What's the square root of 81?" [3]Clever Hans answered by tapping his foot. [4]He was right 90 percent of the time, and the experts found no evidence of cheating. [5]But one day Hans was questioned by someone who didn't know the correct answers. [6]Hans's success rate then fell to 10 percent. [7]Clever Hans, it turned out, did not know math or language, but he did know how to read his questioner's unconscious body movements. [8]Changes in eyes, posture and breathing let Hans know when it was time to stop tapping.

Implied main idea: Experts learned how Clever Hans tapped out correct answers to math questions: he read the questioner's unconscious body movements.

4. According to the paragraph, Clever Hans's ability to understand and answer math questions was examined by
   a. a veterinarian.
   b. horse owners.
   (c.) zoologists and psychologists.
   d. students and teachers.

5. *Fill in the missing number:* At first Clever Hans seemed to be right ____90____ percent of the time.

6. The truth about Hans's ability was discovered when the horse was questioned by
   a. von Osten.
   b. a psychologist.
   c. a zoologist.
   (d.) someone who did not know the answers.

7. It turned out that Hans got clues on when to stop tapping from
   a. questions.
   b. zoologists and psychologists.
   (c.) unconscious body movements.
   d. von Osten.

8. The types of unconscious body movements that influenced Hans can be found in sentence
   a. 5.
   b. 6.
   c. 7.
   (d.) 8.

SUPPORTING DETAILS: Test 5

A. The main idea of each of the following paragraphs is boldfaced. Locate and write down the number of the one sentence in each paragraph that *does not* support the main idea. Read the entire paragraph before making your decision.

1. ¹**Stress is a big part of society's problems.** ²It is, of course, at the heart of many emotional problems. ³What many don't realize is that it is also a contributing factor to many physical problems. ⁴For instance, stress is often a contributor to cancer and heart disease, two leading causes of death. ⁵Exercise is a good method for reducing stress.

   The sentence that does *not* support the main idea: ___5___

2. ¹**The history of toasted bread goes back for thousands of years.** ²The ancient Egyptians toasted bread slices to keep them from getting moldy. ³For thousands of years, people toasted bread basically as the Egyptians had. ⁴They poked sharpened sticks and, later, long-handled forks into bread slices and held them over a fire. ⁵Next came the "toaster oven," which was a wire cage that held four pieces of bread over a coal stove. ⁶An electric toaster was finally developed by Westinghouse in 1910. ⁷Westinghouse has since developed many other household appliances. ⁸Finally in 1926 the Toastmaster, the first electric pop-up toaster, was introduced.

   The sentence that does *not* support the main idea: ___7___

3. ¹**Today, jurors are being asked to make decisions in areas they know little about.** ²One such area is medical malpractice, where the jury must decide if a doctor used correct methods in treating a patient. ³If a doctor is found guilty, the jury must then estimate in dollars what the injured person should get for, say, the loss of a leg. ⁴The increase in malpractice suits has forced doctors to buy a great deal of malpractice insurance. ⁵Another difficult area for jurors is that of libel cases. ⁶In these cases, juries must decide complex legal issues, such as what "truth" is.

   The sentence that does *not* support the main idea: ___4___

(Continues on next page)

B. Answer the questions that follow the paragraph.

> ¹Family therapy may be helpful in certain situations. ²When there are problems between various family members, family therapy should certainly be considered. ³It should also be considered when an individual's therapy is slowed by the family, or when a family member is not adjusting well to the improvement of the person in therapy. ⁴Not all families, however, will benefit from such therapy. ⁵Family members, for example, may not be willing to cooperate, and without them, meeting as a family may be fruitless. ⁶Or one family member may take so much of a session's time that therapy as a family cannot succeed. ⁷In such cases, other types of therapy may be more useful.

Implied main idea: Family therapy may be helpful in certain, but not all situations.

4. Family therapy may be helpful when
    a. problems exist between family members.
    b. an individual's therapy is being slowed by the family.
    c. a family member is adjusting poorly to the improvement of a person in therapy.
    (d.) all of the above.

5. __F__ TRUE OR FALSE? Family therapy should always take place, even when an important family member refuses to cooperate.

6. __F__ TRUE OR FALSE? Where family therapy will not succeed, no other form of therapy will help.

7. The answer to question 6 can be found in sentence
    a. 2.
    b. 4.
    c. 5.
    (d.) 7.

8. __F__ TRUE OR FALSE? The paragraph answers this question: Which therapies should be considered when family therapy won't work?

SUPPORTING DETAILS: Test 6

A. The main idea of each of the following paragraphs is boldfaced. Locate and write down the number of the one sentence in each paragraph that *does not* support the main idea. Read the entire paragraph before making your decision.

1. ¹Vaseline is widely used today as a treatment for chapped skin or minor burns. ²**But Vaseline has had a wide range of uses throughout its history.** ³Fishermen have gobbed it onto their hooks to attract trout. ⁴Stage actresses once smeared it on their cheeks to simulate tears. ⁵Beauty contestants coat their teeth with Vaseline so their lips won't stick during a nervous dry-mouthed moment. ⁶Natives of the Amazon have cooked with it, eaten it on bread, and exchanged jars of it as money. ⁷Vaseline was actually developed by a chemist looking for a new petroleum fuel.

   The sentence that does *not* support the main idea: ___7___

2. ¹**"Buy American—Buy Honda" is not as contradictory as it may seem.** ²Although Honda Motor Company is the third largest automobile manufacturer in Japan, it is also the fourth largest manufacturer of American-made cars. ³In its central Ohio plants, Honda employs thousands of American workers. ⁴And there has rarely been a time when jobs were needed more. ⁵The Ohio-made cars are not only sold in America; they are an American export, shipped world-wide—even to Japan.

   The sentence that does *not* support the main idea: ___4___

3. ¹**Immigrant populations have often presented American schools with special language problems.** ²Today the problem centers mostly on the Spanish-speaking population. ³We have more than fourteen million citizens of Hispanic origin. ⁴That group includes many children who have grown up in homes where only Spanish is spoken. ⁵These children often face serious difficulties once they enter English-speaking schools. ⁶Earlier generations of children from homes where only Italian or Polish or Yiddish was spoken faced similar problems. ⁷English-speaking children would have the same problems if they moved to a foreign country.

   The sentence that does *not* support the main idea: ___6___

(Continues on next page)

B. Answer the questions that follow the paragraph. The main idea is boldfaced.

> ¹**Although water itself has no nutritional value, it is an essential part of our diet.** ²A major reason that water is essential is that it transports nutrients to the cells of our body. ³It also removes waste products from cells. ⁴In addition, water aids in food digestion and regulates the body's temperature. ⁵It cushions vital organs and lubricates the joints. ⁶The cells of our body are partially made up of water. ⁷In fact, our body weight consists of between 60 and 80 percent water. ⁸While the body can survive long periods without food, it can exist for only a few days without water.

4. Water is important to the body's cells because
   a. it removes waste matter from cells.
   b. the cells are partially made of water.
   c. it brings nutrients to the cells.
   (d.) of all of the above.

5. __F__ TRUE OR FALSE? Because the human body stores so much water, it can exist for longer periods without water than it can without food.

6. The answer to question 5 can be found in sentence
   a. 5.
   b. 6.
   c. 7.
   (d.) 8.

7. __F__ TRUE OR FALSE? Water itself contains essential nutrients needed by the body.

8. *Fill in the blank:* As much as _____80_____ percent of our body weight consists of water.

LOCATIONS OF MAIN IDEAS: Test 1

The five paragraphs that follow are on the first level of difficulty. Write the number of each topic sentence in the space provided.

1. ¹They're creepy-crawly, and many people don't like to touch them. ²Nevertheless, earthworms are very helpful creatures. ³People who like to fish, of course, know that worms make great bait. ⁴They also help improve the condition of the soil. ⁵As they dig under the ground, earthworms constantly take soil into their bodies. ⁶Their bodies use part of the soil and pass out the rest in the form of fine powder. ⁷That powder, called cast, makes the earth richer. ⁸In addition, the tunnels that worms create make the earth better able to absorb water and air.

    Topic sentence: _____2_____

2. ¹Unattractive views can be improved inexpensively. ²One way is to block the view with a handmade Japanese-style screen. ³Such a screen can be made by covering a wooden frame with rice paper. ⁴An unpleasant view can also be disguised by attaching a flower box to the window sill. ⁵As the flowers grow, they help to catch the eye and block the view. ⁶Or an inexpensive, plain shade can be painted with a cheerful scene. ⁷An ugly view can even be totally eliminated by painting a window with a stained-glass design.

    Topic sentence: _____1_____

3. ¹When the Social Security system was founded in 1936, most women did not work outside the home. ²They married and raised children, and very few of them got divorced. ³Clearly, women's lives have changed greatly during the life of the Social Security system. ⁴Fifty years after the system was founded, almost half of all married women were working outside of the home, and divorce had become relatively common.

    Topic sentence: _____3_____

4. ¹Don't laugh at Mom's advice to eat your chicken soup. ²Soup is actually good for you. ³First of all, it can help you lose and maintain weight. ⁴Since you can't eat soup on the run, it forces you to eat slowly. ⁵And slow eating usually means a lower calorie intake. ⁶Soup can also help you feel better when you've got a cold or bronchitis. ⁷Hot chicken soup, especially if it's spiced with pepper or garlic, helps to break up the congestion in your throat and chest. ⁸As a result, you can breathe more easily.

    Topic sentence: _____2_____

(Continues on next page)

5.   [1]When English settlers landed in America, they brought tomatoes along only as decorative plants. [2]They believed tomatoes were poisonous. [3]Traveling peddlers, however, eventually learned the truth about tomatoes from foreign visitors, and they spread the word among housewives along their routes. [4]By 1835, a farmer's almanac declared the tomato a useful garden plant, and it found acceptance on most American tables. [5]Thus, the tomato, so familiar to Americans now, is a relatively recent addition to the American diet.

Topic sentence: _____5_____

LOCATIONS OF MAIN IDEAS: Test 2

The five paragraphs that follow are on the first level of difficulty. Write the number of each topic sentence in the space provided.

1. ¹When you find yourself with more on your schedule than you can do in one day, the 4-D approach can help you get your chores under control. ²First, suggests one time-management expert, consider whether a job really needs to be done at all; if not, Drop it. ³If it must be done but can wait until tomorrow, Delay it. ⁴If you can't delay it, think about whether someone else might be able to do it just as well as you, and, if possible, Delegate it. ⁵If you have no other choice, then go ahead and Do the chore.

    Topic sentence: _____1_____

2. ¹A dolphin once played with people for a year off the coast of New Zealand. ²It was said that she even allowed some adults and children to ride on her back. ³There are many such stories about intelligent and caring dolphin behavior. ⁴Another example is the time three dolphins protected a woman from sharks after her boat had exploded. ⁵They stayed with her for over two hundred miles, until she was safe.

    Topic sentence: _____3_____

3. ¹Preventing, not treating, mental health problems is the goal of an increasing number of social programs. ²By teaching teenagers to resist peer pressure, for example, one program helped them avoid serious problems with drinking and drugs. ³In another program, nurses taught poor, young, pregnant women good child care. ⁴These young mothers then gave better care to their babies than mothers who were not taught good child care.

    Topic sentence: _____1_____

4. ¹One way poor spellers can improve their spelling is to keep a list of words they are constantly looking up in the dictionary. ²They can review and test themselves on a few of these words each day. ³Breaking up a word into its parts also makes spelling a less forbidding task. ⁴Third, learning little verbal tricks is helpful. ⁵One such trick is "There's *a rat* in *separate*." ⁶Another is "*Iron* is found in the *environment*." ⁷Using these methods, poor spellers can become reliable spellers.

    Topic sentence: _____7_____

(Continues on next page)

5.   [1]Seeing Eye dogs, those four-legged assistants to the blind, are a common sight in most cities. [2]Now there are dog-helpers called Hearing Ear dogs, trained especially for deaf people. [3]Hearing Ear dogs "tell" their owners when their doorbell or telephone rings. [4]They lead their human master to a crying child. [5]When a smoke alarm goes off, the Hearing Ear dog lets its owner know. [6]The highly trained Hearing Ear dogs are even trained to go "off duty" when there are hearing people around who can take over their job.

Topic sentence: _____2_____

LOCATIONS OF MAIN IDEAS: Test 3

The five paragraphs that follow are on the second level of difficulty. Write the number of each topic sentence in the space provided. Fill in two numbers in the one case where the main idea appears twice.

1. [1]In business meetings with Japanese, laughter may be confusing to Americans. [2]The Americans may think it is a sign of good feeling, but the Japanese tend to laugh if they are embarrassed or uneasy. [3]Americans may also misread Japanese bargaining. [4]The Japanese tend to propose prices close to what they expect to pay; Americans prefer to leave plenty of room for compromise. [5]Thus because of cultural differences, Americans can easily misunderstand business meetings with the Japanese.

    Topic sentence(s): _____5_____

2. [1]Rodents are rightly famous for multiplying quickly. [2]The common vole is a good example. [3]The female of the species is sexually mature and will mate when she is but twelve days old. [4]But the animal that best illustrates rodents' ability to multiply is the tiny female meadow mouse. [5]This most fruitful of all mammals can produce up to seventeen batches of young each year. [6]And each litter can include as many as thirteen offspring.

    Topic sentence(s): _____1_____

3. [1]We believe one man's story because he has an "honest face," but mistrust another's, seeing he has "shifty eyes." [2]It's a fact that a liar's body and voice give clues that he is not telling the truth. [3]When people are lying, they tend to speak in a higher voice than usual. [4]They stumble over their words, saying "uh" and "er" a lot. [5]People smile less when they are lying. [6]When they do smile, the smile tends to look forced. [7]Many people, when they lie, don't use their hands much. [8]They keep them still or out of sight. [9]And yes, "shifty" eyes can indicate a person is lying. [10]Someone telling a lie tends to look away from the person he is speaking to.

    Topic sentence(s): _____2_____

(Continues on next page)

4.   ¹The conditions of work for slaughterhouse employees are unsatisfactory. ²No other workers in the country have a higher rate of injury or illness than they do. ³While one out of ten manufacturing workers has job-related accidents or illnesses each year, the figure for slaughterhouse workers is one out of three. ⁴The turnover rate among slaughterhouse employees is enormously high, indicating great job dissatisfaction. ⁵It is not uncommon for plants in this industry to have annual turnover rates between 60 and 100 percent. ⁶Clearly, slaughterhouse workers find their working conditions troublesome.

Topic sentence(s): _____1, 6_____

5.   ¹No one likes a bully. ²So if your child has been terrorizing other children, you'll be glad to know you can redirect that anti-social behavior in several ways. ³Bullies need a physical outlet for their aggressive feelings. ⁴Encourage the child to join a sports team or do regular physical exercise. ⁵Also, reward the bully for cooperative social behavior, even if you have to arrange a situation where he or she can be pleasant with others. ⁶Point out those good qualities the bully does have, and remind him that those very qualities can get him the attention he so much wants. ⁷Finally, help the bully find a positive role model. ⁸Children often behave like their parents in social situations. ⁹So clean up your own act if you yourself use aggression to accomplish goals.

Topic sentence(s): _____2_____

LOCATIONS OF MAIN IDEAS: Test 4

The five paragraphs that follow are on the second level of difficulty. Write the number of each topic sentence in the space provided. Fill in two numbers in the one case where the main idea appears twice.

1. ¹Sometimes what at first looks like a good investment turns out badly. ²For example, in 1948 NBC was looking for a sure-fire way to establish its new television network as a success. ³They turned to Milton Berle, then a top vaudeville and nightclub entertainer. ⁴To ensure that Berle wouldn't be stolen away by another network, they offered him a thirty-three-year contract. ⁵For several years things worked out well. ⁶Berle became known as "Mr. Television" and gave NBC high ratings. ⁷After eight years, however, audiences tired of Berle, and his show was taken off the air. ⁸NBC was stuck paying Berle full salary for the next twenty-five years of his "retirement."

    Topic sentence(s): _____1_____

2. ¹Everyone knows that women cry more often and more easily than men do. ²Women's more frequent crying actually has a physical basis. ³Scientists have discovered that the hormone prolactin, which stimulates the production of mother's milk, also stimulates the production of tears. ⁴And women have 60 percent more prolactin in their blood than men do.

    Topic sentence(s): _____2_____

3. ¹Some dramatic ads have used musical messages powered by a hidden microchip. ²Musical microchip magazine ads, however, have had their drawbacks. ³One problem is that mail carriers can set a musical ad off just by putting a magazine in a mailbox. ⁴Also, although opening the magazine starts the music automatically, many readers have no idea how to turn it off. ⁵One recent Christmas, several copies of the same magazine were found in the incinerator of a New York apartment building, all playing "Jingle Bells."

    Topic sentence(s): _____2_____

(Continues on next page)

4. [1]Streetcars changed the character of city life. [2]Before their introduction, urban communities were limited by the distances people could conveniently walk to work. [3]The "walking city" could not easily extend more than two and a half miles from its center. [4]Streetcars increased this radius to six miles or more. [5]As a result, the area of the city expanded enormously. [6]Dramatic population shifts resulted as the better-off moved away from the center of the city. [7]In search of air and space, they abandoned the crumbling, jam-packed older neighborhoods to the poor. [8]Such economic segregation speeded the growth of ghettos. [9]Overall, it is difficult to overestimate the impact the streetcar system had on the typical American city.

    Topic sentence(s): ____*1, 9*____

5. [1]Parents are often prepared for a new child through childbirth classes and baby-care books. [2]But older brothers and sisters have gotten no such preparation. [3]Now, however, hospitals around the country are trying to help the siblings of new babies. [4]At Cedars-Sinai Medical Center in Los Angeles, brothers and sisters are given a lesson in baby care and a tour of the maternity floor. [5]At New York's Roosevelt Hospital, they can get two-hour sessions with films, books and toys. [6]And at Pacific Presbyterian Medical Center in San Francisco, siblings actually get to "deliver" a baby doll.

    Topic sentence(s): ____*3*____

LOCATIONS OF MAIN IDEAS: Test 5

The five paragraphs that follow are on the third level of difficulty. Write the number of each topic sentence in the space provided. Fill in two numbers in the one case where the main idea appears twice.

1. [1]Using elements at hand rather than made-to-order materials can often work wonders in emergencies. [2]One below-freezing, blustery night, Morris Berwick of Kansas was awakened by the sound of his aluminum awning banging against the sides of his mobile home. [3]The awning had been pried loose by the heavy winds. [4]To fix it, he took a bath towel, soaked it in water, then ran outside and threw the towel against the break. [5]The towel froze solid. [6]"Fiberglass and resin could not have made a better patch," he says. [7]"Two weeks later, when the temperature rose above freezing, the patch fell off. [8]I then made a permanent repair."

    Topic sentence(s): _____1_____

2. [1]The custom of the wedding ring has its roots in the older tradition of property owners using signet rings to conduct business. [2]Signet rings were rings bearing a male landowner's personal seal. [3]The man would use the ring to put his "stamp of approval" on business papers. [4]When a man gave his signet ring to his wife, it was a symbol of his trust in her. [5]With the ring, she was able to give commands and conduct business in his name. [6]When a couple exchanges wedding rings today, therefore, they are symbolically giving one another authority over their property.

    Topic sentence(s): _____1, 6_____

3. [1]At age 42, he was by far the youngest president in the nation's history up to that time. [2]But Theodore Roosevelt brought solid qualifications to the president's office. [3]Son of a well-to-do New York merchant of Dutch ancestry, he had graduated from Harvard in 1880 and studied law briefly at Columbia. [4]His political experience included three terms in the New York assembly and six years on the United States Civil Service Commission. [5]He had been Assistant Secretary of the Navy. [6]He had served a term as governor of New York. [7]In addition, he had spent time as a rancher in Dakota Territory and a soldier in the Spanish-American War. [8]Roosevelt was also a well-known historian.

    Topic sentence(s): _____2_____

(Continues on next page)

4.   [1]Half of all the plant and animal species in the world live in rain forests. [2]Many of the medicinal drugs used in the United States contain ingredients that originate in rain forests. [3]For instance, 73 percent of the three thousand plants identified as having cancer-fighting properties come from the world's rain forests. [4]Rain forests also help regulate the flow of water on Earth. [5]They soak up the water from heavy tropical rains like enormous sponges. [6]They then release the water slowly, providing a supply for people living hundreds and even thousands of miles away. [7]For all these reasons, it is essential that nations around the world work together to protect the rain forests.

Topic sentence(s): _____7_____

5.   [1]The smiling pumpkin face in your window may strike you as one of the more cheerful Halloween symbols. [2]The term "jack-o'-lantern," however, has a chilling story behind it. [3]According to Irish folklore, there was a young boy named Jack who tried to best the Devil in a game of wits. [4]The Devil, a bad sport, did not take kindly to this. [5]Summoning all his evil power, he condemned the lad to wandering the Earth for all eternity. [6]However, the Devil, in an uncharacteristically charitable act, provided little Jack with something to light his way. [7]Since they didn't have flashlights in days of yore, the Devil gave Jack—you guessed it—a lantern.

Topic sentence(s): _____2_____

LOCATIONS OF MAIN IDEAS: Test 6

The five paragraphs that follow are on the third level of difficulty. Write the number of each topic sentence in the space provided. Fill in two numbers in the one case where the main idea appears twice.

1.   ¹Gestures in sign language may appear to be unrelated to their meanings. ²However, some of the gestures in American sign language are strongly based on their origins. ³For example, the sign for *boy* is made by holding the right hand at the forehead and opening and closing it twice. ⁴This represents the boy tipping his hat and is based on the fact that at one time, most boys tipped their caps when they met an adult. ⁵The sign for *gentleman* combines the signs for *boy* and *polite*; the latter is made by pushing the thumb of the open hand onto the center of the chest. ⁶This sign originally referred to the ruffle on a man's shirt.

Topic sentence(s): _____2_____

2.   ¹According to studies, higher-status people tend to have more impact on others' actions. ²Researchers demonstrated the effect of status by having a poorly dressed man violate the "wait" signal at street corners in Austin, Texas. ³His action triggered little jaywalking from other pedestrians. ⁴Then the same man dressed like a bank president. ⁵After his change in wardrobe, his going against the "wait" prompted many more pedestrians to jaywalk with him. ⁶A separate experiment in Sydney, Australia, had similar results. ⁷Sydney pedestrians were more cooperative when approached by a well-dressed survey taker than one poorly dressed. ⁸A person's apparent status seems to greatly influence others' reaction to him.

Topic sentence(s): _____1, 8_____

3.   ¹Some people assume that primitive societies are mentally backward. ²In fact, primitive people have found ways to control their environment in sophisticated and clever ways. ³Among some Eskimo groups, for example, wolves are sometimes a menace. ⁴They could be hunted down and killed, but this practice involves danger as well as time and energy. ⁵So a simple yet clever device is used. ⁶A sharp sliver of bone is curled into a springlike shape, and seal blubber is molded around it and allowed to freeze. ⁷This is placed where a wolf will discover it and "wolf it down." ⁸Later, the bone uncurls in the wolf's stomach, and its sharp ends cause internal bleeding and death.

Topic sentence(s): _____2_____

(Continues on next page)

4.   [1]One man robs a gas station of $250 and is sent to prison for six months. [2]Another man makes $2.5 million on illegal stock trades and is required only to return the money (plus "interest" in the form of fines). [3]Terrorists plant a bomb in a diplomat's car. [4]When caught, they are charged with conspiracy and criminal homicide. [5]Ford Motor Company sold millions of Pintos, even though its own tests had shown that the rear-mounted gas tank might explode if the car were hit from the back. [6]Over the next eight years, five hundred people were burned to death in accidents involving Pintos. [7]Ford paid millions of dollars in damages, but was found innocent of criminal charges. [8]No one went to jail. [9]As these cases suggest, the social response to corporate and white-collar crime is quite different from the treatment of "common criminals."

Topic sentence(s): _____9_____

5.   [1]The !Kung tribe of southern Africa and the Yanomamo Indians of South America have opposite attitudes towards violence and aggression. [2]The !Kung are known as "the harmless people"; their lives are almost untouched by fighting. [3]The Yanomamo, on the other hand, are called "the fierce people"; for them, violence is a way of life. [4]Women of the !Kung are treated as equals by the men of the tribe. [5]Yanomamo men, however, are often abusive to the women of the tribe. [6]The children of the Yanomamo are taught to resolve their differences by fighting. [7]Yanomamo boys learn that to be men, they must learn to cheat, bully, and kill. [8]Among the !Kung, however, children are taught that problems can be solved without violence.

Topic sentence(s): _____1_____

IMPLIED MAIN IDEAS: Test 1

A. Circle the letter of the general idea that best covers the specific ideas. Remember that the correct general idea will not be too narrow or too broad. It will describe what the specific ideas have in common.

1. *Specific Ideas:* Easter, Thanksgiving, Valentine's Day, New Year's Day

   The general idea is
   a. days.
   b. holidays.
   c. religious holidays.

2. *Specific ideas:* rummy, bridge, hearts, poker

   The general idea is
   a. games.
   b. children's games.
   c. card games.

3. *Specific ideas:* "Yes"; "No"; "Maybe"; "Maybe later."

   The general idea is
   a. words.
   b. answers.
   c. answers to test questions.

4. *Specific ideas:* sneakers, sandals, high heels, loafers

   The general idea is
   a. shoes.
   b. dressy shoes.
   c. men's shoes.

5. *Specific ideas:* OPEN, STOP, FIRE EXIT, YIELD

   The general idea is
   a. words.
   b. words on signs.
   c. words on traffic signs.

6. *Specific ideas:* leaking toilet, no hot water, broken window, roaches

   The general idea is
   a. living problems.
   b. kitchen problems.
   c. apartment problems.

(Continues on next page)

B. (7-8.) Each group below is made up of four sentences with an unstated main idea. Circle the letter of the answer that best states the implied main idea of each group.

Group 1

1. One reason for a growing need for day care is that single-parent households continue to increase.
2. The rise of the divorce rate has contributed to the number of single-parent households.
3. Families with two working parents also need day care.
4. More than half of all mothers now work outside of the home.

Which sentence best expresses the unstated main idea of these sentences?
a. The divorce rate has grown.
b. The number of single-parent households continues to increase.
c. There is a great need for quality day care.
d. Most mothers work outside the home.

Group 2

1. Children sometimes imitate the violent acts they see in cartoons.
2. Extreme acts of violence, such as murder and rape, are common on television.
3. Television viewers may become less sensitive to violence.
4. Lawbreakers sometimes get ideas for crimes from television shows.

The unstated main idea of these sentences is:
a. Cartoons can be bad for children.
b. Television may be contributing to the aggression and violence in society.
c. Television can make viewers less concerned about violence in real life.
d. It is not unusual for television to portray violent acts such as murder and rape.

IMPLIED MAIN IDEAS: Test 2

A. In the following items, the specific ideas are given but the general ideas are unstated. Fill in the blanks with the unstated general ideas.

1. *General idea:* _elected officials_

   Specific ideas: president   mayor
                    governor   council person

2. *General idea:* _team sports_

   Specific ideas: football   baseball
                    basketball   hockey

3. *General idea:* _schools_

   Specific ideas: elementary   junior high
                    nursery   college

4. *General idea:* _games_

   Specific ideas: chess   Chinese checkers
                    Monopoly   dominoes

5. *General idea:* _workers_

   Specific ideas: salesperson   welder
                    hair stylist   insurance agent

6. *General idea:* _wedding preparations_

   Specific ideas: order the invitations   get the tuxedos
                    get the bride's gown   find a photographer

7. *General idea:* _round objects_

   Specific ideas: globe   orange
                    hula hoop   baseball

8. *General idea:* _definitions_

   Specific ideas: *Exploit* means "take advantage of."
                    Patron means "a regular customer."
                    Obstinate means "stubborn."
                    Recipient means "one that receives."

(Continues on next page)

B. Circle the letter of the implied main idea in each of the following two paragraphs.

9. Kentucky Fried Chicken planned to open one hundred stores in Brazil. But it ignored the fact that most Brazilians prefer charcoal-broiled chicken, which is sold on almost every street corner there. Now there are only two Kentucky Fried Chicken stores in Brazil. Similarly, the Singer Company planned to use a certain bright blue in an ad to sell their sewing machines in Hong Kong. The company learned in time that this shade of blue is known there as the death color.

Which sentence best expresses the unstated main idea of the paragraph?
a. Kentucky Fried Chicken's plans for Brazil failed.
b. If companies don't understand other cultures, they may not succeed there.
c. Most Brazilians prefer charcoal-broiled chicken to fried chicken.
d. In Hong Kong, a certain bright blue is associated with death.

10. Many of the "witches" executed in Salem, Massachusetts, in the 1690s were actually mentally ill. Their odd behavior made people believe they were in league with the Devil. In other times and places, mentally ill people have been punished. Often they were beaten or chained up. It was thought that their illness was the result of an evil nature or lack of willpower. Only recently have people accepted the idea that mental illness can be a medical problem.

The unstated main idea is:
a. Mentally ill people were once thought to be witches and were thus executed for being in league with the Devil.
b. Mental illness has become more common since the 1690s.
c. The mentally ill have always been treated badly.
d. Throughout history, there have been different views about the nature of mental illness.

IMPLIED MAIN IDEAS: Test 3

Circle the letter of the implied main idea in each of the following five paragraphs.

1. Some workers skip breakfast and try to make up for it by eating a big lunch. Studies show that workers who do this lose as much efficiency at work as people who've missed a whole night's sleep. Workers who eat a high-protein breakfast and a light lunch, on the other hand, tend to be energetic and efficient throughout the day. A separate study proved that teens who eat breakfast do far better in school than their classmates who don't.

    The unstated main idea is:
    a. Eating breakfast increases one's efficiency throughout the day.
    b. Skipping lunch probably does *not* make one less efficient.
    c. Teens who want to do well in school should eat a good breakfast.
    d. A glass of milk, whole wheat bread, and cheese make for a good breakfast.

2. A famous but unsuccessful television commercial for panty hose began by showing a pair of shapely legs. The camera then panned up the legs slowly. Finally the model's entire body and face were revealed. It was Joe Namath, the famous football quarterback. Marketing research measured the percentage of people who remembered seeing the commercial. That percentage was extremely high. But few people could remember the brand of panty hose it advertised.

    The unstated main idea is:
    a. Joe Namath was once used as a model in a panty hose commercial.
    b. A panty hose ad surprised viewers by revealing that a pair of shapely legs belonged to football player Joe Namath.
    c. An ad can be famous and yet unsuccessful in making people remember the product.
    d. It is difficult to design successful ads for certain products.

3. Outsiders applauded Ronald Reagan's "hands-off" management as exactly what the nation needed after Jimmy Carter. They criticized Carter as too busy with details to inspire or lead. Reagan seemed to set a clear tone and direction. He let his advisers take care of the details. On the other hand, some cabinet officials, including Donald Regan, were worried. They found the new president remarkably ignorant about important matters of policy. Worse, he seemed uninterested in learning more. "The Presidential mind was not cluttered with facts," Regan complained.

(Continues on next page)

The unstated main idea is:

a. Ronald Reagan was by far a better president than Jimmy Carter.

b. People inside and outside the administration had differing views of President Reagan.

c. People outside Reagan's administration felt that he set a clear tone and direction.

d. Officials of Ronald Reagan's cabinet found him to be remarkably ignorant about important matters of policy.

4. Acupressure is a form of ancient Chinese therapy. When you are feeling nervous, try pressing your thumb a hand's width below your collarbone on the right side of your chest. Vibrate your thumb slowly as you press, then rotate your thumb clockwise. You'll be pressing an acupressure point that is supposed to produce calmness. For an aching eye, press the acupressure point at the inside corner of the other eye. To relieve a headache, press your thumb deeply into the fleshy part of the hand beneath your other thumb.

The unstated main idea is:

a. Acupressure can calm you down.

b. The Chinese have developed various useful physical therapies.

c. Acupressure can help you relieve various discomforts.

d. Acupressure is the best ways to relieve various discomforts.

5. Traditionally, situation comedies had been lighthearted and avoided controversy. Then in 1971, producer Norman Lear introduced *All in the Family*. Archie Bunker exploded into prime time. Filled with fears and prejudices, Archie treated his simple-minded, sweet wife like a doormat. He struggled to understand his mildly rebellious daughter. He shouted endless insults at his Polish-American son-in-law. Minority groups, nonconformists, bosses, and liberals all offended him.

The unstated main idea is:

a. *All in the Family* is still the best American situation comedy.

b. Norman Lear is a major figure in American popular culture.

c. Norman Lear has brought America several worthwhile series.

d. *All in the Family* differed from the traditional uncontroversial approach to situation comedy.

IMPLIED MAIN IDEAS: Test 4

A. Circle the letter of the implied main idea in each of the following paragraphs.

1. Women who are poorly nourished before or during pregnancy are at risk for complications during pregnancy and delivery. They are more likely to bear low-birthweight babies or stillborn babies. Their babies are more likely to die soon after birth. The same is true for women who gain too much weight during pregnancy, or who were obese when they became pregnant. Their babies, too, run a greater risk of medical problems.

    The unstated main idea is:
    a. The babies of poorly nourished women are more likely to die soon after birth.
    b. A woman's diet and weight affect her and her baby's health during and after pregnancy.
    c. Pregnant women tend to be poorly nourished or overweight before and during pregnancy.
    d. Obesity is the cause of various medical problems for women and their children.

2. In Indonesia, farmers have taken much land once lived on by elephants. So in order to find food, the elephants have invaded farms. In addition, oil company blasts and helicopters have scared elephants into rioting. Homes, farms, and even lives have been lost. As it is illegal to kill elephants there, another solution had to be found. Thus a reform school for elephants was created. Wild elephants are captured and brought there. Then they are prepared for careers in either entertainment, logging, or farming.

    The unstated main idea is:
    a. Much former elephant territory in Indonesia is now farmland.
    b. Elephants have become dangerous in Indonesia, so a school has been started to make them tame and useful.
    c. Although elephants are dangerous in Indonesia, it is illegal to kill them.
    d. A reform school for elephants has been started.

3. Thomas H. Holmes, a psychiatrist, developed a scale to rate the amount of stress brought on by what he calls Life-Changing Units (LCUs). Some LCUs are obviously negative. They include the death of a spouse (rated at 100 points) or a jail term (63 points). Others may be positive: pregnancy (40 points) or an increase of responsibility at work (29 points). Holmes interviewed more than five thousand hospital patients as part of his study. He

(Continues on next page)

found that half the people who had scored between 150 and 300 LCUs in a year had become ill. About 70 percent of those scoring more than 300 LCUs in a year had gotten sick.

The unstated main idea is:
a. According to a psychiatrist's study, the stress of life-changing events tends to make people sick.
b. Life-changing events can be both positive and negative.
c. For his study, Holmes interviewed more than five thousand hospital patients.
d. According to psychiatrist Thomas H. Holmes, even positive life-changing units cause stress.

B. Write out the unstated main idea in each of the following two paragraphs. A hint will help you figure out the implied main idea of one of the passages. (When scoring, don't count your answers to the hint.)

4. One way to lower fat in your diet is to eliminate meats with marbling. Also, eat more low-fat dairy products, including skim milk and low-fat yogurt. In addition, remember to eat poultry without the skin, which has a lot of fat in it. Finally, look for fat-free or low-fat desserts, or read ingredients labels carefully to see exactly how much fat is part of a certain food item.

The unstated main idea of this paragraph is: _____
_____*There are a few ways to lower the amount of fat in your diet.*_____

5. Returning Vietnam veterans came home with many physical injuries. Many lost limbs or suffered other types of permanent harm, such as hearing damage. These vets have also had many psychological problems. They have suffered from alcoholism, depression, recurring nightmares, and unemployment.

The unstated main idea of this paragraph is: _____
*Vietnam veterans came home with both physical and psychological problems.*

Hint: The author's primary point is that Vietnam veterans have had great
_____*physical*_____ and _____*psychological*_____ problems.

IMPLIED MAIN IDEAS: Test 5

Write out the unstated main idea in each of the following five paragraphs. Occasional hints will help you figure out the implied main idea.

1. One good way to fight stress is to exercise regularly. Exercise releases tensions physically rather than letting them build up inside. Another good method is to use a relaxation technique. It is possible to learn about such methods through classes, audiocassettes, and books. Talking about problems is yet another way to fight stress. If people can't get their feelings off their chests with a friend, they might try to speak to a professional, such as a member of the clergy or a therapist.

   The unstated main idea of this paragraph is: _____
   There are several ways to fight stress.

2. Owning a pet can make a person feel less lonely in life and more connected to the world in general. Another advantage of pet ownership has been described by the National Heart Assocation. Studies show that stroking an animal can lower the blood pressure and slow the heart rate. They also indicate that pet owners are more likely to survive during the first year after a heart attack than people who don't own pets. The elderly also benefit from pet ownership. Older people who own dogs are more likely to get daily exercise than those who don't. And feeding a pet encourages older people to pay more attention to their own diets.

   The unstated main idea of this paragraph is: _____
   Owning a pet has a number of advantages.

   Hint: The topic of this paragraph is owning a pet. What is the author's chief point *about* owning a pet?

3. There is a great deal of salt hidden in the hot dogs, luncheon meats, and dairy products that people eat. And many people do not know that canned products also contain high salt levels. Additionally, snack foods like potato chips, nuts, and pretzels have a surprisingly high salt content. It is not commonly recognized that ketchup, mustard, and salad dressings are also loaded with salt. And MSG, bouillon, soy sauce, and even meat tenderizers are saltier than most people would think.

   The unstated main idea of this paragraph is: _____
   There is a great deal of hidden salt in foods that we eat.

(Continues on next page)

4. Does humor like that on *Sesame Street* interfere with children's learning? To answer that question, a researcher showed educational tapes to four groups of young children. Two groups saw educational programs that included funny parts. Two other groups saw educational programs in which silent, blank screens replaced the funny parts. The children who saw the funny parts answered questions on the material much better than the other children.

The unstated main idea of this paragraph is: _____

One researcher has found that humor may help children learn.

Hint: The topic of this paragraph is humor like that on *Sesame Street*. What is the author's main point *about* that humor?

5. A chimp by the name of Sherman participated in an interesting math experiment. He was given two pairs of cups containing chocolates. One pair contained five candies—three in one cup and two in the other. The second pair held only four candies—three in one and only one in the other. Sherman chose the pair of cups with the most chocolates 90 percent of the time. Also, another chimp, Lana, can match the numbers *1*, *2*, or *3* with a picture of the matching number of boxes 80 percent of the time.

The unstated main idea of this paragraph is: _____

Experiments show that chimps understand numbers.

Hint: The topic of this paragraph is chimps. What is the author saying *about* chimps?

IMPLIED MAIN IDEAS: Test 6

Write out the unstated main idea in each of the following five paragraphs.

1. The first step to a rich summer treat is to defrost a package of frozen raspberries. Next, put the raspberries in the blender with several scoops of vanilla ice cream. Turn the blender on whip until the ice cream and raspberries are partly mixed. Then add a tablespoon of malted-milk powder and several tablespoons of chocolate syrup. Finally, whirl the blender until everything is just mixed.

   The unstated main idea of this paragraph is: _____

   Follow five steps to make a rich summer dessert.
   _____

2. Children with dyslexia, a common learning disorder, often have difficulty seeing the difference between squares, circles, and triangles. A second sign of dyslexia is that they may reverse letters as they read and write, confusing "was" and "saw" or "dog" and "bog." Yet another sign of dyslexia may be a child's failure by age six to develop a preference for using the right or left hand.

   The unstated main idea of this paragraph is: _____

   There are several signs that a child has dyslexia.
   _____

3. Most cases of baldness are caused by heredity. People with hereditary baldness gradually lose the bulbs from which new hair would grow. This type of hair loss is permanent. Some types of hair loss, however, are not permanent. Their causes include high fevers and certain types of drugs.

   The unstated main idea of this paragraph is: _____*Baldness*_____

   may be either_____*permanent*_____ or _____*temporary*_____.

(Continues on next page)

4. One researcher learned that students with several different roles—for example, student, pinball wizard, basketball player, and tutor—were more likely to avoid stress-related illnesses. Likewise, those students with just one or two roles—perhaps student and basketball player—were more likely to suffer a stress-related illness. Apparently, when something went wrong for them, they could not easily strengthen their self-worth in another role.

The unstated main idea of this paragraph is: Research has shown that in

order to avoid _____ *stress-related illnesses* _____,

it is better to have _____ *several different roles in life* _____.

5. After a teenager breaks up, it appears for a while that the sun will never shine again. In the first stage of the breakup, the teen experiences a sense of shock and may have trouble sleeping or concentrating. Grief follows, with the teen mourning the death of the relationship. Next comes blame. In trying to make sense of what has happened, the teenager places blame on someone—himself or herself, the ex-boyfriend or ex-girlfriend, or the ex's new boyfriend or girlfriend. The fourth stage in the process of recovery is known as the goodbye period, during which the person begins to let go of the relationship. The last two stages are rebuilding and resolution. At this point, the teenager can begin to focus on growing stronger and re-entering life ready to love again.

The unstated main idea of this paragraph is: After a _____ *breakup* _____, a

teenager goes through _____ *six* _____ stages in _____

_____ *the process of recovery* _____.

MORE ABOUT SUPPORTING DETAILS: Test 1

A. (1–5.) Major and minor supporting details are mixed together in the list below. The details of the list support the main idea shown. Separate the major, more general details from the minor ones by filling in the outline. Some details have been filled in for you.

Main idea: There are advantages to pursuing a liberal arts program in college.

- Students learn to better understand what they read.
- Writing skills improve.
- Students learn good grammar skills.
- Students learn to organize and clearly state their ideas.
- Students learn to question what they read.

Major detail: 1. Reading skills improve.

Minor details: a. *Students learn to better understand what they read.*

_____

b. *Students learn to question what they read.*

_____

Major detail: 2. *Writing skills improve.*

Minor details: a. *Students learn to organize and clearly state their ideas.*

_____

b. *Students learn good grammar skills.*

_____

(Continues on next page)

B. (6–10.) Number the major details in the following paragraph. Then complete the heading, including the word that ends in *s*. Finally, fill in the major details that fit under the heading. One has been filled in for you.

We all get a kick out of buying a new shirt or record. However, some people are addicted to such kicks, according to one psychiatrist. To distinguish between a happy shopper and an addict, we should look for several signs of addiction. One such sign is if a shopper has buying patterns that put her or him into debt. Also a sign of addiction is shoplifting, especially if this has not been a behavior of the person in the past. A third indicator of addiction is the frequent bouncing of checks. In addition, a shopping addict will experience a mood of tension before shopping and a pleasant release from that tension afterwards. Finally, it's a further sign that a shopper is addicted if he or she suffers from other addictive behaviors, such as overeating, overdrinking or frequent gambling.

Heading: _____*Sign*_____ s _____ *of Shopping Addiction* _____

List of major details:

1. *Buying patterns that put shopper into debt* _____

2. *Shoplifting* _____

3. *Frequent bouncing of checks* _____

4. Tension before shopping and release of tension afterwards

5. *Other addictive behaviors* _____

MORE ABOUT SUPPORTING DETAILS: Test 2

A. (1–5.) Major and minor supporting details are mixed together in the list below. The details of the list support the main idea shown. Separate the major, more general details from the minor ones by filling in the outline. Some details have been filled in for you.

- Margarine and butter have the same number of calories.
- Margarine is less fattening than butter.
- Honey is healthier than regular sugar.
- Many other foods contain as much vitamin A as carrots.
- The nutrients in honey are in too small amounts to be significant.

Main idea: Some of our beliefs about food are myths.

Major detail: **1.** Myth #1: To improve your eyesight, eat carrots.

Minor details: a. *Many other foods contain as much vitamin A as carrots.*

_____

b. Although vitamin A is necessary to the functioning of the eye, it can't improve vision problems.

Major detail: **2.** Myth #2: *Honey is healthier than regular sugar.*

_____

Minor details: a. Honey is a type of sugar.

b. *The nutrients in honey are in too small amounts to be*

significant.

Major detail: **3.** Myth #3: *Margarine is less fattening than butter.*

_____

Minor details: a. Margarine differs from butter only in the type of fat it contains.

b. *Margarine and butter have the same number of calories.*

_____

(Continues on next page)

293

B. (6–10.) Number the major details in the following paragraph. The addition words in italics will help you identify these details. Then, complete the heading, including the word that ends in *s*. Finally, fill in the four major details that fit under the heading.

There are several time-honored ways of getting the audience's attention when giving a speech. *One* way is to surprise your audience. You might begin a speech on nutrition, for example, by saying, "Americans are shortening their lives with dinner." *Another* way to get people's attention is to ask them one or more questions—"What did you have for dinner this evening? Will it add to your good health?" Telling a story of some sort is *also* a good way to begin a speech because everyone enjoys a good story. It could be a true story about the topic of your speech or even a tall tale that makes a point. *Finally*, use a good quotation ("'The preservation of health is a duty,' said the English philosopher Herbert Spencer") to put your speech on the right track.

Heading: _____ Way __s _____ *of Getting the Audience's*

Attention When Giving a Speech

List of major details:

1. Surprise your audience.

2. Ask one or more questions.

3. Tell a story.

4. Use a good quotation.

MORE ABOUT SUPPORTING DETAILS: Test 3

A. (1–5.) Major and minor supporting details are mixed together in the list below. The details of the list support the main idea shown. Separate the major, more general details from the minor ones by completing the outline.

Note: You may find it helpful to put a check (✓) beside each detail that you add to the outline.

- Breed endangered animals
- Jobs as administrators of animal care
- Educational programs on animals
- Giving professionals special work opportunities
- Animals in cages

Main idea: Zoos serve several functions.

I. Acquainting the public with animals

   A. Animal exhibits

     1. *Animals in cages*

     2. Animals to pet

   B. *Educational programs on animals*

     1. Publications for the public

     2. Classes for the public

     3. Special one-time public lectures

II. Participating in important breeding activities

   A. Research on breeding activities

   B. *Breed endangered animals*

     1. To be sure those animals won't become extinct

     2. To eliminate the need for zoos to hunt for endangered animals.

III. *Giving professionals special work opportunities*

   A. Unusual work for veterinarians

   B. Uncommon jobs for zoologists and psychologists

     1. *Jobs as administrators of animal care*

     2. Jobs as public educators

(Continues on next page)

B. (6–10.) Number the major details in the following paragraphs. Then, complete the heading if missing, including the word that ends in *s*. Finally, fill in the missing major details that fit under the heading.

1. Aiming for perfection in all things is a poor strategy. First of all, perfectionists put too much time into unimportant projects, and thus they don't leave enough time for more important activities. At work, for example, someone might put in many hours organizing a professional meeting while neglecting a sales plan. Or a parent might concentrate on a neat home and not have time to spend with the children. Also, perfectionists may limit themselves by resisting new experiences. They discover less because they stick to activities they are sure they can do well. Last, perfectionists are bound to experience disappointment because no one can be perfect at everything he or she does.

    Heading: Reasons Not to Always Aim for Perfection

    List of major details:

    1. *Perfectionists spend too much time on unimportant projects.*

        _____

    2. Perfectionists limit themselves by resisting new experiences.

    3. *Perfectionists experience disappointment because no one can be perfect at everything.*

2. There are a few steps involved in the treatment of a fracture. The first is to put the broken pieces of bone in their proper positions. Next, the bone fragments must be kept from moving out of those positions while they heal. The final step in treatment is therapy for the joints and muscles that have not been used while the bone has been healing.

    Heading: _____ Step ___s *Involved in the Treatment of a Fracture*

        _____

    List of major details:

    1. Put broken pieces of bone in correct positions.

    2. *Keep bone fragments from moving from those positions while healing.*

    3. *Get therapy for unused joints and muscles.*

MORE ABOUT SUPPORTING DETAILS: Test 4

Read each paragraph below and then answer the questions that follow. To help you focus on the details, the topic sentences have been set in boldface.

Note: You may find it helpful to number the major details within the paragraph as you read.

A.   When people are convicted of crimes, they are generally punished. The nature of the punishment depends upon its desired effect or effects. **Punishment has four possible goals.** The most basic is retribution. Retribution means making the convict suffer as he made another suffer. The second is prevention. The fear of punishment may prevent others from committing similar crimes. Rehabilitation is another possible effect. When a convict is reformed during punishment, rehabilitation is taking place. Finally, society feels protected by punishment. People know that while a convict is locked up, he is not committing further crimes.

1. As the topic sentence suggests, the major details of this paragraph are
    a. types of crimes.
    (b.) goals of punishment.
    c. ways to prevent crime.

2. Specifically, the major details of this paragraph are
    a. 1) crime, 2) punishment, and 3) society.
    b. 1) punishment, 2) retribution, 3) the convict, and 4) society.
    (c.) 1) retribution, 2) prevention, 3) rehabilitation, 4) protection of society.

3. *Fill in the blank:* The addition word signaling the third major detail is
    _____*another*_____.

4. Rehabilitation takes place when a convict
    a. suffers.
    (b.) reforms.
    c. is kept from committing further crimes.

5. When revenge is desired, the goal would be
    (a.) retribution.
    b. prevention.
    c. rehabilitation.

(Continues on next page)

B. ¹**There are several types of experiences that influence how people feel about being touched.** ²Our childhood experiences are one thing that affect our attitudes towards touching. ³Little girls, for example, are generally kissed and cuddled more than little boys. ⁴As a consequence, women often like touching more than men. ⁵Our feelings about being touched also depend upon our cultural background. ⁶Latin Americans and southern Europeans, for instance, casually touch each other far more than northern Europeans and most Americans. ⁷Social context, as well, influences our willingness to touch and be touched. ⁸Even men who are generally uneasy about touching may hug one another at an exciting sporting event.

6. A good heading for an outline of this paragraph would be:
    a. Types of Childhood Experiences
    b. Ways People Feel About Being Touched
    c. Types of Experiences That Influence How People Feel About Being Touched

7. The supporting details of the paragraph are
    a. 1) little girls, 2) Latin Americans, 3) southern Europeans, and 4) men at sports events.
    b. 1) childhood experiences, 2) cultural background, and 3) social context.
    c. 1) willingness to be touched and 2) discomfort at being touched.

8. The first major supporting detail is signaled by the addition word or words
    a. *one.*
    b. *for example.*
    c. *also.*

9. Sentence 5 provides
    a. a major detail.
    b. a minor detail.

10. Sentence 6 provides
    a. a major detail.
    b. minor details.

MORE ABOUT SUPPORTING DETAILS: Test 5

A. (1–5.) Number the major details in each of the following paragraphs. Next, complete the heading, including the word that ends in *s*. Finally, fill in the missing major details.

1. While studying sleep at the University of Chicago, a scientist concluded that we have two forms of sleep. The first is now known as REM (Rapid Eye Movement). As the name suggests, during this form of sleep our eyes move very rapidly beneath our closed lids. The other kind of sleep is non-REM sleep, in which we sleep more deeply.

   Heading: _____ *Form* ___ s _____ *of Sleep* _____

   List of major details:

   1. *REM sleep* _____

   2. *Non-REM sleep* _____

2. Many of the stereotypes concerning poor people in the U.S. are untrue. For one thing, the majority of poor people in the U.S. are white, not black. It is true, however, that a larger *percentage* of blacks than white are poor. Although it is widely believed that most poor families are headed by a single woman, that is untrue. The majority of poor families live with both a father and a mother. Also, contrary to popular belief, most poor people do not receive welfare benefits. In fact, only about 35 percent of Americans living below the poverty line are receiving public assistance.

   Heading: _____ *Untrue Stereotype* ___ s ____ *About Poor People* ____

   List of major details:

   3. *Most poor people are white, not black.* _____

   4. Most poor families live with both parents, not a single mother.

   5. *Most poor people do not receive welfare.* _____

(Continues on next page)

B. Read the paragraph below, and then answer the questions that follow. To help you focus on the supporting details, the topic sentences is boldfaced.

Note: You may find it helpful to number the major details within the paragraph as you read.

> ¹**People who become vegetarians often do so to protest the treatment of animals raised for food.** ²First of all, most veal calves are treated horribly. ³They spend their entire lives in cages so small they cannot turn around. ⁴In order to keep their meat pale and tender, they are allowed no exercise and are fed a liquid diet. ⁵The calves are not even allowed straw for bedding, because their hunger for ordinary food would drive them to eat it. ⁶Chickens also receive terrible treatment. ⁷Raised by large producers, they are often crammed into cages with eight or ten others. ⁸They do not even have room to flap their wings. ⁹In their frustration, they often try to peck one another to death. ¹⁰To prevent that from happening, producers cut their beaks off. ¹¹Last, beef cattle, too, are made to suffer. ¹²They are generally castrated in order to make them grow heavier. ¹³The operation is done without anesthetic.

6. In general, the major details of this paragraph are
   a. vegetarians.
   b. where animals raised for food live.
   c. food animals that vegetarians feel are mistreated.

7. *Fill in the blank:* The major details of the passage are signaled by the addition words *first of all*, _____ *also* _____, and *last.*

8. One sentence with a major detail is
   a. sentence 5.
   b. sentence 6.
   c. sentence 7.

9. The minor details of this paragraph
   a. discuss vegetarianism.
   b. provide the specific details of how each animal is treated.
   c. explain the different types of farms.

10. *Complete the sentence:* Chickens' beaks are cut off in order to _____
    prevent the chickens from pecking each other to death.

MORE ABOUT SUPPORTING DETAILS: Test 6

A. (1–6.) Number the major details in each of the following paragraphs. Then complete the heading, including the word that ends in *s*. Finally, fill in the missing major details.

1.   The skillful use of supporting material often makes the difference between a good speech and a poor one. The first type of supporting material is examples. They include brief details as well as extended examples in the form of stories. Statistics can also help in supporting your message. Remember that whatever numbers you cite should be taken from reliable sources, and they should measure fairly what they claim to measure. Expert testimony is also helpful for a speaker. Giving the views of people who are experts is a good way to make your ideas more acceptable. Be sure to quote accurately and to use only sources that present a fair point of view about your subject.

Heading: Types of _____ *Supporting Material for a Speech* _____

List of major details:

1. *Examples* _____

2. *Statistics* _____

3. Testimony of experts

2.   Practically everyone occasionally needs to complain about a product or service that has been unsatisfactory. It's helpful to keep in mind some steps for effective complaints. First, always address your written complaint to a specific individual, such as the head of the company. You can get that person's name by calling the company's switchboard. Next write your complaint briefly, clearly and unemotionally. You'll be taken less seriously if you sound very excited or threatening. Finally, explain exactly what action you want taken. Don't leave it up to the company to figure out what you would consider a satisfactory response.

Heading: _____ *Step* ____s _____ *for Effective Complaints* _____

List of major details:

1. *Address your written complaint to a specific individual.* _____

2. Write complaint clearly, briefly, unemotionally.

3. *Explain exactly what action you want taken.* _____

(Continues on next page)

B. Read the paragraph below, and then answer the questions that follow. To help you focus on the supporting details, the topic sentence is boldfaced.

Note: You may find it helpful to number the major details within the paragraph as you read.

> Children soon realize that they are expected to behave in certain ways depending upon their gender. **There are several sources from which children learn what is "masculine" and "feminine" behavior and that they are to stick to one or the other.** Parents are one powerful source of gender-related conditioning. Studies have shown that parents view even newborn boys as active, independent, and strong, while they regard newborn girls as delicate, dependent, and needy. As their children grow up, parents push sons to give up dependency, clinging, and crying. Meanwhile, they accept these behaviors in girls. Schools, too, help teach typical gender roles to children. Teachers tend to criticize boys when they try out "feminine" behaviors, such as playing with dolls or dress-up toys. Girls receive praise and attention when they remain near their teachers, engaging in quiet activities. The media also play a role in shaping children's gender expectations. Children's TV programs show twice as many male characters as females. The females that do appear generally play unimportant "helping" roles. And last, children's books—even award-winning ones—tend to show males in interesting, active roles and females in more passive roles.

7. In general, the major details of this paragraph are
   a. ways children are expected to behave.
   b. sources from which children learn their gender roles.
   c. "masculine" and "feminine" behaviors.

8. *Fill in the blank:* The four major details are indicated by the addition words

   one, too, _____*also*_____, and *last.*

9. Specifically, the major details of this paragraph are
   a. boys, girls, parents, and teachers.
   b. parents, schools, the media, and children's books.
   c. gender roles, boys who try out "feminine" behaviors, children's TV programs, and books.

10. *Fill in the blank:* According to the paragraph, teachers "teach" children to adopt typical gender roles by criticizing and _____*praising*_____ the children.

TRANSITIONS: Test 1

A. Fill each blank with one of the words in the box. Use each word once.

Note: You may find it helpful to check (✓) each transition after you insert it into a sentence.

next	as a result	for instance
since	similar	

1. Vic has some odd study habits. _____*For instance*_____, he prefers studying for finals in the back seat of his car.

2. The period and the semicolon are marks of punctuation that have _____*similar*_____ uses.

3. To make a Halloween pumpkin, first cut off the top of the pumpkin. _____*Next*_____, scoop out the insides.

4. _____*Since*_____ I started making to-do lists, I get a lot more done each day.

5. The cost of tuition to four-year colleges continues to soar. _____*As a result*_____, enrollment in two-year colleges has risen greatly.

(Continues on next page)

B. Fill each blank with one of the words in the box. Use each word once.

> *Note:* You may find it helpful to check (✓) each transition after you insert it into the passage.

because	but	for example
in addition	then	

Pets can be classified into three categories according to how much they let people get away with. At the bottom are horses, which allow people to ride on their backs. A step above horses are dogs, which usually do not allow people to sit on their backs. However, they often allow themselves to be trained to do tricks for people. (6)_____*In addition*_____, they will readily perform those tricks for nothing more than a pat on the head. At the top of the heap are cats (7)_____*because*_____ they will take no such nonsense. Cats may do tricks, (8)_____*but*_____ only if they dream them up themselves. A cat, (9)_____*for example*_____, will think nothing of making a leap from the floor to the top of a six-foot bookcase when it chooses to. But try getting it to leap up there at your request. Most cats would give you an "Are you serious?" look and (10)_____*then*_____ stroll off in the other direction.

TRANSITIONS: Test 2

Complete each sentence with the appropriate transition word or phrase. Then circle the kind of transition you have used.

1. **a.** The company has a very strict dress code. _____*For example*_____, Kim was at work in her backless sundress for only about fifteen minutes before she was sent home to change.

   In contrast
   For example
   In addition

   b. The relationship of the second sentence to the first is one of

   (illustration.)   contrast.   addition.

2. **a.** Congress passed the bill, _____*but*_____ the President vetoed it.

   but
   therefore
   to illustrate

   b. The relationship between the two parts of the sentence is one of

   illustration.   (contrast.)   cause and effect.

3. **a.** One thing to consider when buying a dog is whether or not you have time to walk it. _____*Another*_____ important factor for some to consider is whether the dog sheds or not.

   Another
   However
   For example

   b. The relationship of the second sentence to the first is one of

   illustration.   contrast.   (addition.)

4. **a.** _____*Before*_____ I turned in the paper, I spent about five minutes proofreading it carefully for obvious errors.

   Because
   Before
   First

   b. The transition signals a relationship of

   (time.)   addition.   cause and effect.

5. **a.** Marva is afraid of making left turns against traffic during rush hour. _____*As a result*_____, she drives blocks out of her way to avoid that situation.

   First
   As a result
   In contrast

   b. The transition signals a relationship of

   time.   (cause and effect.)   contrast.

(Continues on next page)

6. a. Newspapers piled on a porch indicate that people aren't at home, _____*just as*_____ mail overflowing from a mailbox does.

    because
    then
    just as

   b. The relationship between the two parts of the sentence is one of

    addition.   (comparison.)   cause and effect.

7. a. A community college is sponsoring classes at local businesses. _____*Moreover*_____, they are even providing books.

    As a result
    For example
    Moreover

   b. The relationship of the second sentence to the first is one of

    (addition.)   illustration.   cause and effect.

8. a. Begin writing a term paper by choosing the general topic; _____*then*_____ try to narrow that topic.

    therefore
    like
    then

   b. The relationship between the two parts of the sentence is one of

    (time.)   cause and effect.   comparison.

9. a. The Statue of Liberty is truly an immense structure. _____*For instance*_____, her nose measures four feet, six inches in length.

    Also
    For instance
    However

   b. The relationship of the second sentence to the first is one of

    (illustration.)   contrast.   addition.

10. a. As a joke, Theo served jello and shaving cream for dessert at his dinner party. _____*As a result*_____, his friends were slow to accept his next dinner invitation.

    As a result
    On the other hand
    Similarly

   b. The relationship between the two sentences is one of

    comparison.   contrast.   (cause and effect.)

TRANSITIONS: Test 3

A. Fill each blank with one of the words in the box. Use each word once.

Note: You may find it helpful to check (✓) each transition after you insert it into a sentence.

but	in addition	during
because	for example	

1. _____*During*_____ his Presidential campaign, Bill Clinton gained attention by playing the saxophone.

2. The ostrich can't fly, _____*but*_____ it can run thirty-five miles per hour.

3. During its sale, the clothing store was so crowded that Jessica had to wait for a fitting room. _____*In addition*_____, she had to stand in line for twenty minutes to pay for her purchase.

4. _____*Because*_____ there's no gravity to make demands on the body in space, muscles weaken more quickly there.

5. When rulers consistently overstep the limits of their authority, they are often challenged and even overthrown. The late Shah of Iran, _____*for example*_____, built up an incredible fortune at the expense of society before he was driven from power.

(Continues on next page)

B. Fill each blank with one of the words in the box. Use each word once.

Note: You may find it helpful to check (✓) each transition after you insert it into the passage.

for instance	when	despite
because of	as well as	

(6)_____*When*_____ unusual animals are discussed, polar bears frequently come to mind. (7)_____*Because of*_____ their huge size, pure pale yellow color, and habit of living among ice and snow, these bears are like no others. They are powerful athletes who can run twenty-five miles an hour and leap over a six-foot snowdrift (8)_____*as well as*_____ dive fifty feet into the ocean. (9)_____*Despite*_____ their beautiful and even cuddly appearance, polar bears are fierce meat-eaters that are ready to attack if they sense danger. A few years ago in New York, (10)_____*for instance*_____, a child who crawled into a polar bear enclosure at the zoo was killed by the animals.

TRANSITIONS: Test 4

Complete each sentence with the appropriate transition word or phrase. Then circle the kind of transition you have used.

1. a. Children can influence the adult world. One twelve-year old, _____*for instance*_____, led a successful movement to get prostitutes off her playground.

   also
   in contrast
   for instance

   b. The relationship of the second sentence to the first is one of

   contrast.   (illustration.)   addition.

2. a. College students with A averages say they consume, on average, three and a half alcoholic drinks each week. _____*In contrast*_____, students with D or F averages say they average eleven alcoholic drinks a week.

   Because
   In contrast
   Similarly

   b. The relationship between the two sentences is one of

   comparison.   cause and effect.   (contrast.)

3. a. Ned forgot to feed the cats this morning. _____*As a result*_____, by the time he got home from work, they had knocked over the trash and scattered papers and coffee grounds all over the kitchen.

   As a result
   However
   Similarly

   b. The relationship of the second sentence to the first is one of

   contrast.   (cause and effect.)   comparison.

4. a. Authors _____*often*_____ promote their books by going from city to city to appear at bookstores and on local talk shows.

   however
   for instance
   often

   b. The transition indicates

   contrast.   (time.)   illustration.

5. a. My mother didn't see a TV until she was ten. _____*Furthermore*_____, she was almost middle-aged before computers became common.

   Often
   Furthermore
   In contrast

   b. The relationship of the second sentence to the first is one of

   (addition.)   contrast.   time.

(Continues on next page)

6. a. One special feature of parking spaces for the handicapped is that they are close to stores. _____*Another*_____ is that they are wide enough for people to move on wheelchairs and crutches.

   b. The relationship of the second sentence to the first is one of

   (addition.)   cause and effect.   time.

7. a. Animal names can be misleading. _____*For instance*_____, a polecat isn't a cat at all— it's a relative of the weasel.

   b. The relationship of the second sentence to the first is one of

   (illustration.)   cause and effect.   contrast.

8. a. _____*Because*_____ employers can't get enough qualified people to fill certain jobs, many positions remain empty.

   b. The relationship between the two parts of the sentence is one of

   contrast.   (cause and effect.)   time.

9. a. One time Marco locked the car door _____*before*_____ he took the keys out of the ignition.

   b. The transition signals a relationship of

   (time.)   cause and effect.   illustration.

10. a. Many people feel the city of Haifa in Israel looks _____*similar to*_____ San Francisco—they are both beautiful port cities on hilly land.

    b. The transition indicates

    (comparison.)   illustration.   contrast.

TRANSITIONS: Test 5

A. This part of the test will check your ability to recognize the relationships (signaled by transitions) within and between sentences. Read each passage and answer the questions that follow.

Passage 1

¹The ancient Chinese taught that it was distasteful to serve meat in large pieces that resembled the original animal. ²They also believed it rude to expect diners to struggle at the table to cut up hunks of meat. ³Instead, the Chinese preferred to cut the meat into bite-size pieces in the kitchen. ⁴Therefore, they used chopsticks, the logical solution for the problem of how to eat such small morsels of meat.

1. The relationship of sentence 2 to sentence 1 is one of
   (a.) addition.   c. illustration.
   b. time.   d. contrast.

2. The relationship of sentence 4 to the previous sentence is one of
   a. time.   (c.) cause and effect.
   b. addition.   d. comparison.

Passage 2

¹Couples often mistake a powerful sexual attraction for "love at first sight." ²But couples who consider themselves happily married rarely fell in love so quickly. ³More often they say that their first impressions of one another were only mildly positive. ⁴More intense feelings came along later. ⁵Later, too, they developed a feeling of "being understood" by their partners. ⁶Furthermore, the better they knew each other, the more attractive they considered their partners to be.

3. The relationship of sentence 2 to sentence 1 is signaled by the word
   (a.) *but.*   c. *who.*
   b. *so.*   d. *quickly.*

4. The relationship of sentence 6 to the sentences that come before it is one of
   a. time.   c. cause and effect.
   (b.) addition.   d. contrast.

(Continues on next page)

Passage 3

[1]Today, the only sure way to know if someone has Alzheimer's disease is to examine his brain after death. [2]However, researchers in Boston believe the nose might be a key to early detection. [3]Their reason is that Alzheimer's victims lose their sense of smell at an early stage. [4]Also, Japanese studies have found a possible link between Alzheimer's and people with older than average parents. [5]This could be important because more couples are having families later in life. [6]Another method of prediction might be related to diet. [7]Aluminum in food additives has surfaced as a possible cause.

5. The relationship of sentence 2 to sentence 1 is one of
   a. addition.
   b. contrast.
   c. cause and effect.
   d. illustration.

6. The relationship of sentence 6 to the sentences that come before it is one of
   a. time.
   b. contrast.
   c. addition.
   d. illustration.

B. The following four transitions have been removed from the passage below. Read the passage carefully to see which transition logically fits in each answer space. Then write in each transition.

Note: You may find it helpful to check (✓) each transition after you insert it into the passage.

| however | including | although |
| in addition | | |

(7)_____*Although*_____ caffeine is the world's most widely consumed drug, few of its users realize how potent it is. Caffeine is a drug that acts fast. In less than five minutes after you've drunk a cup of coffee, caffeine is racing to every part of your body. Its effects are many, (8)_____*including*_____ increasing the flow of urine and stomach acid, relaxing involuntary muscles, and stepping up the intake of oxygen. (9)_____*In addition*_____, caffeine heightens the pumping strength of the heart. Therefore, too much caffeine can cause an irregular heartbeat. A small dose of caffeine can improve your performance as you type or drive; (10)_____*however*_____, too much caffeine will make you shaky and unsteady.

TRANSITIONS: Test 6

A. This part of the test will check your ability to recognize the relationships (signaled by transitions) within and between sentences. Read each passage and answer the questions that follow.

Passage 1

[1]There are actually two types of smog: the London type and the Los Angeles type. [2]The London variety is caused by the burning of fossil fuels, mainly coal with high sulfur content. [3]Los Angeles smog results when cool ocean air slips under a layer of warmer air and becomes trapped, along with exhaust emissions from automobiles. [4]Carbon monoxide and hydrocarbons are examples of such emissions. [5]This type of smog occurs in valleys and other areas with poor air circulation.

1. Sentences 2 and 3 each express a relationship of
   a. addition.
   (b.) cause and effect.
   c. time.
   d. illustration.

2. The relationship of sentence 4 to the last part of sentence 3 is one of
   a. time.
   b. contrast.
   c. comparison.
   (d.) illustration.

Passage 2

[1]A Nayar girl who lives in Kerala, India, is encouraged to have several lovers during her adolescence. [2]If she becomes pregnant, one or more of these lovers pays the costs of delivering the baby. [3]Beyond this, however, the mother's family are completely responsible for care of the child and support of the mother. [4]This is only one aspect of how the Nayar way of life would seem strange to us. [5]The Nayar do have a form of marriage, but it is simply a ritual that marks a girl's passage into adulthood. [6]The woman's relatives choose a man to be her husband for three days. [7]Afterward, husband and wife may never see each other again.

3. The relationship of sentence 3 to sentence 2 is one of
   a. addition.
   (b.) contrast.
   c. comparison.
   d. illustration.

4. The relationship of sentence 7 to sentence 6 is one of
   (a.) time.
   b. addition.
   c. cause and effect.
   d. illustration.

(Continues on next page)

Passage 3

¹The National Association of Broadcasting enforces some rules on liquor ads. ²First, no hard liquor can be advertised on radio or TV. ³Also, broadcasters cannot show anyone drinking beer or wine in an ad. ⁴It is all right, however, to show characters in programs drinking liquor. ⁵Finally, active sports figures cannot appear in beer and wine commercials. ⁶In spite of these rules, a dispute over alcohol ads continues. ⁷Opponents of such ads say that advertisers often equate drinking with attractiveness and "the good life." ⁸Thus, their ads are particularly effective with young people wanting to appear attractive and popular.

5. The relationship of sentence 3 to sentence 2 is one of
   a. time.
   b. addition.
   c. contrast.
   d. cause and effect.

6. The relationship between sentences 7 and 8 is one of
   a. addition.
   b. contrast.
   c. comparison.
   d. cause and effect.

B. The following four transitions have been removed from the passage below. Read the passage carefully to see which transition logically fits in each answer space. Then write in each transition.

Note: You may find it helpful to check (✓) each transition after you insert it into the passage.

include therefore	finally	another

Every year it is reported that some 35,000 Americans have committed suicide. The actual number is probably higher. Yet many people who attempt or succeed in suicide could be helped in regaining their desire to live. (7)_____*Therefore*_____, it is important for those around them to recognize the warning signs of a potential suicide. Such signs (8)_____*include*_____ severe depression and withdrawal, often combined with the inability to sleep or eat. Extreme mood swings, from joy to deep depression, are (9)_____*another*_____ danger sign. Suicidal people may begin giving away valued belongings. (10)_____*Finally*_____, any life crisis, such as the death of a loved one or the loss of a job, may make a potentially suicidal person feel that he or she can't go on.

PATTERNS OF ORGANIZATION: Test 1

Identify the pattern used in each item below by writing in the letter of one of the following:

a Time order
b List of items
c Comparison and/or contrast
d Cause and effect
e Definition and example

Each pattern is used twice.

___*d*___ 1. Eleanor Roosevelt received many threatening letters after her husband became President. Therefore, the Secret Service insisted she carry a pistol in her purse.

___*a*___ 2. To open, tear off the plastic tip. Then, before trying to spray, rotate the nozzle until the two dots are in line with each other.

___*b*___ 3. Over the next five to ten years, there is expected to be a big demand for certain types of jobs, including teacher's aides, accountants, restaurant cooks, and nurses.

___*e*___ 4. Transitions are words and phrases that show relationships between ideas. For instance, time transitions such as *before, soon,* and *now* show time relationships.

___*c*___ 5. Friendships with my old high-school buddies are often different from those with my newer friends. I can share many memories with my old friends, but my newer pals are more likely to share my current interests.

___*b*___ 6. To borrow money, consumers can choose among several sources: banks, credit unions, finance companies, and insurance companies.

(Continues on next page)

___d___ 7. Pam decided to save money by washing her dark clothes with her white ones. As a result, her underwear and gym socks are now an ugly grayish pink.

___a___ 8. A group of English musicians began playing together in their teens, during the 1950s. They eventually made up a group called Johnny and the Moondogs. By the sixties, the group was known as the Beatles.

___e___ 9. One method used by psychologists is observation. Observation involves watching others and recording what happens. For example, child psychologists often observe children through one-way mirrors.

___c___ 10. Like butter, all margarines (except for the low-calorie versions) are 99 percent fat and contain about one hundred calories per tablespoon. Margarine, however, contains less saturated fat than does butter.

PATTERNS OF ORGANIZATION: Test 2

Arrange the groups of scrambled sentences into logical paragraphs by numbering the sentences in an order that makes sense. Then circle the letter of the main pattern of organization used.

Group 1

___3___ When the interview is over, thank the interviewer for his or her time.

___1___ When going for a job interview, it's important to be on time and dressed as you might if you worked where you're being interviewed.

___2___ When speaking to the interviewer, keep eye contact and speak clearly, without slouching or fidgeting.

    (a.) time order   c. cause and effect

    b. comparison   d. definition and example

Group 2

___1___ Boys who mature early have an advantage over those who mature late.

___3___ In contrast, late maturers are underdeveloped physically and thus feel inadequate.

___2___ Early maturers become heroes in sports and leaders in various other activities.

    a. time order   (c.) contrast

    b. items in a list   d. definition and example

Group 3

___3___ For instance, if you believe that a particular group is pushy, you will automatically judge someone who belongs to that group to be pushy— without waiting to see what that person is really like.

___1___ Stereotyping is holding a set of beliefs about the personal nature of a group of people.

___2___ It can greatly interfere with our making accurate judgments about others.

    a. time order   c. cause and effect

    b. comparison   (d.) definition and example

(Continues on next page)

Group 4

__2___ By the ninth grade, one child in six will have tried marijuana, and one in three will have experimented with alcohol.

__3___ A much worse effect is the fact that the suicide rate for youths under fifteen has tripled since 1960.

__1___ Stresses of the modern world have a great deal of impact on today's children.

a. time order   c. cause and effect
b. contrast   d. definition and example

Group 5

__3___ Finally, many feel that being strongly motivated and quitting cold turkey is the best way to conquer the habit.

__2___ Another method is acupuncture, in which a tiny needle is placed in a smoker's earlobe to remove the craving for a cigarette.

__1___ Many ways have been suggested for quitting smoking, including being hypnotized and chewing a special nicotine gum.

a. time order   c. comparison
b. list of items   d. contrast

PATTERNS OF ORGANIZATION: Test 3

For each passage, write the sentence number of the main idea in the space provided. Then circle the letter of the chief pattern of organization of the passage.

1.   [1]If you'd like a raise or promotion, there are a few steps you can take. [2]Begin by outlining your on-the-job accomplishments. [3]That is, write an "achievement memo" listing the duties of your job and how you have performed them. [4]Include any special ways that your work has contributed to the company. [5]This list will help both you and your boss evaluate your work. [6]Next, type up the memo neatly and give it to your boss. [7]Then ask to hold a private meeting with him or her. [8]Explain at the meeting your desire to advance and why your record shows you deserve it.

Sentence with the main idea: _____*1*_____

Passage's pattern of organization:
(a.) time order
b. comparison and/or contrast
c. definition and example

2.   [1]Americans spend some $2.5 million each year to repair termite damage to their homes. [2]However, much of that money could be saved if a few anti-termite precautions were observed. [3]Firewood, a favorite snack of termites, should be stored on a metal platform well away from the house. [4]Fences, playhouses and other wooden structures that touch the soil should be pre-treated with a protective coating. [5]And tree stumps near the home should be removed.

Sentence with the main idea: _____*2*_____

Passage's pattern of organization:
a. time order
(b.) list of items
c. comparison and/or contrast

(Continues on next page)

3. [1]When I turned thirty last week, I couldn't help thinking about how I had changed over the last ten years. [2]When I was twenty, I acted as if I was confident, but I was really filled with huge doubts. [3]Now I really am somewhat confident, so I don't feel the need to impress others so much. [4]At twenty I had girls on my mind day and night. [5]Now that I'm married, I don't have to put all that energy into hustling up dates. [6]I'm also emotionally calmer now. [7]Ten years ago I wasted a lot of energy being angry at people. [8]I realize now that I'm more likely to accept people the way they are. [9]At least I don't blame them any more for my own problems.

Sentence with the main idea: _____1_____

Passage's pattern of organization:
a. comparison and/or contrast
b. cause and effect
c. definition and example

4. [1]An altruistic person will help others even when he or she expects no benefits in return. [2]Consider the example of one of the passengers on a plane that crashed into the Potomac River one cold January day in 1982. [3]Most of the passengers died under the ice, but six passengers escaped into the icy waters. [4]Every time a life preserver was lowered by a helicopter, one man passed it on to one of the other five. [5]When the helicopter had lifted out all five, it returned to pick up that last survivor. [6]But he had disappeared under the ice.

Sentence with the main idea: _____1_____

Passage's pattern of organization:
a. list of items
b. cause and effect
c. definition and example

PATTERNS OF ORGANIZATION: Test 4

For each passage, write the sentence number of the main idea in the space provided. Then circle the letter of the chief pattern of organization of the passage.

1. ¹People often feel that domestic cats and their larger relatives, the jungle cats, are very different. ²In reality, however, cats at home and cats in the wild have many traits in common. ³Both have eyes suited for night vision, and both prefer to sleep by day and move about at night. ⁴Also, just as pet cats use their tails to keep their balance and to signal emotions, so do lions and other large cats. ⁵In addition, both kinds of cats can leap great distances. ⁶Pet cats are often found on top of bookcases or refrigerators. ⁷Similarly, the puma, the champion jumper of the cat family, has been known to jump twenty feet up and forty feet ahead. ⁸Finally, little cats are not the only ones that purr; the cheetah, puma, and snow leopard all purr when content.

Sentence with the main idea: ___2___

Passage's pattern of organization:
a. time order
(b.) comparison and/or contrast
c. cause and effect

2. ¹Imagine a runner who has torn a leg muscle and is prescribed a drug to control the pain. ²She finds that the drug acts quickly to soothe her discomfort. ³As a result, she unconsciously begins to lower her level of "tolerable" pain. ⁴The memory of what the welcome rush of relief feels like leads her to take the medication for lower and lower pain levels. ⁵She also takes the medication more and more often. ⁶A torn muscle may thus turn an injured runner into one of the many persons dependent upon legal, doctor-prescribed medications.

Sentence with the main idea: ___6___

Passage's main pattern of organization:
a. list of items
b. comparison and/or contrast
(c.) cause and effect

(Continues on next page)

3. [1]A primary group is one that is made up of a small number of people who relate intimately with each other over a long period. [2]The members of such a group know each other personally and behave informally together. [3]Examples of the primary group are families and small circles of friends. [4]Such groups are important units within the larger social structure. [5]In fact, in some traditional small-scale societies, the social structure is based almost totally on primary groups.

    Sentence with the main idea: ___1___

    Passage's pattern of organization:
    a. time order
    b. cause and effect
    (c.) definition and example

4. [1]Gary began stealing liquor from his parents when he was fourteen, and by age seventeen he regularly came to school drunk. [2]In his early twenties, he realized he was completely dependent on alcohol. [3]Gary's moment of truth came at age twenty-five, when he narrowly escaped death in a drunk-driving accident. [4]He soon committed himself to the local alcohol-recovery center. [5]After an intensive four-week treatment and a ninety-day follow-up program, Gary was free of alcohol for the first time in over ten years. [6]He then returned to college and received a degree. [7]Now he works as a counselor in the same treatment center that gave him his second chance. [8]Gary's story should inspire many of his own patients at the alcohol-recovery center.

    Sentence with the main idea: ___8___

    Passage's pattern of organization:
    (a.) time order
    b. list of items
    c. comparison and/or contrast

PATTERNS OF ORGANIZATION: Test 5

A. For each passage, write the sentence number of the main idea in the space provided. Then circle the letter of the chief pattern of organization of the passage.

1. ¹When life inflicts setbacks and tragedies on optimists, they weather those storms better than pessimists do. ²Optimists bounce back from defeat, and, with their lives somewhat poorer, they pick up and start again. ³Pessimists give up and fall into depression. ⁴Because of their ability to spring back, optimists achieve more at work and in school. ⁵Optimists have better physical health and may even live longer. ⁶Americans want optimists to lead them. ⁷Even when things go well for pessimists, they are haunted by fears of catastrophe.

    Sentence with the main idea: ___*1*___

    Passage's pattern of organization:
    a. definition and example
    b. time order
    (c.) contrast

2. ¹The history of books is marked by many important milestones. ²One of the greatest of these would have to be the establishment of the first public library. ³This event took place in Athens, Greece, in 540 B.C. ⁴Books had to be copied by hand until 1456. ⁵Then, German inventor Johann Gutenberg built a printing press capable of producing multiple copies of one book. ⁶During the 1800s American publishing houses began pumping out works to satisfy a reading-hungry public. ⁷One such book, *Uncle Tom's Cabin*, published in 1852, sold seven million copies. ⁸It was credited with helping to begin the Civil War. ⁹By the 1980s, the publishing of "electronic books"— books on audiotape—began a new chapter in the fascinating history of books.

    Sentence with the main idea: ___*1*___

    Passage's pattern of organization:
    a. definition and example
    (b.) time order
    c. comparison

(Continues on next page)

B. In the space provided, write the sentence number of the main idea of the following passage. Then circle the letter of the chief pattern of organization.

Finally, complete the outline by 1) finishing the heading and incomplete major detail and 2) filling in the two missing major details.

[1]Television advertising is what pays for much of television programming. [2]But parents and others have several objections to television advertising for children. [3]First of all, some critics object to the whole idea of kids'commercials. [4]Young children, they point out, do not understand the nature of advertising. [5]They thus tend to simply accept ads as true. [6]The promotion of war-related toys is another area of concern for many parents. [7]Others complain about the many ads that promote sugar-coated cereals and other unhealthful "kiddie" foods. [8]Still others campaign against TV ads that invite children to call special "900" telephone numbers to, for example, "hear a story from Santa." [9]Parents have been horrified to find their children racking up huge phone bills calling these advertised numbers.

Sentence with the main idea: __2__

Passage's pattern of organization:
a. definition and example
b. time order
(c.) list of items

Objections to _____*Television Advertising for Children*_____

1. Children, being too young to understand advertising, accept it as true.
2. *War-related toys are promoted on TV.*

   _____

3. *Sugar-coated cereals and other unhealthful food for children are promoted on TV.*

4. Some ads encourage children to *rack up huge phone bills by calling special telephone numbers.*

PATTERNS OF ORGANIZATION: Test 6

A. For each passage, write the sentence number of the main idea in the space provided. Then circle the letter of the chief pattern of organization of the passage.

1. ¹For 250 million years, reptiles—which appeared on earth long before the first mammals—have been fighting over territory. ²Today, human beings do battle over property as well. ³But the reptiles' way of fighting is generally more civilized and humane than the humans'. ⁴Lizards will take a few rushes at one another to test which one is stronger. ⁵After a few passes, the loser rolls over on his back to signal defeat. ⁶The winner allows him to leave unharmed. ⁷Rattlesnakes, similarly, will duel over territory. ⁸But they do it with the necks twined together so that they cannot injure each other with their fangs. ⁹Humans, of course, generally fight with the intent of injuring one another. ¹⁰The victor often seems to feel he hasn't really won until he's wounded and humiliated his opponent, if not killed him.

   Sentence with the main idea: ___3___

   Passage's pattern of organization:
   a. cause and effect
   b. list of items
   (c.) comparision and/or contrast

2. ¹Each year, thousands of square miles of rain forest are burned or cut down in tropical countries, causing much damage to land, animals, and humans everywhere on Earth. ²Destroying the forests results in lifeless, useless desert. ³Much of the variety of Earth's life consists of creatures who live in the rain forests. ⁴Destruction of the rain forests thus threatens those animals. ⁵Many species are becoming extinct before scientists ever find out about them. ⁶The destruction of the rain forests threatens human life as well as animals. ⁷As we breathe, we use up oxygen. ⁸The oxygen is constantly being resupplied by plants—and the tropical rain forests provide a major share of that fresh oxygen. ⁹As we burn or hack down the rain forests, we are destroying more and more of the very oxygen supply we depend on to breathe.

   Sentence with the main idea: ___1___

   Passage's pattern of organization:
   a. definition and example.
   (b.) cause and effect
   c. comparison and/or contrast

(Continues on next page)

B. In the space provided, write the sentence number of the main idea of the following paragraph. Then circle the letter of the chief pattern of organization.

Finally, complete the outline by filling in the major details of the paragraph. Also, number the major details. (Note that the number of details may differ from the number of answer lines shown.)

[1]For recycling to succeed, four distinct steps need to be completed. [2]First of all, the material to be recycled must be collected. [3]Next, the recyclables need to be sorted by type. [4]For example, glass must be separated from aluminum. [5]Then the materials have to be reclaimed in a form that can be used in some way. [6]Finally, the materials must actually become part of something new once again, as when newspapers become comic books.

Sentence with the main idea: ___1___

Passage's pattern of organization:
a. definition and example
b. comparison and/or contrast
(c.) time order

Steps Needed for Recycling to Succeed:

1. *Collect material to be recycled.*

2. *Sort recyclables by type.*

3. *Reclaim materials in a form that can be used.*

4. *Make materials part of something new.*

_____

_____

INFERENCES: Test 1

After reading each passage, put a check by the **two** inferences that are most firmly based on the given information.

1. The best places for a magazine ad are the first right-hand page or the outside back cover. The next best spots are the other cover positions or the front section of the magazine.

    ✓ a. The success of a magazine ad is influenced by its location.

    ✓ b. More people see the front section of a magazine than the back section.

    ___ c. Newspaper ads are more successful than magazine ads.

2. An old saying states, "Three people can keep a secret if two of them are dead."

    ✓ a. Secrets are very difficult to keep.

    ___ b. It is dangerous to keep secrets.

    ✓ c. People should not assume that others will keep their secrets.

3. Smoking cigarettes is a major cause of lung cancer. Although adult men have cut back on their smoking in recent years, adult women and teenage girls have increased theirs. Lung cancer recently passed breast cancer as the leading cancer-killer among women.

    ✓ a. Increased lung cancer among women is linked to smoking.

    ✓ b. Lung cancer may decrease among adult men.

    ___ c. There are still more teenage boys smoking than teenage girls.

4. There's an old story about a certain state legislator who had spent some time in a mental institution. For years after, when debate in the legislature got heated, he would wave his release papers and declare: "I've got papers that prove I'm sane! What about the rest of you?"

    ___ a. The legislator was ashamed of having been in a mental institution.

    ✓ b. When he left the institution, the legislator was considered sane.

    ✓ c. The legislator had been re-elected despite his mental problems.

(Continues on next page)

5. A well-known prayer goes as follows: "Oh, God, grant me the courage to change what I must change, the patience to bear what I must bear, and the wisdom to know the difference."

✓ a. It sometimes takes courage to change one's life.

___ b. Courage is more important than patience.

✓ c. We sometimes aren't wise enough to know when we must simply accept a situation.

INFERENCES: Test 2

A. After reading the passage, put a check by the **two** inferences that are most firmly based on the given information.

> A Dallas disk jockey asked his listeners to send him money, and they did. One day, Ron Chapman of station KVIL simply told his listeners, "Go to your checkbooks. Write a check payable to KVIL Fun and Games. Make it in the amount of $20 and mail it to this address." He never stated why listeners should send the money, only that they should. Chapman expected that about three or four hundred listeners would respond. He intended to return their checks and send them a bag of goodies from his sponsors. However, instead of four hundred checks, over twelve thousand were received, amounting to $244,240. The station donated the money to charity.

  ✓   1. People will sometimes do what they're told without knowing exactly why.

  ___   2. The station gave the money to the homeless.

  ✓   3. Chapman made his announcement to play a trick on his listeners.

  ___   4. Chapman's sponsors were furious about the stunt.

  ___   5. Chapman had tried the same stunt once before.

B. After reading the passage, put a check by the **three** inferences that are most firmly based on the given information.

> At Wellness Community meetings, cancer patients give each other various types of support, including the opportunity to laugh. They laugh with each other about things that would make outsiders uneasy. One joke told by patients is about a man with cancer who has just learned that he has only one more night to live. He asks his wife to come to the bedroom with him for one last sexual encounter. His wife says, "Gosh, Hugo, I'd love to, but I'm too tired." Hugo says, "Oh, come on." And his wife says, "That's easy for you to say. You don't have to get up in the morning."

  ___   1. In real life, cancer patients cannot participate in sex.

  ✓   2. Cancer patients can laugh about their problems.

  ✓   3. The author feels that healthy people may be uncomfortable over jokes about death.

(Continues on next page)

___✓___ 4. The wife in the joke is aware that Hugo will die the next morning.

_____ 5. All cancer patients in the Wellness Community meeting will die from their illness.

INFERENCES: Test 3

A. Read the following passage. Then circle the letter of the most logical answer to each question, based on the given information.

> In Brazil, life moves slowly, and personal relationships are more important than financial success. Social life revolves around friends, relatives, and special occasions, like weddings or communions. People greet each other with a peck on each cheek or a hearty embrace, and being too much on one's own is seen as abnormal. Business men and women in the cities go home to nearby apartments for lunch. Shops close from noon to 2:00 P.M. so the family can be together. No one feels a need to always be "on time," and people get there when they get there. The important thing is to enjoy life.

1. We can conclude that life in Brazil is
   a. more difficult than life in the United States.
   b. different from life in the United States.
   c. very similar to life in the United States.

2. We can infer that Brazilians tend to be
   a. more materialistic than Americans.
   b. less materialistic than Americans.
   c. equally materialistic as Americans.

3. We can conclude that Brazilians place a high value on
   a. family life.
   b. promptness.
   c. being alone.

B. Read the following passage. Then circle the letter of the most logical answer to each question, based on the given information.

> Two psychiatrists—one young, the other nearing retirement—shared an office suite. As each workday began, both were well-groomed and calm, but by quitting time it was a different story. The younger doctor was exhausted; his hair was wild, his shirt damp with perspiration. But the older man was still fresh as a flower, cheerful and relaxed. Finally, the young psychiatrist could stand it no longer. "I don't understand it!" he exclaimed. "You spend your days as I do—listening to your patients pour out their troubles and tragedies. But I'm a wreck, and you're cool as a cucumber. How do you do it?" The older man turned his calm smile on the young doctor and answered, "So who listens?"

(Continues on next page)

1. We can infer that listening to other people's problems
   a. can be difficult.
   b. is impossible.
   c. is easy.

2. When he says, "So who listens?" the older man implies that
   a. he has no patients.
   b. the way to stay cool is to not listen to patients.
   c. his patients have fewer troubles than the younger man's patients.

INFERENCES: Test 4

A. After reading the passage, put a check by the **two** inferences that are most firmly based on the given information.

> When a Minnesota newspaper held a taste test for fudge sauces, Sweet Mary's Fudge Sauce was included. The sauce is made by a local woman, Mary Riley, who also sells the sauce to other companies to sell under their own label. A sauce sold by Dayton's, a well-known and highly respected department store, was also included in the taste test. The judges did not rank Sweet Mary's Fudge Sauce very highly. One said the sauce had an aroma "like old rubber tires." In contrast, the judges liked Dayton's Marketplace Fudge Sauce very much and gave it a second-place rating. That sauce, agreed the judges, had a "nice blend of bitter and sweet." Mary Riley, to say the least, was angry over the ratings. Why? Dayton's Marketplace Fudge Sauce, as it happens, is none other than her own hot-fudge sauce.

____ 1. It is clear that the judges did not taste any of the sauces.

✓ 2. The judges probably did not know that Mary Riley made Dayton's sauce.

____ 3. Sweet Mary's Fudge Sauce should have come in first.

✓ 4. The judges were probably influenced by Dayton's reputation.

____ 5. Fudge sauce is probably Mary Riley's only product.

B. After reading the passage, put a check by the **three** inferences that are most firmly based on the given information.

> Research has shown that there is more to medicine than lab reports, pills, and surgery. One doctor, for example, has found that the most "difficult" patients—those who ask lots of questions and participate actively in their treatment—are the patients who make the best recoveries. In addition, insurance companies have found that husbands who get kissed goodbye by their wives in the morning have fewer accidents. Also, these husbands live five years longer than those who don't get kissed. Finally, in Israel, researchers have come up with a sure way to predict heart problems in a group of men at risk: When asked "Does your wife show you that she loves you?" those who answer "No" will sooner or later develop chest pains.

____ 1. Men have more accidents than women.

✓ 2. Emotions and attitudes influence health.

(Continues on next page)

✓ 3. Expressing love can be healthy for those you love.

✓ 4. Doctors find unquestioning patients easier to deal with.

___ 5. Bachelors obviously have the most accidents of any group.

INFERENCES: Test 5

A. After reading the following newspaper report, circle the letter of each inference that is most firmly based on the given information.

> *Seattle, Wash. (UPI)*—Ten years ago a man wrote a love poem to his wife, slipped it into a bottle with an envelope, and dropped it into the Pacific Ocean halfway between Seattle and Hawaii.
>
> Chris Willie, an employee of the National Wildlife Federation, found the bottle recently while jogging on a beach in Guam. After replacing the envelope—the ten-cent stamp was a bit behind the times—he dutifully mailed the letter to Seattle.
>
> When it was returned with "no longer at this address," Willie sent it to the *Seattle Times.*
>
> The printed note was unabashed, old-fashioned romanticism.
>
> "If, by the time this letter reaches you, I am old and gray, I know that our love will be as fresh as it is today.
>
> "It may take a week or it may take years for this note to find you. Whatever the case may be, it shall have traveled by a strange and unpredictable messenger—the sea.
>
> "If this should never reach you, it will still be written in my heart that I will go to extreme means to prove my love for you. Your husband, Bob."
>
> The woman to whom the letter was addressed was reached by phone, and the note was read to her. She burst out laughing—and the more she heard, the harder she laughed.
>
> "We're divorced," she said, slamming down the phone.

1. At the time the poem was written, its author probably
   a. was leaving home for good.
   b. loved his wife.
   c. was old and gray.

2. Between the time that the love poem was written and it was found,
   a. ten years had passed.
   b. the couple's love had ended.
   c. both of the above.

(Continues on next page)

B. After reading the following textbook passage, put a check by the **three** inferences that are most firmly based on the given information.

> In our society, the unwritten rules of communication discourage the direct expression of most emotions. Count the number of genuine emotional expressions you hear over a two- or three-day period and you'll discover that emotional expressions are rare.
>
> Not surprisingly, the emotions that people do share directly are usually positive. For example, one study of married couples revealed that the partners shared complimentary feelings ("I love you") or face-saving ones ("I'm sorry I yelled at you"). They also willingly disclosed both positive and negative feelings about absent third parties ("I like Fred," "I'm uncomfortable around Gloria"). On the other hand, the husbands and wives rarely verbalized face-threatening feelings ("I'm disappointed in you") or hostility ("I'm mad at you").
>
> Surprisingly, social rules even discourage too much expression of positive feelings. A hug and kiss for Mother is all right, though a young man should shake hands with Dad. Affection toward friends becomes less and less frequent as we grow older, so that even a simple statement such as "I like you" is seldom heard between adults.

✓   1. Positive feelings are easier to communicate than negative ones.

___   2. The couples in the above study are likely to get divorced.

✓   3. In American culture, women are permitted greater freedom to express emotions than men are.

___   4. Many people in our society are insensitive to the needs of others.

✓   5. Most couples find it easier to express their negative feelings about other people than to express their negative feelings about each other.

INFERENCES: Test 6

A. After reading the following textbook passage, put a check by the **three** inferences that are most firmly based on the given information.

It isn't necessary to travel overseas to encounter differing cultural perspectives. Within this country there are many subcultures, and the members of each one have backgrounds that cause them to see things in unique ways. Failure to recognize these differences can lead to unfortunate and unnecessary misunderstandings. For example, an uninformed Anglo teacher or police officer might interpret the downcast expression of a Latin female as a sign of avoidance, or even dishonesty. But, in fact, this is the proper behavior in her culture for a female being addressed by an older man. To make direct eye contact in such a case would be considered undue brashness or even a sexual come-on.

Eye contact also differs in traditional black and white cultures. Whites tend to look away from a conversational partner while speaking and at the other person when listening. Blacks do just the opposite, looking at their companion more when talking and less when listening. This difference can cause communication problems without either person's realizing the cause. For instance, whites are likely to use eye contact as a measure of how closely the other person is listening. The more others look, the more they seem to be paying attention. A white speaker, therefore, might interpret a black partner's lack of eye contact as a sign of inattention or rudeness. However, quite the opposite could be true.

___✓___ 1. In Anglo culture, downcast eyes are often viewed as a sign of avoidance or dishonesty.

_____ 2. The act of flirting, or letting someone know you are sexually interested, is basically the same in all cultures.

___✓___ 3. Much can be communicated without words.

_____ 4. Latin women have greater freedom in conversations with men than do Anglo women.

___✓___ 5. The same expression can have different meanings in different cultures.

(Continues on next page)

B. Read the following textbook passage. Then circle the letter of the most logical answer to each question, based on the given information.

The pupils of our eyes have long been known to show emotional arousal. Many magicians have an act that makes use of this response. A subject is asked to pick a card from a deck. After the card is returned to the deck, the subject is shown the cards one at a time. By carefully observing the subject's pupils to see which card produces increased pupil size, the magician is able to identify the correct card. If you try this trick on your friends, do not be discouraged if you don't meet with immediate success. Only a great deal of training will sensitize you to the very subtle changes in pupil size. In fact, a special device, called the pupillometer, was devised especially to measure changes in pupil size.

1. We can conclude that magicians
   a. rely on involuntary clues from their subjects.
   b. can read their subjects' minds.
   c. rely on pupil size only when performing the card trick described.

2. We can infer that an emotional response causes the pupils
   a. to first enlarge and then shrink to smaller than usual.
   b. to enlarge very noticeably.
   c. to enlarge slightly.

COMBINED SKILLS: Test 1

After reading the passage, circle the letter of the best answer to each question.

[1]Students sitting quietly in a lecture hall are not all involved in the lecture. [2]If you shot off a gun at sporadic points during a lecture and asked the students to reveal their thoughts at that moment, you would find that very few of them were actually listening to the lecturer. [3]During a typical lecture, about 20 percent of the students are thinking sexual thoughts. [4]Another 20 percent are reminiscing about various events in their lives. [5]Only 20 percent are actually paying attention to the lecture. [6]And only 12 percent are actively listening. [7]The others are worrying, daydreaming, or thinking about lunch or—surprise—religion.

1. In sentence 2, the word *sporadic* means
   a. zero.
   b. expected.
   c. high.
   d. occasional.

2. In sentence 4, the words *reminiscing about* mean
   a. forgetting about.
   b. talking about.
   c. looking back on.
   d. not thinking of.

3. The relationship of sentence 4 to the sentence before it is one of
   a. time.
   b. addition.
   c. illustration.
   d. cause.

4. The main pattern of organization of this paragraph is
   a. time order.
   b. definition and example.
   c. cause and effect.
   d. list of items.

5. __T__ TRUE OR FALSE? We can conclude that a researcher must have asked students what they were thinking at various points during school lectures.

(Continues on next page)

6. We can conclude from this passage that a professor who lectures may improve student attention to class material by

   a. changing the topic of his lectures.

   b. having students participate in the lectures in a direct way.

   c. shooting a gun at various times during the lecture.

   d. lecturing for longer periods of time.

7. We can conclude from this passage that

   a. there is a difference between paying attention to something and actively listening to it.

   b. only very few people have the ability to listen actively.

   c. active listening is easy.

   d. most lectures are not very important.

8. The sentence that best expresses the main idea of the passage is

   a. sentence 2.

   b. sentence 3.

   c. sentence 4.

   d. sentence 7.

COMBINED SKILLS: Test 2

After reading the passage, circle the letter of the best answer to each question.

¹Touching is vital to human development. ²During the nineteenth and early twentieth centuries a large percentage of children died from a disease then called *marasmus*. ³In Greek this word means "wasting away." ⁴In some orphanages the mortality rate was nearly 100 percent. ⁵However, even children in the most "advanced" homes and institutions died regularly from the disease. ⁶Researchers finally found that the infants suffered from lack of physical contact with parents or nurses. ⁷The children hadn't been touched enough, and as a result they died. ⁸From this knowledge came the practice in institutions of picking the baby up, carrying it around, and handling it several times each day. ⁹At one hospital that began this practice, the death rate for infants fell from between 30 to 35 percent to below 10 percent.

1. In sentence 1, the word *vital* means
   - necessary.
   - beside the point.
   - superior.
   - an added bonus.

2. In sentence 4, the word *mortality* means
   - health.
   - death.
   - Greek.
   - touching.

3. *Marasmus* is
   - incurable.
   - mainly a Greek illness.
   - an illness that killed children in orphanages and elsewhere.
   - all of the above.

4. The relationship between the first and second parts of sentence 7 is one of
   - illustration.
   - contrast.
   - cause and effect.
   - time.

5. *(Fill in the blank)* Within the context of the passage, touch is (*a cause* or *an effect?*) _____.

(Continues on next page)

6. From this passage, we can assume that in the nineteenth and early twentieth centuries, children tended to get less attention
   a. at home, from their parents.
   b. in orphanages.
   c. in Greece.
   d. at hospitals where *marasmus* was understood.

7 From this passage, we can infer that touching is one advantage of
   a. giving birth to a child.
   b. breastfeeding a child.
   c. putting a child in a hospital.
   d. giving a child vitamins.

8. The topic sentence of the paragraph is
   a. sentence 1.
   b. sentence 2.
   c. sentence 8.
   d. sentence 9.

COMBINED SKILLS: Test 3

After reading the passage, circle the letter of the best answer to each question.

¹More and more working parents are seeking family benefits. ²Such benefits include unpaid leave to take care of a new baby and day-care assistance. ³Providing family benefits is also helpful to companies. ⁴Employees with such benefits perform better and miss less work.

⁵Although attractive, the concept of family benefits is only getting started. ⁶Now, one out of ten companies provides child-care assistance of some sort. ⁷Such assistance ranges from handing out lists of local community services to providing day-care facilities on the premises. ⁸At least six hundred firms now offer day-care. ⁹Over 50 percent of American firms offer some form of maternity leave. ¹⁰Moreoever, many firms also offer parental leave to fathers. ¹¹In a pioneering move, IBM has started a program allowing an employee to take a leave of absence of up to three years. ¹²The employee can take care of a child or a sick relative without losing company benefits and with a guaranteed job on return.

1. In sentence 11, the words *leave of absence* mean a
   a. vacation time.
   b. job elsewhere.
   c. period of working part time.
   c. period of time away from work.

2. The author states that family benefits
   a. are helpful to companies as well as employees.
   b. cost too much for most companies to provide.
   c. have been offered for many years.
   d. are unfair to workers who are unmarried.

3. The relationship of the second sentence to the first sentence is one of
   a. time.
   b. addition.
   c. illustration.
   d. contrast.

4. The relationship of sentence 10 to sentence 9 is one of
   a. illustration.
   b. addition.
   c. time.
   d. contrast.

(Continues on next page)

5. The main pattern of organization of the second paragraph is
   a. time order.
   b. list of items.
   c. definition and example.
   d. cause and effect.

6. The paragraph suggests that family benefits result in
   a. more productive workers.
   b. more productive companies.
   c. both of the above.
   d. neither of the above.

7. The passage suggests that in the future, companies will probably
   a. offer fewer and fewer family benefits.
   b. hire fewer and fewer women.
   c. provide more and more family benefits to workers.
   d. give more financial bonuses to workers.

8. Which of the following statements best expresses the main idea of the passage?
   a. Although they are still fairly new, family benefits help both employees and companies.
   b. Many working parents are looking for special benefits from their employers.
   c. One out of ten companies now provides child-care assistance.
   d. IBM has begun a program allowing employees to take a personal leave of absence of up to three years.

COMBINED SKILLS: Test 4

After reading the passage, circle the letter of the best answer to each question.

¹In making its pricing decision, a company needs to consider the other members of the pricing chain. ²The consumer price of a product is often the result of several separate decisions.

³Consumer goods usually pass from manufacturer to wholesaler to retailer. ⁴The manufacturer makes the product and decides on an initial price. ⁵Then the manufacturer sells the item to a wholesaler, who sells the item to a retailer at a new price. ⁶The retailer then tries to sell the product to the consumer at yet another price. ⁷If nobody buys the item, the retailer may reduce the price. ⁸At every level in the chain, the price of the product is increased enough for that member to make a profit.

⁹Because a number of parties are involved in setting the final price of a product, no one has total control. ¹⁰The manufacturer may recommend a certain pricing strategy for a product. ¹¹But there is no guarantee that other links in the chain will abide by the recommendation.

1. In sentence 4, the word *initial* means
   a. final.
   b. large.
   c. first.
   d. unfair.

2. In sentence 11, the words *abide by* mean
   a. follow.
   b. remember.
   c. know.
   d. argue against.

3. The price of a product is increased in each step of the pricing chain
   a. too much.
   b. too little.
   c. enough for each member of the chain to make a profit.
   d. strictly according to the instructions of the manufacturer.

4. The relationship between the first and second parts of sentence 9 is one of
   a. comparison.
   b. contrast.
   c. addition.
   d. cause and effect.

(Continues on next page)

5. The relationship between sentences 10 and 11 is one of
   a. cause and effect.
   b. comparison.
   (c.) contrast.
   d. time.

6. The main pattern of organization of the second paragraph is
   a. list of items.
   b. contrast.
   (c.) time order.
   d. definition and example.

7. Why might the author have used the image of a chain to describe the pricing process?
   a. The pricing process is a rigid system in which prices not flexible.
   b. The pricing system protects the manufacturer, like a strong chain-link fence.
   c. The pricing process is unfair and chains people to high prices.
   (d.) The steps in the process are linked one to another, like the parts of a chain.

8. The passage suggests that in addition to manufacturer, wholesaler and retailer, the price of a product is also influenced by
   a. state governments.
   b. guarantees.
   (c.) the consumer's attitude toward the product.
   d. last year's prices.

COMBINED SKILLS: Test 5

After reading the passage, circle the letter of the best answer to each question.

[1]Research shows that we do make assumptions about people based on their style of clothing. [2]In one study, a man and woman were stationed in a hallway so that anyone who wished to go by had to respond to them in some way. [3]They could either politely excuse themselves or rudely ignore them. [4]Sometimes the conversationalists wore "formal daytime dress." [5]At other times they wore "casual attire." [6]Passers-by behaved differently toward the couple, depending on the style of clothing. [7]They responded positively to the well-dressed couple and negatively when the same people were casually dressed. [8]Similar results in other situations show the influence of clothing. [9]We are more likely to obey people dressed in a high-status manner. [10]Pedestrians were more likely to return lost coins to well-dressed people than to those dressed in low-status clothing. [11]We are also more likely to follow the lead of high-status dressers, even when it comes to violating social rules. [12]For example, 83 percent of the pedestrians in one study followed a well-dressed jaywalker who crossed the street when a traffic light flashed "wait." [13]But only 48 percent followed a jaywalker dressed in lower-status clothing.

1. In sentence 2, the word *stationed* means
   a. imagined.
   b. avoided.
   c. forced.
   (d.) placed.

2. In sentence 11, the word *violating* means
   (a.) breaking.
   b. understanding.
   c. following.
   d. learning.

3. According to the experiment, we are more likely to return lost coins to
   a. men.
   b. women.
   (c.) people in high-status clothing.
   d. people in low-status clothing.

(Continues on next page)

4. People tend to react more positively toward
   a. men who are casually dressed.
   b. women.
   (c.) people who are dressed formally or in a high-status manner.
   d. couples who are dressed alike.

5. The relationship of sentence 8 to sentence 7 is one of
   a. time.
   b. illustration.
   (c.) comparison.
   d. contrast.

6. The relationship of sentences 12 and 13 to sentence 11 is one of
   a. time.
   (b.) illustration.
   c. contrast.
   d. comparison.

7. We can infer from this passage that our reactions to people are sometimes
   a. not thought out.
   b. based on appearances.
   c. illogical.
   (d.) all of the above.

8. Which statement best states the main idea of the selection?
   a. In one experiment, people who passed a casually dressed couple responded negatively to them.
   (b.) The way people dress affects the way we view them and the level of influence they have over us.
   c. To get ahead in a career, dress in a high-status manner.
   d. Pedestrians were more likely to return coins to well-dressed people than to those dressed in low-status clothing.

COMBINED SKILLS: Test 6

After reading the passage, circle the letter of the best answer to each question.

¹It is human nature to prefer doing business with those we know and like. ²For this reason, many people practice networking, the art of making and using contacts. ³Networking is the way people find out about jobs that aren't advertised in the newspaper. ⁴It is the way they learn about valuable new developments in their field before the crowd does.

⁵There are three main elements in networking. ⁶The first is *visibility*, making your presence known. ⁷The more people who meet you, the more who are likely to remember you. ⁸The next element is *familiarity*, letting people get to know you. ⁹It takes courage to expose your skills, attitudes, and opinions, but people are more likely to deal with you if they have some idea of how you think and react. ¹⁰The last element, *image*, means giving people positive impressions of you. ¹¹Image provides people with the impression that you are competent. ¹²No one wants to hire someone who lacks the necessary skills for the job.

1. In sentence 10, the word *competent* means
   a. friendly.
   b. eager to begin work.
   c. well-dressed.
   (d.) properly qualified.

2. The relationship between sentences 1 and 2 is one of
   a. contrast.
   (b.) cause and effect.
   c. comparison.
   d. addition.

3. The relationship of sentence 10 to the several sentences that come before it is one of
   a. time.
   b. illustration.
   (c.) addition.
   d. comparison.

4. The main pattern of organization of the second paragraph is
   a. time order.
   (b.) list of items.
   c. contrast.
   d. definition and example.

(Continues on next page)

5. (Fill in the blank): The transitions that introduce the major supporting details of the second paragraph are *first*, *next*, and _____ *last* _____.

6. The passage suggests that networking
   a. can be used to improve your standing after you have a job as well as in finding the job.
   b. should never involve stating your opinions.
   c. can be used only in large corporations.
   d. should get you a job within a few weeks.

7. The main idea of the second paragraph is best expressed in
   a. sentence 4.
   b. sentence 5.
   c. sentence 9.
   d. sentence 12.

8. Which statement best expresses the main idea of the entire passage?
   a. There are three main elements in networking.
   b. There are many more ways to find a job than simply looking through newspaper advertisements.
   c. People prefer to do business with those they know and like.
   d. Networking, the art of making and using contacts, involves three elements: visibility, familiarity, and image.

Part III

TEN READING SELECTIONS

1

Disaster and Friendship
Chuck Wilson

Preview

Some situations are especially good for showing what people are really like. During a trip south, Chuck Wilson lived through such a situation, an unexpected one. Much of what he found people to be really like was also unexpected. This selection is his account of that experience.

Words to Watch

relate (1):	tell
bearing (3):	advancing
stereotyped (4):	oversimplified and prejudiced
stocky (4):	solidly built
severe (5):	harsh
intensified (5):	increased
mocking (6):	scornful
trusty (7):	a convict who has been given special privileges

I shall relate° to you as accurately as possible what happened 1 when I, a black man, had a car accident in North Carolina during a trip to Florida. I am by profession a golf caddy. I usually caddy in the Philadelphia area during the spring, summer, and fall, and find some other type of work during the winter months. One particular winter was a poor one in the area for work, so I decided to go to Florida and caddy until spring. I packed my clothes in my car, made my goodbyes to my wife and three children, and left for Florida on a Saturday around noon.

The trip was very long and boring, especially since I was traveling 2 alone. I drove straight through Delaware and Virginia until about 3:00 A.M., when I noticed a cafe open in a small town in North Carolina. I stopped with the intention of getting a cup of coffee and perhaps a sandwich. However, it just so happened that the cafe sold not only coffee but also beer and bootleg liquor. Not realizing how tired I really was or how a drink or two would affect me, I had a hamburger, two beers, and, worse, a drink of North Carolina's special "white lightning."

When I got back on the road, it was almost 5 A.M. I didn't think 3 the drinks would have an adverse effect on my driving, but I was wrong. About 5:30, soon after I passed a sign informing me I was passing through the town of Warrendale, I went to sleep behind the wheel and missed a curve around an island in the center of the road. When I suddenly awoke I could see that I was bearing° onto the island, and I was too late in snatching the wheel quickly to the right. The front wheels hit the curb, causing my car to flip over on its top and slide across the grass of the island. After the car stopped, I must have spent a minute in total darkness, upside down and having no clear idea of what had happened to me. Eventually I realized that I was physically all right, and I rolled down the driver's window and managed to climb through it and out of the car. A passing motorist, a white man, stopped to see if I needed help. After convincing me and himself that I was all right, he said he would contact the local sheriff and drove off.

Because of the chilly weather, and the fact that I had only a light 4 golf jacket on, I climbed back into my car through the open window. I was lying there with my feet hanging out the window when the sheriff arrived. I heard him exclaim, "My God, not another one!" and I then crawled out from the car. The sheriff explained to me that another accident had happened at the same spot just a week before, but the driver had been killed. My first reaction on seeing the sheriff was apprehension, for he looked like the stereotyped° image of the white Southern country sheriff—short, stocky°, and red-necked.

But he turned out to be just the opposite of what I feared. He 5 called for a wrecker to take away my car and took me to his office. He listened sympathetically to my account of how the accident happened and of my intentions of travelling to Florida to make a living for myself and my family. He searched his violation book for the violation that carried the least severe° fine and finally decided that I had "failed to yield right of way." He told me that I would have to accompany him to Chester, North Carolina, which was the county seat, and appear before the magistrate there. We then drove the eighteen miles to Chester, and that was where my troubles really intensified°.

I was brought before a white magistrate who, to put it mildly, was   6
very peeved at having been awakened at 6:00 A.M. to hear a case. The
magistrate read the charges and swore at the sheriff for writing out a
ticket that wasn't consistent with what actually happened. The sheriff
explained that I had limited money and that I was going to Florida to
try to make a living for my family. The magistrate then turned to me
and said, "Boy, how much money have you got?" His eyes were filled
with a hard, mocking° look; calling me "Boy" clearly gave him great
pleasure. I was very angry, but knowing where I was, I tried to control
myself. I told him that I had $24.50, just enough money to get to
Florida. He then said, "The fine's $24.50." I paid the fine with my last
money and then requested that I be given lodging for the rest of the
night, since I had no money and no place to go. He said all right and
turned me over to the jailer, who took me upstairs to the county jail and
put me in one of the cells.

I fell asleep very quickly, exhausted by everything that had   7
happened. I was awakened about 7:30 that morning by a black trusty°
bringing breakfast. There was a small tray with a cup of cold coffee,
two hard biscuits, and a small helping of grits. When I said I didn't
want anything to eat, the fellow in the next cell asked me for mine,
which I readily gave to him. I went back to sleep and woke up at about
3:00 P.M. Thinking that I was free to go, I asked the trusty to get the
jailer for me. When he came, my spirits, which were low anyway,
really got a jolt. The jailer looked at me with amusement through the
bars and said that I owed an additional $2.50 for lodging and
breakfast. I really felt that the bottom had fallen out of things now, and
had visions of working on a chain gang somewhere. I wondered if this
was the reason the magistrate had been so ready to let me stay in the
jail to sleep.

My salvation was that the trusty took a liking to me and offered   8
me the $2.50 that I needed. I was taken downstairs and when I paid the
magistrate, his final words were, "Now, boy, git out of my town." I
found out the name of the small town where I had the accident and
which direction it was. I also learned that it was eighteen miles away. I
began walking the dusty, lonesome road to Warrendale in the chilly
evening air. As I did, a police car with two white officers who had been
in the magistrate's office sped by me. I had heard that they were going
on a patrol to the city's limits, but certainly wasn't surprised that they
declined to offer me a ride. I did notice the officer in the passenger's
seat looking out at me as the car went by, and I expected to get an
obscene finger gesture or a mocking smile. I was surprised, then, to see
that his face showed an expression more like that of regret.

The first person to see me as I completed my eighteen-mile 9
marathon at 11:30 P.M. was the white sheriff. He picked me up and
asked me what I was doing on the road at this hour. After I explained
what had happened in Chester, he told me that he would find me a
place to stay for the night. He stopped at about three houses before he
finally found a young black couple who agreed to take me in for the
night. I don't think I could have accepted a complete stranger in my
house the way they did. They may have been intimidated by the
presence of the white sheriff. But beyond that, they were simply a very
good and friendly couple. They gave me a clean bed to sleep in and the
next morning, which was Monday, gave me breakfast and left to take
their children to a babysitter and to go to work themselves. They told
me to leave whenever I wanted and just be sure to lock the door.

I left their home at about 9:00 A.M. and walked over to the garage 10
where my car was being held. The owner of the garage was white and
hostile, and told me that there was a thirty-five-dollar towing charge
even though the accident had occurred approximately seventy-five
yards from his garage. I tried to explain my situation to him, but he
made it clear by quickly walking away that the only thing he would
listen to was the money. He even refused to let me open the trunk of my
car to get out the clothes and things I thought I would need if I had to
stay in the area until I earned the money. After looking around the town
of Warrendale for a while I realized I would have to go back to Chester
to try to find work.

I started hitchhiking, and who but the friendly sheriff picked me 11
up. I told him my situation, and he agreed to take me to Chester. In
Chester, I went to the chamber of commerce and asked the lady in
charge to help me find a job. When she understood my situation, she
got in touch with the minister heading the local church federation and
the president of the local bank. Within an hour they had gotten money
for the release of my car and another twenty-five dollars to help me
reach Florida. The minister drove me back to Warrendale, got my car
for me, and sent me on my way. The remainder of the trip proceeded
without incident, giving me plenty of time to think about all the good
and bad things that had happened to me.

VOCABULARY QUESTIONS

A. Use context clues to help you decide on the letter of the best definition for each italicized word.

1. The word *adverse* in "I didn't think the drinks would have an adverse effect on my driving, but I was wrong" (paragraph 3) means
   a. positive.
   b. unfavorable.
   c. humorous.
   d. impossible.

2. The word *apprehension* in "My first reaction on seeing the sheriff was apprehension, for he looked like the stereotyped image of the white Southern country sheriff—short, stocky, and red-necked" (paragraph 4) means
   a. joy.
   b. confusion.
   c. fear.
   d. romance.

3. The word *peeved* in "a white magistrate who, to put it mildly, was very peeved at having been awakened at 6:00 A.M." (paragraph 6) means
   a. pleased.
   b. flattered.
   c. annoyed.
   d. fearful.

4. The word *jolt* in "Thinking that I was free to go, I asked the trusty to get the jailer for me. When he came, my spirits . . . really got a jolt. The jailer . . . said that I owed an additional $2.50" (paragraph 7) means
   a. sudden shock.
   b. encouragement.
   c. inspiration.
   d. something expected.

5. The word *intimidated* in "a young black couple . . . agreed to take me in for the night. . . . They may have been intimidated by the presence of the white sheriff. But beyond that, they were simply a very good and friendly couple" (paragraph 9) means
   a. pleased.
   b. angered.
   c. frightened.
   d. discouraged.

B. Below are words, or forms of words, from "Words to Watch." Write in the one that best completes each sentence.

bearing	intensified	related
severely	stereotyped	

6. Dora hardly fits the _____*stereotyped*_____ image of a grandmother—she jogs fifteen miles a week and manages her own catering company.

7. Once the flames ate into the logs, the heat from the fireplace _____*intensified*_____.

8. Elvin sat down by his son, who had just lost his job, and _____*related*_____ the story of how he too had lost his very first job.

9. When he saw three tacklers _____*bearing*_____ towards him, the quarterback quickly stepped back and passed the football.

10. If you punish your child too _____*severely*_____, he or she may resent you rather than learn from the experience.

READING COMPREHENSION QUESTIONS

Central Point and Main Ideas

1. Which sentence best expresses the central point of this selection?
   a. Drinking and driving can be disastrous.
   b. Sometimes kindness is found where it is least expected.
   c. Always carry extra money for emergencies when you travel.
   d. A small Southern town is never a good place for a black stranger.

2. Which sentence best expresses the main idea of paragraph 9?
   a. Once again, good people helped Wilson, this time with a ride and a place to stay.
   b. Wilson had to walk the eighteen miles.
   c. The sheriff had a little trouble finding a place for Wilson to stay.
   d. A young black couple let Wilson stay overnight.

Supporting Details

3. Wilson
   a. usually had to go to Florida to find work in the winter.
   b. knew that he was too tired to drive after drinking.

c. couldn't remember why he lost control of his car.

(d.) was not hurt in the accident.

4. The white magistrate fined Wilson
   a. $2.50.
   (b.) all the money Wilson had.
   c. $50.00.
   d. $25.00.

5. The owner of the garage
   a. was located far from the accident.
   b. was willing to forget the towing charge.
   (c.) refused to let Wilson open his car trunk.
   d. offered Wilson work so he could work off his debt.

Transitions

6. Narratives naturally benefit from time transitions. Write here two of the time transitions Wilson uses in paragraph 3.

When	*after*

7. The sentence below begins with a transition that shows
   a. time.
   b. addition.
   (c.) cause and effect.
   d. comparison.

   > Because of the chilly weather, and the fact that I had only a light golf jacket on, I climbed back into my car through the open window. (Paragraph 4)

Patterns of Organization

8. Like paragraphs, longer selections use patterns of organization. This selection, like all narratives, mainly uses the pattern of organization of
   (a.) time order.
   b. a list of items.
   c. cause and effect.
   d. definition and example.

Inferences

9. From the story, we can conclude that Wilson never expected
   a. to find a job in Florida.
   (b.) to pay for staying in jail.
   c. to see his car again.
   d. any trouble with the local sheriff.

10. From the story, we can conclude that
   a. Wilson preferred working in Florida to working in the Philadelphia area.
   b. the white magistrate treated everyone equally, regardless of color.
   c. people rarely go out of their way to help others.
   (d.) not all Southern police officers fit the old stereotype of them as racists.

OUTLINING

Following is a general outline of "Disaster and Friendship." Complete the outline by filling in the letters of the missing major supporting details, which are listed below in random order.

Central point: Trouble can be an opportunity to experience unexpected kindness.

1. ___b___

2. Wilson's stop at the cafe and the resulting accident

3. A passing driver's help

4. ___d___

5. ___c___

6. ___a___

Major Supporting Details Missing from the Outline
   a. Help in finding a place to sleep after jail
   b. The reason for Wilson's trip to Florida
   c. A racist magistrate's treatment and a day in jail
   d. The sheriff's efforts to help Wilson get off easily

DISCUSSION QUESTIONS

1. Wilson was worried that the sheriff would be just "like the stereotyped image of the white Southern country sheriff." What is that image?

2. Wilson asked the woman in charge at the Chester Chamber of Commerce to help him find a job. Instead, she arranged for him to get some money and his car so he could go on to Florida. Why might she have done that?

3. Wilson's experience was notable partly because it showed how wrong stereotypes can be. What experiences have you had in which people did not fit their stereotypes?

4. How do stereotypes influence our treatment of other people?

Check Your Performance   DISASTER AND FRIENDSHIP

Skill	*Number Right*	*Points*	*Total*
VOCABULARY			
Vocabulary in Context (5 items)	_____	x 10 =	_____
Words to Watch (5 items)	_____	x 10 =	_____
		SCORE =	_____%
COMPREHENSION			
Central Point and Main Ideas (2 items)	_____	x 8 =	_____
Supporting Details (3 items)	_____	x 8 =	_____
Transitions (2 items)	_____	x 8 =	_____
Patterns of Organization (1 item)	_____	x 8 =	_____
Inferences (2 items)	_____	x 8 =	_____
Outlining (4 items)	_____	x 5 =	_____
		SCORE =	_____%

FINAL SCORES: Vocabulary _____%   Comprehension _____%

Enter your final scores into the reading performance chart on the inside back cover.

2

Read All About It
Fran DeBlasio

Preview

When are people too old to really turn their lives around? Ten? Twenty? Twenty-five? Here is the story of someone who made her life *very* different and better beginning at the age of thirty-five.

Words to Watch

decipher (1):	read or make sense of something
unique (2):	unusual
pass the buck (4):	pass the responsibility on to someone else
chaos (5):	disorder
landmarks (8):	objects or structures that help people find their way
stunned (10):	shocked

For most of her life Fran DeBlasio, 36, tried to conceal her shame. Unable to read the street signs or subway maps in her native Manhattan, let alone decipher° warning labels on medicine bottles, she lived, like many illiterates, in constant fear of the unknown. An even greater terror was that friends would discover her secret. "I was embarrassed," DeBlasio says. "I thought there must be something wrong with me."

DeBlasio's case is not unique°. Studies suggest that perhaps one in ten adult Americans is unable to read well enough to complete this article. The costs to society—in terms of welfare and unemployment payments and underproductivity—are enormous. With a growing *awareness of the literacy crisis, a lucky few are getting help. DeBlasio enrolled last year in a program sponsored by Literacy Volunteers of New York City, a nonprofit organization, and can now read and write at a junior high school level. She described her personal triumph to reporter Jane Sugden.*

3 By the time I reached junior high school I could read a little, but not very much. Whenever I was asked to read aloud in class, I felt terrible. I was afraid and nervous. I tried to tell myself, "Fran, you're smart. You have something up there." But I was confused and didn't know where to turn. My parents had separated when I was young and my mother supported me and my two brothers by working as a cleaning lady. She was a traditional Italian woman who always told us how important it was to get a good education. But even after she went to my school to try to find out why I was having problems, nothing changed.

4 I was going to public school in a working-class neighborhood in Manhattan. When I had to take written tests, I scribbled down some answers. I almost always flunked, but they still passed me on to the next grade anyway. When I told my teachers I was scared I wouldn't be able to keep up, they all gave me the same story: "Go home this summer and study hard on your vacation. If you work hard, you'll do better next year." But the impression I really had was they thought I was just too stupid to learn and would drop out sooner or later anyway. It's as if everyone just wanted to pass the buck° and get rid of me as quickly as possible. No one ever tried to give me any special help with my reading, and there weren't any experts at the school who knew how to teach people who didn't catch on right away. They just made me feel it was all my fault—that I didn't try hard enough. Meanwhile, I felt rejected and alone. Very alone. I get so angry when I think about that now.

5 Even though I had never been a discipline problem, in the seventh grade they put me in a class for kids who were troublemakers or wise guys. It was total chaos°. All day, the teacher yelled at the students and they yelled back. It was no good for learning.

6 High school was worse. I went to an all-girl school where a lot of the kids were tough. Fights broke out almost every day. I was too frightened to use the john because girls had been attacked there, sometimes sexually attacked by other girls. When I turned 17, I couldn't take it any more and quit. I figured, "What's the difference? I'm not learning anything anyway."

7 After quitting school, I didn't know what to do. Babysitting was one of the few jobs I could handle. I also worked at an amusement park in New Jersey taking tickets for kiddie rides. Once I went to apply for a city job. I didn't understand most of the application, so I asked to take

it home. But she said I had to fill it out there. I said, "Never mind. I don't want this job anyway," and ran out. I didn't want to be a bum, but I was very afraid of being rejected.

Trying to get a driver's license was impossible because I knew I couldn't pass the written test. Even simple street directions were a problem because I was not able to read signs. At the same time, I was ashamed to tell my friends I couldn't read, so I bluffed a lot. I memorized landmarks° in order to get around. Since I couldn't understand the menus at restaurants, I learned to be a good actress. I asked my friends, "What are you having? What looks good?" Sometimes at parties, people wanted to play games like Scrabble, and I had to fake a headache. When people talked about the books they were reading—maybe a best-seller—I'd say, "I read sports books," because sports was one of the few subjects I could talk about. 8

By the time I was 25, my reading had improved slightly from studying the sports pages of the newspaper. Then a friend helped me fill out an application to work in the mail distribution department of a bank and—I couldn't believe it—I got the job. I had a tough time at first, learning to tell the difference between hundreds of different names. But my boss was very helpful. I learned to do the job well and began to feel much better about myself. 9

In June 1985, after ten years on the job, I was offered a promotion to assistant supervisor, but I was terrified because the new position involved a lot of paperwork. Luckily, a friend told me about Literacy Volunteers and arranged for me to meet with Barbara Greenfield, one of the coordinators of the program. When I told Barbara about my fears of taking on the new position, she volunteered to tutor me during her own free time. I was stunned° that someone would go out of her way to help me like that. When I walked out of her office, I felt born again. 10

Within a few months, I joined a small reading group which meets for two-hour sessions three times a week. When I first began, I would read a passage twenty-five times and not know what it meant. Or I would get hung up on one word for a half hour without getting the sense of a whole sentence. But during one session a few weeks later, one of my tutors asked me questions about something I read, and I suddenly realized I was giving her the answers. She said, "Fran, you understand!" I said, "Holy Christ! This is me. I can read." 11

The tutors also encouraged me to write. At first I had trouble putting down a single sentence, but before long I was writing stories and even poetry. I particularly like to write about my family. At a special meeting of my reading group one night, I recited a story I had written on my birthday about my mother, who died three years ago. 12

When I finished everyone had tears in their eyes. I've written other pieces about my grandfather, who is ninety years old and lives with me. When he was in the hospital for a stroke three months ago, I sat with him every day and wrote about my feelings.

Things that once seemed impossible are now fun. I've read books 13 about George Washington and Babe Ruth. I'm studying for my high school equivalency exam and my driver's license test. I recently went to see an opera and was able to read an English translation of the story that they projected above the stage. Wow, that made me feel good! Even watching TV is different. Now I can read the ads. I understand street signs, menus, all those things. It's like a great burden has been lifted off my back.

Recently, I've confessed to my friends about the problem I always 14 had reading. One very close friend I used to play softball with moved to Florida several years ago and kept writing to me. She didn't know I couldn't write back, so she called me one time to ask why she hadn't received any letters from me. I said, "Oh, I'm just not very good about writing." I was ashamed to tell her the whole truth, so I had a friend write a letter for me. A few months ago, I wrote her a letter in my own handwriting and explained my problem. I told her how much I was learning and how exciting it was to finally be able to read. She wrote back and said, "I'm very proud of you. Very proud. I'm glad you told me." She understood.

VOCABULARY QUESTIONS

A. Use context clues to help you decide on the best definition for each italicized word. Then circle the letter of each choice.

1. The word *rejected* in "I said, 'Never mind. I don't want this job anyway,' and ran out. . . . I was very afraid of being rejected" (paragraph 7) means
   a. refused.
   b. hired.
   c. honored.
   d. forgotten.

2. The word *bluffed* in "I was ashamed to tell my friends I couldn't read, so I bluffed a lot. I memorized landmarks. . . . I learned to be a good actress" (paragraph 8) means
   a. coughed.
   b. talked.
   c. questioned.
   d. pretended.

3. The word *recited* in "At a special meeting of my reading group one night, I recited a story I had written. . . . When I finished everyone had tears in their eyes" (paragraph 12) means
   a. thought about.
   b. sang.
   c. read aloud.
   d. examined.

4. The word *projected* in "I . . . was able to read an English translation of the story that they projected above the stage" (paragraph 13) means
   a. read out loud.
   b. made appear.
   c. erased.
   d. forgot.

5. The word *burden* in "I understand street signs, menus, all those things. It's like a great burden has been lifted off my back" (paragraph 13) means
   a. shirt.
   b. load.
   c. bump.
   d. pleasure.

B. Below are words, or forms of words, from "Words to Watch." Write in the one that best completes each sentence.

chaos	decipher	landmark
stunned	unique	

6. The birthday party for my three-year-old created such _____*chaos*_____ in the living room that it took me all afternoon to clean up.

7. Norm and I have been going together for two years now, but my parents were still _____*stunned*_____ to learn that we plan to get married.

8. Because the statue of President Grant is in the middle of town, everyone uses it as a _____*landmark*_____.

9. The statues on the top of the wedding cake had a _____*unique*_____ touch—the bride wore a maternity wedding dress.

10. Pharmacists always manage somehow to _____*decipher*_____ doctors' prescriptions.

READING COMPREHENSION QUESTIONS

Central Point and Main Ideas

1. Which sentence best expresses the central point of the selection?
   a. DeBlasio could not read.
   b. Learning to read has changed DeBlasio's life.
   c. DeBlasio felt ashamed that she couldn't read.
   d. DeBlasio didn't learn to read in school.

2. Which sentence best expresses the main idea of paragraph 7?
   a. DeBlasio could handle babysitting.
   b. DeBlasio once worked at an amusement park taking tickets for children's rides.
   c. DeBlasio couldn't fill out the application form for a city job.
   d. DeBlasio's inability to read limited job opportunities and made applying for jobs difficult.

3. Which sentence best expresses the main idea of paragraph 13?
   a. DeBlasio is enjoying activities she thought she would never be able to do.
   b. DeBlasio can now read books.
   c. DeBlasio is studying for a high-school equivalency exam and a driver's license test.
   d. DeBlasio can even read the English translation of an opera.

Supporting Details

4. Before she was tutored by a coordinator of Literacy Volunteers, DeBlasio
   a. could not read at all.
   b. never even wished she could read.
   c. could read a little.
   d. could read enough to feel very capable at work.

Transitions

5. Paragraph 7 begins with a transition that shows
   a. addition.
   b. time.
   c. illustration.
   d. cause and effect.

6. The sentence below expresses a relationship of
   a. contrast.
   b. cause and effect.
   c. time.
   d. addition.

   Trying to get a driver's license was impossible because I knew I couldn't pass the written test. (Paragraph 8)

Patterns of Organization

7. The pattern of organization of paragraph 13 is
   a. time order.
   ⓑ list of items.
   c. definition-example.
   d. contrast.

Inferences

8. DeBlasio implies that
   a. she was too stupid to learn to read in public school.
   b. her teachers did the best they could for her.
   ⓒ none of the schools she went to were good places for her to learn in.
   d. in school she managed to keep her self-image strong despite the fact that she couldn't read.

9. __*T*__ TRUE OR FALSE? DeBlasio implies that she should not have been put in a class for students who were discipline problems.

10. From this article we can conclude that
    a. people can get along very well without reading.
    ⓑ those who can't read may find ways of hiding that fact.
    c. when people don't learn to read in school, it is all their own fault.
    d. once people reach their thirties, it is almost impossible for them to learn new skills.

SUMMARIZING

Complete the following summary of "Read All About It" by filling in the blanks.

DeBlasio didn't learn to read in her schools, which did a poor job of teaching her. After quitting high school, there were few jobs she could tackle, and her everyday activities were restricted by her inability to read. Ashamed that she couldn't read, DeBlasio hid it from her friends. By the time she was twenty-five, however, her reading had improved a little and she got a job _____*distributing mail in a bank*_____. After working at the bank for ten years, _____*DeBlasio was offered a promotion*_____. She wasn't sure, however, that she could handle the paperwork of the new job. Luckily, a friend told her about Literacy Volunteers, and she began to learn to read through a tutor. Later she also joined ____*a reading group*____ and began to write. DeBlasio is now able to enjoy many activities she once thought impossible for her. She feels much happier with herself and has even told_____*her friends about the problems she has had with reading*_____.

DISCUSSION QUESTIONS

1. Do you know anybody who has trouble reading? How does that trouble affect his or her life?

2. Just how difficult is it to live in our society without being able to read? To get an idea of the answer to this question, think about your activities at home, shopping, in restaurants, and driving. How much of what you've done involves reading?

3. DeBlasio gives a pretty bleak picture of the schools she attended. In what ways were your own schools like, or unlike, hers? Why do you think her teachers behaved as they did?

4. We tend to think that people don't learn important new skills as they get older, but DeBlasio's story contradicts that idea. Are there people you know of who have been able to learn new skills as they get older?

Check Your Performance   **READ ALL ABOUT IT**

Skill	Number Right	Points	Total
VOCABULARY			
Vocabulary in Context (5 items)	_____	x 10 =	_____
Words to Watch (5 items)	_____	x 10 =	_____
		SCORE =	_____%
COMPREHENSION			
Central Point and Main Ideas (3 items)	_____	x 8 =	_____
Supporting Details (1 item)	_____	x 8 =	_____
Transitions (2 items)	_____	x 8 =	_____
Patterns of Organization (1 item)	_____	x 8 =	_____
Inferences (3 items)	_____	x 8 =	_____
Summarizing (4 items)	_____	x 5 =	_____
		SCORE =	_____%

FINAL SCORES: Vocabulary _____%   Comprehension _____%

Enter your final scores into the reading performance chart on the inside back cover.

3

Adult Children at Home
Marilyn Mack

Preview

Parents used to expect their children to leave home not long after high school or college. Nowadays, however, children leave home later than ever, and even then they may not be gone for good. Marilyn Mack explains this new pattern and its ups and downs.

Words to Watch

ruefully (2):	with regret
phenomenon (10):	important happening
cope (12):	manage
fixed (13):	unchanging
precautions (18):	actions taken in advance to protect against possible problems
consent (22):	agreement

Ruth Patterson remembers the day the last of her children left home. "Dan was 18 and headed off to the state university," said the Pennsylvania housewife. "I cried a while, and then told myself, 'Cheer up! At last you and Dave have the house to yourselves!'" 1

Six years later, Mrs. Patterson laughs a little ruefully° at that memory. Since her youngest son left for college, three of her four children—one with a three-year-old daughter—have moved back to the family home for at least six months at a time. 2

"The 'empty nest' hasn't been quite as empty as we expected," 3
says Mrs. Patterson.

The Pattersons' situation is becoming less unusual all the time. 4
Adult children have been "nesting," or moving back to the family
home, in increasing numbers in recent years. In 1970, according to the
U.S. Census Bureau, 54 percent of men and 41 percent of women
between the ages of 18 and 24 depended on their parents for housing.
In 1988, those figures had risen to 59 percent of men and 47 percent of
women. For men and women ages 25 to 34, the figures had risen from
9.5 percent and 6.6 percent in 1970 to 14 percent and 8 percent in 1988.

Why are adult children coming home? The case of the Pattersons 5
provides some typical reasons.

Oldest daughter Suzanne, 35, a bank teller, returned home with her 6
toddler after a painful divorce. Two years later she is still there, with her
mother caring for her little girl. "She needed a place to lick her wounds,"
said her mother. "We thought it would be for just a few months, but
when we realized what it would cost her to keep Jenny in day care while
she worked, it didn't make sense for them to move out again."

Five years after high school, son Peter, now 28, spent a year at 7
home working on a painting crew while he and his fiancée saved
money for the down payment on a house.

Daughter Lesley, 30, has moved in and out of the house so many 8
times "we've lost count," says her mother. A legal secretary, Lesley
"earns enough to have her own place, if she'd learn to live within her
means. But she wants to live like the lawyers she works with." That
translates into an expensive car, lots of evenings out and a wardrobe
that burst the limits of her modest salary.

Only the Pattersons' youngest, Dan, now 24, has followed the 9
route his parents expected. He graduated from college, found a job
teaching high school social studies, and lives on his own in a city
apartment.

Many factors have contributed to the phenomenon° of nesting. 10
They include the rise in the divorce rate, increased housing costs, a tight
job market, college debts, and the trend to delay marriage. Once out on
their own, many young people are finding it unexpectedly difficult to
maintain the standard of living they hoped for. Apartment rentals,
particularly in major cities, can make living alone an impossible option.
Buying a house is even less likely for most—a first-time home buyer
can expect to pay over 40 percent more today than in 1977.

Returning home can be a financial life-saver for struggling young 11
people. Some credit counselors recommend nesting as a solution for
people who've gotten in over their heads with credit cards and utility

bills. "I was really in a mess financially when I moved back in with Mom and Dad," said Tony Woelk, a 28-year-old stereo equipment salesman. "I don't know what I would have done if they hadn't helped me pay off my bills and make a fresh start." Today, after two years of living with his parents, Tony is on his own again and determined to keep his spending under control.

Another advantage mentioned by some nesters is the emotional support they were shown by their parents in a time of need. Judy Loewen, 31, moved back in with her family for a month after breaking up with her long-time boyfriend. "I quit my job and left the city where he was," she remembers today. "I really felt that I couldn't cope° unless I got away immediately, and where could I go with no money and no job except to my folks? And bless them, they said, 'Just take it easy here for a while and don't rush into anything.' After a few weeks, I was ready to take a lot more realistic view of the situation and make some good decisions." 12

Parents, too, can find some practical and emotional benefits when their adult children return home. A child's contribution to room and board can help out with household expenses, particularly if the parents are living on a fixed° income. Parents may enjoy as well having a younger person around to help out with household repairs and other chores. "As I get older, taking care of the house and yard has become more of a burden for me," said Bill Robinson, a widower whose 35-year-old son has been sharing the house for the last two years. "Joseph pays some rent, but his real contribution has been to take a lot of those worries off my shoulders." 13

But the nesting phenomenon has its gloomy side as well. Parents and children report the number-one problem as the lack of space and privacy experienced by everyone involved. 14

"Never, never, never again," vowed Vicki Langella, 32, who lived with her parents for six months after losing her job as a word processor. "We get along fine when we visit, but within ten minutes of moving back in, I felt like I was 12 years old. It was constantly, 'Where are you going? When will you be back? Who are you going to be with?' And I found myself reacting to them as if I really were 12. The worst part of it was knowing that it was my own fault—I'd chosen to move back in with them." 15

"Believe it or not, 60-year-olds enjoy some privacy too," said Ella Purcell, whose two adult daughters have both returned home for brief periods. "Coming into my own living room to find my daughter and a date smooching on the couch made me feel like an intruder. I finally had to say, 'I love you—but out already!'" 16

Finances can be another difficult area for parents and returned 17 children. Parents often struggle with the decision of whether to ask their children for rent. "When you're letting them stay with you in order to save money, it seems silly to charge rent. But when we saw the way Ed was throwing money around, we began to feel taken advantage of," said the mother of one adult nester.

Despite its possible pitfalls, psychologists, family counselors and 18 others believe that nesting can succeed for many families if some precautions° are taken. They offer the following tips on maintaining a happy "nest."

- Regardless of their financial situation, adult children should 19 pay some room and board. Monica O'Kane, the author of *Living with Adult Children*, admits that this can be difficult. "It's hard to squeeze blood from a turnip, especially when it's your own turnip. But paying for room and board helps children grow in financial independence."

- Establish clear expectations about household duties. "I 20 remembered all too well being treated like the family servant when the kids were teenagers," said one experienced mother of a nester. "So when Rob moved back in, I said, 'Fine. Here is your share of the laundry, grocery-shopping and cleaning duties.' Once it was clear that I was serious, he pitched right in."

- Respect one another. Children should not expect to be treated 21 as guests or to use the parental home as a hotel, coming and going at all hours with no explanations. Parents, on the other hand, should recognize that the nester is no longer a youngster whose activities need constant supervision.

- And, most importantly: Don't let it go on forever. "When a child 22 returns home, everyone should agree on a tentative date for him to move out again," said one family therapist. "If that date is changed later by the mutual consent° of everyone concerned, that's OK, but everyone should understand that this isn't a permanent arrangement."

VOCABULARY QUESTIONS

A. Use context clues to help you decide on the best definition for each italicized word. Then circle the letter of each choice.

1. The word *modest* in "she wants. . . . a wardrobe that bursts the limits of her modest salary" (paragraph 8) means
   a. noble.
   b. strange.
   c. small.
   d. large.

2. The word *maintain* in "many young people are finding it unexpectedly difficult to maintain the standard of living they hoped for" (paragraph 10) means
   a. avoid.
   b. keep up.
   c. remember.
   d. sum up.

3. The word *option* in "Apartment rentals . . . can make living alone an impossible option" (paragraph 10) means
   a. choice.
   b. discovery.
   c. failure.
   d. limit.

4. The word *tentative* in "'When a child returns home, everyone should agree on a tentative date for him to move out again,' said one family therapist. 'If that date is changed later . . . that's OK. . . .'" (paragraph 22) means
   a. unchangeable.
   b. public.
   c. according to law.
   d. agreed upon for the time being.

5. The word *mutual* in "'If that date is changed later by the mutual consent of everyone concerned, that's OK. . . .'" (paragraph 22) means
   a. shared.
   b. mistaken.
   c. spoken.
   d. divided.

B. Below are words, or forms of words, from "Words to Watch." Write in the one that best completes each sentence.

consent	fixed	phenomenon
precautions	ruefully	

6. The disappearance of the dinosaurs is a _____*phenomenon*_____ that scientists are still trying to figure out.

7. My mother can keep a good poker face; when she plays cards, her expression is totally _____*fixed*_____.

8. Martin looked around _____*ruefully*_____ at the messy house; as usual, he had reason to feel regretful once he was sober.

9. Sexually active teenagers must learn to take _____*precautions*_____ against pregnancy.

10. In order to go on the field trip, students must get the _____*consent*_____ of their parents.

READING COMPREHENSION QUESTIONS

Central Point and Main Ideas

1. Which sentence best expresses the central point of the selection?
   a. Parents are not sure if they should ask their grown children who live at home for rent money.
   b. The Pattersons are a good example of nesting.
   c. Nesting, which has increased, has advantages and disadvantages, but it can succeed if families take precautions.
   d. Between 1970 and 1988 nesting has greatly increased among children aged 18–24.

2. The main idea of paragraph 10 is expressed in its
   a. first sentence.
   b. second sentence.
   c. third sentence.
   d. last sentence.

3. The main idea of paragraph 13 is
   (a.) in the first sentence.
   b. in the second sentence.
   c. in the last sentence.
   d. implied.

Supporting Details

4. Adult children return home
   a. after divorces.
   b. when it's hard to find a job.
   c. to better pay off their bills.
   (d.) for all of the above reasons.

5. ___F___ TRUE OR FALSE? There are no disadvantages to having adult children return home to live.

6. According to the article, when adult children return home they
   a. gain privacy.
   b. should be allowed to stay indefinitely.
   c. should be treated like guests.
   (d.) should help out financially and physically.

Transitions

7. The sentence below begins with a transition that shows
   (a.) contrast.
   b. time.
   c. addition.
   d. illustration.

   But the nesting phenomenon has its gloomy side as well. (Paragraph 14)

8. The relationship between the two sentences below is one of
   a. addition.
   b. illustration.
   (c.) contrast.
   d. time.

   Children should not expected to be treated as guests or to use the parental home as a hotel, coming and going at all hours with no explanations. Parents, on the other hand, should recognize that the nester is no longer a youngster whose activities need constant supervision. (Paragraph 21).

Patterns of Organization

9. The pattern of organization of paragraph 10 is
   a. comparison.
   b. contrast.
   c. list of items.
   d. time order.

Inferences

10. ___T___ TRUE OR FALSE? The author implies that money problems are the main reason that adult children return home to live.

OUTLINING

Complete the following outline of the article by filling in the letters of the missing major details, listed below.

Central point: The growing phenomenon of nesting, which has advantages and disadvantages, can work well for families if precautions are taken.

1. Introductory anecdote (paragraphs 1–3)

2. Increase in nesting (paragraph 4)

3. __b__ (paragraphs 5–10)

4. __a__ (paragraphs 11–13)

5. __d__ (paragraphs 14–17)

6. __c__ (paragraphs 18–22)

Major Details Missing from the Outline

   a. Advantages of nesting
   b. Reasons for increased nesting
   c. Precautions for successful nesting
   d. Disadvantages of nesting

DISCUSSION QUESTIONS

1. Do you know any cases of nesting? Why did the children return home? How did it work out?

2. Do you think today's young adult children are having a harder time financially than their parents' generation? Or is the "standard of living they hoped for" higher? Or both?

3. Mack mentions the "people who've gotten in over their heads with credit cards and utility bills." Why do you think people get into this situation?

4. Do you agree that adult children who return home, "regardless of their financial situation," should pay some room and board? If not, what financial situations should exclude adult children form paying room and board?

Check Your Performance		ADULT CHILDREN AT HOME	
Skill	*Number Right*	*Points*	*Total*
VOCABULARY			
Vocabulary in Context (5 items)	_____	x 10 =	_____
Words to Watch (5 items)	_____	x 10 =	_____
		SCORE =	_____ %
COMPREHENSION			
Central Point and Main Ideas (3 items)	_____	x 8 =	_____
Supporting Details (3 items)	_____	x 8 =	_____
Transitions (2 items)	_____	x 8 =	_____
Patterns of Organization (1 item)	_____	x 8 =	_____
Inferences (1 item)	_____	x 8 =	_____
Outlining (4 items)	_____	x 5 =	_____
		SCORE =	_____ %

FINAL SCORES: Vocabulary _____ %   Comprehension _____ %

Enter your final scores into the reading performance chart on the inside back cover.

4

Winners, Losers, or Just Kids?
Dan Wightman

Preview

Did you believe a high-school teacher who may have thought you'd never amount to anything? Did you sometimes feel in high school that happiness and success were going to come for other people, but not for you? If so, like the author of this selection, you should realize that "A" students sometimes earn D's in life, and high-school losers sometimes turn out to be winners.

Words to Watch

coyly (1):	with pretended shyness
flaunted (1):	showed off
blotto (2):	very drunk
swank (3):	ritzy
metamorphoses (4):	great changes
morose (7):	gloomy
fare (8):	make out
endeared (9):	made dear
sheepish (11):	shamefaced
presumptuous (11):	taking too much for granted
regressed (13):	gone backward
quick (15):	the sensitive flesh under the fingernails
stride (17):	pace

If I envied anyone in high school, it was the winners. You know   1
who I mean. The ones who earned straight A's and scored high on their

Scholastic Aptitude Tests. The attractive ones who smiled coyly°, drove their own sport cars and flaunted° those hard, smooth bodies that they kept tan the year round.

By contrast, my high-school friends were mostly losers. We spent a lot of time tuning cars and drinking beer. Our girlfriends were pale and frumpy, and we had more D's than B's on our report cards. After graduation, many of us went into the Army instead of to a university; two of us came back from Vietnam in coffins, three more on stretchers. On weekends, when we drank Colt 45 together in my father's battered Ford, we'd laughingly refer to ourselves as the "out crowd," But, unless we were thoroughly blotto°, we never laughed hard when we said it. And I, for one, rarely got blotto when I was 16. 2

The reason I mention this is that last month 183 winners and losers from my Northern California high-school graduating class got together at a swank° country club for a revealing fifteen-year reunion. 3

Predictably, only happy and successful people attended. The strange thing, though, was that the people I once pegged as losers outnumbered the winners at this reunion by a visible margin. And, during a long session at the bar with my informative friend Paula, I got an earful about the messy lives of people I'd once envied, and the remarkable metamorphoses° of people I'd once pitied. 4

Paula reported that Len, a former class officer, was now a lost soul in Colorado, hopelessly estranged from his charming wife. Tim, one of the sorriest students I'd ever known, was a successful sportswriter, at ease with himself. 5

Estelle, who was modestly attractive in her teens, was now a part-time stripper in the Midwest, working to support her young son. Connie, a former car-club "kitten," had become a sophisticated international flight attendant. 6

Paula told me that Gary, a college scholarship winner, was overweight, underemployed and morose°. Ron, who had shown little flair for music, had become a symphony violinist. 7

Sipping a Piña Colada, I thought to myself how terribly mistaken my senior counselor had been when she told me that high-school performance indicates how one will fare° later. 8

I looked at Paula, a high-school troublemaker with a naughty smile, whose outgoing personality and rebellious spirit had endeared° her to me so long ago. Together, we once stole a teacher's grade book, changed some of our low marks, then dropped the book in the lost-and-found box. The savvy teacher never said a word about the incident, but at the end of the year, when report cards were issued, gave us the D's we deserved. 9

Now Paula was a housewife, a volunteer worker and the mother 10
of two sons. She wore a marriage-encounter pin on her modest dress,
and sat at the bar tippling Perrier on ice.

She shook her head when I reminded her of the grade-book 11
escapade, and the sheepish° look on her face reminded me how
presumptuous° it is to predict the lives of others.

It also got me thinking about my own life since high school—how 12
I'd gradually shaken my loser's image, gotten through college, found a
decent job, married wisely, and finally realized a speck of my potential.

I thought about numerous situations where I could have despaired, 13
regressed°, given up—and how I hadn't, though others had—and I
wondered why I was different, and had more luck, less guilt.

"The past is fiction," wrote William Burroughs. And, although I 14
don't subscribe to that philosophy entirely, the people I admire most
today are those who overcome their mistakes, seize second chances and
fight to pull themselves together, day after day.

Often they're the sort of people who leave high school with 15
blotchy complexions, crummy work habits, fingernails bitten down to
the quick°. And of course they're bitterly unsure of themselves, and
slow to make friends.

But they're also the ones who show up transformed at fifteen-year 16
reunions, and the inference I draw is that the distinction between
winners and losers is often slight and seldom crucial—and frequently
overrated.

In high school especially, many people are slow getting started. 17
But, finding their stride°, they quickly catch up, and in their prime
often return to surprise and delight us—their lives so much richer than
we'd ever imagined.

VOCABULARY QUESTIONS

A. Use context clues to help you decide on the best definition for each italicized
word. Then circle the letter of your choice.

1. The word *pegged* in "the people I once pegged as losers outnumbered the
winners" (paragraph 4) means
a. feared.
b. classified.
c. admired.
d. envied.

2. The word *estranged* in "a lost soul . . . hopelessly estranged from his charming wife" (paragraph 5) means
   a. enriched.
   b. free.
   c. separated.
   d. rich.

3. The word *flair* in "Ron, who had shown little flair for music, had become a symphony violinist" (paragraph 7) means
   a. dislike.
   b. inability.
   c. talent.
   d. money.

4. The word *savvy* in "the savvy teacher . . . gave us the D's we deserved" (paragraph 9) means
   a. foolish.
   b. cruel.
   c. misled.
   d. knowing.

5. The words *subscribe to* in "'The past is fiction,' wrote William Burroughs. And although I don't subscribe to that philosophy entirely, the people I admire . . . are those who overcome their mistakes" (paragraph 14) means
   a. agree with.
   b. disagree with.
   c. understand.
   d. pay for.

B. Below are words, or forms of words, from "Words to Watch." Write in the one that best completes each sentence.

endeared	flaunted	metamorphosis
morose	sheepish	

6. For the first week after her engagement, Janice _____*flaunted*_____ her diamond ring at the office.

7. Dark skies often made Ron feel _____*morose*_____.

8. The boss's absentmindedness only _____*endeared*_____ him even more to the workers.

9. Five-year-old Richie looked _____*sheepish*_____ after his mother found his pet worms in the bathtub.

10. Having to work for a living brings about a _____*metamorphosis*_____ in young people's attitude toward money.

READING COMPREHENSION QUESTIONS

Central Point and Main Ideas

1. Which sentence best expresses the central point of the selection?
   a. High-school winners get good grades and are attractive.
   b. High-school losers drink beer and fix cars.
   c. The author attended his fifteen-year reunion.
   d. High-school performance doesn't show how well a student will do later in life.

2. The main idea of paragraph 2 is best expressed in the
   a. first sentence.
   b. second sentence.
   c. third sentence.
   d. last sentence.

Supporting Details

3. The author's old friend Paula, a troublemaker in high school,
   a. become a part-time stripper.
   b. become a housewife, mother, and volunteer worker.
   c. remained a troublemaker.
   d. told the author nothing about their classmates' lives.

4. According to the author, high-school losers
   a. are less interested than other people.
   b. have little potential for success.
   c. have a lot of potential for success.
   d. should try to become friends with winners.

Transitions

5. The relationship of the second paragraph to the first is one of
   a. comparison.
   b. contrast.
   c. illustration.
   d. time.

6. The relationship of the second sentence in paragraph 17 to the first sentence of that paragraph is one of
   a. addition.
   b. illustration.
   c. comparison.
   (d.) contrast.

Patterns of Organization

7. The details in paragraphs 5–7 are organized in a pattern of
   a. time order.
   (b.) a list of items.
   c. cause and effect.
   d. definition and example.

Inferences

8. From the article, we can conclude that in high school, the author
   a. thought the winners would not always be winners.
   b. thought the winners did not deserve their grades.
   c. felt the winners did not know they were winners.
   (d.) might have traded places with the winners.

9. The author implies that
   (a.) people often think that high-school losers will remain losers.
   b. the difference between winners and losers in high school is usually very important to their futures.
   c. fifteen-year reunions change losers to winners.
   d. everyone knows that high-school losers often become winners.

10. The author implies that
    a. being a winner in high school is a poor start in life.
    b. being a high-school winner is more important to one's future than determination.
    (c.) determination and hope change people's lives.
    d. people's abilities are fully developed by high school.

SUMMARIZING

1. Circle the letter of the statement that best summarizes the central point of "Winners, Losers, or Just Kids?" as expressed in the first four paragraphs.
   a. In high school the author was a loser who envied the winners.
   b. High-school reunions can teach us important lessons about life in general.
   (c.) The reunion showed that many high-school winners and losers had turned out differently than the author had expected.

2. Circle the letter of the statement that best summarizes the first set of supporting details for the central point (paragraphs 5–12).
   a. At his reunion, the author found out what had happened to his classmates.
   b. The author's friend Paula had turned her life around and was now happily married and a contributor to society.
   c. The author realized that some losers in his high-school class, including himself, had done more with their lives than some of the winners he had once envied.

3. Circle the letter of the statement that best summarizes the second set of supporting details for the central point (paragraphs 13–17).
   a. The winners in life include those who overcome early mistakes and problems and persist in building good lives for themselves.
   b. The winners in life are the ones who leave high school as attractive people with impressive records.
   c. The author began life as a loser but ended up as a winner.

DISCUSSION QUESTIONS

1. What does Wightman really mean by "winners" and "losers"? Why does the title also say, "or Just Kids"?

2. What do the first two paragraphs of this selection accomplish?

3. What is the meaning of the sentence "the past is fiction"? To what extent do you think it's true, if at all? In what ways isn't it true?

4. Wightman writes that he "wondered why he was different, and had more luck, less guilt" than others. What factors do you suppose are involved in determining whether or not people shake their "loser's image"? What factors does Wightman name?

Check Your Performance

WINNERS, LOSERS, OR JUST KIDS?

Skill	*Number Right*	*Points*	*Total*
VOCABULARY			
Vocabulary in Context (5 items)	_____	x 10 =	_____
Words to Watch (5 items)	_____	x 10 =	_____
		SCORE =	_____ %

COMPREHENSION			
Central Point and Main Ideas (2 items)	_____	x 8.5 =	_____
Supporting Details (2 items)	_____	x 8.5 =	_____
Transitions (2 items)	_____	x 8.5 =	_____
Patterns of Organization (1 item)	_____	x 8.5 =	_____
Inferences (3 items)	_____	x 8.5 =	_____
Summarizing (3 items)	_____	x 5 =	_____
		SCORE =	_____ %

FINAL SCORES: Vocabulary _____ %   Comprehension _____ %

Enter your final scores into the reading performance chart on the inside back cover.

5

Shyness
Richard Wolkomir

Preview

Have you ever not raised your hand in class because you would be embarrassed to draw attention to yourself? Does it sometimes take courage for you to pursue a new friendship? If so, like many people, you know what it's like to feel shy. Fortunately, as this magazine article by writer Richard Wolkomir explains, no one has to suffer such distress forever.

Words to Watch

equate (5):	make equal
initiated (9):	started
attributes (10):	explains the cause of something
genetic (11):	inherited at birth
invariably (12):	always
extroverted (15):	friendly, outgoing
encroaching (19):	trespassing, intruding
perceptions (25):	impressions

He's tall and interesting looking, dressed in a business suit. He smiles and says "Hi" when Carol Johnson, a twenty-five-year-old typist in Rochester, New York, gets on the bus, but her tongue freezes and she glances away, hating herself. It's a familiar reaction. Since speaking at staff meetings also makes her nervous, she lets co-workers take credit for her new ideas; at parties, she stands to one side, wishing someone would notice her, and praying he won't.   1

Carol suffers from a problem that almost everyone experiences at some time: shyness. For her, shyness is neither cute nor sweet, nor easy to overcome. It makes her distant when she wants to be friendly; cold when she wants to be warm—and lonely when she wants company. 2

It was four years ago, when Carol broke up with her boyfriend, that her shyness began to bother her. "He was talkative and very domineering in conversations, so I sort of sat back, not talking much," she says. "We'd been going together since high school, and after we split I suddenly found I didn't have much to say to people." 3

For three years, Carol had little social life. Then, one day, she told herself, "If you don't try something, you'll just slip further and further back." She forced herself to become more active. She volunteered for the Special Olympics, and began to meet other people who shared her interest in handicapped children. It was an important first step. "I'm making progress . . . slowly," she says. 4

Carol is not alone. At some time in their lives, over 80 percent of all Americans report feeling shy, according to Stanford University psychologist Philip Zimbardo, Ph.D., a shyness authority and author of *The Shy Child*. It's a special problem for women, many of whom are still raised to equate° bashfulness with femininity. 5

Yet, in today's intensely competitive work place, shyness can be a severe handicap. What will happen if your stomach knots every time you meet a new client? How far will you rise if you're too shy to be assertive with the workers you supervise? 6

"Whenever I had to talk to new people I'd get sick to my stomach and sweat," recalls Sylvia Madden, now a Purdue University counselor in her late twenties, who conducts a shyness workshop for college students. "It used to be awful to make a speech—forget about talking to boys." 7

Sylvia says her shyness began in childhood. Her parents were quiet people who kept to themselves, and she was a tall, awkward and self-conscious girl who was never encouraged to socialize with others. Throughout college, she depended upon her boyfriend for her social life. But when she moved away for graduate school, she resolved not to become isolated. 8

"I made myself go to parties—I had a miserable time at first, but I was determined to do it," she says, recalling that it took all her courage to invite someone out for coffee. "For the first time, I actively initiated° friendships, and I could feel myself changing." Oddly enough, it was a rejection that convinced her she'd won her battle. "I invited a guy to go to a party," she says. "When he turned me down, instead of being crushed, I decided that the loss was his—it felt wonderful!" 9

Sylvia Madden attributes° her own early shyness to poorly 10 developed social skills and a negative self-image—two common causes of the problem. Sometimes teenagers develop poor self-images because they're physically different from their peers, whether they're shorter or taller, fatter or thinner—or even prettier, says Dr. Zimbardo. But often shyness develops because parents' expectations make a child feel self-conscious regardless of her attributes. A parent's love may depend on a child's performance—such as a good report card, or trying to meet unrealistic expectations. A mother, trying to fulfill her own fantasies, for instance, may want her daughter to become a ballerina, even though the girl has no special talent for dance. "Failing as a dancer, she may feel she's failed completely as a person," says Dr. Zimbardo.

11   According to recent studies, shyness is one of a number of behavioral characteristics that can even be hereditary. Jerome Kagan, a Harvard University psychologist, found that up to one-third of all shy children are born bashful. And a study of identical and fraternal twins by Robert Plomin, Ph.D., of the University of Colorado at Boulder, and David C. Rowe, Ph.D., of the University of Oklahoma at Norman, shows that shyness, which is evident in infancy, is largely genetic°.

12   However or whenever shyness develops, it can be debilitating. Fortunately, it can be overcome. The first step is invariably° the same: a sudden decision to change.

13   Angela Dix, for example, a forty-year-old publicist for a New England health agency, was a painfully shy child of a shy mother. When her parents divorced and her mother became dependent on her, Angela's shyness increased. But subconsciously she knew she had to break out into a larger world; against her mother's wishes, she enrolled in a large, urban university.

14   "By the time we drove up to the dormitory, my mother was so upset about 'losing' me that we were barely speaking," Angela remembers. "I was terrified of being alone in this large, strange place, but I knew that meeting people and making a life for myself were completely up to me, and I resolved right then to do something about it."

15   She forced herself to walk through the dormitory, cheerfully saying, "Hi!" to the other freshmen. A few nights later she was nominated floor president. "At first, I thought they had made a mistake—they were voting for the fake, outgoing me," she says. "But it was then that I realized that if I acted extroverted°, then that's what I was."

16   Shyness is so common that psychologists have recently been focusing considerable attention on the problem. There are now over forty "shyness workshops" at universities around the country. Many of the participants are women, often because men are reluctant to admit they have a problem.

At her Purdue University workshops, Sylvia Madden starts each 17 session with exercises to help participants become comfortable with one another. For instance, each member of the group talks about herself to another member who takes notes. Then the note-taker introduces her partner to the group as a whole.

She also leads the participants in such psychological games as 18 "sculpting," in which participants pretend they are statues that express the feeling of shyness or its opposite. "Often, when they express how it feels not to be shy, they will reach out a hand toward someone else," she says.

Group members also work on conversational skills, discussing the 19 physical symptoms of shyness and how to say things more effectively in situations that bother them. For instance, a woman who wants to ask a co-worker to stop encroaching° on her area of responsibility acts out the scene, asking another member to take the part of the "villain."

All participants sign a "behavioral contract" that specifies their 20 own goals. For instance, one goal might be, "I want to say hello to three strangers every day."

Such techniques do work. A twenty-year-old woman majoring in 21 mathematics recently enrolled in a shyness workshop at Pennsylvania State University, where these programs developed, after she'd dropped out of the university's public-speaking course for her sixth time.

Her first assignment was to return a bulky, blue wristwatch she'd 22 just bought. She really wanted a small watch, but had been too shy to tell the clerk. With the help of her counselor, she wrote out a precise plan of action: "At 3:30 this afternoon I will go to the store, find the clerk who sold me the blue watch and explain that I want a small one."

At the next class, proudly wearing a delicate wristwatch, she had 23 enough confidence to try public speaking. "Afterward, she just stood at the lectern whispering, 'Wow, wow!'" says Herman Cohen, Ph.D., a professor of speech communication who ran the workshop. "Even after she sat down, I could still hear her saying, 'Wow!'"

Even if there's no workshop near you, you can use some of these 24 techniques. Dr. Zimbardo suggests becoming your own friendly coach. Instead of telling yourself bad things about yourself—"I'm dumb"; "I'm fat"; "I have nothing to say"—give yourself compliments: "My hair looks good today"; "I'm a good cook." And, try to improve. "Although I started off just right—what can I do next time to get the results I want? Speak louder? Look her right in the eye? Reveal a little about myself before I ask questions?"

"I'm fascinated by the distorted perceptions° shy people have of 25 themselves," says Dr. Cohen. "For instance, almost invariably they consider themselves far less attractive or talkative than they actually are. You're responsible for no more than fifty percent of any conversation— if a conversation is a dud, why are you so sure it's all your fault?"

Gerald Phillips, Ph.D., who directs the shyness program at Pennsylvania State University, tells people to put their goals in writing. " 'I will become an interesting conversationalist' is an unrealistic goal," he says. "You can't be sure what others will find interesting; some people actually find nothing interesting except themselves. It's much better to say: 'At the office tomorrow I'll start a conversation with Bill and I'll talk to him for at least three minutes.' Include in your plan of action three or four subjects to talk about." 26

Afterward, he says, check off the goals you accomplish and celebrate each victory with a reward to boost your self-confidence. 27

Dr. Phillips also advises shy people to imitate particular traits they admire. Does the woman you respect look people in the eye? Speak loudly enough to be heard? How does she use her expressions and body language to make what she says seem lively? How does she make transitions from one subject to another? He also suggests "active listening" to master conversation. If you look attentive when the other person talks, and ask appropriate questions, it puts the burden of conversation on them, rather than on you. And it makes you less self-conscious. 28

"Even if you hardly say two words all evening, the other person will probably think you're a terrific conversationalist," says Dr. Phillips. "And most people worth knowing will reciprocate by asking you questions." 29

A bit of bashfulness can be an asset: "The people who join our program are much more considerate, much more sensitive to the needs of others, than most people," says Dr. Phillips. And that's no compliment to shy away from. 30

VOCABULARY QUESTIONS

A. Use context clues to help you decide on the best definition for each italicized word. Then circle the letter of each choice.

1. The word *distant* in "For her, shyness is neither cute nor sweet, nor easy to overcome. It makes her distant when she wants to be friendly; cold when she wants to be warm. . . . " (paragraph 2) means
   a. pleasant.
   b. unfriendly.
   c. confused.
   d. tired.

2. The word *domineering* in "He was talkative and very domineering in conversations, so I sort of sat back" (paragraph 3) means
   a. quiet.
   (b.) controlling.
   c. pale.
   d. sour.

3. The word *resolved* in "But when she moved away for graduate school, she resolved not to become isolated" (paragraph 8) means
   (a.) decided.
   b. avoided.
   c. enjoyed.
   d. regretted.

4. The word *debilitating* in "whenever shyness develops, it can be debilitating. Fortunately, it can be overcome," (paragraph 12) means
   a. encouraging.
   (b.) weakening.
   c. stylish.
   d. catching.

5. The word *reciprocate* in "If you look attentive when the other person talks and ask appropriate questions, it puts the burden of conversation on them, rather than on you. . . . And most people worth knowing will reciprocate by asking you questions" (paragraphs 29–30) means
   a. envy you.
   b. hurt you.
   c. interrupt rudely.
   (d.) return the favor.

B. Below are words, or forms of words, from "Words to Watch." Write in the one that best completes each sentence.

attributes	encroaching	extroverted
genetic	perceptions	

6. The salesclerk realized her _____*perceptions*_____ of customers might sometimes be wrong when the shabbily-dressed man turned out to be the owner of the store.

7. Gerald _____*attributes*_____ his good looks to his parents and his personality to his grandparents.

8. The young woman felt that her roommate was _____*encroaching*_____ on her personal space.

9. Some doctors believe that couples should be tested for _____*genetic*_____ diseases before they become parents.

10. We were all surprised when our shy co-worker married an _____*extroverted*_____ woman.

READING COMPREHENSION QUESTIONS

Central Point and Main Ideas

1. Which sentence best expresses the central point of the selection?
   a. More shyness workshops are available than ever before.
   b. Shyness is hereditary.
   c. Shy people are likely to be failures.
   d. Shyness, a common problem with various causes, can be overcome.

2. Which sentence best expresses the main idea of paragraph 26?
   a. Shy people have unrealistic goals, according to one expert.
   b. Most shy people are uninteresting.
   c. According to one expert, putting realistic goals in writing helps people overcome shyness.
   d. One expert says that some people are only interested in themselves.

Supporting Details

3. __*T*__ TRUE OR FALSE? According to the author, many women are raised to feel being shy is feminine.

4. According to one shyness expert, shy people
   a. are good supervisors.
   b. don't recognize all the good things about themselves.
   c. are happy being shy.
   d. are unable to boost their own self-confidence.

Transitions

5. The relationship between the two sentences on the next page is one of
   a. cause and effect.
   b. comparison.
   c. contrast.
   d. illustration.

Throughout college, she depended upon her boyfriend for her social life. But when she moved away for graduate school, she resolved not to become isolated. (Paragraph 8)

6. The relationship of the second sentence below to the first is one of
   a. contrast.
   b. illustration.
   c. time.
   d. comparison.

   "I'm fascinated by the distorted perceptions shy people have of themselves," says Dr. Cohen. "For instance, almost invariably they consider themselves far less attractive or talkative than they actually are." (Paragraph 25)

Patterns of Organization

7. The main pattern of organization of paragraph 10 is
   a. time order.
   b. cause and effect.
   c. comparison and contrast.
   d. definition and example.

8. The main pattern of organization of paragraphs 22–23 is
   a. time order.
   b. list of items.
   c. comparison and contrast.
   d. definition and example.

Inferences

9. The author implies that overcoming shyness
   a. is easy.
   b. is impossible.
   c. can only be done at workshops.
   d. takes determination.

10. In paragraph 29, Dr. Phillips implies that
    a. all shy people are good conversationalists.
    b. shy people shouldn't try to speak much.
    c. many people's idea of a good conversationalist is someone who listens to them.
    d. shy people should avoid talking to people who aren't worth knowing.

SUMMARIZING

1. Circle the letter of the statement that best summarizes the central point of "Shyness," as expressed in the first twelve paragraphs.
   a. Shyness is a special problem for women in our society.
   (b.) Shyness, which is a common problem caused by various factors, can be defeated.
   c. Nearly everyone experiences shyness at some time or other.

2. Circle the letter of the statement that best summarizes the first set of supporting details (paragraphs 12–15) for the central point.
   a. A forty-year-old publicist was painfully shy.
   (b.) To overcome shyness, people must be determined to change.
   c. To overcome shyness, people must understand their subconscious goals.

3. Circle the letter of the statement that best summarizes the second set of supporting details (paragraphs 16–23) for the central point.
   (a.) Attending shyness workshops is a good way to learn to overcome shyness.
   b. A Purdue University workshop uses psychological games to help shy people.
   c. One shyness workshop helped a woman exchange a wristwatch she didn't want.

4. Circle the letter of the statement that best summarizes the third set of supporting details (paragraphs 24–30) for the central point.
   a. One expert feels shy people have distorted images of themselves.
   (b.) Some techniques used at shyness workshops are useful even if people don't attend a workshop.
   c. Shy people can benefit by imitating qualities of people they admire.

DISCUSSION QUESTIONS

1. Are there certain situations—such as a job interview, a particular classroom or workplace, or a party most of whose guests you don't know— where you become shy or feel shyness taking over? If so, what techniques mentioned in the article might help you combat your shyness?

2. What are the similarities and differences between Carol Johnson (paragraphs 1–4) and Sylvia Madden (paragraphs 7–10)? Consider the causes of their shyness and their approaches to overcome it.

3. The author uses many examples of shy people and workshop exercises throughout his article. Why do you think he chose to use so many examples? What would the article be like without any examples?

4. Do you feel that a person should deal with his or her problems alone, or with other people, as in a workshop, helping out? Does the group approach make it easier—or harder—to deal with personal problems?

Check Your Performance   **SHYNESS**

Skill	Number Right	Points	Total
VOCABULARY			
Vocabulary in Context (5 items)	_____	x 10 =	_____
Words to Watch (5 items)	_____	x 10 =	_____
		SCORE =	_____ %
COMPREHENSION			
Central Point and Main Ideas (2 items)	_____	x 8 =	_____
Supporting Details (2 items)	_____	x 8 =	_____
Transitions (2 items)	_____	x 8 =	_____
Patterns of Organization (2 items)	_____	x 8 =	_____
Inferences (2 items)	_____	x 8 =	_____
Summarizing (4 items)	_____	x 5 =	_____
		SCORE =	_____ %

FINAL SCORES: Vocabulary _____ %   **Comprehension** _____ %

Enter your final scores into the reading performance chart on the inside back cover.

6

False Ideas About Reading
Robert and Pam Winkler

Preview

Some people see reading as a real chore. They try to make it part of their lives, but doing so seems impossible. Such people may be the victims of certain false ideas about reading. This selection explains three such false notions and how they may keep people from becoming everyday readers.

Words to Watch

sound (3):	logical
dry (5):	plain
commentary (5):	explanations or interpretations
plow (5):	labor
assert (6):	claim
imprinted (7):	clearly impressed
passively (9):	inactively
resources (10)	knowledge and skills that can be beneficial

There are a few false ideas, or myths, that people have about the reading process. These myths prevent them from becoming better readers. 1

MYTH 1: YOU MUST READ EVERY WORD

Perhaps the most common such myth is that whenever you read a book, you have to read every word. Victims of this myth may not feel it's their duty to read every word in a newspaper or magazine story, but 2 put a book in their hands and their attitude changes. They treat the book like sacred Scripture and regard every word as a holy thing. Because they think that every word must be carefully read, they are not likely to read anything.

In contrast to popular belief, there are two sound° reasons why you need not read every word. First of all, your purpose in reading may not require it. Perhaps you are reading a textbook chapter and all you need to cover are main ideas. You know this from past tests the teacher has given or because the teacher has said directly, "All you have to know are the high points of the chapter." In such cases, there may be no need to read many of the supporting details that may occupy 75 percent or more of the space in the chapter. Instead, you might skim quickly through the chapter, skipping secondary information and reading only main points and enough details to help you understand those main points. You then have more time to study, learn, and remember those main ideas.   3

Or perhaps you are using the textbook only to supplement class notes, which will be the real basis for a test. All you may need, then, are certain key points from the text to round off ideas in your notes. In that case, you can just scan the text—that is, look it over quickly with the goal of finding the few points you need.   4

The second reason not to read every word is simply that certain material may not interest you. It may bore you because of your personal interests or because the material is dull, or both. If the material is in a class textbook and is important, you have no choice. But if it is in personal reading, you do have a choice—you can simply skip the uninteresting material. Some people, for instance, often skip passages of nature description or dry° commentary°. But many others feel it is their duty to plow° through long, dull passages they could not care less about. In fact, they are so unwilling to skip anything that they are more likely to quit reading altogether.   5

Here is a story that will help you feel less guilty about omitting words. One British writer recalls in her autobiography how shocked she was when her professor at Oxford University said to her, "You will never be a reader unless you learn the art of skipping." She explains how from her earliest years she had been taught that skipping a word in reading was like cheating at cards. Her professor pointed to the books jamming the shelves in his office and said, "Do you mean to assert° that every word in all these volumes is worth reading? You must choose in life what is worth and what is not worth your attention." After this talk with her professor, the woman was able to skip, without guilt, sections of many of the books she read.   6

MYTH 2: READING ONCE IS ENOUGH

Students who believe they must read every word are often victims 7
of a related myth—the idea that reading something once is enough.
Such students think that since they forced themselves to read every
word, they've done all the work that is necessary. Whatever is
important in the book should be imprinted° by then in their brain, ready
for them to transfer to a test paper upon command. If there's something
they don't know, or don't remember, they think, "It's a lost cause. I'm
not going to waste any time trying any further." Or they think, "If one
reading isn't enough, it's because I'm stupid. There's no point in my
trying to read any more." Students with such a crazy attitude are good
candidates for failure, for one reading is seldom enough for study
purposes. Instead, it is often the first step in the mastery of material.
Any person with normal intelligence will have to go back, reread the
material, and then take notes on the material if he or she hopes to
master and remember it.

MYTH 3: READING HAS TO BE WORK

A final myth about reading, perhaps the worst one of all, is that 8
reading has to be work. It is true that reading is at times a most
demanding (and rewarding) effort. But reading doesn't always require
hard work. It can be simply for fun, for relaxing pleasure.

Unfortunately, students are unlikely to read for fun for two 9
reasons. First, most or all of the reading in school is associated with
work. One must do it and then be tested and graded on it. The result of
such school experience is that reading is seldom connected with
pleasure. Second, students, and people in general, are unlikely to read
for entertainment because it is easier to turn on the television. The fact
that many people watch television is understandable. Some shows are
good, and while many others are trash, even trash can be fun to watch,
at least once in a while. After a long, hard day of work, it is relaxing to
sit passively° and unthinkingly, soaking up the bright images that flash
across the screen. The danger is that one will sit night after night, for
many hours on end, doing nothing but watching television. Then it
truly becomes an "idiot box."

What many people need to do, in order to widen their experience 10
and resources°, is to learn how to read for pleasure. Unfortunately,
people are likely to have the false idea that reading is a chore, not
entertainment. The fact is that such people haven't given reading a
chance. They should expect to do a bit of work at first, until they
become accustomed to the reading process. But if they persist, and if

they give a book time to gain their interest, they will almost certainly experience a pleasant surprise. And if one book does not gain their interest, there are many more that will. They will soon find a whole new source of enjoyment open up to them. It is helpful to remember, too, that reading for pleasure will provide bonuses that other forms of recreation cannot. It will develop word power, improve spelling, increase reading speed, and help people discover and explore parts of themselves that they may not know existed.

A simple way to learn pleasure reading is to set aside some time 11 for a book each day. It might be a half an hour ordinarily spent watching television or time before going to bed. What is important is that it be a realistic time slot that you can use for reading more or less regularly. What is important, too, is that you persist—that you give a book a chance to catch on, and yourself a chance to get into a book.

To review, then, there are three damaging myths that interfere 12 with good reading. They are that every word must be read, that reading something once should be enough, and that all reading must be work. Be aware of these myths and how they may affect your own attitudes about reading. Don't let any of them prevent you from developing into a better reader.

VOCABULARY QUESTIONS

A. Use context clues to help you decide on the best definition for each italicized word. Then circle the letter of each choice.

1. The word *skim* in "you might skim quickly through the chapter, skipping secondary information and reading only main points and enough details" (paragraph 3) means
   a. read slowly.
   b. glance through.
   c. stare.
   d. labor.

2. The word *supplement* in "perhaps you are using the textbook only to supplement class notes, which will be the real basis for a test" (paragraph 4) means
   a. skip.
   b. avoid.
   c. add to.
   d. decrease.

3. The word *jamming* in "Her professor pointed to the books jamming the shelves in his office and said, 'Do you mean to assert that every word in all these volumes is worth reading? . . . '"(paragraph 6) means
   (a.) crowding.
   b. lying flat on.
   c. coloring.
   d. absent from.

4. The word *seldom* in "one reading is seldom enough for study purposes. Instead, it is often the first step in the mastery of the material" (paragraph 7) means
   a. usually.
   (b.) rarely.
   c. always.
   d. luckily.

5. The word *persist* in "They should expect to do a bit of work at first, until they become accustomed to the reading process. But if they persist . . . , they will almost certainly experience a pleasant surprise" (paragraph 10) means
   a. quit.
   b. forget.
   c. run.
   (d.) stick with it.

B. Below are words, or forms of words, from "Words to Watch." Write in the one that best completes each sentence.

asserted	dry	passive
resources	sound	

6. Our history teacher's lectures are so _____ *dry* _____ that half the students never listen.

7. Parents too often encourage the _____ *passive* _____ activity of watching TV over more noisy but more healthy pastimes.

8. A good argument must include _____ *sound* _____ reasoning.

9. Part-time jobs in high school provide students with _____ *resources* _____ that they can use to succeed in full-time jobs later.

10. "Wrinkles," _____ *asserted* _____ Mark Twain, "should merely indicate where smiles have been."

READING COMPREHENSION QUESTIONS

Central Point and Main Ideas

1. Which sentence best expresses the central point of the selection?
   a. Reading requires effort.
   b. Certain myths prevent people from becoming better readers.
   c. It is a myth that you must always read every word.
   d. Reading once is often not enough.

2. Which sentence best expresses the main idea of paragraph 7?
   a. Some students believe one reading should be enough for study purposes.
   b. Some students believe that reading more than once is a lost cause.
   c. Some students think only a stupid person needs to read something more than once.
   d. It is a myth that reading once is enough for study purposes.

3. Which sentence best expresses the main idea of paragraph 11?
   a. Pleasure reading can be learned by reading regularly.
   b. Pleasure reading can be learned by reading regularly and giving a book a chance to catch your interest.
   c. One good time for pleasure reading is a half hour that is usually spent watching television.
   d. You must give a book a chance to catch on.

Supporting Details

4. According to the authors, one reason for not reading every word is
   a. you don't have the book.
   b. certain material may not interest you.
   c. the vocabulary may be too difficult.
   d. grades are of secondary importance in a learning experience.

5. For study purposes,
   a. one reading is enough.
   b. read every word.
   c. use only class notes.
   d. reread material and take notes.

Transitions

6. The relationship between the two parts of the sentence below is one of
   a. contrast.
   b. time.
   c. cause and effect.
   d. addition.

   Because they think that every word must be carefully read, they are not likely to read anything. (Paragraph 2)

7. The relationship of the second sentence below to the first sentence is one of
   a. addition.
   (b.) contrast.
   c. illustration.
   d. time.

   > It is true that reading is at times a most demanding (and rewarding) effort. But reading doesn't always require hard work. (Paragraph 8)

Patterns of Organization

8. Just as paragraphs are organized in patterns, so are longer selections. The main pattern of organization of this selection is
   a. time order.
   b. definition and example.
   c. cause and effect.
   (d.) list of items.

Inferences

9. The authors imply that
   a. schoolwork interests people in reading for pleasure.
   b. all television shows are trash.
   c. you should stop reading a book if you don't like the first page.
   (d.) too few people read purely for enjoyment.

10. __T__ TRUE OR FALSE? The authors imply that reading for pleasure takes some will power.

OUTLINING

Prepare an outline of "False Ideas About Reading" by filling in the central point and the three major supporting details.

Central point: ___*Three myths about reading keep people from becoming better*___

___*readers.*___

1. ___*The first myth is that every word must be read.*___

2. ___*The second myth is that reading once is enough.*___

3. ___*The third myth is that reading has to be work.*___

DISCUSSION QUESTIONS

1. Which one of the myths about reading is most helpful for you to know about? How has this myth affected your reading and study habits?

2. Give an example of someone you know who has been influenced by one of the reading myths. What would you tell this person to change his or her attitude?

3. What do you think are the benefits and dangers of not reading every word?

4. The Winklers write that books can "help people discover and explore parts of themselves that they may not know existed." What do they mean by this? Use examples, if possible, from one or more books you have read.

Check Your Performance   **FALSE IDEAS ABOUT READING**

Skill	Number Right	Points	Total
VOCABULARY			
Vocabulary in Context (5 items)	_____	x 10 =	_____
Words to Watch (5 items)	_____	x 10 =	_____
		SCORE =	_____%
COMPREHENSION			
Central Point and Main Ideas (3 items)	_____	x 8 =	_____
Supporting Details (2 items)	_____	x 8 =	_____
Transitions (2 items)	_____	x 8 =	_____
Patterns of Organization (1 item)	_____	x 8 =	_____
Inferences (2 items)	_____	x 8 =	_____
Outlining (4 items)	_____	x 5 =	_____
		SCORE =	_____%

FINAL SCORES: Vocabulary _____%   Comprehension _____%

Enter your final scores into the reading performance chart on the inside back cover.

7

Are You a Good Listener?
Robert L. Montgomery

Preview

You may imagine that a good conversation requires only people who speak well. But if speaking is important to a conversation, so is listening. In this selection, Robert L. Montgomery explains the skills of good listening.

Words to Watch

dynamic (5):	energetic
distraction (6):	something that turns attention away
prospect (10):	a potential customer
curb (27):	control
dividends (27):	bonuses
check (28):	control; hold back
prone (28):	having a tendency
stifle (29):	put down
bias (33):	prejudice
demeanor (34):	manner

Do you listen to others as you like to be listened to? It takes skill 1
and determination to speak, but it takes even more skill and determination to listen to others. It also takes energy.

We listen more than we do any other human activity except 2
breathe. Listening is essential to our personal, professional, social and family success. If working people were taught to listen effectively, the efficiency of American business could be doubled.

Listening is the most neglected and the least understood of the communications arts. It has become the weakest link in today's communications system. Poor listening is a result of bad habits that develop because we haven't been trained to listen. Fortunately, it is a skill that can be learned.   3

Here are six basic guidelines for better listening. You can improve your listening the day you start practicing them.   4

First, look at the other person. Look at the person who is talking to you. Also, always look at the person you're talking to. Looking directly at the person who is speaking shows dynamic° interest. I don't mean staring at the other person, just looking into his or her eyes, but looking toward the person as he or she talks to you. You can look at the hairline, the neckline, watch the mouth as the person speaks, even notice the color of the eyes of the speaker.   5

But don't look at the floor or ceiling or out the window. And don't turn your eyes to view every distraction° around you. People tell me they don't trust the person who doesn't look at them. They also sense suspicion, trickery or distrust from such people. And distrust will block communication. It's a huge block also to motivation. There's little or no motivation when there is no respect. Concentrate on the other person as you listen. Looking at the person will enable you to judge the intent of the message as well as the content. So give your undivided attention as you listen to others. If you project genuine, active attention, you will convey sincere interest. When the eyes are elsewhere, the mind is elsewhere.   6

Rule Two is ask questions. This is the best way for anyone to become a better listener fast. It's a necessity for parents, teachers, managers and salespeople. To keep from doing all the speaking yourself and to get the other person talking, develop the tools of the reporter, the art of asking questions. Master the different types of questions you'll learn now. Start using them today. Practice is the best instructor.   7

Some types of questions help you discover facts. You might want to know where someone works or lives, what they do, where they're from. Questions that get specific, concise facts for answers are called closed-end questions. You rarely get more than a word or two in reply. "What is your name?" is one example. "How old are you?" is another.   8

The opposite type is called open-ended questioning. You can find out most of the facts about a person by asking just one or two open-ended questions. For example, I might ask you, "How did you get into the line of work you're in now?" That question will usually get a person talking for at least five minutes and more likely for fifteen. Of   9 course, you could simply say to someone, "Tell me about yourself." That's open-ended and will accomplish the same purpose.

I've often wondered how many sales are lost each week because the salesperson doesn't listen to the prospect° or customer. There has been a revolution in selling. The change has taken us from the product-pusher of the past to the counselor-type salesperson who asks questions first. Contrary to the belief of many people, you actually save time and make the sale faster by asking the prospect some questions to discover his or her needs, problems or objectives. 10

To illustrate the power of questions, I think of the experience of a famous sales trainer and speaker, the late Fred Herman. Herman was introduced on the Mike Douglas television show one day as "the greatest salesman in the world." What happened next was purely spontaneous; Herman vowed he had no idea what Mike Douglas would ask him. 11

Douglas began by saying, "Fred, since you're hailed as the number-one salesman in the world, sell me something!" Without any hesitation, Fred Herman responded instantly and instinctively with a question: "Mike, what would you want me to sell you?" 12

Mike Douglas, who is paid a couple of million dollars a year for asking questions, was now on the defensive. Surprised, Douglas paused, looked around and finally answered, "Well, sell me this ashtray." 13

Fred Herman again spoke instantly, "Why would you want to buy that?" And again, Mike Douglas, surprised and scratching his head, finally answered, "Well, it's new and shapely. Also, it's colorful. And besides, we are in a new studio and don't want it to burn down. And, of course, we want to accommodate guests who smoke." 14

At this point, Mike Douglas sat back in his chair, but not for long. Instantly Fred Herman responded, "How much would you pay for the ashtray, Mike?" 15

Douglas stammered and said, "Well, I haven't bought an ashtray lately, but this one is attractive and large, so I guess I'd pay eighteen dollars or twenty dollars." And Fred Herman, after asking just three questions, closed the sale by saying, "Well, Mike, I'll let you have the ashtray for eighteen dollars." 16

That's selling by questioning and listening. I call it selling with a professional ear. The whole sale took less than one minute. Fred Herman said he simply reacted as he always does in selling, by asking questions. 17

Make it your personal goal to ask a lot of questions. But have a purpose for each question. There are two basic categories: to get specific information or to learn opinions and feelings. It's easier to gain 18 rapport and get a person to open up by relating your questions to the other person's background or experience. Use open-ended questions to draw him out. Remember, closed-end questions will make it difficult to get another person to speak and share ideas or information. Nobody likes to feel he's being investigated.

Finally, remember the advice of the famous statesman of some 19 years ago, Bernard Baruch, who said: "You can win more friends in two months by showing interest in others than you can in two years by trying to interest others in you." Looking at people as you converse with them and asking questions will help show genuine interest.

Rule Three is don't interrupt. It's just as rude to step on people's 20 ideas as to step on their toes.

It's a human tendency to want to jump right into a conversation 21 when we get an idea or are reminded of something by someone's words. And that's why there's a problem. We need to continually practice letting other people finish their sentences or ideas. Speak only in turn is the answer.

Most of us avoid interrupters. We even go out of our way to avoid 22 them. In fact, a desire to prevent interruptions motivated Thomas Jefferson to invent the dumbwaiter, a mechanical lift to take food and drink by pulley from the kitchen to an upstairs dining room. Jefferson disliked being interrupted in conversation by servants; with the dumbwaiter, no servants were necessary and he couldn't be interrupted.

Nobody likes to be cut off while speaking. So work at letting 23 others finish what they have to say. Bite your tongue and count to ten if you have to, but practice Rule Three.

Rule Four is don't change the subject. This is a little different 24 from Rule Three. Interrupting is bad enough, but going right on and changing the subject at the same time is positively rude. Some people do this so much they are dodged by others who don't want to be their next victim.

Consider a group of people who are talking and one of the 25 members says, "I was watching television the other night and Senator Hayakawa of California spoke about . . ." Now at this point another member of the group, hearing the word *California*, interrupts immediately and changes the subject. "Oh, California, have you been out there to Disneyland? It's terrific! We took the kids there last summer and had a ball. You know, they have an island there, Tom Sawyer Island. And they have tree houses, caves, all kinds of things to do. Why, you could spend a couple of days there. You get to the island on a raft or one of those old Mississippi steamboats. Boy, it was just like being Robinson Crusoe on that island. Now what were you saying?"

Well, the speaker who was going to say something about Senator 26
Hayakawa of California has no doubt buried that idea forever. In fact,
the person who was cut off will not offer any more ideas and will
probably find a reason to get out of the presence of the interrupter who
also changed the subject.

Interrupting and changing the subject are sure ways to alienate 27
people quickly. So try to curb° both tendencies. You can be certain of
this: If you cut people off while they're speaking and also change the
subject, you'll be cutting them out of your life as friends or associates
as well. A little restraint will pay big dividends°.

Rule Five is to check° your emotions. Some people are prone° to 28
anger and get excited about certain words. It doesn't pay to get
overstimulated and overreact to the words and ideas of others.

Words such as *gasoline, taxes, abortion,* and *communism* can stir 29
one's emotions instantly. Curb your emotions. Control your urge to
interrupt and stifle° the other person's idea. It's a free country. People
are entitled to their opinions and the right to complete their thoughts.
Hear others out.

Let them explain their points of view. Cutting them off won't 30
accomplish anything. Try to understand them first. Then give your own
ideas in a controlled manner. Little is gained through arguing and
fighting. On the contrary, loss of time and injured relationships usually
result.

Evaluate when the idea is complete, not before, or only when you 31
fully understand the other person's meaning.

I know a fellow who went storming into his boss's office. He was 32
shouting and complaining that someone not as long with the company
had received a promotion he thought he should have gotten. The boss
told him that because of his quick temper he wouldn't be trusted to
manage others.

Besides, getting overly excited causes us to mentally debate or 33
fight any idea that differs from our personal conviction, experience or
bias°. So we don't hear what the speaker is saying at these times.
Remember, the biggest problem in listening is failing to concentrate on
the other person's communication. Getting overly emotional about
something is one of the causes of the problem. Check your emotions.
Hear the other person out first.

Rule Six stands for an essential principle of better listening and 34
therefore better understanding: responsiveness. Be a responsive
listener. Be responsive in your demeanor°, posture and facial
expression. Let your whole being show you are interested in other
people and their ideas.

As you listen, look at the other person and show some signs of hearing and understanding. Nod your head occasionally—gently, not vigorously. Nod slightly with a yes for agreement or a no when it's something sad or unhappy. Show through your posture, whether seated or standing, that you are concentrating on listening totally. 35

We show our interest in others also when we say occasionally "Um-mm or "Uh-huh." These simple signs encourage speakers. They show that we're interested in them and that we're listening to what they're saying. However, others won't talk long unless we are responsive in our listening and offer some nonverbal and even some slight verbal signs of understanding. 36

To understand this important principle of being responsive, it helps to ask, "How do we turn people off?" The answers come quickly, by not looking at them, not asking questions, not showing any positive response; by looking out the window, shuffling papers, interrupting or giving other negative types of feedback. 37

But we want to turn people on, not off. Whether we're teachers, managers, doctors, parents or salespeople, we want to encourage others to communicate with us so that we can gain understanding. 38

And there's one more important part to being responsive in listening to others: The one time it is all right, even desirable, to interrupt is to clarify what is said. 39

For example, as soon as you hear someone's name when you are introduced, inquire right at that moment how to spell the name if it is a difficult one. Or if you aren't sure of a statistic, date, place or other fact someone mentions, it shows responsive, concentrated listening to interrupt to clarify. 40

You can cushion your interruption with "Pardon me." But sometimes that isn't necessary. You might simple inquire, "How many?" or "When did it happen?" or "What's the name?" The interruption to clarify will actually help you focus on the other person's message more actively. 41

With a little knowledge and practice you can double your listening ability. 42

Listening is a gift you can give, no matter who you are. And you can give it to anyone. It doesn't cost a cent, but it is priceless to a person who needs a listener. 43

VOCABULARY QUESTIONS

A. Use context clues to help you decide on the best definition for each italicized word. Then circle the letter of each choice.

1. The word *concise* in "questions that get specific, concise facts for answers are closed-end questions. You rarely get more than a word or two in reply" (paragraph 8) means
   a. angry.
   b. easy.
   (c.) brief.
   d. tall.

2. The word *alienate* in "Interrupting and changing the subject are sure ways to alienate people quickly. . . . If you cut people off . . . and also change the subject, you'll be cutting them out of your life" (paragraph 27) means
   (a.) make unfriendly.
   b. welcome.
   c. make enthusiastic.
   d. praise.

3. The word *restraint* in "If you cut people off . . . you'll be cutting them out of your life as friends or associates as well. A little restraint will pay big dividends" (paragraph 27) means
   a. interruption.
   (b.) control.
   c. punishment.
   d. lack of discipline.

4. The word *stir* in "Words such as *gasoline, taxes, abortion*, and *communism* can stir one's emotions instantly" (paragraph 29) means
   a. calm.
   b. delay.
   c. educate.
   (d.) excite.

5. The word *vigorously* in "Nod your head occasionally—gently, not vigorously" (paragraph 35) means
   a. slightly.
   b. rarely.
   (c.) forcefully.
   d. accidentally.

B. On the next page are words, or forms of words, from "Words to Watch." Write in the one that best completes each sentence.

curb	demeanor	distraction
prone	prospects	

6. At night, my father is _____ *prone* _____ to fall asleep while watching television.

7. "You can't expect _____ *prospects* _____ to buy something if you don't offer them help," the manager said to the new salesclerk.

8. Thoughts of the argument with Julie were a _____ *distraction* _____ to Mickey—he kept reading the same page over and over.

9. Mr. Mills had the _____ *demeanor* _____ of a pussy cat but the intentions of a tiger.

10. I decided to _____ *curb* _____ my spending by putting some money in a savings account each week.

READING COMPREHENSION QUESTIONS

Central Point and Main Ideas

1. Which sentence best expresses the central point of the selection?
   a. Good listening is an important skill everyone can learn by following a few guidelines.
   b. The best listener looks at the person speaking.
   c. Bad habits and being overly emotional cause us to be poor listeners.
   d. Listening skills can help people do better in business.

2. Which sentence best expresses the main idea of paragraph 6?
   a. When you're listening, don't look out the window.
   b. People don't trust a person who doesn't look at them.
   c. Look at a person you're listening to and concentrate on him or her.
   d. Distrust can block communication and motivation.

Supporting Details

3. Looking directly at the person who is speaking
   a. is rude.
   b. blocks communication.
   c. helps the speaker trust the listener.
   d. alienates people quickly.

4. The two types of questions good listeners ask are
   a. closed-end and open-ended questions.
   b. questions with either "yes" or "no" answers.

c. humorous and serious questions.

d. sales or personal questions.

5. ___F___ TRUE OR FALSE? A good listener will never interrupt a speaker.

Transitions

6. The author begins two sentences in paragraph 5 with transitions that show addition. Find those transitions and write them here.

    First   *Also*

_____   _____

7. Throughout the article, the author uses illustrations to help make his points. What are two illustration signals that he uses?

         example; for example; to illustrate; such as

_____

Inferences

8. ___T___ TRUE OR FALSE? The author implies that good listening requires mental and physical effort.

9. The author implies that improving listening skills

a. takes a long time.

(b.) can help people's careers.

c. is not important for everyone.

d. is always very easy.

10. In which publication do you think the article may have first appeared?

a. *Newsweek* magazine

b. A psychology textbook

(c.) A business publication

d. *People* magazine

OUTLINING

Complete the outline of "Are You a Good Listener?" by filling in the central point and the missing major supporting details.

Central point: *Following six basic guidelines can help you become a better*

           listener.

1. *Look at the other person.*

2. *Ask questions.*

3. Don't interrupt.

4. *Don't change the subject.*

5. Control your emotions.

6. *Be responsive.*

DISCUSSION QUESTIONS

1. Which of Montgomery's six rules for better listening are most helpful for you personally to remember?

2. Which trait of poor listening bothers you most when you are speaking to others? Give examples.

3. In paragraph 10, Montgomery contrasts the "product-pusher" with the "counselor-type salesperson." What does he mean by each of those terms, and what are the differences between them? What experiences have you had with either of those types? If you've encountered them both, which do you prefer?

4. Montgomery writes in paragraph 2, "Listening is essential to our personal, professional, social and family success." In what specific ways might listening contribute to success in each of those areas of our life? Give examples for each.

Check Your Performance		**ARE YOU A GOOD LISTENER?**	
Skill	*Number Right*	*Points*	*Total*
VOCABULARY			
Vocabulary in Context (5 items)	_____	x 10 =	_____
Words to Watch (5 items)	_____	x 10 =	_____
		SCORE =	_____ %
COMPREHENSION			
Central Point and Main Ideas (2 items)	_____	x 8 =	_____
Supporting Details (3 items)	_____	x 8 =	_____
Transitions (2 items)	_____	x 8 =	_____
Inferences (3 items)	_____	x 8 =	_____
Outlining (5 items)	_____	x 4 =	_____
		SCORE =	_____ %

FINAL SCORES: **Vocabulary** _____ %   **Comprehension** _____ %

Enter your final scores into the reading performance chart on the inside back cover.

8

Getting Words on Paper: Where to Begin
Richard P. Batteiger

Preview

Have you ever sat down determined to write a paper or essay only to find yourself staring in frustration at a blank sheet of paper? If so, Richard P. Batteiger has some suggestions that will help you develop the skills you need to write more effectively. In this selection from his textbook *Business Writing* (Wadsworth, 1985), he also explores the reasons why writing is often viewed as a difficult, frustrating, or even terrifying experience.

Words to Watch

equivalent (1):	the equal in some way
efficiently (5):	effectively with a minimum of effort
practitioners (7):	people who practice a profession or an art
distinguish (8):	separate according to differences
thoroughly (13):	completely
conventional (14):	traditional

You probably do not think of yourself as a writer. You have 1 chosen a career in management, marketing, accounting, finance, or some other related business subject because you want to work with objects, numbers, or people, not words. But working with any of these will also require you to use words. Perhaps you have already discovered that writing is an important, daily part of almost every management or technical job in business and industry. In fact, many people in business may write the equivalent° of a medium-length book each year, even though they do not consider themselves to be writers.

Writing is a tool that you use to do your job. And employers will expect you to write as effectively as you do the rest of your job. Your company's success, and your own, may depend on how well you can present your ideas on paper.

WHAT DOES IT MEAN TO WRITE EFFECTIVELY?

Too many people find writing frustrating, difficult, and even terrifying. After all, writing *looks* easy. It appears to be simply a matter of picking up a pen and putting words on paper, one after another. Begin at the beginning and keep going until you reach the end. What could be simpler? **2**

The notion that writing is easy, or that it ought to be easy, comes in part from our reading. When we read a book, a magazine article, a business report, or even a brief memo, we see only the finished text. We have no way of knowing whether it was easy or difficult to write. We can't see the false starts, the rough drafts, or the hours of work that went into it. We read from beginning to end, and the finished, polished text seems to say that it came from someone's pen just the way we see it. Certainly our own writing ought to go as smoothly, and as well. **3**

People find writing difficult and frustrating for a variety of reasons. Perhaps someone has told them that their writing is no good, that they make too many mistakes, or that their writing too often doesn't make sense. Perhaps their writing does not accomplish the goals they had in mind for it (whatever those goals might be). Perhaps they have received low grades on their writing assignments in school. Or the writing itself may be difficult to do. It becomes an ordeal, something to be faced, rather than something to do. They spend too much time staring at a blank page or waiting for inspiration and end up rushing through a draft at the last minute. For these reasons and others, many people find writing difficult to do. They avoid writing, or they are constantly unhappy with their own writing. **4**

To say that you should write effectively is to identify two separate but related goals. The first is to learn how to write a finished draft that says what you want it to say and accomplishes its goal. The second is to learn how to use working methods that will actually help you produce a finished draft efficiently°, with a minimum of frustration. Most inexperienced writers concentrate on the first of these goals, without realizing that their ability to produce a well-written final draft depends, to a larger extent than they are aware, on the working methods they use. That is, writing is difficult or ineffective for them because their working methods get in the way. **5**

Writing is not a gift, but a skill you can learn. The goal of this book is to help you learn that skill by focusing not only on what to say and how to say it, but also on the working methods that are most likely to help you write successfully. 6

TAKING TIPS FROM EXPERIENCED WRITERS

One way to learn any skill is to seek advice from experienced, successful practitioners°. If you want to improve your golf or tennis game, you will probably take lessons from a local pro and read articles and books that explain how championship players play the game. You can learn to make a long, difficult putt or to improve your serve by taking tips from the experts. What works for golf or tennis can work for writing. We can learn a great deal about how to write by looking at what experienced, successful writers do when they write. 7

Who are the experts? Some of them are professional writers, people who write for a living. Others are not professional writers. That is, writing is not their livelihood, but something they must do as part of their jobs. They are engineers, managers, executives, teachers, and students just like you who use writing as a tool. In recent years a number of researchers have observed these experienced writers, as well as inexperienced writers, to discover what they do when they write. As a result of this research, we can distinguish° experienced writers from inexperienced ones in a number of ways, not only by the quality of their final drafts, but also, and especially, in the working methods they use. As you read the following list of comparisons, think about your own working methods and decide whether you are closer to the experienced or inexperienced group. How could you change your own methods to bring you closer to those used by experienced writers? 8

1. *Experienced* writers spend from 50 to 80 percent of their time planning, thinking about what they will write, before they attempt to write a draft.
   Inexperienced writers often spend less than 30 percent of their time planning. 9

2. *Experienced* writers delay attempting to produce a draft until they believe they have a workable plan.
   Inexperienced writers often begin to write immediately. 10

3. *Experienced* writers take time to identify the goals they want their writing to accomplish.
   Inexperienced writers seldom think about goals. 11

4. *Experienced* writers spend a considerable amount of their   12
planning time thinking about their readers. They try to see
their subjects and their goals from a reader's point of view and
to find ways to adapt their writing to their audience.
Inexperienced writers spend comparatively little time thinking
about readers, if they think about them at all.

5. *Experienced* writers take time to explore and thoroughly°   13
understand their subjects. They often gather more information
than they will need, but they focus their search on information
that will help them achieve their goals.
Inexperienced writers tend to extremes when they explore
their subjects. On the one hand, they may gather only the
absolute minimum that they think they will need. Or they may
attempt to gather all information that is available about their
subjects.

6. *Experienced* writers use a variety of methods to organize their   14
information before they write.
Inexperienced writers frequently use only a conventional°
outline to help them organize.

7. *Experienced* writers often consider their first draft to be a   15
"discovery draft" in which they try to find out what they know
and how well their plan will work. As they write this draft,
they pay little attention to such details as spelling, punctuation,
and other editorial details.
Inexperienced writers often write their first drafts with
considerable attention to editorial details. They may work to
get everything "right" the first time; they often believe they
should be able to write from beginning to end and that the
writing should flow smoothly and easily.

8. *Experienced* writers expect to revise their drafts, perhaps   16
several times. And revision often involves a complete
rethinking and restructuring of the draft. They may add or
delete large sections. They may abandon their original draft
and start over.
Inexperienced writers do not often thoroughly revise their
drafts. When they do, their revisions often focus on the
editorial details of spelling, word choice, and punctuation.

9. *Experienced* writers edit and proofread carefully, perhaps   17
several times.

Inexperienced writers seldom pay close attention to editing and proofreading.

Of course, not all writers work in exactly the same way, and one writer may use different methods at different times. But these distinctions between experienced and inexperienced writers show that, in general, experienced writers have learned or discovered a reasonably well-defined working method that seems to help them get their writing done. 18

- They plan.
- They consider their readers.
- They investigate their subject.
- They organize.
- They write.
- They revise.
- They edit and proofread.

It makes sense to give this method a try, to see if it makes writing both easier to do and more effective. It is not necessary to go through these stages in the sequence in which they are listed here. In fact, it is unlikely that you will do so. When you write, many things happen at once. As you plan you may discover that you are thinking of facts and ideas that you want to include in your draft, or that you know something important about your reader. As you organize you may find that you are once again investigating your subject. The steps listed here are guidelines, not rigid rules. You are free to change and adapt them so that they fit your own situation. 19

VOCABULARY QUESTIONS

A. Use context clues to help you decide on the best definition for each italicized word. Then circle the letter of your choice.

1. The word *notion* in "The notion that writing is easy, or that it ought to be easy, comes in part from our reading" (paragraph 3) means
   a. correct idea.
   b. law.
   c. belief.
   d. debate.

2. The word *ordeal* in " . . . the writing itself may be difficult to do. It becomes an ordeal, something to be faced, rather than something to do" (paragraph 4) means
   a. experience.
   b. good experience.
   (c.) difficult experience.
   d. satisfying task.

3. The word *livelihood* in "Others are not professional writers. That is, writing is not their livelihood, but something they must do as part of their jobs" (paragraph 8) means
   (a.) means of support.
   b. favorite task.
   c. hobby.
   d. assignment.

4. The word *distinctions* in "But these distinctions between experienced and inexperienced writers show that, in general, experienced writers have learned or discovered a reasonably well-defined working method. . . ."(paragraph 18) means
   a. problems.
   b. arguments.
   c. questions.
   (d.) differences.

5. The word *rigid* in "The steps listed here are guidelines, not rigid rules" (paragraph 19) means
   a. unimportant.
   b. careless.
   c. flexible.
   (d.) firmly set.

B. Below are words from "Words to Watch." Write in the one that best completes each sentence.

conventional	distinguish	equivalent
practitioner	thoroughly	

6. The bride decided against the _____*conventional*_____ all-white wedding cake. Instead she ordered a strawberry one with pink icing.

7. Kyle _____*thoroughly*_____ enjoyed every spoonful of the chocolate marshmallow ice cream.

8. To get into that business graduate program, a person needs a B.S. in business or the _____*equivalent*_____ in business experience.

9. Before writing her report on alternative health treatments, Tricia consulted an acupuncture _____*practitioner*_____.

10. In a paper for my writing class, I _____*distinguish*_____ true friends from false ones and new friends from old ones.

READING COMPREHENSION QUESTIONS

Central Point and Main Ideas

1. Which sentence best expresses the central point of the selection?
   (a.) Writing is not a gift, but a skill that can be learned by studying the methods used by experienced writers.
   b. Writing is important for many jobs in business.
   c. Experienced writers take time to plan and think about what they will write before they attempt to write a draft.
   d. Writing can often be a frustrating experience because it looks easy.

2. The main idea of paragraph 3 is expressed in its
   (a.) first sentence.
   b. second sentence.
   c. third sentence.
   d. last sentence.

3. Which sentence best expresses the main idea of paragraph 5?
   a. A finished draft should say what you want it to say and accomplish its goal.
   b. Writing effectively is not an easy process.
   (c.) Effective writing involves both writing a finished draft and using good working methods; inexperienced writers focus on the former without learning how to do the latter.
   d. The working methods of inexperienced writers can get in their way.

Supporting Details

4. Experienced writers do not
   a. spend a great deal of time planning what they will write.
   b. think about the goals of their writing.
   c. think about their audience.
   (d.) pay attention to spelling errors during the first few drafts.

5. Writing effectively involves
   a. producing final drafts that accomplish the writer's goal.
   b. using working methods that enable you to write efficiently, with a minimum of frustration.
   c. both of the above.
   d. neither of the above.

Transitions

6. The relationship between the two parts of the sentence below is one of
   a. illustration.
   b. addition.
   c. time.
   d. contrast.

   They often gather more information than they will need, but they focus their search on information that will help them achieve their goals. (Paragraph 13)

7. If a transition were added in the blank to the excerpt below, which of the following would be most appropriate?
   a. In addition
   b. For instance
   c. In contrast
   d. Next

   One way to learn any skill is to seek advice from experienced, successful practitioners. _____, if you want to improve your golf or tennis game, you will probably take lessons from a local pro and read articles and books that explain how championship players play the game. (Paragraph 7)

Patterns of Organization

8. The main pattern of organization of paragraph 4 is
   a. cause and effect.
   b. time order.
   c. contrast.
   d. definition and example.

Inferences

9. __T__ TRUE OR FALSE? The author implies that much of "writing" actually involves mental planning and researching.

10. Which of the following ideas is *not* implied by the author?
    a. Writing is a process in which one never returns to an earlier stage, such as reworking a section after a first draft has already been written.
    b. Your writing will probably improve if you try the method used by experienced writers.
    c. As they work on a piece of writing, writers often need to pare down the information they have gathered on their topic.
    d. There are a number of ways to organize information other than the traditional outline.

OUTLINING

Following is a general outline of "Getting Words on Paper." Complete the outline by filling in the letters of the missing details. (The list of missing details appears on the next page.)

Central Point: Writing is a skill that can be learned.

A. What Does It Mean to Write Effectively?
   1. The idea that writing should be easy comes from our reading.
   2. There are a number of reasons why people find writing to be difficult.
      a. _e_
      b. Their writing doesn't accomplish the goals they had in mind for it.
      c. _a_
      d. The writing itself may be difficult to do.
   3. Writing effectively involves two goals.
      a. The first is to write a finished draft that accomplishes its goal.
      b. _d_
B. Taking Tips from Experienced Writers
   1. Like any skill, to learn writing you should consult the experts in the area.
   2. Who are the experts?
      a. _b_
      b. Others write as part of their job, but they are not professional writers.
   3. A comparison of the practices of experienced writers and inexperienced writers will aid you in improving your own writing.
   4. The methods of experienced writers can be used as guidelines for your own writing.
      a. They spend a lot of time on planning.
      b. They delay writing until they have a workable plan.
      c. They identify goals.

   d. They consider their readers.

   e. They take time to explore and thoroughly understand their subjects.

   f. They use a variety of methods to organize their information before writing.

   g. They consider their first draft to be a "discovery draft" and pay little attention to editorial details.

   h.   _c_

   i. They edit and proofread carefully.

Details Missing from the Outline

   a. They have received low grades in their writing assignments in school.

   b. Some are professional writers, people who write for a living.

   c. They revise or start over as necessary.

   d. The second is to learn how to use working methods that will help you produce a finished draft efficiently.

   e. They may have been told their writing is no good in some way.

DISCUSSION QUESTIONS

1. Do you find writing to be a difficult and frustrating task? What are some of the problems you face when you attempt to write? How might Batteiger's article help you to overcome these problems?

2. How does viewing writing as a skill, and not a gift, change your attitude toward it? In what ways have you learned other skills? Can those same ways be applied to learning writing?

3. The author writes, "Experienced writers spend a considerable amount of their planning time thinking about their readers." Do you consider your audience when you write? How does considering your readers change your writing? Consider, for example, how you might write the same idea differently when you are writing for your instructor as compared to writing for your peers.

4. Batteiger writes that, in addition to considering their audience, authors must consider their goals for writing. For example, think about the differences that might result between a person who is reporting on a fire for the local evening newspaper and someone who is writing about the fire for a book about the history of the town. What will be the differences in the information they find important? How do you think their writing styles would be different?

Check Your Performance   GETTING WORDS ON PAPER

Skill	Number Right	Points	Total
VOCABULARY			
Vocabulary in Context (5 items)	_____	x 10 =	_____
Words to Watch (5 items)	_____	x 10 =	_____
		SCORE =	_____%
COMPREHENSION			
Central Point and Main Ideas (3 items)	_____	x 8 =	_____
Supporting Details (2 items)	_____	x 8 =	_____
Transitions (2 items)	_____	x 8 =	_____
Patterns of Organization (1 item)	_____	x 8 =	_____
Inferences (2 items)	_____	x 8 =	_____
Outlining (5 items)	_____	x 4 =	_____
		SCORE =	_____%

FINAL SCORES: Vocabulary _____%   Comprehension _____%

Enter your final scores into the reading performance chart on the inside back cover.

9

Dealing with Feelings
Rudolph F. Verderber

Preview

Is it sometimes useful to conceal your feelings when you're hurt? Is it usually best to simply yell out and get your feelings off your chest when you're angry? Is there a risk to telling others how you really feel? Think of your answers to these questions. Then read the following excerpt from the college textbook *Communicate!*, Sixth Edition (Wadsworth, 1990), to see what the author says.

Words to Watch

self-disclosure (1):	revealing
decipher (2):	interpret
seethe (2):	boil with emotion
perceived (3):	seen
undemonstrative (3):	tending not to express feelings
inconsequential (4):	unimportant
interpersonally (7):	involving relations between people
potential (12):	possible
net (14):	final
triggered (16):	set off
elated (17):	very happy

An extremely important aspect of self-disclosure° is the sharing of feelings. We all experience feelings such as happiness at receiving an unexpected gift, sadness about the breakup of a relationship, or anger when we believe we have been taken advantage of. The question is whether to disclose such feelings, and if so, how. Self-disclosure of feelings usually will be most successful not when feelings are withheld or displayed but when they are described. Let's consider each of these forms of dealing with feelings.   1

WITHHOLDING FEELINGS

Withholding feelings—that is, keeping them inside and not giving 2 any verbal or nonverbal cues to their existence—is generally an inappropriate means of dealing with feeling. Withholding feelings is best exemplified by the good poker player who develops a "poker face," a neutral look that is impossible to decipher°. The look is the same whether the player's cards are good or bad. Unfortunately, many people use poker faces in their interpersonal relationships, so that no one knows whether they hurt inside, are extremely excited, and so on. For instance, Doris feels very nervous when Candy stands over her while Doris is working on her report. And when Candy says, "That first paragraph isn't very well written," Doris begins to seethe°, yet she says nothing—she withholds her feelings.

Psychologists believe that when people withhold feelings, they 3 can develop physical problems such as ulcers, high blood pressure, and heart disease, as well as psychological problems such as stress-related neuroses and psychoses. Moreover, people who withhold feelings are often perceived° as cold, undemonstrative°, and not much fun to be around.

Is withholding ever appropriate? When a situation is 4 inconsequential°, you may well choose to withhold your feelings. For instance, a stranger's inconsiderate behavior at a party may bother you, but because you can move to another part of the room, withholding may not be detrimental. In the example of Doris seething at Candy's behavior, however, withholding could be costly to Doris.

DISPLAYING FEELINGS

Displaying feelings means expressing those feelings through a 5 facial reaction, body response, and/or spoken reaction. Cheering over a great play at a sporting event, booing the umpire at a perceived bad call, patting a person on the back when the person does something well, or saying, "What are you doing?" in a nasty tone of voice are all displays of feelings.

Displays are especially appropriate when the feelings you are 6 experiencing are positive. For instance, when Gloria does something nice for you, and you experience a feeling of joy, giving her a big hug is appropriate; when Don gives you something you've wanted, and you experience a feeling of appreciation, a big smile or an "Oh, thank you, Don" is appropriate. In fact, many people need to be even more demonstrative of good feelings. You've probably seen the bumper sticker "Have you hugged your kid today?" It reinforces the point that you need to display love and affection constantly to show another person that you really care.

Displays become detrimental to communication when the feelings 7 you are experiencing are negative—especially when the display of a negative feeling appears to be an overreaction. For instance, when Candy stands over Doris while she is working on her report and says, "That first paragraph isn't very well written," Doris may well experience resentment. If Doris lashes out at Candy by screaming, "Who the hell asked you for your opinion," Doris's display no doubt will hurt Candy's feelings and short-circuit their communication. Although displays of negative feelings may be good for you psychologically, they are likely to be bad for you interpersonally°.

DESCRIBING FEELINGS

Describing feelings—putting your feelings into words in a calm, 8 nonjudgmental way—tends to be the best method of disclosing feelings. Describing feelings not only increases chances for positive communication and decreases chances for short-circuiting lines of communication, it also teaches people how to treat you. When you describe your feelings, people are made aware of the effect of their behavior. This knowledge gives them the information needed to determine whether they should continue or repeat that behavior. If you tell Paul that you really feel flattered when he visits you, such a statement should encourage Paul to visit you again; likewise, when you tell Cliff that you feel very angry when he borrows your jacket without asking, he is more likely to ask the next time he borrows a jacket. Describing your feelings allows you to exercise a measure of control over others' behavior toward you.

Describing and displaying feelings are not the same. Many times 9 people think they are describing when in fact they are displaying feelings or evaluating.

If describing feelings is so important to communication 10 effectiveness, why don't more people do it regularly? There seem to be at least four reasons why many people don't describe feelings.

1. *Many people have a poor vocabulary of words for describing* 11 *the various feelings they are experiencing.* People can sense that they are angry; however, they may not know whether what they are feeling might best be described as annoyed, betrayed, cheated, crushed, disturbed, furious, outraged, or shocked. Each of these words describes a slightly different aspect of what many people lump together as anger.

2. *Many people believe that describing their true feelings reveals too much about themselves.* If you tell people when their behavior hurts you, you risk their using the information against you when they want to hurt you on purpose. Even so, the potential° benefits of describing your feelings far outweigh the risks. For instance, if Pete has a nickname for you that you don't like and you tell Pete that calling you by that nickname really makes you nervous and tense, Pete may use the nickname when he wants to hurt you, but he is more likely to stop calling you by that name. If, on the other hand, you don't describe your feelings to Pete, he is probably going to call you by that name all the time because he doesn't know any better. When you say nothing, you reinforce his behavior. The level of risk varies with each situation, but you will more often improve a relationship than be hurt by describing feelings. 12

3. *Many people believe that if they describe feelings, others will make them feel guilty about having such feelings.* At a very tender age we all learned abut "tactful" behavior. Under the premise that "the truth sometimes hurts" we learned to avoid the truth by not saying anything or by telling "little" lies. Perhaps when you were young your mother said, "Don't forget to give Grandma a great big kiss." At that time you may have blurted out, "Ugh—it makes me feel yucky to kiss Grandma. She's got a mustache." If your mother responded, "That's terrible—your grandma loves you. Now you give her a kiss and never let me hear you talk like that again!" then you probably felt guilty for having this "wrong" feeling. But the point is that the thought of kissing your grandma made you feel "yucky" whether it should have or not. In this case what was at issue was the way you talked about the feelings—not your having the feelings. 13

4. *Many people believe that describing feelings causes harm to others or to a relationship.* If it really bothers Max when his girlfriend, Dora, bites her fingernails, Max may believe that describing his feelings to Dora will hurt her so much that the knowledge will drive a wedge into their relationship. So it's better for Max to say nothing, right? Wrong! If Max says nothing, he's still going to be bothered by Dora's behavior. In fact, as time goes on, Max will probably lash out at Dora for others things because he can't bring himself to talk about the behavior that really bothers him. The net° result is that not 14

only will Dora be hurt by Max's behavior, but she won't understand the true source of his feelings. By not describing his feelings, Max may well drive a wedge into their relationship anyway.

If Max does describe his feelings to Dora, she might quit 15 or at least try to quit biting her nails; they might get into a discussion in which he finds out that she doesn't want to bite them but just can't seem to stop, and he can help her in her efforts to stop; or they might discuss the problem and Max may see that it is a small thing really and not let it bother him as much. The point is that in describing feelings the chances of a successful outcome are greater than they are in not describing them.

To describe your feelings, first put the emotion you are feeling 16 into words. Be specific. Second, state what triggered° the feeling. Finally, make sure you indicate that the feeling is yours. For example, suppose your roommate borrows your jacket without asking. When he returns, you describe your feelings by saying, "Cliff, I [indication that the feeling is yours] get really angry [the feeling] when you borrow my jacket without asking [trigger]." Or suppose that Carl has just reminded you of the very first time he brought you a rose. You describe your feelings by saying, "Carl, I [indication that the feeling is yours] get really tickled [the feeling] when you remind me about that first time you brought me a rose [trigger]."

You may find it easiest to begin by describing positive feelings: "I 17 really feel elated° knowing that you were the one who nominated me for the position" or "I'm delighted that you offered to help me with the housework." As you gain success with positive descriptions, you can try negative feelings attributable to environmental factors: "It's so cloudy; I feel gloomy" or "When the wind howls through the cracks, I really get jumpy." Finally, you can move to negative descriptions resulting from what people have said or done: "Your stepping in front of me like that really annoys me" or "The tone of your voice confuses me."

VOCABULARY QUESTIONS

A. Use context clues to help you decide on the best definition for each italicized word. Then circle the letter of your choice.

1. The word *exemplified* in "withholding feelings is best exemplified by the good poker player who develops a 'poker face,' a neutral look" (paragraph 2) means
   a. contradicted.
   b. illustrated.
   c. surprised.
   d. stolen.

2. The word *detrimental* in "a stranger's inconsiderate behavior at a party may bother you, but because you can move to another part of the room, withholding may not be detrimental" (paragraph 4) means
   a. useful.
   b. private.
   c. helpless.
   d. harmful.

3. The word *premise* in "Under the premise that 'the truth sometimes hurts' we learned to avoid the truth by not saying anything or by telling 'little' lies" (paragraph 13) means
   a. question.
   b. choice.
   c. theory.
   d. disagreement.

4. The word *wedge* in "Max may believe that describing his feelings to Dora will hurt her so much that the knowledge will drive a wedge into their relationship" (paragraph 14) means
   a. something that divides.
   b. loyalty.
   c. friendship.
   d. many years.

5. The words *attributable to* in "As you gain success with positive descriptions [of feelings], you can try negative feelings attributable to environmental factors: 'It's so cloudy; I feel gloomy'" (paragraph 17) mean
   a. that cannot be explained by.
   b. that can be explained by.
   c. unrelated to.
   d. confused by.

B. Below are words from "Words to Watch." Write in the one that best completes each sentence.

decipher	elated	inconsequential
perceived	seethe	

6. Charlene was _____*perceived*_____ as being cold, but in reality she was just very shy.

7. Reading about all the tax breaks that the rich get makes me _____*seethe*_____.

8. Ellie recognized her baby's various cries so well that she could _____*decipher*_____ what each one meant.

9. By the time people have several years of career success, their school records usually become _____*inconsequential*_____.

10. Howard was _____*elated*_____ to learn he got an A in biology.

READING COMPREHENSION QUESTIONS

Central Point and Main Ideas

1. Which sentence best expresses the central point of the selection?
   a. Everyone has feelings.
   b. There are three ways to deal with feelings; describing them is most useful for educating others about how you want to be treated.
   c. Withholding feelings means not giving verbal or nonverbal clues that might reveal those feelings to others.
   d. Expressing feelings often leads to problems with others.

2. Which sentence best expresses the main idea of paragraph 3?
   a. Withholding negative feelings may lead to physical problems.
   b. Withholding negative feelings may lead to psychological problems.
   c. Withholding positive feelings can make one seem cold.
   d. Withholding feelings has several disadvantages.

3. Which sentence best expresses the main idea of paragraph 8?
   a. Describing your feelings favorably influences others' behavior toward you.
   b. It is possible to encourage friends to visit you again.
   c. It is possible to encourage friends to ask before they borrow things from you.
   d. It is possible to encourage friends.

Supporting Details

4. According to the author, you are more likely to create problems for yourself by
   a. withholding your feelings.
   b. displaying your positive feelings.
   c. describing your positive feelings.
   d. describing your negative feelings.

5. Describing your feelings means
   a. keeping your feelings inside.
   b. giving a nonverbal response to feelings.
   c. putting your feelings into words.
   d. telling "little" lies.

Transitions

6. The two parts of the sentence below express a relationship of
   a. time.
   b. addition.
   c. contrast.
   d. comparison.

   Although displays of negative feelings may be good for you psychologically, they are more likely to be bad for you interpersonally. (Paragraph 7)

7. The two illustration transitions in paragraph 4 are _____*for instance*_____ and _____*example*_____.

Patterns of Organization

8. The author develops paragraph 5 with
   a. a contrast.
   b. a comparison.
   c. a definition and examples.
   d. time order.

Inferences

9. From the reading we can conclude that describing feelings
   a. is usually easy for people.
   (b.) is a good way to solve some problems.
   c. should be done only for positive feelings.
   d. usually makes you feel guilty.

10. Which sentence can we conclude is an example of displaying a feeling?
    a. Jane refused to tell Tom that she hated his haircut.
    b. Betty told her son, "I enjoy reading your letters so much."
    (c.) The father clapped joyfully when the baby said, "Dada."
    d. Martin avoided Karen because he had forgotten her birthday.

OUTLINING

Below is an outline for "Dealing with Feelings." Complete the outline by filling in the central point (which Verderber presents in the first paragraph of the passage) and the three major supporting details.

Central point: *There are three ways that people deal with their feelings; while*

each is appropriate at times, the last one is especially useful for

educating others about how you want them to treat you.

1. *Withholding feelings means keeping them inside.*

2. *Displaying feelings means expressing them through a nonverbal or verbal*

   reaction.

3. *Describing feelings means putting them into words.*

DISCUSSION QUESTIONS

1. What is the difference between describing feelings and expressing them? How might Doris describe her feelings to Candy after Candy says, "That first paragraph isn't very well written" (paragraph 2)?

2. What do you think would be Verderber's advice on "little lies"? (See paragraph 13.)

3. Why do you think Verderber emphasizes describing feelings over the other two methods of dealing with feelings?

4. What are some examples from your own experience of withholding, expressing or displaying, and describing feelings? How useful was each?

Check Your Performance   **DEALING WITH FEELINGS**

Skill	*Number Right*	*Points*	*Total*
VOCABULARY			
Vocabulary in Context (5 items)	_____	x 10 =	_____
Words to Watch (5 items)	_____	x 10 =	_____
		SCORE =	_____%

COMPREHENSION			
Central Point and Main Ideas (3 items)	_____	x 8 =	_____
Supporting Details (2 items)	_____	x 8 =	_____
Transitions (2 items)	_____	x 8 =	_____
Patterns of Organization (1 item)	_____	x 8 =	_____
Inferences (2 items)	_____	x 8 =	_____
Outlining (4 items)	_____	x 5 =	_____
		SCORE =	_____%

FINAL SCORES: **Vocabulary** _____%   **Comprehension** _____%

Enter your final scores into the reading performance chart on the inside back cover.

10

Childhood Stress and Resilience
Diane E. Papalia and Sally Wendkos Olds

Preview

Have you ever met people who, despite misfortunes, seem to be able to recover unharmed? Have you ever wondered why those people could successfully deal with problems that would have stopped others? In the following selection from the college psychology textbook *A Child's World* (McGraw-Hill, 1993), the authors search for answers to these questions. They explore factors that enable some children to bounce back from hardship, and they note that any person may find the strength to rise above difficult circumstances.

Words to Watch

resilience (title):	ability to recover strength or good spirits quickly
sibling (1):	brother or sister
subject to (4):	to cause to experience
resourceful (6):	able to deal well with new situations and problems
hereditary (8):	passed down genetically from generation to generation
adaptable (9):	able to adjust well
consoles (9):	comforts
adverse (12):	unfavorable, harmful
compensate (13):	provide a balance

Stressful events are part of every childhood. Illness, the birth of a   1
sibling°, frustration, and parents' temporary absence are common
sources of stress. Other nonroutine stresses are all too likely to occur in

a child's world. Divorce or death of parents, hospitalization, and the day-in, day-out grind of poverty affect many children. Some children survive wars and earthquakes. The increase in the number of homeless families in the United States has brought severe psychological difficulties to children. Violent events like kidnappings and playground sniper attacks make children realize that their world is not always safe and that parents cannot always protect them. This realization is stressful to children in the short run and may affect them in the long run as well. Children's fears reflect their awareness of many modern stresses, as seen in Box 13-3.

Box 13-3: What Children Are Afraid Of

Adults have become increasingly concerned about the number of dangers facing children and worry about children's own fears of personal or global catastrophe. Children do have anxieties about homelessness, AIDS, drug abuse, crime, and nuclear war, but most childhood fears are about things much closer to youngsters' daily lives. According to research in six countries—Australia, Canada, Egypt, Japan, the Philippines, and the United States—children from many different cultures are remarkably alike in what they are afraid of.

When third- through ninth-grade children were asked to rank a list of twenty events in order of how upsetting they would be, the primary fear among children in each country was the same: fear of losing a parent. Close in importance to this were events that would embarrass children—being kept back in school, wetting their pants in public, or being sent to the principal. Surprisingly, children of every country rated the birth of a new sibling least upsetting of all (perhaps, at this age, children are so busy outside the home that they are less affected by a new arrival—or at age 8 and older, few were dealing with the birth of a new baby). Boys and girls rated events abut the same; by and large, so did children of different ages.

For most children, school is a source of insecurity—partly because it is so important in their lives and partly because so many belittling practices (like accusing children of lying, or ridiculing them in class) flourish there. Adults can stem fears by respecting children, encouraging them to talk about their worries, and not expecting fears to simply disappear.

Most childhood fears are normal, and overcoming them helps children grow, achieve identity, and master their world.

Children today have new pressures to cope with. Because families move around more than they used to, children are more likely to change schools and friends and less likely to know many adults well. They know more than children of previous generations did about technology, sex, and violence; and when they live in single-parent homes or have to consider parents' work schedules, they are likely to shoulder adult responsibilities.

The child psychologist David Elkind has called today's child the "hurried child." Like some other thoughtful observers, he is concerned that the pressures of life today are making children grow up too soon and are making their shortened childhood too stressful. Today's children are pressured to succeed in school, to compete in sports, and to meet parents' emotional needs. Children are exposed to many adult problems on television and in real life before they have mastered the problems of childhood. Yet children are not small adults. They feel and think like children, and they need these years of childhood for healthy development.   3

Sometimes a child's healthy development is thwarted by the very people expected to help it—the parents, who subject° their children to physical abuse or psychological maltreatment. Some children, however, known as "resilient" children, are able to overcome enormous life stress.   4

COPING WITH STRESS: THE RESILIENT CHILD

The effects of stress are unpredictable because people are unpredictable. Children's reactions to stressful events may depend on such factors as the event itself (children respond differently to a parents' death and to divorce), the child's age (preschoolers and adolescents react differently), and the child's sex (boys are more vulnerable than girls). Yet of two children of the same age and sex who are exposed to the same stressful experience, one may crumble while the other remains whole and healthy. Why is this so?   5

Resilient children are those who bounce back from circumstances that would blight the emotional development of most children. They are the children of the ghetto who go on to distinguish themselves in the professions. They are the neglected or abused children who go on to form intimate relationships, be good parents to their own children, and lead fulfilling lives. In spite of the bad cards they have been dealt, these children are winners. They are creative, resourceful°, independent, and enjoyable to be with. What is special about them?   6

Several studies have identified "protective factors" that may operate to reduce the effects of such stressors as kidnapping or poor parenting. Several of these factors may also protect children who have been psychologically abused.   7

Are some children born with stress-proof personalities? Or can children *develop* resilience? There has been little research on hereditary° factors in handling stress or on the effect of differences in   8 temperament, which seems to be partly hereditary. Factors like the following seem to contribute to children's resilience:

- *Personality.* Resilient children tend to be adaptable°. They are usually positive thinkers, friendly, sensitive to other people, and independent. They feel competent and have high self-esteem. Intelligence, too, may be a factor: good students seem to cope better (Rutter, 1984). These children are often able to diminish the importance of their problems by the way they look at them—as does the child hero of the movie *My Life As a Dog*, who consoles° himself by thinking, "It could always be worse." 9

- *Family.* Resilient children are likely to have good relationships with parents who are emotionally supportive of them and each other, or, failing that, to have a close relationship with at least one parent. If they lack even this, they are likely to be close to at least one other adult who shows interest in them and obviously cares for them, and whom they trust. Resilient abused children are likely to have been abused by only one parent rather than both and to have had a loving, supportive relationship with one parent or a foster parent when growing up. 10

- *Learning experiences.* Resilient children are likely to have had experience solving social problems. They have seen parents, older siblings, or others dealing with frustration and making the best of a bad situation. They have faced challenges themselves, worked out solutions and learned that they can exert some control over their lives. 11

- *Reduced risk.* Children who have been exposed to only one of a number of factors strongly related to psychiatric disorder (such as discord between the parents, low social status, overcrowding at home, a disturbed mother, a criminal father, and experience in foster care or an institution) are often able to overcome the stress. But when two or more of these factors are present, children's risk of developing an emotional disturbance increases fourfold or more. When children are not besieged on all sides, they can often cope with adverse° circumstances. 12

- *Compensating experiences.* A supportive school environment and successful experiences in sports, in music, or with other children or interested adults can help make up for a dismal home life. In adulthood, a good marriage can compensate° for poor relationships earlier in life. 13

All this research, of course, does not mean that what happens in a 14
child's life does not matter. In general, children with an unfavorable
background have more problems in adjustment than children with a
favorable background. What is heartening about these findings is the
recognition that childhood experiences do not necessarily determine the
outcome of a person's life, that many people do have the strength to
rise above the most difficult circumstances, and that we are constantly
rewriting the stories of our lives as long as we live.

VOCABULARY QUESTIONS

A. Use context clues to help you decide on the best definition for each italicized
word. Then circle the letter of your choice.

1. The word *shoulder* in "when children today live in single-parent homes or
have to consider parents' work schedules, they are likely to shoulder adult
responsibilities" (paragraph 2) means
   a. resent.
   b. take on.
   c. desire.
   d. remember.

2. The word *thwarted* in "Sometimes a child's healthy development is thwarted
by the very people expected to help it—the parents" (paragraph 4) means
   a. encouraged.
   b. taken care of.
   c. known.
   d. prevented.

3. The word *blight* in "Resilient children are those who bounce back from
circumstances that would blight the emotional development of most
children" (paragraph 6) means
   a. satisfy.
   b. have no effect on.
   c. greatly harm.
   d. encourage.

4. The word *discord* in "Children who have been exposed to only one of a
number of factors strongly related to psychiatric disorder (such as discord
between the parents, low social status . . .) are often able to overcome the
stress" (paragraph 12) means
   a. agreement.
   b. conversation.

    c. closeness.

    (d.) conflict.

5. The word *besieged* in "When children are not besieged on all sides, they can often cope with adverse circumstances" (paragraph 12) means
    a. behind.
    b. agreeable.
    (c.) surrounded by unfriendly forces.
    d. encouraged to do better.

B. Below are words or forms of words from "Words to Watch." Write in the one that best completes each sentence.

adverse	compensate	console
resilience	subject	

6. Gina decided to stay at home when she heard about the _____*adverse*_____ weather conditions.

7. One of the duties of a camp counselor is to _____*console*_____ young campers who are homesick.

8. To _____*compensate*_____ for her poor athletic skills, Jill decided that she would make herself a superior student.

9. Fred was impressed by the _____*resilience*_____ of the weeds in his garden; they returned even after he sprayed them with weed killer.

10. The concerned mother left the movie theater because she didn't want to _____*subject*_____ her child to the obscene language in the film.

READING COMPREHENSION QUESTIONS

Central Point and Main Ideas

1. Which sentence best expresses the central point of the selection?
    a. Children today experience much more stress than children did in the past.
    b. A supportive school environment and successful experiences in activities such as sports or music can help make up for a troubled home life.
    (c.) Although nearly all children experience stress that may affect them negatively later in life, much can be learned by studying resilient children.
    d. The increase in the number of homeless families in the United States has brought severe psychological difficulties to children.

2. The main idea of paragraph 1 is best expressed in its
   a. first sentence.
   b. second sentence.
   c. next-to-the-last sentence.
   d. last sentence.

3. The main idea of paragraph 2 is best expressed in its
   a. first sentence.
   b. second sentence.
   c. last sentence.
   d. none of the above.

4. Which sentence best expresses the main idea of paragraph 3?
   a. Today's children are pressured to succeed in school and compete in sports.
   b. The pressure of life today forces children to grow up quickly and often makes their shortened childhood too stressful.
   c. Children are exposed to many adult problems on television.
   d. There are many pressures on today's children.

Supporting Details

5. Resilient children tend to have
   a. low self-esteem.
   b. little experience solving social problems.
   c. a close relationship with at least one parent.
   d. foster parents.

Transitions

6. The relationship of the second sentence to the first is one of
   a. illustration.
   b. contrast.
   c. addition.
   d. time.

   Children are exposed to many adult problems on television and in real life before they have mastered the problems of childhood. Yet children are not small adults. (Paragraph 3)

7. The sentence below expresses a relationship of
   a. time.
   b. illustration.
   c. contrast.
   d. cause and effect.

   Because families move around more than they used to, children are more likely to change schools and friends and less likely to know many adults well. (Paragraph 2)

Patterns of Organization

8. The main pattern of organization of paragraph 6 is
   (a.) definition and example.
   b. comparison.
   c. list of items.
   d. time order.

Inferences

9. From the information in Box 13-3, we can conclude that
   a. childhood fears have remained the same throughout the centuries.
   b. boys and girls have remarkably different fears.
   c. parents are less important to third- to ninth-graders than people think.
   (d.) educators add to children's fears.

10. We can conclude that compensating experiences
    a. always occur in groups.
    (b.) provide a sense of support and achievement.
    c. can occur only during childhood.
    d. can harm the development of children who have a lot of stress at home.

SUMMARIZING

Complete the following summary of "Childhood Stress and Resilience" by filling in the blanks.

Stressful events are part of every childhood. However, children today have new pressures to deal with. These pressures, such as *divorce or death of parents, hospitalization, poverty, wars, earthquakes, homelessness, and violence* , result in more stress for children. In addition to the stresses of the modern world, some children experience physical or *psychological* maltreatment from the very people who are supposed to support their healthy development: their parents. The effects of these stresses on children are unpredictable because children are unpredictable. However, it is known that some children seem to be able to bounce back from unfortunate circumstances that other children would not have been able to overcome. These children are known as *resilient children* .

Factors which researchers feel contribute to childhood resilience cover the following areas: personality, *family, learning experiences, reduced risk, and compensating experiences.*

Such findings are encouraging in that they show we are able to overcome even very difficult circumstances and make positive changes in our lives.

DISCUSSION QUESTIONS

1. How has childhood changed since you were young? How was your own childhood different from that of your parents? What was better about your childhood as compared to that of children's today? Compared to your parents' childhood? What was worse?

2. Do you recall any experiences that you found particularly stressful as a child? If so, how did you deal with them?

3. The author states that children today are forced to grow up too quickly. What are some of the things that you believe children need time to learn and experience as children?

4. Sometimes a child's healthy development is hindered by the very people who are supposed to encourage it—the child's parents, relatives, or friends. What do you believe could be done to prevent child abuse (both physical and mental)? Why do you think child abuse is so common in the United States?

Check Your Performance   CHILDHOOD STRESS AND RESILIENCE

Skill	Number Right	Points	Total
VOCABULARY			
Vocabulary in Context (5 items)	_____	x 10 =	_____
Words to Watch (5 items)	_____	x 10 =	_____
		SCORE =	_____ %
COMPREHENSION			
Central Point and Main Ideas (4 items)	_____	x 8 =	_____
Supporting Details (1 item)	_____	x 8 =	_____
Transitions (2 items)	_____	x 8 =	_____
Patterns of Organization (1 item)	_____	x 8 =	_____
Inferences (2 items)	_____	x 8 =	_____
Summarizing (4 items)	_____	x 5 =	_____
		SCORE =	_____ %

FINAL SCORES: Vocabulary _____ %   Comprehension _____ %

Enter your final scores into the reading performance chart on the inside back cover.

Limited Answer Key

An Important Note: To strengthen your reading skills, you must do more than simply find out which of your answers are right and which are wrong. You also need to figure out (with the help of this book, the teacher, or other students) *why* you missed the questions you did. By using each of your wrong answers as a learning opportunity, you will strengthen your understanding of the skills. You will also prepare yourself for the review and mastery tests, for which answers are not given here.

ANSWERS TO THE PRACTICES IN PART I

1 Dictionary Use

Practice 1

1. fishbowl, fiscal, firing squad
2. glow, gnaw, glue
3. liver, load, lizard
4. during, duplicate, dunk
5. stumble, subcompact, style

Practice 2

1. decided
2. occasion
3. duty
4. accident
5. neighbor
6. experiment
7. remember
8. attention
9. character
10. photocopy

Practice 3

2. dis please, 2
3. hur ri cane, 3
4. as par a gus, 4
5. suf fi cient, 3
6. in hu man i ty, 5

Practice 4

1. a
2. b
3. a
4. a
5. b
6. a
7. b
8. b
9. b
10. b

Practice 5

A. 1. discipline, 1
   2. encounter, 1
   3. artificial, 2
   4. majority, 1
   5. natural, 2

B. 2. sĭn′ĭk
   3. ĕm′ə-nāt′
   4. fē′zə-bəl
   5. prŏg-nō′sĭs

Practice 6

1. 3; third
2. 4; second
3. 3; first
4. 4; third
5. 3; second

Practice 7

1. verb, noun
2. adjective, noun, verb
3. adverb, preposition, noun
4. noun, verb
5. noun, adjective, verb, adverb

Practice 8

1. verb; *shook; shaken; shaking*
2. adjective; *liveliest*
3. noun; *qualities*

Practice 9

1. Definition 1
2. Definition 2
3. Definition 2

2   Vocabulary In Context

Practice 1

1. Examples: *numerous paper cups, ticket stubs, cigarette butts*; c
2. Examples: *white bread, rice, mashed potatoes*; c
3. Examples: *Uzi machine guns, plastic explosives*; a
4. Examples: *backing his car into the side of the boss's Cadillac, hurting himself while trying to walk through glass doors*; b
5. Examples: *a man with 4,831 tattoos, a Chinese priest with twenty-two-inch fingernails*; b

Practice 2	*Practice 3*	*Practice 4*
1. *used up*	1. *neat*; c	1. c
2. *cloudy*	2. *temporary*; a	2. a
3. *in secret*	3. *allowed*; c	3. a
4. *standards*	4. *old*; a	4. c
5. *powerful*	5. *order*; b	5. a

3   Main Ideas

Practice 1

A.
1. liquid
2. snacks
3. car
4. entertainment
5. containers
6. music
7. jewelry
8. timepiece
9. symptoms
10. communicating

B.
1. insect
2. dessert
3. leader
4. tool
5. citrus fruit
6. instrument
7. mathematics
8. beverage
9. gem
10. noise

Practice 2

1. 2, 3, 1
2. 1, 3, 2
3. 2, 3, 1
4. 2, 1, 3
5. 3, 1, 2
6. 3, 1, 2
7. 1, 3, 2
8. 1, 3, 2
9. 2, 3, 1
10. 2, 3, 1

Practice 3

1. B
   N
   T
   names
   faces

2. N
   T
   B
   memories
   senses

3. B
   T
   N
   phobias
   phobias
   example
   medical needles

Practice 4

1. B
   T
   N

2. T
   B
   N

3. B
   N
   T

Practice 5

1. SD
   SD
   MI
   T
   habits
   general

2. MI
   T
   SD
   SD

3. MI
   T
   SD
   SD

4. T
   MI
   SD
   SD

5. MI
   SD
   T
   SD

Practice 6

A.
1. c
   broad, narrow, marijuana
2. 1
   specific, general, 1

B.
1. a
2. 1

C.
1. a
2. 1

4   Supporting Details

Practice 1

1. c
2. b
3. b
4. a

Practice 2

1. 2
2. 3
3. 4
4. 7

Practice 3

A.
1. c
2. c
3. c
4. c
5. F

B.
1. F
2. d
3. a
4. fish
5. d

C.
1. a
2. Many
3. rules
4. c
5. T

5   Locations of Main Ideas

Practice, p. 88

1. 1
2. 4
3. 2
4. 1, 7
5. 3

Practice: Level 1

1. 6
2. 1
3. 2
4. 3
5. 2

Practice: Level 2

1. 1
2. 1, 6
3. 5
4. 1
5. 6

Practice: Level 3

1. 2
2. 1
3. 1, 6
4. 7
5. 2

6   Implied Main Ideas

Practice 1
1. b
2. c
3. a
4. c
5. c
6. a
7. a
8. b
9. b
10. c

Practice 2
1. hair colors
2. containers
3. cold symptoms
4. building materials
5. types of music
6. furniture for seating
7. people who work at a restaurant
8. household chores
9. insults
10. steps in making pizza

Practice 3
Group 1. a
Group 2. c
Group 3. a

Practice 4
1. b
2. c
3. d

Practice 5
1. There are several factors that workers feel are most important to job satisfaction.
   Hint: factors, important
2. VCRs have several advantages.
   Hint: several advantages
3. Lonnie's grades suffered because of his heavy work schedule.
   Hint: work schedule

7   More About Supporting Details

Practice 1

List 1
1. My mother's longer methods
   a. Makes chicken broth for cream soups
2. My aunt's shortcut methods
   b. Uses only frozen and canned vegetables

List 2
1. a. Is the work interesting?
2. Some factors have to do with the environment.
   b. Is the workplace safe?
3. b. Is there room to advance?

List 3
1. It allows me to be antisocial.
2. It is useful for dates with my girlfriend.
   a. Watching TV movies is cheaper for us than going to the movies.
3. It is educational.
   b. It's possible to learn about law from shows like *People's Court.*

Practice 2
1. two . . . one . . . song . . . 6 7 . . . second . . . communicate . . . call . . . 8 . . . minor
2. steps . . . first . . . major . . . dress carefully . . . next . . . 5 . . . Put on insect repellent . . . finally . . . Shower as soon as you return from a tick-infested area . . . minor
3. describe useless objects . . . 2 . . . 3–4 . . . flopcorn . . . spirobits . . . 5 . . . names for frustrating actions . . . two . . . examples

Practice 3
A. *Heading:* Ways *to Protect Yourself from Skin Cancer*
   1. Use a sunscreen with a sun-protection factor of fifteen or more.
   2. Limit your exposure when the sun's rays are strongest (10 a.m. to 3 p.m.).

B. *Heading:* Followers *Who Broke Away from Freud*
   1. Carl Jung, who believed there were two levels of the unconscious.
   2. Alfred Adler, who emphasized the ego more.

C. *Heading:* Words *Based on People's Names*
   1. *Guillotine* was named for Dr. Guillotin, who wanted a kinder method ofexecuting criminals.
   2. *Sandwich* comes from the Earl of Sandwich, who invented the sandwich.
   3. *Nicotine* is named for Jean Nicot, who introduced tobacco into France.

Practice 4
A. 1. a
   2. b
   3. b
   4. people can't snore if they don't open their mouths.
   5. 5

B. 1. b
   2. b
   3. finally
   4. b
   5. c

8   Transitions

Wording will vary throughout these practices.

Practice 1
1. Another
2. In addition
3. Also
4. First of all
5. furthermore

Practice 2
1. often
2. Then
3. before
4. When
5. during

Practice 3
1. but
2. even though
3. on the other hand
4. Although
5. However

Practice 4
1. just as
2. Similarly
3. as
4. In like manner
5. as if

Practice 5
1. For instance
2. including
3. Once
4. for example
5. To illustrate

Practice 6
1. Because
2. As a result
3. Since
4. Therefore
5. reason

Practice 7
1. but
2. so
3. and
4. but
5. Moreover
6. consequently
7. on the other hand
8. consequently
9. furthermore
10. but

Practice 8
1. but
2. and
3. so
4. but
5. nevertheless
6. also
7. Therefore
8. but
9. Furthermore
10. Therefore

9 Patterns of Organization

Wording will vary throughout these practices.

Practice 1a
A. 1. pouch.
   2. drinks concentrated milk solution.
   3. a more diluted form of milk.
   4. When almost ready to give up mother's milk, the joey leaves pouch as it pleases.
B. 2. movable type was invented
   3. after the newspaper was born, the first newspaper ad was published in London.
   4. By the end of the 1800s, magazines became another place for ads.
   5. In the 20th century, radio and TV ads are common.

Practice 1b
A. 2, 5, 3, 4, 1   B. 5, 1, 4, 2, 3

Practice 2
A. Ways to raise your self-esteem; 4
B. Defense mechanisms used by opossums; 3; b

Practice 3
A. Contrasting; high school and college
B. Both; goat's milk and cow's milk

Practice 4a
1. *Cause:* left casserole in oven too long
   Effect: family ate out
2. *Cause:* dog's barking
   Effect: family awoke in time to escape fire
3. *Cause:* worked in garden for three hours
   Effect: back pain
4. *Cause:* witness kept contradicting himself
   Effect: jury didn't believe witness
5. *Cause:* taking large amounts of carotene
   Effect: skin turns orange

Practice 4b
1. cause, cause, effect
2. effect, cause, cause
3. cause, cause, effect
4. effect, effect, cause
5. cause, effect, effect

Practice 4c
1. cause, cause, effect
2. effect, effect, cause

Practice 5
A. *Definition:* 1; *Example 1:* 3; *Example 2:* 3
B. *Definition:* 1; *Example 1:* 3; *Example 2:* 4

Practice 6
1. b
2. b
3. a
4. c
5. c

10 Inferences

Practice 1
1. c
2. a
3. b

Practice 2
1. b
2. c
3. c

Practice 3
1. b
2. a
3. b

Practice 4
2, 3, 6

Practice 5
2, 3, 5

Acknowledgments

The American Heritage Dictionary, Paperback Edition. Copyright © 1983 by Houghton Mifflin Company. *The American Heritage Dictionary*, Second College Edition. Copyright © 1991 by Houghton Mifflin Company. Reprinted by permission.

Bassis, Michael S., Richard J. Gelles, and Ann Levine. "Behind Closed Doors: Violence in the Family." From *Sociology: An Introduction*. Copyright © 1991 by McGraw-Hill, Inc. Reprinted by permission.

Batteiger, Richard. "Getting Words on Paper: Where to Begin." From *Business Writing*. Copyright © 1985 by Wadsworth Publishing. Reprinted by permission.

DeBlasio, Fran, as told to Jane Sugen. "Read All About It." From *People Weekly*, © 1986 by Time, Inc.

DeLeon, Clark. "Victims Versus Oppressors." From *The Philadelphia Inquirer*, February 5, 1985. Reprinted by permission.

Hinkle, Tom. "The Gentle Giant and the Reluctant Robber." Adapted with the permission of the *Camden Courier-Post*.

Mack, Marilyn. "Adult Children at Home." Reprinted by permission of the author.

Miller, Warren. Drawing on page 200. Copyright © 1992 by The New Yorker Magazine, Inc.

Montgomery, Robert L. "Are You a Good Listener?" Reprinted by permission of the publisher, from *Listening Made Easy* by Robert L. Montgomery. Copyright © 1981 by AMACOM, a division of American Management Association. All rights reserved.

Morris, Charles G., and John J. Chiodo. "Exam Anxiety and Grandma's Health." From *Psychology*, 7/e. Copyright © 1990 by Prentice-Hall. Reprinted by permission.

O'Keeney, Brian. "How To Make It in College, Now That You're Here." Reprinted by permission.

Papalia, Diane E., and Sally Wendkos Olds. "Childhood Stress and Resilience." From *A Child's World*, 6/e. Copyright © 1993 by McGraw-Hill, Inc. Reprinted by permission.

Parish, Ramona. "Messages from a Welfare Mom." From *Newsweek*, issue of May 23, 1988.

Peck, M. Scott. "Responsibility." Copyright © 1978 by M. Scott Peck, M.D. Reprinted by permission of Simon & Schuster, Inc.

Ruth, Beth Johnson. "Body Language." Reprinted by permission.

Spangler, Phyllis. "Touch Sparks Love." From *Good Housekeeping*, August 1971. Reprinted by permission.

Stark, Rodney. "Group Pressure." From *Sociology*, 3rd ed., by Rodney Stark. Copyright © 1989 by Wadsworth Publishing. Reprinted by permission.

Verderber, Rudolph. "Dealing with Feelings." From *Communicate!* 6th ed. Copyright © 1990 by Wadsworth Publishing. Reprinted by permission.

Wightman, Dan. "Winners, Losers, or Just Kids?" *Los Angeles Times*, July 25, 1979.

Wilson, Chuck. "Disaster and Friendship." Reprinted by permission.

Winkler, Robert, and Pam Winkler. "False Ideas About Reading." Reprinted by permission.

Wolkomir, Richard. "Shyness." Reprinted by permission.

Index

Accent marks in dictionary entries, 16-17
"Adult Children at Home," Marilyn Mack,
    370-378
"Are You a Good Listener?" Robert L.
    Montgomery, 405-414
Addition, words that show, 131-132, 148-149,
    174
Antonyms as context clues, 33-34

Bassis, Michael S., and others, "Behind Closed
    Doors: Violence in the Family," 141-144
Batteiger, Richard P., "Getting Words on
    Paper: Where To Begin," 415-425
"Behind Closed Doors: Violence in the
    Family," Michael S. Bassis and others,
    141-144
"Body Language," Beth Johnson Ruth, 97-100

Cause and effect:
    pattern of organization, 179-183
    words that show, 154-155; 180
"Childhood Stress and Resilience," Diane E.
    Papalia and Sally Wendkos Olds, 436-444
Combined skills mastery tests, 339-350
Comparison and/or contrast:
    pattern of organization, 177-179
    words that show, 150-153; 171, 177
Context clues:
    antonyms, 33-34
    examples, 30-31
    general sense of the sentence or passage,
        34-36

synonyms, 32-33
Contrast, words that show, 150-151; 171

"Dealing with Feelings," Rudolph F.
    Verderber, 426-435
DeBlasio, Fran, "Read All About It," 362-369
DeLeon, Clark, "Victims Versus Oppressors,"
    40-42
Definition and example pattern of
    organization, 183-185
Definitions
    in the dictionary, 19-20
    in textbooks, 36-37
Details, supporting, 51-61
    definition of, 68-69
    major and minor, 125-137
    reading carefully for, 71-75
    ways to locate:
        addition words, 131-132
        opening phrases, 129-131
Dictionary use, 9-27
    definitions, 19-20
    guide words, 10-11
    parts of speech, 17-18
    pronunciation, 13-17
    spelling, 11-12, 18-19
    synonyms and antonyms, 20-21
    usage labels, 21
    word origins, 21
Directions, series of, 172-172
"Disaster and Friendship," Chuck Wilson,
    353-361

Events or stages, as type of time order, 170-172

"Exam Anxiety and Grandma's Health," Charles G. Morris and John J. Chiodo, 211-213

Examples:
  as context clues, 30-31
  with definitions, 36-37; 183-185
  words that introduce, 184

"False Ideas About Reading," Robert and Pam Winkler, 397-404

Finding words in dictionary, 10-12

General versus specific ideas, 47-54, 106-111

"Getting Words on Paper: Where To Begin," Richard P. Batteiger, 415-424

"The Gentle Giant and the Reluctant Robber," Tom Hinkle, 24-26

"Group Pressure," Rodney Stark, 63-65

Guide words in dictionary, 10-11

Hinkle, Tom, "The Gentle Giant and the Reluctant Robber," 24-26

"How To Make It in College, Now That You're Here," Brian O'Keeney, 190-196

Illustration, words that show, 153-154; 184

Implied main ideas, 103-124

Inferences, 199-216
  with implied main ideas, 103-124
  mastery tests for, 327-338
  review tests for, 207-216

Irregular spellings, 18-19

Limited answer key, 445-448

List of items pattern of organization, 174-176

Mack, Marilyn, "Adult Children at Home," 370-378

Major and minor supporting details, 125-137

Main ideas, 45-67, 85-102
  and topics, 26-30
  definition of, 26
  implied, 103-124
  location of, 267-278
  and topic sentences, 45-47, 55-59
  mastery tests for, 243-254, 267-278, 279-290
  review tests for, 60-67, 94-102, 116-124

"Messages from a Welfare Mom," Ramona Parish, 120-122

Montgomery, Robert L, "Are You a Good Listener?" 405-414

Morris, Charles G., and John J. Chiodo, "Exam Anxiety and Grandma's Health," 211-213

O'Keeney, Brian, "How To Make It in College, Now That You're Here," 190-196

Opening phrases, 129-130

Papalia, Diane E., and Sally Wendkos Olds, "Childhood Stress and Resilience," 436-444

Parish, Ramona, "Messages from a Welfare Mom," 120-122

Parts of speech in dictionary, 17-18

Patterns of organization, 168-198
  cause and effect, 179-183
  comparison and/or contrast, 177-179
  definition and example, 183-185
  list of items, 174-176
  mastery tests for, 315-327
  review tests for, 186-198
  time order, 169-173
  topic sentences and, 185-186

Peck, M. Scott, "Responsibility," 163-165

Pronunciation symbols in dictionary entries, 13-16

"Read All About It," Fran DeBlasio, 362-369

Reading performance chart, inside back cover

"Responsibility," M. Scott Peck, 163-165

Ruth, Beth Johnson, "Body Language," 97-100

Schwa, 14
Sense of the passage, as context clue,
    34-36
"Shyness," Richard Wolkomir, 387-396
Spangler, Phyllis, "Touch Sparks Love,"
    79-83
Specific versus general ideas, 47-54,
    106-111
Spelling of words, 11-13, 18-19
Stages or events, as type of time order,
    170-172
Stark, Rodney, "Group Pressure," 63-65
Steps, series of, as type of time order,
    172-173
Supporting details, 68-84, 125-146
    definition of, identifying, 68-71
    by reading carefully, 71-75
    major and minor, 125-137
    mastery tests for, 255-266, 291-302
    review tests for, 75-84, 137-146
    ways to locate:
        addition words, 131-132
        opening phrases, 129-131
Synonyms:
    as context clues, 12
    in dictionary, 20-21

Thesaurus, 20-21
Time, words that show, 149-150; 170
Time order pattern of organization, 169-173
    series of events or stages, 170-172
    series of steps (directions), 172-173
Topic, 26-30
Topic sentences:
    and patterns of organization, 185-186
    definition of, 45
    locations of, 85-102
"Touch Sparks Love," Phyllis Spangler,
    79-83

Transitions, 147-167
    the logic of, 155-159
    and patterns of organization, 168-169
    mastery tests for, 303-314
    review tests for, 160-167
    that show addition, 148-149
    that show cause and effect, 154-155
    that show comparison, 152-153
    that show contrast, 150-151
    that show illustration, 153-154
    that show time, 149-150
    using a variety of, 155-159

Usage labels in dictionary, 21

Verderber, Rudolph F., "Dealing with
    Feelings," 426-436
"Victims Versus Oppressors," Clark DeLeon,
    40-42
Vocabulary in context, 29-44
    antonyms, 33-34
    examples, 30-31
    general sense of the sentence, 34-36
    mastery tests for, 231-242
    review tests for, 37-44
    synonyms, 32-33

Wightman, Dan, "Winner, Losers, or Just
    Kids?" 379-386
Wilson, Chuck, "Disaster and Friendship,"
    353-361
Winkler, Robert and Pam, "False Ideas About
    Reading," 397-404
"Winners, Losers, or Just Kids?" Dan
    Wightman, 379-386
Wolkomir, "Shyness," 387-396
Word origins in dictionary, 21